SHRINES AND MIRACULOUS IMAGES

A VOLUME IN THE RELIGIONS OF THE AMERICAS SERIES

Series Editors: DAVÍD CARRASCO and CHARLES H. LONG

Shrines and Miraculous Images

Religious Life in Mexico Before the Reforma

William B. Taylor

UNIVERSITY OF NEW MEXICO PRESS ALBUQUERQUE

© 2010 by the University of New Mexico Press
All rights reserved. Published 2010
Printed in the United States of America

First paperback edition, 2019
Paperback ISBN: 978-0-8263-4854-8

LIBRARY OF CONGRESS CATALOGING-IN-PUBLICATION DATA

Taylor, William B.
 Shrines and miraculous images : religious life in Mexico before the Reforma / William B. Taylor.
   p. cm. — (Religions of the Americas)
 Includes bibliographical references (p.).
 ISBN 978-0-8263-4853-1 (cloth : alk. paper)
 1. Christian shrines—Mexico—History. 2. Catholic Church—Mexico—History. 3. Mexico—Religious life and customs. I. Title.
 BX2320.5.M6T38 2010
 263'.04272—dc22
                    2010021107

Cover illustrations: (*front*) *Our Lady of Light* by Miguel Cabrera (d. 1768), n.d. (1760s?). Courtesy of the Patronato del Colegio de San Ignacio de Loyola, Vizcaínas, Mexico City. (*front and back, detail*) *Novena en honra de Nuestra Señora de los Dolores, que con el renombre de las Aguas* . . . (México: Colegio de San Ildefonso, 1761), second leaf. Courtesy of the Sutro Branch of the California State Library, San Francisco.

Designed by Melissa Tandysh

Text is composed in Minion Pro Regular 10.5/14
Display type is Incognito

To Inga Clendinnen
For her friendship, encouragement, and example

Contents

Figures ix

Foreword xi

Acknowledgments xv

Introduction 1

Part I   Images and Shrines 13

1. Images and Immanence in Colonial Mexico 15
2. Two Shrines of the Cristo Renovado: Religion and Peasant Politics 63

Part II   Our Lady of Guadalupe: Toward a History of Devotion 95

3. Mexico's Virgin of Guadalupe in the Seventeenth Century: Hagiography and Beyond 97
4. Places of Our Lady of Guadalupe in Eighteenth-Century Mexico 117
5. Guadalupe, Remedios, and Cultural Politics of the Independence Period 139

Part III   Beyond the Colonial Period 163

6. Shrines and Marvels in the Wake of Mexican Independence 165

Notes 207

Index 281

Figures

Chapter 1 Images and Immanence in Colonial Mexico

Fig. 1.1 *Portrait of a Lady,* attributed to Baltasar de Echave Orio, 1615–1620 — 21

Fig. 1.2 Ink drawing of a charred handprint, presented in an Inquisition investigation of an apparition of a recently deceased soul, 1648 — 28

Fig. 1.3 Print of Our Lady of Zapopan from an engraving by Sotomayor, ca. 1772 — 34

Fig. 1.4 Painting of a procession of Indians with statue of Jesús Nazareno to the Hospital of the Immaculate Conception, Mexico City, 1781 — 40

Fig. 1.5 Print of Madonna and Child from an engraving by Ortuño, 1760 — 42

Fig. 1.6 Painting of the Virgin of Guadalupe by Miguel Cabrera, 1766 — 44

Fig. 1.7 Print of sketch of "Interior of an Indian Hut, El Bozal," San Luis Potosí, by Mr. and Mrs. H. G. Ward, 1827 — 45

Fig. 1.8 Title page and engraving from booklet of prayers to Our Lady of Solitude, 1817 — 46

Fig. 1.9 Print of Nuestra Señora de las Aguas from an engraving by Ortuño, 1761 — 48

Fig. 1.10 Print of the Cruz de Huaquechula, 1809 — 51

Fig. 1.11 *Our Lady of Light* by Miguel Cabrera, n.d. (1760s?) — 55

Fig. 1.12 Print of Our Lady of Light from an engraving by Tomás de Suría, 1790 — 57

Chapter 2 Two Shrines of the Cristo Renovado: Religion and Peasant Politics

Fig. 2.1	Print of the Cristo Renovado in Alfonso Alberto de Velasco's *Exaltación de la divina misericordia* . . . , 1698	62
Fig. 2.2	Print of the Cristo Renovado in Alfonso Alberto de Velasco's *Exaltación de la divina misericordia* . . . , 1807	69
Fig. 2.3	Print of the Cristo Renovado in Alfonso Alberto de Velasco's *Exaltación de la divina misericordia* . . . , 1820	70
Fig. 2.4	Map of the Shrine of Mapethé and surroundings	74
Fig. 2.5	Map of the reach of Otomí alms collectors for the Cristo Renovado	84

Chapter 3 Mexico's Virgin of Guadalupe in the Seventeenth Century: Hagiography and Beyond

Fig. 3.1	Annual Income Tabulated from the Visita Records, 1634–1698	106
Fig. 3.2	Annual Expenditures Tabulated from the Visita Records, 1634–1698	107

Chapter 6 Shrines and Marvels in the Wake of Mexican Independence

Fig. 6.1	Print of Our Lady of los Remedios with Fernando Cortés and Juan Rodríguez de Villafuerte, from an engraving by Sylverio, 1759	189
Fig. 6.2	Ink drawing of a proposed medal of Our Lady of los Remedios, 1803	190

Foreword

In his introduction to this volume, William B. Taylor writes, "A key to imagining colonial territories in the future Mexico is to keep larger and smaller in mind at the same time, to cultivate a more synoptic historical practice." Taylor has developed just this synoptic work during a highly productive career as a Latin American historian inquiring into small places and large spaces, intricate social processes and pervasive political and religious institutions, sacred and profane practices in Mexican history. Fortunately for our Religions of the Americas series, this book reveals what turning this key in the many doors of places and peoples in Mexico's history of religions opens for us to understand and appreciate. Taylor takes his pen and eyes into neglected locations and subtle, slow changes in Mexican religions, dividing his book into three sections: "Images and Shrines," "Our Lady of Guadalupe: Toward a History of Devotion," and "Beyond the Colonial Period." In six carefully written, lengthy essays (accompanied by twenty relevant images) about the miraculous power of images and shrines, plus the politics of religious practices at ordinary places that became extraordinary sites for local and sometimes national populations, we learn the variety of ways the "sensual faith of Catholic Christianity" was transmitted to, received by, and reworked in various local communities in Mexico during five centuries.

One of the added offerings of this excellent book, *Shrines and Miraculous Images: Religious Life in Mexico Before the Reforma*, is Taylor's autobiographical and methodological introduction that traces his personal and professional journey as an historian, in which he sought to fulfill the goal of helping students "to reach beyond personal experience for what it means to be human, to promote a bond between them and the subject by practicing what Inga Clendinnen calls 'exact imagining.'" Taylor notes that his work of history and imagination has been marked by endless hours in archives but also "epiphanies, encounters, and *inquietudes*" that led him to an awareness that historical study is "a restless kind of discipline of context." Taylor's understanding of context changed significantly as he was immersed in his studies of drinking, homicide, and rebellion in colonial Mexican villages when he came to realize that "priests and religious institutions were everywhere in the record. I came to realize that I had entered a cul-de-sac in my studies of Latin American history. If I wanted to go deeper into a more synoptic history of Mexico and Mesoamerica, and the workings of a colonial regime, I had to make room for close attention to church and religion." We have already benefited substantially by this realization in the award winning magnum opus, *Magistrates of the Sacred: Priests and Parishioners in Eighteenth-Century Mexico*. Fortunately, this book moves in new directions and provides innovative interpretations of religious practices and the religious imagination of many Mexicos not addressed in *Magistrates of the Sacred*.

One epiphany that contributes substantially to the focus and importance of this book came to Taylor painfully, when a moving van transporting family and office possessions caught fire, destroying almost all his teaching and research materials. Left mainly with his slide collection he was forced, as he scrambled to teach through his next semester, to depend in more than ornamental ways on images of paintings, fountains, altars, ground plans, pots, benches, sculptures, and doodles made in the sixteenth through eighteenth centuries by various classes and kinds of Mexicans. Drawn to look more closely at these illustrations, Taylor saw the necessity and benefit of thinking *in terms of images* as well as in terms of written texts that had been central to his previous works. This book's essays are the interpretive fruit of this nearly fifteen-year labor of putting "the picture on the same plane as a means of communication with written texts and spoken words, as they surely were to their original audience." The reader of these chapters and images will find discerning discussions of a religious supermateriality of Mexican places, crosses, saints, shrines, churches, and images, plus fresh views of how local peoples worshiped the Virgin of Guadalupe but also worshiped other Virgins who sometimes overshadowed Guadalupe as their protector and numinous object of faith and emotion. We see again and again how, in Mexico, many different images including miraculous images of Jesus Christ in many different locations were experienced as dynamically filled with the presence of divinities and worshiped as "essential to personal and collective well-being."

Collective well-being in Taylor's historical view leads him to link the specific sites, stories, and actors of miracles to the interaction of official religion and peasant politics, the changes in spiritual geography, and the politics of miraculous images during and after social conflicts and movements for Mexican independence. For those truly interested in the roles of religious attitudes and practices in social history, this book weaves us in and out of numerous Mexican shrines and the endless marvels and miracles that magnetized and changed countless lives and institutions—small and large. In the end we are faced with more than a sociology of religion or a history of religion. We are reading a history of many lives and living things—lives of individuals, places, saints, and periods of social order, disorder, and the miracles that sometimes turned misery into the work of devotion.

Readers will also be pleased to know that a companion volume of primary documents and interpretive essays by William Taylor entitled *Marvels and Miracles in Late Colonial Mexico: Three Texts in Context* will soon be published by the University of New Mexico Press. This sourcebook contains three largely ignored documents about miracles and shrines in late colonial Mexico, plus introductory essays on faith practices and colonial politics. This volume is being produced so as to provide for students of colonial Mexico important primary sources and invite them to enter more vigorously into the dialogues about historical understandings of religious devotion and practice in Mexico. The three documents, in Taylor's words, help us "glimpse news of miracles in their first, unfinished stages—more singular and idiosyncratic in ways that restore some rough edges, personalities, and contingencies to the compressed, authorized miracle stories." Taylor's interpretive essays in both the present book and the upcoming sourcebook help us keep "larger and smaller" always in mind—at the same time.

—Davíd Carrasco
Harvard University

Acknowledgments

I owe much to the generosity of talented friends who followed what I was doing these past ten years and offered encouragement, help with sources and permissions, and excellent advice on drafts of the essays. I thank especially Inga Clendinnen, Kenneth Mills, Davíd Carrasco, Brian Connaughton, William A. Christian Jr., David Weber, Allen Wells, Isabel Estrada Torres, Alicia Mayer González, Esteban Sánchez de Tagle, Óscar Mazin, Jorge Traslosheros, Ana Carolina Ibarra, Álvaro Matute, Ethelia Ruiz Medrano, Jaime Cuadriello, Martín de Jesús Sánchez Espinosa, Susan Deans-Smith, Michael Hironymous, Nancy D. Mann, Cecilia Brown, Mieko Nishida, Peter Bakewell, Theresa Alfaro-Velcamp, Luis Gordo Peláez, and my Berkeley colleagues Sylvia Sellers-García, Paul Ramírez, Sean McEnroe, Karen Melvin, José Refugio de la Torre Curiel, Jessica Delgado, Brianna Leavitt-Alcántara, Jennifer Hughes, Brian Madigan, Rachel Chico, Kinga Novak, Beatriz Reyes-Cortés, Michel Estefan Gutiérrez, Dan Nemser, Walter Brem, David Kessler, Theresa Salazar, Susan Snyder, Rus Sheptak, Rosemary Joyce, William F. Hanks, Yuri Slezkine, Leslie Peirce, and Wen-hsin Yeh. A special thanks to Karin E. Taylor and Jennifer S. Edwards, who came to my rescue as I prepared the images for this volume.

There was time to begin working on several of the essays during the winter and spring of 2002 thanks to a residential fellowship at the Center for Advanced Study in the Behavioral Sciences, Palo Alto, CA, funded by the Andrew W. Mellon Foundation, Grant #29800639.

Introduction

IT HAS ALWAYS SEEMED STRANGE TO BE ASKED HOW MY "OWN work" is going, meaning my research and writing, because teaching has been my main work and how I have made a living for forty years. It is honest work, creative work when I've been up to it. Whether or not I was a successful teacher, I always had in mind that being a responsible and responsive teacher was my first priority during the school year. I have been less interested in the information or line of interpretation students might acquire in my classes or whether they were convinced by my presentations and perspectives than in their engagement with the subject and primary sources in a spirit of inquiry, exchange, and constructive criticism. John Dewey expressed my ambition as a learner and teacher:

> Thinking is a process of inquiry, of looking into things, of investigating. *A*cquiring is always secondary, and instrumental to the act of *in*quiring. It is seeking, a quest for something that is not at hand. We sometimes talk as if "original research" were a peculiar prerogative of scientists or at least of advanced students. But all thinking is research, and all research is native, original with him who carried it on, even if everybody else in the world is sure of what he is still looking for.[1]

My grander goal as a historian in U.S. classrooms has been to help students reach beyond personal experience for what it means to be human, to promote a bond between them and the subject by practicing what Inga Clendinnen calls "exact imagining." We have obligations to those we study and the sources that can be mustered; we are not at liberty to make carefree claims because it is not just our story we are trying to tell. I think of historical study as a restless kind of discipline of context. It is not just mastery of assorted facts; it is the attempt to study past human experience in all of its paradoxes, uncertainties, and silences. It is never done. As historical geographer Donald Meinig said, history "is not the study of any particular kind of thing, but a particular way of studying almost anything"; reckoning with "how all kinds of things exist [and change] together" in place and time.[2] The effort at comprehension usually is more synoptic than deductive, holding in mind quite different possibilities and trying to understand how they might coexist.[3] Of course, no one can know enough to master it all, but in pushing Sisyphus's rock and accepting an aching sense of ignorance, sound choices can be made about which contexts are salient in a particular episode. There is the challenge, and I have never tired of working with students toward that kind of understanding through primary sources—doing some history as well as talking about it. While my first teaching job at the high school level was fulfilling, I wanted to inquire and learn through more open-ended research and writing, too, which led to a research degree and a career of university teaching and scholarship.

In the film *My Architect*, Louis Kahn speaks of the place of accident and circumstance in his life. He was thinking especially of the high school course that turned him toward architecture. It has been a privilege to do the work I have done, but it hasn't unfolded with me acting alone or in a straight line. There were bound to be fortuitous turning points and setbacks, and I have had crucial help along the way. I won't take up space here to record all the surprises and the teachers, colleagues, friends, and family who made what I have done seem possible, but several small epiphanies, encounters, and *inquietudes*[4] stand out in my memory of becoming a teacher and scholar of Latin American history. A youth soccer team from Mexico City on tour in southern California in 1959 visited my high school to show us what the sport was about. Over lunch, the inevitable conversation of sixteen-year-old boys shifted in a surprising direction when one young man asked me what I thought about the U.S.-Mexican War. He was curious to know what a contemporary of his from *el otro lado*—the "other side"—thought about something he assumed was as important to me as it was to him. The fact was that I thought nothing about the war and had only the dimmest recollection from a U.S. history textbook of a paragraph about marines in the Halls of Montezuma. I felt my ignorance then, but I also glimpsed a different historical awareness—that events a hundred years old can still be unfinished business and have the urgency of today's headlines.

Then, in college, I had an opportunity to study and travel in Jalisco and central Mexico one summer. We visited several great monastic church complexes built in the sixteenth century in what are now rather small, unprepossessing communities. This was another revelation to me—this Gothic America in an earthquake belt centuries before my ancestors arrived. I wondered who built and maintained those durable buildings, how they were used, and why they were located there. After college, I returned to Mexico to study comparative law at the National University; but when we arrived in Mexico City, the university was on strike, so my wife and I were in central Mexico for a year with nothing particular to do. I began to visit historical archives, attend classes at the Universidad de las Américas on the old highway to Toluca, and traveled some more. I was beginning to understand what L. B. Simpson meant by the title of his survey of Mexican history, *Many Mexicos*, and I was finding Mexicos Simpson hadn't described.[5] I remember especially the days spent in Mexico's national archive that year, learning to read colonial-era manuscripts and sitting across the big study tables from *campesinos* and their country lawyers poring over the land records of their communities, teaching me that there was life and tragedy in those papers, information that was vital to their well-being, if I would look for it. I was hooked and wanted to share as much as I could of the complexities I found with Americans who were exposed to little more than Frito Bandito and Chiquita Banana–type simplicities about Latin America. Away flew my thoughts of law school. During my PhD studies I returned to Mexico in the summers looking for something of my own that seemed worthwhile and possible, something that might interest Mexican scholars and students as well as open the way for me and my future students and readers to understand Mexican history more fully.

My goal as a historian has been to enlarge the view of history, especially Mexican history, by making Mexico both larger and smaller—larger territorially and in subject matter; smaller in terms of manageable, place-centered research and identities. Mexico did not exist in its current territorial limits before 1848. So, what existed before and how were people connected there? Answering these questions often has led me to the many smaller Mexicos of a then-overwhelmingly rural society: regions and affiliations within regions, centers, and peripheries, villages and towns, each regarded by its people as pivotal.[6] These significant places and clusters of places are not timeless. They change in long ripples more than loops of repetition or revolutionary turns. They change even in the supposedly slow-moving colonial history of rural Mexico in the seventeenth and eighteenth centuries, and the more eventful nineteenth century, before the Mexican Revolution of 1910. New market systems developed, as did a centralized state that drew people into wider networks in particular ways as laborers, Christians, "Indian" vassals of the crown, and litigants defending their rights and resources or serving more selfish purposes. The impetus during the colonial period was toward smaller groupings, too. The larger city-states of precolonial Mesoamerica fractured as subject communities sought the political status of head town standing and separated in other ways. A key to imagining colonial territories in the future Mexico is to keep larger and smaller in mind at the same time, to cultivate a more synoptic historical practice.

In 1969, I was fortunate to find full-time employment at the University of Colorado, Denver, a commuter school where nearly everyone was a reentry student. More experienced than I was, and thirsty for learning, the students there carried me through the first exciting, exhausting years of college teaching. And I continued research on rural Mexico, especially *pueblos de indios* in colonial circumstances. From land tenure and wealth in the Valley of Oaxaca,[7] I took up the abundant, but little-known and then uncatalogued late-colonial criminal and civil court records for a study of village life through documentation on drinking behavior, homicide, and rebellion. I knew from the study of land and society in Oaxaca that no one place can stand for Mexico or Mesoamerica, even though the history of a place might well reveal processes of change experienced elsewhere. For this second study,[8] I concentrated on one well-documented district in Oaxaca and various places in central Mexico that were also well-documented. The juxtaposition of places, small and large, in different parts of Mexico has become a strategy to gain some comparative perspective and wider scope in most of my work since then.

In those studies of land tenure and social life in rural Mexico, priests and religious institutions and activities were everywhere in the record. I came to realize that I had entered a cul-de-sac in my studies of Latin American history. If I wanted to go deeper into a more synoptic history of Mexico and Mesoamerica, and the workings of a colonial regime, I had to make room for close attention to church and religion. It was clear to me that the history of parish priests, in particular, opened out to local affairs, colonial relationships of authority and power, as well as faith, in countless ways. As agents of the state religion and as intermediaries both between parishioners and higher authorities and between the sacred and the profane, they were a promising point of entry into a history of connections and perspective. Heartened by conversations with Davíd Carrasco about the vibrant field of religious studies and central places, and his budding Mesoamerican Archive, I launched research on church and religion in Mexican history during my last years in Colorado. This led first in the direction of a study of priests in their rural parishes during the late colonial period, reaching for the social, political, cultural, and devotional relationships between them and their parishioners in the Archdiocese of Mexico and the Diocese of Guadalajara. *Magistrates of the Sacred: Priests and Parishioners in Eighteenth-Century Mexico* was the result.[9] Organized as three related studies—a social history of parish priests at work; the religious culture of parishioners; and local politics in which priests exercised influence along with village officials, royal governors, hereditary chiefs, popular spokesmen, community groups, and neighboring landlords—it was especially concerned with how the inescapable intimacies of those contacts and relationships in colonial circumstances meant conflict, fear, violence, and painful disappointment, as well as warmth, hope, trust, and communion.

When we moved to Dallas, TX, and Southern Methodist University in 1993, another small epiphany imposed itself. The moving van carrying our belongings caught fire and nearly everything we sent was destroyed. Except for the fifteen boxes of slides stored in the driver's cab, most of my recent research notes and writings and all of my teaching materials were lost. Those slides became touchstones for my teaching during the next few years, and opened for me a new appreciation in my research for the making and uses of images and other things. I found myself starting a new semester without my class notes, reading journals, books, research materials, and other working papers, but with several thousand transparencies that I had gathered with the idea of helping students imagine a vast area of the world becoming "America," and conveying that the lives of people in earlier times were as extraordinary and passionate and problematic as our own. That was only a fond hope in 1993, for I had not put those images to much more than ornamental use, and I had not looked closely at many of them in ways that might advance the cause of teaching and learning as I have tried to practice them. What was I going to do with these pictures of town plans, buildings, altarpieces, paintings, drawings, prints, statues, fountains, pots, benches, and doodles made in the sixteenth, seventeenth, and eighteenth centuries? I had no real choice but to look at them more closely—look harder at what they seemed to depict and how, and try to learn more about who had made them, why, and for whom. That is, I was interested in how they might be viewed more in their own right, with their own puzzles and surprises, how they moved people to tears and action, and how they could be contextualized in their time and beyond. Sometimes I cannot help talking about parts of these things, but I try to remember E. B. White's amiable warning about disassembling a good joke. "Humor," wrote White, "can be dissected, like a frog can, but the thing dies in the process and the innards are discouraging to any but the pure scientific mind."[10] I am trying to study some religious objects from the colonial period in a somewhat different way, trying to look at, add to, and situate more than take apart.

What I have been after, both for myself and early modern people is the "thinking in terms of images" that Italo Calvino emphasized, inspired by his boyhood reading of Ignatius of Loyola's *Spiritual Exercises* and U.S. comic strips like "Felix the Cat" and "the Katzenjammer Kids." His Italian newspapers redrew the cartoons without speech balloons, replacing them with a few rhymed lines under each picture. "Those simple-minded rhyming couplets provided no illuminating information," wrote Calvino. "Often they were stabs in the dark.... I preferred to ignore the written lines and to continue with my favorite occupation of daydreaming with the pictures and their sequence." I am still the historian—a contextualizer who sees images especially as residues of episodes—but I like Calvino's idea of "daydreaming within pictures." The aim is to put the pictures, as a means of communication, on the same plane with written texts and spoken words, as they surely were to their original audience. As Calvino wrote, "We may distinguish between two types of imaginative process: the one that starts with the word and arrives at the visual image, and the one that starts with the visual image and arrives at its verbal expression." This is not to say that images and language are neatly separable orders of representation. They are likely to be interwoven in all sorts of ways (as Calvino does in *The Castle of Crossed Destinies*), but his thought about *starting* with an image or words is a way of not automatically reducing the value of images from other times and places or making them always into illustrations, as if we and the people we want to understand always start with the word.[11]

Lately, my curiosity about reception and changes in the history of church and religion has taken me further into material culture, especially sculpture and painting. It was an obvious step considering that Mexican shrines—my special interest now—were image shrines and most art was religious art then. As Clara Bargellini observes, "What most differentiated the circumstances of New World painters from those of their European counterparts, even the Spanish, was the overwhelming role of the church as patron and arbiter of the arts."[12] Catholic Christianity has always been a sensual faith, based on belief in an incarnate God and understood in seventeenth- and eighteenth-century Mexico as a kind of supermateriality, in which sculpted and painted images, altars, candles, and ephemeral decoration aid in lifting the viewer into an exalted emotional state of contrition and faith "where men and gods are held to be transparent to one another."[13] Signs of divine presence in the world were apparent and much anticipated then, and images of Christ or saints, especially Mary, were the focal points of that presence, where the divine was revealed. Makers, authorities, and beholders of images had high hopes—to make and honor images that somehow gave physical form to the invisible and fleeting, inviting divine presence with an out-of-this-world beauty created as much by the heartfelt devotion of believers as by the talent of the sculptors and painters, whose best efforts were attributed to divine inspiration, if not direct divine intervention. Under the right circumstances, and if it was God's will, images literally came to life and wondrous healings and protection followed.

I have not gone very far with this interest in reception, material culture, and geographies of faith. I am still inclined to surround images with written sources that suggest their audience and how they were made, received, and used, and used again. But I mean to think about images from colonial places as more than auxiliary evidence, more than illustrations of things I had already concluded from written sources, as things made and used in certain times and places, with certain values, for good reasons. Above all, the challenge is to reckon with the idea that images were a vital medium of divine presence in the world and often regarded as essential to personal and collective well-being. It has made me more alert to how history, art, religion, and geography intersect[14]; how a revered statue can also be a place in time that expresses the longing to be both here—fulfilled at home—and elsewhere.

The essays in this collection, written over the last ten years, are fruits of these lines of inquiry into the power of images, the history and politics of religious practices, place and space, and reception, and how they might be addressed with the sources I could find. The attention to art and objects of devotion in the history of shrines is best represented in the opening essay, "Images and Immanence in Colonial Mexico," but all of the essays have to do with revered statues and paintings—what they meant to people then, and how they might be studied from the sources available. The second essay in Part I, "Two Shrines of the Cristo Renovado," also introduces an overarching theme in my historical studies of Mexican shrines that goes back to another *inquietud* from my first years of research and teaching in the 1960s and 1970s. In my first studies of communities in the state of Oaxaca where the indigenous presence still is powerfully felt—where native languages continue to be spoken and most village communities date from precolonial times—I expected devotion to Our Lady of Guadalupe to thread through the colonial records. I had read my Octavio Paz and various social science historians who regarded *guadalupanismo* as a Native American devotion from the beginning, with colonial *indios* turning to the maternal embrace of Mary as Guadalupe in their "spiritual orphanhood," as Paz put it.[15] If this was so, and if Oaxaca was among the most "Indian" areas of Mexico, then Guadalupe should be evident just about everywhere there. She was not absent, especially in the city of Antequera from the late seventeenth century, but Guadalupan devotion was overshadowed by local and regional shrines to other images of Mary and Christ; among others, the Virgin of Juquila, Our Lady of La Soledad in Antequera, the cross of Huatulco, and the Lord of Tlacolula. Clearly, there was not just one dominant symbol presiding over a soaring hierarchy of interlocking sacred places and images. With many shrines and images in play, the subject reached far beyond Our Lady of Guadalupe. "Two Shrines of the Cristo Renovado" takes up the history of one of the many shrines to miraculous images of Christ for an examination of the politics of faith in two places during the seventeenth and eighteenth centuries, how Catholic Christianity was becoming an American religion, and how people with seemingly conflicting and subversive interests collaborated in its making.

To move the spotlight in other directions is not to discount the fundamental place of Our Lady of Guadalupe in the history of Mexican devotion.

Since the early eighteenth century, no image has meant so much to so many people. She has become the greatest sign of divine presence in Mexico, and the shrine at Tepeyac today is the most visited in the Americas, and perhaps Christendom. A man from Oaxaca working as a gardener in Berkeley, CA, in the mid-1990s shared this sense of Guadalupe's presence in the face of historical doubts with one of my former undergraduate students, Sergio Rodas: "Only your faith can guide you to decide whether it [the apparition to Juan Diego] was a miracle or an invention of the friars of that time. Whatever the case, the Virgin of Guadalupe came to Mexico and she was well received."[16] This conviction of her presence in Mexico—that the Virgin Mary in the guise of Guadalupe came to stay and was well received—has been repeated endlessly, from colonial sermons that proclaimed her "arrival with no goodbyes" and "Now she never leaves us even though she has ascended to Heaven" to street interviews by journalists during times of crisis in which people say again and again "We all know that the government has failed us and the Virgin of Guadalupe has not."[17]

As much as I am drawn to the many Mexican shrines dedicated to figures of Christ and other images of Mary and the saints for a fuller history of shrines and images that centers on place, Guadalupe inevitably comes into the narrative, as I think she would for anyone interested in faith and religious practice in Mexico. She is featured in the three essays in Part II and mentioned in the other essays, but in somewhat different ways than most writings about Guadalupan devotion. My interest in the array of devotees and their devotions leads me to be less concerned with the sixteenth century—the poorly documented but fascinating earliest stages of guadalupanismo and the debates over the historicity of the apparition story and whether the cultus was mainly precolonial in spirit and Indian in practice from the beginning. Devotees and their devotions in place have led toward the better-documented history of the seventeenth, eighteenth, and early nineteenth centuries, and to a curiosity about two paradoxes in colonial Mexico's spiritual geography. First, that the image of Guadalupe was revered almost everywhere in the Viceroyalty of New Spain by the late eighteenth century, yet the shrine at Tepeyac, with its famous cloak on which the image was impressed during the time of Mary's reported apparitions to Juan Diego, was not yet much visited by distant pilgrims. And second, that the image of Guadalupe had a thousand meanings, but not a thousand faces. Many copies circulated in the colonial period, but nearly all sought to copy as exactly as possible the image at Tepeyac. Only recently have Mexican American and Mexican artists altered the image in more spectacular ways.

The last essay in the collection brings Tepeyac and other shrines together for an exploration of the little known, thinly recorded subject of changes in the spiritual geography and politics of miraculous images and faith during the eventful years after Mexico's national independence in 1821. Focusing on shrines and news of miracles, it highlights surprising growth of old and new shrines at the time and a more conspicuous, leading role for the laity. But it also points to eventful continuities, especially the ongoing importance of images and divine presence in the practice of faith in Mexico. Reported theophanies seem to have been as frequent as ever and shared across classes, not just among villagers and the urban poor. Regional shrines developed, but nearly all of them began in the seventeenth century and were well established before the end of the colonial period. Marian devotion intensified, especially in the second half of the nineteenth century, but this, too, was a great continuity. Devotion to the infant Jesus became more popular, and some miraculous images of Christ's Passion rose to prominence for the first time or became more prominent than they had been in the colonial period, but miracle shrines dedicated to images of Christ had long been the most numerous of all in Mexico.

Annie Kriegel, the French political commentator and social historian of labor movements, once made a wicked appraisal of the arc of the scholar in our time: for the junior scholar, the monograph; for the mature scholar, the magnum opus; for the senior scholar, the preface. I have written my share of prefaces and dust jacket blurbs, but I've also become more quixotic—or maybe just reckless—in my ambitions as an elder scholar trying to figure out what people have understood about religion and how they understood it. By veering off into local histories of hundreds of shrines, celebrated images, and episodes of sacred movement, piecing together parts of biographies of some objects, searching for devotees and reception as well as promotion and regulation, I am pursuing and trying to enlarge upon Émile Durkheim's idea of the contagiousness of the sacred over the course of five centuries and across many places, without reducing it all to a sociology of religion. It is a vast field with scattered documentation and patchy secondary literature that spills out in too many directions. It is more than I could hope to master in a lifetime of study.

But letting it get out of hand is part of the pleasure, as well as a research strategy. The great benefit of academic tenure, beyond the luxury of coming to feel undivided about my priorities during the school year, has been that it freed me to fail, to explore unlikely lines of investigation and contexts, to do more hopeful reading along tangents, to "pursu[e] the matter to the last ditch and the final hill because that is where the fun is and the balm of accomplishment," as E. B. White put it.[18] Of course, success is not always in the cards. I have started more than a few lines of inquiry that did not pan out. The evidence is likely to be favorable rather than conclusive, in any case, and somehow we have to attend to what J. H. Hexter called the historian's second record—"everything the individual mind brings to bear on the record of the past in order to elicit the best account possible of what seems to have actually happened."[19] When I think about all this in the abstract, it puts me in need of a nap, and I've struggled against the impulse to throw in the towel. But the mysteries and doubts have kept me in the archive and at my desk. As poet Wesley McNair says, "The fear of being washed up is a necessary part of the writer's process. The only proof of your ongoing life as a writer" is the next thing you write[20]; next perhaps a more continuous narrative of shrines and images in Mexican history.

PART I

Images and Shrines

Images and Immanence in Colonial Mexico

IN 1656, FRANCISCANS OF THE PROVINCE OF THE HOLY GOSPEL in central Mexico complained to the viceroy about Antonio de Gandía, caretaker of a chapel at Tulantongo on the edge of the Valley of Mexico. Fourteen years earlier Gandía, then a blind beggar, reportedly received a special favor from the Virgin Mary. While praying before a crude, worm-eaten painting of the Madonna and Child on wooden boards that belonged to a local Indian, he heard a woman's voice say that she intended to restore his sight and that he should build her a chapel by the well in his yard. Once it was completed he would see again. As news of the apparition spread, many Indians from nearby Texcoco were moved to visit Gandía and the painting and to give money, building materials, and labor for the promised chapel. Before long, it was completed and Gandía recovered his sight. Now the little shrine was thriving, and Gandía refused to allow the Franciscans from Texcoco who celebrated Mass there to supervise his activities. He had profited from the proceeds, establishing a textile workshop, bakery, and butcher shop on the premises. The Franciscans claimed Gandía had influential friends who protected him in his encroachments on ecclesiastical jurisdiction and that he encouraged superstitious practices among gullible Indians—blessing those who came to visit the chapel, hearing their petitions, and offering advice that he said came to him from the Virgin. They added that during a pastoral visit the archbishop's delegate ordered Gandía to submit a financial report to the Franciscan guardian at Texcoco every six months and turn over to him the collections not spent on routine expenses. But Gandía had not complied, and now bogus copycat miracles were cropping up in the district. The Franciscans wanted to assign one of their own to reside at the shrine and supervise its spiritual and financial affairs.

The viceroy's office issued Gandía a warning to follow orders and avoid excesses in his enterprises near the shrine. It did not specify the orders or excesses, and I have not found further action against him, but the Franciscans would have their way before long as Gandía's name drifted out of the judicial record and into legend. A fine new church was dedicated in 1676, and during his pastoral visit in 1683 Archbishop Aguiar y Seijas, an enthusiast of miraculous images and shrines, ordered that a Franciscan pastor-administrator fluent in Nahuatl be placed there "in order to inflame this devotion." When Franciscan chronicler Agustín de Vetancurt published his *Teatro mexicano* in 1697, a Franciscan pastor was in residence and the shrine continued to receive many visitors thanks to its reputation for cures and other divine favors. By the middle of the eighteenth century the legend of Our Lady of Tulantongo had been worn smooth, reduced and simplified in writing by expectations for a proper founding miracle. Without openly questioning the role of the Virgin in the reported restoration of Gandía's sight, the Franciscan petition in 1656 repeatedly identified him as a *mestizo*, in effect an outsider with a sharp eye for personal power and profit. By the 1740s he had become a virtuous Indian who, when he washed his face in the well water and opened his eyes to sight "more than two hundred years ago," saw the decrepit image of the Madonna and Child restored to fine condition.[1]

During Mexico's War of Independence, in late June 1812, a company of royalist soldiers, including a detachment of Tlaxcalan nobles, drove insurgents and their local supporters from the town of Calpulalpan, in the mountains that drop down to the Valley of Mexico about fifty miles east of Mexico City. In celebration of this victory, the royalist commander granted his troops one hour to pillage the town. The Tlaxcalans declined to take part. Instead, in the spirit of calculated mayhem they had directed against their old enemies, the Aztecs, and, for a time, against Hernán Cortés in 1519 before becoming his indispensable allies, they asked for something that would cut deeper into the well-being of the community of Calpulalpan than random looting. They wanted the miraculous statue of St. Anthony of Padua from the parish church. The royalist commander granted their request, and for nearly two months Calpulalpan was without its Palladium. We know of these events only because within a week of the statue's removal, the viceroy, in response to urgent appeals from the elders of Calpulalpan, issued a formal order for the Franciscans to send in a pastor as soon as possible and to keep the statue temporarily in their convent church at Texcoco. The friar assigned to Calpulalpan reported on August 12 that he had arrived to a warm welcome by townspeople whose only lament, he said, was that he had not brought with him their beloved statue. He pointedly requested that the statue be returned, and the viceroy responded the following day with an order for restitution, which was soon fulfilled.[2]

When Father Antonio Flores Flores went home to Zapotlán del Rey, Jalisco, in the mid-1980s, he looked forward to a tranquil retirement after his busy ecclesiastical career. In 1995 he wrote a little book about the community that celebrated the local statue of the Madonna and Child known as Nuestra Señora del Socorro. Brimming with filial pride, he recounted how he had worked with the parish priest to gain special recognition for the beloved image—an official coronation authorized by the Archbishop of Guadalajara and celebrated in Zapotlán with a special Mass and fiesta in June 1985. Nuestra Señora del Socorro had long "visited" hamlets in the parish following the rainy season, but Father Flores assumed that once it gained this exalted standing, like the renowned images of the Virgin Mary at Talpa, San Juan de los Lagos, and Zapopan, it was too precious to chance the mishaps of the road. The archbishop concurred, adding that another statue of Mary in the parish church could circulate. When the season for Mary's visits came in October that year and angry parishioners from outlying settlements objected and appealed to the archbishop, the auxiliary bishop responded that they could visit the crowned image in the parish church, but only the other image would travel. The parish priest was equally adamant that the crowned image should no longer leave the church. When threats were made against the parish priest, he fled for his safety and never returned. Father Flores also decided it was best to leave town for a while. Upon his return two years later, he asked the new pastor if the celebrated image had been allowed to circulate. The pastor replied, "The people of Zapotlán think of nothing else." A chastened Father Flores recognized the wisdom of this answer. "It seemed to me prudent and respectful of the traditions of the community. With that phrase alone he countered all my reasons for why the image should no longer go out."³

These episodes spanning several centuries suggest how vital religious images have been to individual and collective well-being in Mexico, and how deep the politics of images still run. Clearly, the images at the heart of the action were more than objects or "representations." But how so? Why were they so important to so wide a range of people of different class, caste, and ethnicity? How was their vitality understood and nurtured? How did they connect this world of direct experience to imagined worlds beyond? The idea of immanence, of divine presence, might seem a key to how the potency of a particular image was understood, but that presence could not simply be summoned at will like the djinn of Aladdin's lamp. Presence was God's will. Yet images—some more than others—were seen as potential bridges to the sacred, their allure as "sweet magnets of souls," coaxing feelings of awe and contrition so pleasing to God that devout believers might be admitted, briefly, into the divine presence.

So it might seem, but a scattering of episodes from the remote and recent past, no matter how various and suggestively documented, cannot be made to sustain a continuous history of immanence manifested in religious images. More modestly, this introductory essay seeks to add in some patterned tendencies from a large, scattered, and partial written record in order to construct a scaffolding for other essays in this collection that explore particular images, shrines, and the sometimes conflicted relations among their human custodians.⁴

Shared Anticipation

Religious images carried meaning in various official and unofficial ways during the colonial period, but the notion that they could come alive with the sacred was widely shared. In 1801, Fr. Pedro Pablo Patiño, the Franciscan chaplain of the shrine of Nuestra Señora de los Ángeles at Tlatelolco, expressed a narrower, but frequently voiced clerical view that was in keeping with worries about idolatry in these American places new to Christianity and the Council of Trent's cautious endorsement of images:

We revere images with a relative devotion, in honor of the excellence of the original [the holy personage represented]. The submission we show before a sacred image expresses our respect for the saint who is represented, . . . an internal submission to the original is set in motion. The Council of Trent teaches this when it says: "By way of the images we kiss, to which we remove our hats and kneel, we worship Christ and venerate the saints they resemble."[5]

Extending the teaching metaphor and the act of looking, church authorities in New Spain regarded religious images as aids to instruction and memory. It was through visual images—paintings, statues, altarpieces, plays, processions, tableaux, and the liturgy—that scripture and the mysteries of the faith would be conveyed to and remembered by the ignorant laity.[6] Dr. Juan José de Eguiara y Eguren, the pioneering bibliographer and member of the cathedral chapter in Mexico City, seemed to echo this purpose when he wrote in 1731 that "images are silent sermons."[7]

The didactic impulse notwithstanding, images were more than mute sermons to Indian Christians. For that matter, images were more than that to most people in colonial Mexico, including priests and viceroys. After declaring pictures to be silent sermons, even Eguiara y Eguren suggested in the next breath an equivalence of images and words more than a precedence for words that reduced images to illustrations of doctrine and Christian history: "Sermons also are eloquent images that make themselves seen through the ears."[8] Put another way by Antonio Paredes, S.J., in 1759, "images are eloquent orators that evoke piety." That is, inspired words and beautiful images together invited the kind of devout response that could lead to direct apprehension of the divine, where official and popular understandings of images met in colonial Mexico.[9] Italo Calvino described the connection between images and the pathway to enlightenment and presence in Ignatius of Loyola's key text of the time, the *Spiritual Exercises*, as "through the emotional stimulus of sacred art, the believer was supposed to grasp the meaning of the verbal teachings of the Church," without the image being only a vehicle for a given text. What Calvino found distinctive about Loyola's approach to images was "the shift from the word to the visual image as a way of attaining knowledge of the most profound meaning." Starting with an image and seeking spiritual insight and communion was not unusual, but, says Calvino of Loyola, "in the middle there opens up a field of infinite possibilities in the application of the individual imagination, in how one depicts characters, places, and scenes in motion."[10] This view of images and imagination culminated in the best of baroque art during the seventeenth and eighteenth centuries.

Reaching for divine presence began with sight, with seeing the image, but did not end there. Christian doctrine and ecclesiastical practice seemed to privilege visibility, but apprehending in this way depended on a more active engagement of all the senses in ways reminiscent of South Asian *darsan*, that is, "seeing" the god means more than visibility—beholding or "taking in" the image and presence of the divine, *and* being beheld by that presence, with sound, smell, sight, touch, gesture, and exertion all in play. This beholding was not simply an act initiated by the devotee—"Under the right circumstances, the deity present[s] itself to be seen in its image"[11]—but approaching the divine in the right way, in the right spirit could make a difference. Colonial sources from Motolinía on emphasize the acts of ardent devotion that made miracles possible. The usual route to the active company of a divine being was contemplative (as in Fig. 1.1), but not always. Facing grave danger, a devotee's urgent appeal for protection could be answered. For example, in Motolinía's telling, an Indian maiden was rescued by angels from two lascivious suitors intent on raping her because "she continually beseeched God with tears and a good heart."[12]

Shared notions of redemptive beauty strengthened the connection between images and immanence in the colonial period.[13] Beauty and a sense of completion in the world turned on comprehension of God. For Francisco de Florencia, the indefatigable Jesuit devotee and promoter of miraculous images and their shrines in New Spain during the late seventeenth century, beauty was a function of the tender awe and wonder the image inspired, drawing the beholder closer to God. As he put it in his description of the statue of Our Lady of Loreto, "The image of Our Lady is marvelously beautiful. . . . To look directly at its face stirs devotion, respect, and tenderness."[14] The author of a report for the district of Querétaro in 1743 described a famous painting of the Virgin of Guadalupe there as "a beautiful and divine canvas whose most beautiful image is so like its prodigious original that it attracts the faithful like a sweet magnet, enriching the world with celestial favors."[15] Beauty here meant a perfection of proportion and technique that was pleasing to God, asserted the being of the figure represented, and invited that presence and favor.[16] The form was important to the effects. For these authorities, the richer the materials and the more polished, exquisite, and seemly the rendering, the more beautiful and

Fig. 1.1. The posture of prayer. A young aristocrat approaches God in a fitting way, with hands joined, her eyes uplifted and glistening with tears, probably on her knees. *Portrait of a Lady*, attributed to Baltasar de Echave Orio, 1615–1620. Courtesy of the Museo Nacional de Arte, Mexico City.

perfect—and holy—the result.¹⁷ The finery added to the preciousness of the image itself. It testified to the generosity and sacrifice of devotees, a tangible display of their ardent devotion, a kind of good work.

Ecclesiastical authorities generally regarded decorum,¹⁸ an appropriate setting, and exquisite trappings as indispensable features of a beautiful image. Painstaking, conventional representations of the appearance and spirit of the subject were said to be especially pleasing to God. But popular taste could rub against these prescriptions for what was decorous. Favorite local images in their niches might appear ugly, tired, and in need of a makeover to church authorities who knew them only from a distance. Still, there was general agreement that the measure of beauty was the response it evoked, and feelings associated with beauty converged for all concerned on awe, love, tearful rapture, contrition, and a sense of grandeur and wholeness that brought them close to God.

Faith in these terms was not always decorous. To devotees, the reputation of an image for supernatural favors or signs of life could make a crude image beautiful. Images that showed their age, especially the signs of loving caresses by one's ancestors or minor alterations from a remote past could add to its aura of preciousness and permanent favor.¹⁹ Pastors who demoted, removed, or retouched treasured local images in keeping with their own ideas about beauty and fitting appearance could expect an angry reaction from parishioners that made a quick escape their only recourse.²⁰ Ecclesiastical judges routinely cautioned local officials not to be too eager to enforce sweeping directives against unseemly images. Better to condone a vulgar practice, if necessary, than chance a rebellion was the message.²¹

Leading authors of devotional texts encouraged this subjective truth of beauty and miracles. Admitting that fewer primary sources for the early history and miracles of Our Lady of Los Remedios and Our Lady of Guadalupe had come to light than he hoped for, Florencia concluded that the fact that miracle stories were widely retold and an image's favors were known by reputation (*voz pública y fama*) was the best evidence of their truth. "The miracles of this image are themselves voices that publicize it," he wrote, "Human faith alone makes them certain."²² Testimonials about miracles, in particular, were regarded as evidence of God's grace and an image's singular beauty. Sometimes images were understood to come alive, literally, and make God's will known directly—trembling, groaning, weeping, bleeding, speaking, changing posture, growing heavy, sprouting hair, restoring themselves to fine condition, resisting attack, appearing in mysterious ways, healing, and protecting. Another learned priest, Dr. Alfonso Alberto de Velasco, summed up this shared understanding of the mystique of religious images in 1699 when he wrote that Divine Providence had always provided miraculous images to her church for four purposes: (1) as proof of the efficacy of faith in sacred images against heretics and doubters; (2) for instruction of the ignorant; (3) as a perpetual reminder of the "Sovereign Mysteries of our Redemption"; and (4) to stir tender feelings of devotion.[23] An object became more beautiful when it was associated with divine favor—*maravillas* that responded to the concerns of devotees, protecting them from harm, bestowing the benefits of health, abundance, or a good death—and an inclination toward good works by devotees. Beauty, then, was a manifestation of the divine as much as a stimulus toward it. Beauty, itself, was a kind of miracle, regarded as the product of divine inspiration, rather than an artist's personal ingenuity, although church leaders remained alert to the possibility that art could be an enticing deception by the devil, too.

The powerful appeal of Christian images in colonial Mexico is not surprising given the widely shared sense of beauty and immanence in Spanish American Catholicism, and the synesthesia of devotion in both precolonial and colonial practices. Images tend to cross cultures more readily than words, but their reception in this case was bound to be equivocal. As Ernst Gombrich suggested in his reflections on the difference between word statements and pictorial statements,

> Looking at communication from the vantage point of language, we must ask first which of these functions the visual image can perform. We shall see that the visual image is supreme in its capacity for arousal, that its use for expressive purposes is problematic, and that unaided it altogether lacks the possibility of matching the statement function of language.[24]

With their own long experience of making and using effigies, native peoples of Mesoamerica made and beheld Christian images in ways theologians and ecclesiastical courts did not fully comprehend and could not easily manage or remove by persuasion and force. And the church's emphasis on reception—the feelings evoked—in their conception of beauty added yet another layer of subjectivity to the exuberance of images. Despite the Christian hunt for idols, the issue was not that the meaning and uses of images were absolutely different and antagonistic, with little room for shared experience beyond imposition, but that the similarities that drew people to images were important enough to make for subtle misunderstandings. In different ways, the human body was understood in indigenous and Christian cultures as a living vessel of sacred being, although in precolonial Mesoamerica humans merged more completely with natural forms and forces, much as the materials from which effigies were made—the stones, wood, maize stalks, and other plant material—contained the sacred in themselves.[25] Like special Christian images and relics, Mesoamerica's "supremely sacred sculptures" might be carried in procession or, like Calpulalpan's St. Anthony, stolen by enemy states. Or, like Christian reliquaries, the sacred energy of an effigy might be enhanced by inserting precious stones associated with a divine being or ashes of the totemic ancestor it represented into a recess in the body. Deities in precolonial Mesoamerica sometimes were conceived anthropomorphically, and the majestic annual cycle of rituals, which often involved effigies, was associated with divine power that blended with Christian practices in the colonial period: celestial creation and protection; fertility; and war and sacrifice.[26] The abundance of anthropomorphic ceramic figurines found in the remains of precolonial house sites suggests a widely shared use of images in daily life at home before and after the Conquest. Just what the uses were is not certain, but they may have been associated with health, curing, and protection through divine intervention, much like the saints and offerings on home altars since the early colonial period.

These similarities invited acceptance and enthusiasm, but they were not equivalents and there were bound to be misunderstandings. Precolonial deities were more than emblems of "natural" forces; they were those forces. The divinity in and of nature, represented in figures that incorporated human forms but were not simply human effigies, is more a part of Mesoamerican worldviews, and was expressed in the premise that powerful dualities of creation and destruction were contained in the same manifestation of divine power. Christian views of Christ, Mary, and the saints involved judgment and punishment, but they were more about protection and salvation, and focused on the human form and humanity of holy personages. Female divinity was associated with fertility in both (and to a lesser extent, purity), but the most common representation of divine females in Mesoamerica attached them literally, not just metaphorically, to the sacred food plant maize as much as to motherhood.[27] The remarkable maize stalk and paste figures of Mary, Christ, and some saints made in the sixteenth and seventeenth centuries are colonial creations rich in these similarities with multiple meanings that may not have challenged Christian teachings, but were not limited by them.[28]

Historical Patterns

Images of Christ and the Virgin Mary were part of New Spain's colonial history from the beginning. If we can believe Bernal Díaz del Castillo, Hernán Cortés left a string of statuettes of the Virgin Mary at native ceremonial sites along his route to the Aztec capital in 1519. And images of both Christ and Mary became the celebrated objects of devotion at several miracle shrines before the end of the sixteenth century, including Our Lady of Guadalupe at Tepeyac, Our Lady of los Remedios at Naucalpan, Our Lady of Guanajuato, the Christ of Totolapa, the Christ of the Dominican Novitiates' chapel in Mexico City, and La Conquistadora and Our Lady of la Defensa of Puebla. But, for the most part, miraculous images of these two central figures in Catholic Christianity and the shrines that sheltered them began or gained their lasting fame later, in the seventeenth century.

Eruptions of the sacred in human affairs seem almost commonplace in the sixteenth-century Spanish chronicles of conquest and colonization, but most were apparitions rather than numinous images. On the Spanish side, early friars, fixed on their evangelizing mission, anticipated providential signs of divine presence and found them in dream visions, apparitions of Christ and the saints, and miraculous healings and protection.[29] But they were ambivalent about the use and meaning of images. The Council of Trent affirmed the importance of images in Christian practice, but cautiously, and the debate continued. There was no rush to images or flood of reports of images coming to life or working miracles in Spain, much less Spanish America. Sixteenth-century chronicles of the "spiritual conquest" by mendicant friars reflecting on the evangelization enterprise of their orders, rarely mention wonder-working images or shrinemaking, but speak often of free-ranging apparitions to, and marvelous healings associated with, exemplary members of their orders. These early chronicles also describe apparitions reported to them by Indian neophytes. These reports may well be more than pious fabrications by the friars since visions, omens, and other overt signs of divine presence were familiar features of precolonial life throughout Mesoamerica. Native interest in apparition stories is apparent in Nahuatl miracle narratives from the sixteenth century and occasional reports of Indians claiming to be Christ or Mary incarnate later in the colonial period.[30]

Among the Franciscans, Motolinía (writing in the mid-sixteenth century) includes miraculous healings and conversions worked by God that focused on St. Francis, especially his signature knotted girdle. In his account, several mortally ill Indians who urgently requested last rites had visions of being taken to Hell by "some black men." When they cried out to God and the Blessed Mary, an angel protected them. In one case the angel took the lost soul to a place of "great delights and happiness" (*mucho placer y alegría*). Motolinía also associated the sign of the cross with protection from harm and enlarged upon its meaning by adding that Indians in the Valley of Mexico began making crosses to protect against flood, a practice that he said was especially popular in Texcoco and Huejotzingo, as well as Mexico City. But other images enter his account mainly as liturgical objects. He mentioned statues of saints in the procession of Corpus Christi at Tlaxcala in 1538, but did not associate them with miracles.

Franciscan chronicles from the late sixteenth and early seventeenth centuries, including the *Oroz Codex* (1585), Gerónimo de Mendieta's *Historia eclesiástica indiana* (completed 1596), and Juan de Torquemada's *Monarquía indiana* (published 1615) continued to chart Christian enchantment of central Mexico, including apparitions and visions to Indian neophytes. The *Oroz Codex* recounts eight apparitions to Indians, sometimes of friars or a deceased soul, and one Indian vision of devils and angels. Mendieta's text, which overlaps the *Oroz Codex* in content, expands on the theme of apparitions and revelations to Indians with three twists that grew out of the early evangelization by mendicant missionaries and anticipate the central importance of images to Catholic faith in New Spain during the seventeenth century. First, like Motolinía, Mendieta emphasized Indian devotion to the cross and miracles associated with this devotion. He mentioned some particular cases, including a refulgent cross in the sky at Tlaxcala when the great wooden cross was planted there and crucifixes radiating a great light.[31] Early friars apparently saturated the native landscape with crosses, planting them in the atria of new churches and at native sacred sites in the fields and mountains where they imagined the devil lurked. Second, in Mendieta's account elderly Indians and children, especially girls, were the favored seers because of their "simplicity"; adult women are notably absent. And third, the apparitions he mentioned now pointed to Christ and the Virgin Mary: an Indian of Tula watching a priest raise the consecrated Host saw a baby in a snow white diaper appear in his hands; another Indian man came to confess a second time in two days, insisting that a voice spoke to him when he dropped a crucifix, "Woe is thee. You intend to receive me tomorrow and you have not completely confessed your sins"; and during the great epidemic of 1576 a fisherman in his canoe saw a woman in Indian dress on the water who consoled him and told him to ask Mendieta to warn the people to repent, that God was offended by their conduct.

Unlike his predecessors, Torquemada introduced a miraculous image—the cross of Huatulco on the coast of Oaxaca, which could not be destroyed by devilish English Protestant pirates. Otherwise, his vast chronicle finds the miraculous in astonishing healings and in visions and apparitions to Indians, especially young girls (again, because of their "santa simplicidad"). He described only a few cases, but suggested that others of this kind could fill a volume as large as his *Monarquía indiana*, if only they were recorded as they occurred. Again, as in other early chronicles, there are visions of devils and angels; a dream vision of two paths, one stony and fetid, the other smooth and smelling of roses; and consoling visits by the Virgin Mary, bringing a good death or spoonfuls of healing tonic. Franciscans were Torquemada's main witnesses. One friar at Tzintzuntzan reported seeing the Host levitate and fly into the mouth of an Indian woman standing in line for communion.

News of apparitions did not end in the sixteenth century,[32] but they became less frequent, largely displaced by other signs of immanence. And another kind of apparition—by souls in Purgatory—was reported and treated with great seriousness in the seventeenth century. One case is especially well documented. News came to the Inquisition in 1648 from the mining town of Pachuca that the soul in limbo of Juan Mexía, a recently deceased miner, had appeared to a young Spaniard he had befriended. According to the young man, Juan González, Mexía appeared three times during Holy Week, in the company of a shadowy Augustinian friar and a murmuring multitude of souls, calling upon him to ask the forgiveness of Juan Cortés Ramírez, against whom he had born false witness. As a sign of his anguished, urgent presence, Mexía's spirit left the mark of his flaming hand on the blanket that covered González the night of the third apparition. Although the case file lacks a final judgment, suggesting that it was discreetly left unfinished (like many other Inquisition dossiers that never went to trial), it contains a lengthy, cautious,

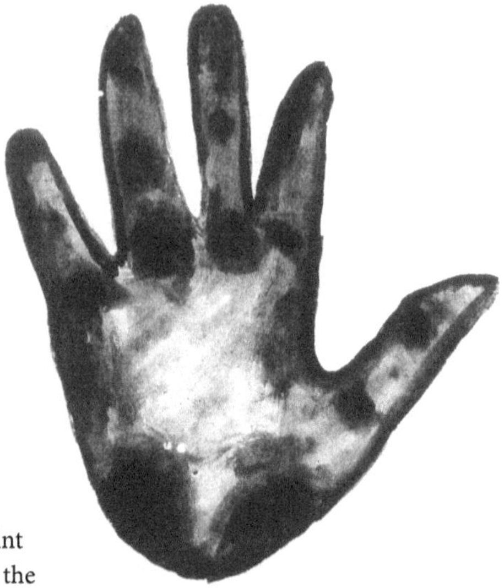

Fig. 1.2. The immanence of images in Christian New Spain was always about awe, but not always about beauty and sweet magnetism. Especially in nominally Spanish settlements during the seventeenth century, the supernatural could break in on the living with dramatic signs that fed anxieties about the journey of the soul after death. Here is the ink drawing from 1648 of a charred handprint on a wool blanket presented in the investigation of Juan González's claim that he had been visited by the soul of his recently deceased neighbor and mentor, Juan Mexía. Courtesy of the Library of Congress, Henry A. Monday Collection.

and not incredulous investigation, with detailed testimony from character witnesses and witnesses to the scene after the fact. The prospect of Purgatory was palpable to pious Christians of the time, anxiously alert to the consequences of their sins.[33]

But when new apparition stories involving Indians were reported later in the seventeenth century, they were rarely greeted with the enthusiasm found in Mendieta and Torquemada or afforded to Juan Diego and Our Lady of Guadalupe. Jacinto de la Serna was not incredulous when he reported in the 1650s that Indian shamans in the Valley of Toluca claimed that Our Lady of los Remedios, the Madonna in a *huipil*, and the archangels Gabriel and Michael appeared to them and brought healing herbs and special recipes; nor was Pedro Ponce when he reported shamans at Zumpahuacan claiming to have encountered Christ and angels in drugged visions. But they attributed these apparitions to the devil.[34] And when individuals declared themselves to be Christ, God Almighty, or the Virgin Mary in the eighteenth century, their cases were dispatched without serious attention to the claim. The more modest and less threatening claim by

Francisco Diego, an Indian of Atenco in the parish of Metepec, in 1728, that the Virgin of Guadalupe had appeared to him, promising money that he was to spend on fruit for the poor was also suppressed without further ado.[35] By the mid-seventeenth century, the concern mainly was that these seers and shamans might appeal to a wider audience than just local Indians, and their activities needed to be nipped in the bud.

As apparitions declined in official favor and the written record during the seventeenth century, miraculous images took their place. More than three hundred Mexican miracle shrines drawing devotees from beyond the immediate community were founded in the colonial period. Most of them began in the seventeenth century and nearly all were associated with an image that was believed to have shown life or worked wondrous cures. Nearly all of them prospered during the eighteenth century. Agustín de Vetancurt's chronicle, *Teatro mexicano. Descripción breve de los sucesos exemplares, históricos, políticos, militares y religiosos del nuevo mundo occidental de las Indias*, published in 1697, can serve as a coda for this trend toward image shrines in the seventeenth century. Unlike his fellow Franciscans Torquemada, Mendieta, and Motolinía, Vetancurt's providential New World homeland was a web of shrines housing images that worked miracles and showed life. The only apparition story he featured was the now canonical one of the image of the Virgin of Guadalupe.[36] Many of the miraculous images had an aura about their activation that went beyond the personal presence of the saint, angel, or Christ. Their existence and location often was heralded by celestial lights and music, or church bells that rang on their own, or the images gave off a sweet smell, or grew too heavy to move, or were found on the back of a mule that would not budge from the spot where the shrine would be built. Or handsome young men—sometimes Indians—dressed in white whom no one recognized appeared then disappeared, leaving behind images that were too beautiful to be the work of human hands.

Images and the numinous were not confined to the shrines in which they were celebrated. Since the uniqueness of a particular image was less important than the faith devotees brought to it, any image anywhere might be a place to encounter the divine. As the next section suggests, it could be a copy hundreds of miles from the original image, even a cheap print; or it might be found on a corner table at home displaying prints, small statues, candles, food, and other offerings; or activated by a procession or a novena. Home altars belonging to all classes of people are a feature of the popular practice of Christianity in colonial Mexico.[37] How the meaning of images on home altars in Indian pueblos expressed indigenous traditions is an elusive subject, but several threads of continuity are apparent. The ceramic figurines frequently found by archaeologists in the debris of home sites in precolonial central Mexico, and the pictorial and written references to household *oratorios*, suggest the use of images as sources of protection for the home.[38] However, the widespread use of tables to display home altar goods appears to have been a colonial innovation. John Monaghan makes the suggestive surmise that ritual home use of this new kind of furniture by colonial Indians to invite divine protection and favor expressed their understanding of authority under the new regime. Tables begin to appear in native pictorial manuscripts after the conquest mainly as objects associated with colonial officials, who were shown seated behind them.[39] Appealing for divine favor at a table with offerings, and making gestures of respect and submission, resembled the expected manner of approaching colonial officials, he suggests.

The origin stories and signature miracles for various image shrines reported in devotional histories, novena booklets, civil and religious reports, and ecclesiastical court records are one way to discuss the appeal of images that came to life in some way. Of the ninety-four origin stories I have collected so far,[40] fifty were for shrines dedicated to images of the Virgin Mary, forty-one to images of Christ, and six to images of saints other than Mary. Of the forty-one shrines to images of Christ, thirty-three (80.5 percent) originated with activations of the image; twenty-seven of the fifty Marian origin stories involved activations (54 percent), as did four of the six devotions to other saints. These aggregate numbers point to some striking tendencies and comparisons. The two obvious patterns are that the overwhelming majority of miracle shrines in the colonial period were dedicated to images of Christ and Mary, and images of Christ were more likely to show signs of life. An array of saints other than Mary were known and venerated as patron saints of particular communities and were displayed and invoked by individuals in local churches, chapels, and homes, but images of Christ and Mary were the ones that gained widespread fame for signs of immanence and favor. Of course, Christ's immanence was understood to be ever present in the Mass and communion wafer, but images of him as an infant and in the Passion, especially on the cross, brought him closer to the tribulations of the faithful than the mediation of saints might suggest. Miraculous images of Christ were numerous and often called "santos" by their devotees, intimately present in the way of a patron saint or guardian angel. While miraculous images of Christ were more likely than images of Mary to be animated, their presence rarely took the form of apparitions separate from the statue or painting, and rarely did Christ speak in these activations.[41] Christs trembled, grew heavy, became bigger, perspired, bruised, oozed or spurted blood, groaned, and restored themselves to pristine condition, simulating His crucifixion and resurrection. The Holy Child of San Juan de la Penitencia in Mexico City famously changed his pose to keep a wall from collapsing in an earthquake. Figures of Mary also changed posture, but, for obvious reasons, representations of the Passion of Christ, especially the crucified Christ, had standard poses that rarely changed. More often than the figures of Mary, the miraculous Christs and crosses were found in nature, indeed were often *of* nature—embedded in a tree or rock or appearing suddenly in the sky. One unusual symbolic representation of Christ in and of nature—the unusual wild green grass that grew in the form of a cross at Tepic, Nayarit—pointed to His resurrection and the promise of life everlasting in a different way.[42] In the early 1750s Fernando Bustillo Varas y Gutiérrez, a patriotic lawyer from Guadalajara, wrote a treatise celebrating his American homeland in providential terms that highlighted this cross:

> There in the town of Tepic is the amazing grassy cross that remains always green and beautiful even when the land around it is bone dry. It is so hardy that as soon as a piece is cut off as a relic—which happens many times a day—the next day it is full again. But this is not the only marvel, because part of the way down the trunk of the cross is a hole, like a wound, corresponding to the wound in the side of Our Divine Lord, full of whitish soil that replenishes itself no matter how much is taken away as a relic and medicine. Also remarkable is the fact that the chapel there has never been successfully roofed over, just as the site where Christ our Lord ascended to his Heavenly Father could never be covered.[43]

Some Marian images perspired, grew heavy, and changed posture, and a few restored themselves or mysteriously completed themselves in their New World homes,[44] but their signs of life usually differed from the animated Christs in ways that displayed womanly virtues of the time. Many were diminutive, welcoming statues. Unlike the Christs, none of the animated Marian images I know of was said to grow in size, and few displayed much physical prowess (although several statues of Mary in Mexico City were famous for wet hems and caked mud on their dresses, and were believed to have become the living Mary at night and gone out on the causeways to hold back flood waters).[45] They expressed more emotion than physical suffering, often weeping. Mary's face and hands were the center of attention, and it was her perennial purity and perfection they were said to convey. The renowned images were known as beautiful and unblemished, or they reputedly changed color or expression to show sorrow, anger, or love. Sometimes a mole on the Virgin's cheek grew or shrank, or a star appeared on her forehead. While rarely restoring themselves, they were often said to have remained in fine condition despite exposure to the elements. While figures of Christ that came to life rarely spoke, Mary was known to speak in the presence of her image, with instructions, warnings, and consolation.

Decent Images, Indecent Acts

As Durkheim would have anticipated, the proper appearance and presentation of images was on the minds of church leaders from the beginning. Although not a major concern, proper depiction was a topic of discussion in all three sixteenth-century synods and, in the spirit of the Council of Trent, early prelates spoke of encouraging the cult of images, especially paintings.[46] Promotion of images in devotional practice and the accompanying worries about idolatry came to the fore in the seventeenth century. Bishops then, from Juan de Palafox y Mendoza in Puebla to Archbishop Francisco de Aguiar y Seijas, promoted shrines and miraculous images and took care that images were kept in good repair and displayed properly.[47] Perhaps no one was as enthusiastic a promoter of shrines as Aguiar y Seijas during his 1683 pastoral visit.[48]

One particular concern that runs through much of the seventeenth- and eighteenth-century administrative record of the church, and culminated in a concerted campaign by government officials during the 1820s, was the display of crosses and other religious images outdoors, in "indecent places," where they were exposed to mundane activities, if not sacrilege. The intimacies of daily life were liable to look "indecent" to authorities in any case, but there was the larger worry about the devil's tireless ubiquity in the world. War had to be waged against him. In

1641 the Inquisition banned celebrations on the day of the Holy Cross because crosses were being placed or painted in "indecent places."[49] Then in August 1690 and March 1691 the Inquisition issued a more sweeping decree meant to "eliminate the abuse of placing and painting crosses at public corners and other indecent places, in order to rescue then from everyday indecencies" and end outdoor celebrations of Mass, sermons, and processions, as well as profane fiestas.[50] Decrees about removing crosses and other religious images from inappropriate public places were reissued several times by the crown as well as ecclesiastical authorities in the late eighteenth century, but by then they were less concerned about idolatry and the devil lurking behind irregular practices. Now there was a more insistent royal program to reduce routine religious celebrations in public places.[51] In 1786, when residents of the Calle del Aguila neighborhood in Mexico City petitioned for an exemption so they could continue to venerate their beloved image of Our Lady of Sorrows, which had always been displayed in a protected street corner niche, the Inquisition said no.[52] Times had changed. A similar request by officials of the Mexico City mint in May 1654 for permission to celebrate the annual feast of the Holy Cross at the corner of the offices where a cross was displayed was approved by the archbishop's council without debate.[53] The campaign against religious images in public places took another turn in the 1820s when national and state politicians moved to remove religious images from public places in a way that seemed to be less about dignifying the cult than reducing its importance in public life.

Within a generation of the conquest, bishops were policing what they took to be abuses of images, but efforts to control their use intensified in the seventeenth and eighteenth centuries. To describe patterns in the record of abuse of images, I am relying on ninety-one judicial cases of *desacato de imágenes* (irreverence toward images) dating from the 1550s to 1810, nearly all of them from the Inquisition's archive.[54] The acts of irreverence and disrespect included physical abuse—burning, smashing, slashing, whipping, throwing, dropping, or otherwise damaging an image; spitting on it; leaving it lying on a filthy floor; wiping it with a dirty sock; folding or crumpling a religious print and putting it in one's shoe or pocket, using a print for a rag or toilet paper, or allowing it to be displayed in poor condition; and speaking provocatively to it or about it by mocking its appearance and powers or dismissing it as just a piece of wood, stone, canvas, or paper.

Fig 1.3. One of the cheap religious prints that priest-imposter Joseph Lucas de Aguayo y Herrera wore folded up in his shoes in the Guanajuato jail. The print shows wear and is spotted with dirt. The back of the print is soiled along the fold lines. Circulating in the city of Guanajuato, this print also documents the reach of devotion to Our Lady of Zapopan and its shrine beyond the Diocese of Guadalajara. From an engraving by Sotomayor in AGN Inquisición 1096, exp. 9, 1772. Courtesy of the Archivo General de la Nación, Mexico.

As another kind of documentation of the long history of images and their reception, these cases of mistreatment present us with a perennial conundrum: Do they mainly reflect an administrative history in which colonial ecclesiastical and royal authorities were concerned about abuse of images at particular times? Or did they mark important changes in religious practice among the kinds of people who were accused of provocative behavior? By themselves, these cases of desacato de imágenes investigated by the Inquisition cannot answer these questions, but they suggest some outlines of a history of persistence through change.

Gender differences and perverse enactments of the life stories of Christ and Mary—provocative inversions of the self-renovating crucifixes and perpetually perfect images of Mary—are especially clear patterns in these cases of irreverence toward images. Women occasionally were brought before ecclesiastical courts for misusing or physically mistreating images, but the accused were overwhelmingly men, especially younger *casta* men of humble origins, a disproportionate number of whom labored in the textile workshops of Mexico City, where the Inquisition held court. At the other end of the ethnic spectrum, peninsular Spanish men, both minor royal officials and misanthropes, were also overrepresented. And the images abused were mostly representations of men. Statues of the Virgin Mary sometimes were mistreated, but figures of Christ, especially crucifixes, were the usual objects of abuse. Most often they were whipped, reiterating the physical abuse of Christ on the road to Calvary and in his crucifixion.

The nature of recorded abuses shifted somewhat over time. In most of the nine sixteenth-century cases, the accused was charged with acts of physical abuse of images that appeared to express disillusionment and anger of the moment rather than iconoclasm or mockery. The more provocative, cynical acts of abuse were rare then and mainly date from the late seventeenth and eighteenth centuries.[55] But it would be a mistake to imagine a neat, linear progression from enchantment to disenchantment or medieval to modern sensibilities in these records. For the most part, these desacato cases and the regulations that foresaw or responded to them were signs of disillusionment, anger, egocentrism, and official anxiety about contagion, rather than a watershed in disenchantment. Basic patterns in the kinds of abuse, objects of abuse, and abusers continued more than changed, and the notable concentration of cases during the 1610s–1620s and 1750s–1790s points to administrative preoccupations of the time more than an explosion of abuses or widespread change in devotional life. The preoccupations of these two times *were* different. The peak of accusations in the 1610s–1620s included people from many walks of life during a time of anxious concerns about spirituality, sin, idolatry, contamination, decline, and omnipresence of the devil. From the early 1600s to about 1650—during and shortly after the union of the crowns of Spain and Portugal (1580–1640)—Portuguese immigrants, stereotyped as crypto-Jews, were prominent among those accused of mistreating images. And eight of the nineteen cases in this first peak of desacatos de imágenes date from 1616–1617. Perhaps an administrative order about such abuses was published in 1615 or 1616 to trigger this judicial activity then, much as an edict against the use of peyote in the 1620s elicited reports and accusations about use of hallucinogenic drugs.[56] They tell us something about popular practice, but even more about an administrative history.

The second peak—with thirty-two cases, eleven of them clustered in the 1790s—was longer and coincided with a concerted reform program directed by royal governors who presented themselves as keepers of a more sober, dignified faith, as much as by sympathetic prelates and an Inquisition court that participated in the new politics of religion. The contrast between Torquemada's account of friars filling the landscape with crosses during the great sixteenth-century evangelization and the archbishop of Mexico's call in 1792 for crosses venerated in the mountains and other remote places to be brought into the parish church for proper care and reverence is one example of the change in official attitude toward images in public places.[57] The bishops' concern for "decency," restraint, and convention in images documented in their pastoral visits, administrative circulars to parish priests, and moves against particular practices by the mid-eighteenth century[58] was echoed in the late eighteenth century by the restrictions on alms-collecting missions with images; the efforts to remove images from public view; restrictions on their use in processions; the campaign against "ridiculous" images; and the array of incidents of disrespect for images recorded in the late eighteenth-century Inquisition and criminal cases.

What seems especially new in these late colonial cases—although not yet dominant patterns—is more open contempt for traditional religious practices by some public officials, mainly lower-level royal governors and army personnel; more examples of wanton destruction of images[59]; and more robberies of church treasures in the years shortly before and during the independence war.[60]

A Synoptic Record

Occasionally a set of documents from the late colonial period displays an array of actors and accumulated history for a closer view of the uses of images in rural Mexico. The *relaciones geográficas* for the Archdiocese of Mexico in 1743 have been useful to me in this way, but I have used them piecemeal. The reports by bishops and intendants about processions with images in 1796–1797 are less well known. They cover a larger area in some suggestive ways, and touch on both devotional practices in Indian communities where images were alive with the sacred and the longstanding, now mounting efforts of governors and regalist clergy to contain popular religiosity—especially its expression in processions, lavish fiestas, alms-collecting missions for image shrines, and display of images in public places—and redirect the devotional "economy" toward more productive uses.

The chain of administrative action and report writing in this instance was touched off by a complaint to Puebla's bishop from the pastor of Tzompantepec (Tlaxcala)—the kind of complaint royal governors, bishops, and the Inquisition encouraged in the late eighteenth century in their moves to dignify, if not eliminate, traditional devotional practices, control "disorder and abuses," and reduce religious expenses. Using the official language of "desórdenes y abusos," the pastor complained of wasteful local collections to pay for excessive feast day celebrations, especially the processions of images from outlying villages to the parish seat that led to drunkenness, lewd behavior, and "ridiculous" embellishment of the images on these occasions, as well as lavish spending.[61] Bishop Salvador Bienpica y Sotomayor forwarded the pastor's complaint to the viceroy with a request for action, insisting that there would be no resolution without the intervention of royal authority. He noted that in response to similar abuses in San José de Chiapa in 1775, his predecessor, Bishop Victoriano López Gonzalo, prohibited the movement of religious images outside their communities, especially in processions to the parish seat. Bienpica claimed that López Gonzalo's prohibition was at least nominally in force from 1775–1792. Included with Bienpica's appeal to the viceroy was a brief by his legal adviser that the order would benefit both civil society and religious practice because the Indians generally were rebellious and disorderly people (*tumultuaria y desarreglada*) who required "the greatest vigilance." He suggested that the bishop issue a general order against such processions in his diocese and urge the viceroy to commission reports from other parts of the viceroyalty. The result of this petition was an official inquiry with reports by the Archbishop of Mexico, the bishops of Valladolid, Guadajalara, Nuevo León, Puebla, and Antequera, and the intendants of Guanajuato, San Luis Potosí, Valladolid, Veracruz, and Guadalajara, culminating in a viceregal decree in December 1797 that images could not be carried in processions beyond the local community. They were not to be processed from village to village nor taken out to the fields or on alms-collecting tours. Indians could go in processions of up to one league, but only with a cross and *ciriales* (tall candles carried by acolytes in certain Catholic ceremonies).

Considering the origin of the inquiry and the political climate of the time, I expected resounding endorsements of the Bishop of Puebla's complaint by the prominent officials solicited for information and advice. Some of the reporters obliged, apparently without bothering to collect evidence from district governors and parish priests. Bishop Cabañas of Guadalajara wrote a lengthy disquisition against processions of images from afar in the spirit of the hoary Spanish proverb, "Romería de cerca, mucho vino y poca cera" (On short pilgrimages much wine is spilled, but little candlewax). He appealed mainly to theological principles, especially that "holy things should be treated in a holy manner."[62] Intendant Manuel de Flon of Puebla, who came under scrutiny for provocative comments about Catholic devotional practices and beliefs earlier in his political career in New Spain,[63] weighed in with a short opinion that when Indians left home and work for these diversions they committed all sorts of "stupidities and irreverence toward images" (*torpezas y desacato de imágenes*). Oaxaca's Intendant Antonio de Mora y Peysal followed suit, offering a sketchy report of some "excesses" by Indians who gathered in the city Antequera during Corpus Christi with "ridiculous images," extravagantly adorned. The Bishop of Antequera also added his support for the Bishop of Puebla's view.[64] But these records also document the hesitation of prelates and royal authorities to act decisively. For one, the Archbishop of Mexico did not challenge the viceroy's edict, but he warned that during his pastoral visits since 1774 he had issued similar instructions without much effect "because the Indians are very tenacious about keeping their customs, and they are very fond of carrying images, crosses, ciriales, banners, and flags considerable distances to the sound of rockets and musical instruments."[65]

Judging by the district reports submitted for some of the intendancies and dioceses in this dossier, the practice of processions with images to parish seats on special feast days was widespread, but not universal. Within the report for Zacatecas, district governors at Sombrerete, Sierra de Pinos,

Chimaltitán, Nieves, and Mazapil reported either that the custom was absent or there were no pueblos de indios. But the reporter for Fresnillo stated that all Indian pueblos in the district came there with their images, traveling up to five leagues (roughly five and a half to fourteen miles). He found the practice unseemly, with novice musicians playing too loud and off key, and people incensing their images with *copal* from little braziers rather than proper censers. He mentioned some drunkenness (without saying there was provocative behavior), but allowed that after the processions ended at the parish church, the Indians immediately took the images back to their villages. The Intendant of Veracruz reported that all pueblos de indios in the district of Jalapa processed with their images to the parish church there for Corpus Christi, and in the district of Acayucan they gathered without incident in the parish seat with their images to celebrate the cotton harvest, but he reported that the procession by people from Papantla to Tecolutla to celebrate their image and collect alms from devotees had been suspended because of unspecified abuses. The alms-collecting mission of Tuxtla's favorite image also was no longer permitted because celebrations en route had caused "disturbances."[66]

These reports document the fact of processions with images to the parish seat on certain holidays, to the fields at planting time, and in circumambulations of the pueblo, but not much more. However, some of the twenty-seven reports from districts in the Diocese of Michoacán are detailed enough for a closer view of these images on the move, as objects of immanence. These Michoacán reports on processions from the 1790s are reminiscent of Gilberto Giménez's description of festive pilgrimages to Chalma from rural Indian communities in the state of México during the 1970s.[67] Giménez observed that the groups of people from different communities walking with their images viewed themselves as companions, conveying the images in the right way. They regarded the images as the real pilgrims, the beating heart of the pueblo: "Where the *santos patronos* are, there is the pueblo."[68] It was the images that were obliged to make the journey for the sake of the pueblo, to pay their respects to the great Lord of Chalma and return recharged with spiritual energy.[69] Without the image, the most essential part of the journey was missing.

The overview reports of both the Bishop and Intendant of Michoacán describe Indians on procession with their images as exemplary Christians in their demeanor and actions. Limiting his remarks to the city of Valladolid, the bishop said the practice was not prejudicial because Indians paraded there only from places close to the city and were models of piety and decorum for the rest of society. Speaking of Michoacán more generally, the intendant acknowledged that many pueblos took their most cherished images to the parish seat on special holidays, but in "an edifying manner ... that fills me with satisfaction."[70] These were unusually strong endorsements for a practice that was being challenged by powerful colleagues, but, reading the district reports they received, it would have been a surprise if they reported otherwise. Ten of the district reports said there was no problem because extended processions were not undertaken there. Another mentioned that the only processions were to the community cemetery. The other sixteen noted that longer processions with images were made by most, often all, Indian villages in their districts. Without exception, they reported no "excesses" or "unruliness."[71] Several were positively glowing in their praise of Indian conduct in these processions. For Taretan, Carlos José de Contreras reported that the processions from Ziraquarétiro "bring their devotion and reverence to life" (*vivifica su devoción y reberencia*). At Yndaparapeo, Francisco Xavier de Lezo had this to say about the processions with images from Queréndaro, Pio, and Singio on February 2, Maunday Thursday, Corpus Christi, and for publications of the bulls of the crusade: "to see that ardent desire and care which those natives show not

Fig. 1.4. Procession of Indians with flags, musicians, and a statue of Jesús Nazareno to the Hospital of the Immaculate Conception in Mexico City. This 1781 painting depicts a 1663 event. Courtesy of the Patronato del Hospital de Jesús, México City.

only to the image they bring, but also to the flowers, candles, incense, and embellishment of the image is a source of admiration"[72]; and Vicente Lelo reported from Huetamo that Indian villages in the vicinity brought their images there at Corpus Christi and during Holy Week, always "with great devotion, singing the Rosary in rustic tones that, even though unconventional, are not disagreeable to the ear."[73]

The most detailed description of processions in these reports comes from the district of Motines on the coastal lowlands of Michoacán (the modern municipio of Aquila). The reporter, Juan Joseph Aguilar, drew special attention to the processions themselves and the gravitas of local devotion during the reciprocal visits of images between two pairs of communities, Ostula and Maquilí, and Coire and Pómaro. Here is his account of the processions between Ostula and Maquilí:

> The Indians of Ostula bring the Most Holy Virgin to Maquilid for two feast days annually, one at the end of February and the other in January. Their way of bringing her is for the alcalde, members of the community, and the "cargadoras" [women carriers], as they call them, to come out of the [Ostula] church singing litanies and as many prayers as the cantor chooses. Someone guides them along the entire route. Not even the women carrying the image don their hats at any point, and they are perfumed with incense, all of which is undertaken with exceedingly great seriousness and much reverence and devotion. The Indians of Maquilid carry their Most Holy Mary to Ostula for two other events and collect alms from her devotees. Both pueblos do this with civility, and I know first hand of the great devotion and reverence with which the aforementioned Indians frequent their churches and the tidiness and [proper] decoration of their images. On holy days when Mass is not celebrated, they gather and pray the rosary, sing litanies and hymns of praise, then return to their homes.[74]

Copies and Prints Alive and Sometimes Dangerous

In the Western tradition, paintings of the Virgin Mary by Renaissance artists like Raphael, Michelangelo, Titian, and Caravaggio have long been celebrated as great artistic and devotional images, but the mixing of beauty and devotion in New Spain's many popular religious images seems

Fig. 1.5. This especially fine, iconlike print from an engraving of a sweet Madonna and Child was treated as an original object of devotion. The caption announces that Archbishop of Mexico Manuel José Rubio y Salinas (1749–1765) and Bishop of Puebla Pantaleón Alvares de Abreu (1743–1763) grant forty days' indulgence to those who pray a Salve Regina in its presence. Engraving by Ortuño in José Joaquín de Ortega y San Antonio, *Mes mariano, o lección mensal, mystico-panegyrica, por las treinta y una letras de la cláusula: Ave María, gratia plena, Dominvs tecvm. Con varios symbolos, geroglíficos, epitetos, anagrammas, exemplos, y otras historias, y noticias, todas acomodadas a la Soberana Madre de Dios, y al fin de cada dia, un recuerdo de sus Dolores* (México: La Imprenta de la Bibliotheca Mexicana, 1760). Courtesy of the Bancroft Library, University of California, Berkeley.

closer in spirit to Byzantine icons. In Eastern Orthodoxy, the beauty and spiritual presence of a particular religious image was not about an artist's singular creative genius or the lush, trompe l'oeil perfection of its depiction of the human form and pose. How an image captured the spirit of the holy figure and invited its presence was about awe, which meant more than beauty, but the notion of beauty in the creation of the image was more restricted. Byzantine icons by the late Middle Ages were modeled on earlier ones, reaching for the sublime by repeating pictorial conventions of paintings that were understood to have captured the transcendent spirit of the figure and were associated with miracles of healing and protection.[75] This valorization of conventional expression closely modeled on earlier icons is similar to the power of copies in New Spain and the way that use, guided by laity and priests more than artists and connoisseurs, established what was beautiful. In New Spain, a painting or statue reputed to be "most like" a beautiful and renowned image could attract a large following of its own, as did paintings of Our Lady of Guadalupe at Querétaro and the Santuario del Desierto outside the city of San Luis Potosí. This was a notion of beauty that valued replication and embellishment of copies as the real thing.[76]

The possibility of divine presence in images did not make every religious image and object equally beautiful and beckoning.[77] There was still great value placed on the unique object, the matrix image or "original," as it was sometimes called.[78] This was the judgment of Miguel Cabrera and his fellow experts in their evaluation of the image of Our Lady of Guadalupe at Tepeyac in 1751. It was so beautiful, they judged, and so unique, that it could not be the work of human hands. And, as Cabrera's former pupil, José de Ibarra, observed, no painter had been able to make a perfect copy, try as he might.[79] Yet copies of images renowned for their beauty were not just regarded as imitations, of little value to the discerning observer. On the contrary they could prompt awe and wonder, too, even without showing signs of life. Copies that had touched the celebrated matrix image were enhanced by the contact. And the copy of Our Lady of Guadalupe in the Franciscan Colegio de Nuestra Señora de Guadalupe at Zacatecas that was commissioned by its famous founder, Fr. Antonio Margil de Jesús, was said to have turned out so well because it was painted only while Margil celebrated Mass.[80]

Rather than regarded as lesser, powerless images because they were cheap and less exact, prints of Christ and the saints also had special claims on

Fig. 1.6. One of the fine painted copies of the image of the Virgin of Guadalupe at Tepeyac signed by Miguel Cabrera. The caption declares that this one touched the original image on October 28, 1766. Courtesy of the Museo de la Basílica de Guadalupe, México City.

INTERIOR OF AN INDIAN HUT, EL BOZAL.

Fig. 1.7. This print of the sketch of "Interior of an Indian Hut, El Bozal" depicts a "fine collection of religious plates" including Christ, various saints, and the Virgin of Guadalupe, displayed against a woven reed mat in "a wretched hovel" at El Bozal, near Real de Catorce, San Luis Potosí, in 1827. Depicted and described by Mr. and Mrs. H. G. Ward, in *Mexico*, 2nd ed. (London: H. Colburn, 1829), II, facing p. 261. From author's copy.

truth and an allure that church officials enlisted and worried about.[81] Printed matter was still unusual during the colonial period, and anything printed had a certain aura of authority and presence. Everyone had seen printed decrees of the Inquisition and the crown posted on the great doors of the parish church, and even the poorest homes and workplaces were likely to display several religious prints on a table or wall (see Fig. 1.7).

By the late seventeenth century, presses in Mexico City and Puebla were publishing devotional literature containing small prints of Christ and the saints with the encouragement and support of bishops, the religious orders, and pious individuals as aids to spiritual renewal and perfection. Fig. 1.8 displays two pages from a pocket size devotional book consisting of eight different booklets bound together in the early nineteenth century, including three-, seven-, and nine-day rounds of prayers to miraculous images, various saints, and advocations of Mary. Four of the booklets include engraved

IMAGES AND SHRINES   45

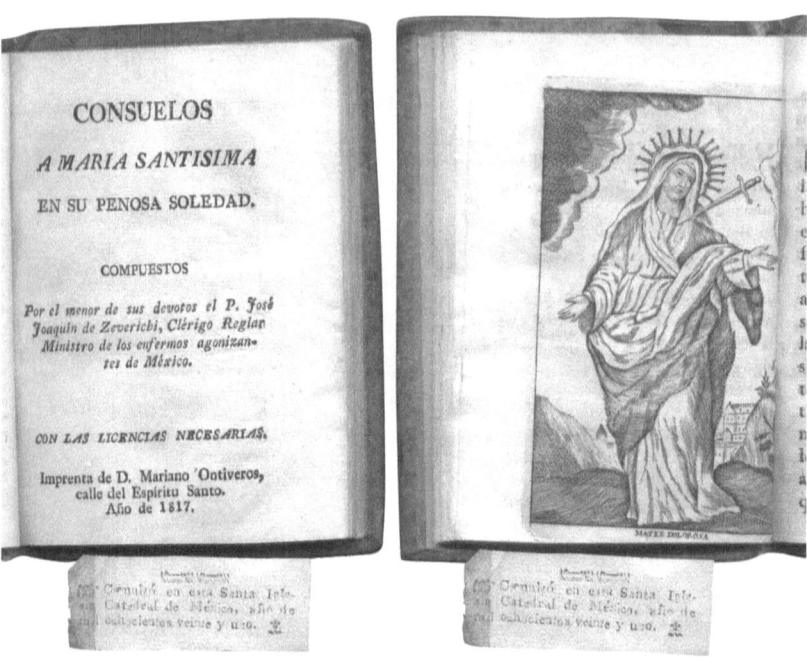

Fig. 1.8a and b. Title page and engraving from an 1817 booklet of prayers in honor of Our Lady of Solitude. From a pocket book of eight booklets printed in Mexico City. Tipped into this little volume (and displayed below the booklet pages) is a printed slip known as a *cedulilla* that the bearer received after performing his or her Easter duty to confess and take communion in 1821. From author's copy.

images to pray with. These booklets and prints were published with the permission of the Archbishop of Mexico (*con las licencias necesarias*).

Why copies, even the many cheap black-and-white prints modeled after a celebrated painting, statue, or standard representation, were valued reaches beyond the decorative and didactic into a theological point noticed by Hans Belting.[82] A copy could still be "an 'original' in the religious sense— an image exercising power over believers by its actual presence." Not surprisingly, local copies of all kinds sometimes were reported to show life and work wonders—sweating, crying, bleeding, changing expression, healing, protecting—signs of divine presence that made them compelling sites of the sacred to devotees. For instance, in the 1720s a painting of the celebrated crucifix of Our Lord of Chalma in the convent church at Chalma was visited by D. Vicente Moya y Escaño, a desperately ill gentleman from Mexico City who recovered the next day and attributed his sudden good health to the Lord of Chalma through this copy.[83] Then in 1748 a small, framed print of Christ was reported to have perspired under its protective glass in the new chapel of the Holy Trinity in the Jesuit church of Parras, Coahuila. In addition to the Jesuit rector's summary, the report included testimony from eight local notables who had witnessed the event and described the throng of people that gathered to see for themselves.[84] In Patino's text on Our Lady of los Ángeles (1801), the "original" was not the painting on an adobe wall in Tlatleloco—a singular image that never lost its beautiful face and hands despite centuries of exposure to the weather and human neglect. Rather, the original was the Blessed Mary herself, and even the most exquisite images of her were only proximate copies. In this sense, all images were approximations. As surrogates for what they represented, images served to elicit public displays of attachment or rejection and invite God's presence.[85] With a fine copy of the image in a church within reach, or even a cheap print on a home altar, the promise of that presence was already at hand.[86]

Late colonial officials were concerned about the evocative power of prints and their availability in hundreds of places at once. They repeatedly ordered that prints, like religious images of other kinds, depict their sacred subjects in prescribed ways and not arouse excessive or otherwise inappropriate interest. They were particularly concerned about prints that might encourage "fanaticism" and impure thoughts. In 1770, a viceregal circular banned prints that mocked the recently expelled Jesuits because they might lead to "fanaticism" against priests in general.[87] At the same time, church officials tried to make sure that the Virgin Mary was depicted only in timeless "biblical" garb. There should be no hint of immodesty in them—no buxom Virgins in contemporary styles of dress that accentuated their curves[88] (see Fig. 1.9. Also see figures 1.6, 1.8, 1.10, and 1.11 for the kind of timeless attire prelates attending the Fourth Provincial Synod recommended).

Other late colonial prints were dangerous because they drew attention to places, religious images, and providential events that officials meant to erase from memory. When devotions developed around new images at that time and news spread with the distribution of prints that could, themselves, be portals to the sacred, they usually were greeted with less credulity and theological seriousness than had Our Lady of Tulantongo or the

Fig. 1.9. This print from an engraving by Ortuño of a statue of Our Lady of los Dolores in the Mexico City convent of Jesús María known as Nuestra Señora de las Aguas, with flowing hair and a tight bodice in the style of the day, is the kind of image late colonial bishops and ecclesiastical courts were inclined to censor. *Novena en honra de Nuestra Señora de los Dolores, que con el renombre de las Aguas* . . . (México: Colegio de San Ildefonso, 1761), second leaf. Courtesy of the Sutro Branch of the California State Library, San Francisco.

charred hand on the blanket at Pachuca in the mid-seventeenth century. Late colonial bishops, even those who were not among the outspoken regalist reformers, were wary of new devotions and popular euphoria. As long as interest in new images and places remained local and did not attract great notoriety, church officials tended to ignore them or seek to have them brought to the parish church. But those that gained a wider fame and following without supervision or were promoted too zealously by a parish priest were more likely to be suppressed.

A case of initial endorsement followed by suppression is the long forgotten miraculous cross of Huaquechula, Puebla. In August 1806 local Indians discovered a mysterious painted cross on a boulder in the river at the edge of town. They moved it to shore and petitioned the viceroy in 1808 for permission to honor this cross with a proper shrine—"*una capilla rural o pequeña iglesia*"—in the woods near the river. Over two thousand pesos were collected from townspeople for the project, and a design by a licensed architect was presented to the authorities in Mexico City. With the endorsement of the parish priest and the *fiscal protector de indios* of the Audiencia of México, a viceregal license was issued and a small shrine was quickly erected. A silver disk skillfully embossed with a fine cross, flanked by Mary Magdalene and John the Baptist, was commissioned to cover the crude cross on the rock, and a copper plate engraving of the disk was cut and prints from it began to circulate.

By 1809, the Cross of Huaquechula had gained a following far beyond the town. The prints circulated widely in and beyond the Diocese of Puebla, and pilgrims began to stream in from as far away as Veracruz on the Gulf coast and Acapulco on the Pacific, especially during the annual fiesta period around the Day of the Holy Cross (May 3). News of personal favors to visitors spread and were commemorated in paintings on the walls of the little shrine. In early 1810, Bishop Manuel Ignacio González del Campillo went to see for himself, alert to the wiles of Satan and troubled by "the implications of such exuberance for episcopal authority and decorous devotion." Styling himself a vigilant protector of "the purity of the cultus" against "the hysterics of incredulity ... and superstition" (*los vapores de la incredulidad ... [y] la superstición*), he quickly concluded that this was a false and dangerous devotion. In his judgment, the supposed miracles associated with the painted cross were false or at best incomplete: the most notable of them, a crippled man who began to walk, was not credible because he had been seen limping around town long before the "miracle" and he still walked with a limp. The bishop also judged the image itself to be unremarkable. What had been called a "perfect" cross in the 1808 petition was, he said, no more than a crude crossing of lines, perhaps simply a boundary marker or the work of a passing priest. The handsome prints in wide circulation were an abominable superstition because they purported to show the actual cross when, in fact, they reproduced the image on the silver disk that covered the crude original. The devotion, he concluded, did not honor a genuine apparition and had nothing miraculous about it. It was little more than a promotional scheme hatched by people of Huaquechula. He ordered that within three days all the prints, scapularies, and chips of stone from the boulder and dirt from the site of the shrine in the hands of his flock be confiscated. As quickly and quietly as possible he had the stone with the cross pulverized, the shrine razed, and prints destroyed. The Cross of Huaquechula and its shrine were effectively erased from the face of the earth and, eventually, from public memory. The only copy of the print I have seen or seen mentioned is filed in the administrative record of the case.[89]

Church authorities regarded another late colonial religious print as even more dangerous, and they moved with equal determination to collect and destroy all known copies. Apparently none survives even in the archive of the Inquisition. In January 1743, Matheo de Reyna Lasso de la Vega, a priest in the household of the Bishop of Chiapas who was visiting Mexico City, appeared before the Inquisition with a print of the Madonna and Child he had noticed on the wall of a merchant in the city of Chiapas. When he asked about it, the merchant said it was an image of the Virgin of Cancuc. During his travels in the diocese Father Reyna had seen other copies of this print and understood that they were being introduced into the provinces of Chiapas and Tabasco by Dutch traders through ports on the coast of Laguna de Términos, Campeche, and Tabasco. He knew that "the Virgin of Cancuc" was associated with the Tzeltal Rebellion that had convulsed the highlands of Chiapas in 1712 and resulted in the deaths of Catholic priests and laymen. As he understood it, Tzeltal rebels set themselves up as apostles and bishops and removed the statue of Our Lady of Intercession from the cathedral's main altar, replacing it with the living tableau of a young Indian woman dressed in a Dominican habit with an Indian baby in her arms. This young woman was known as the Virgin of Cancuc.[90] Father Reyna was worried that the dissemination of the print was meant to incite Indians in the region to rise up again.

Fig. 1.10. Perhaps the only surviving example of the 1809 *estampa* of the Cruz de Huaquechula suppressed by Bishop González del Campillo in 1810. AGN Clero Regular y Secular 215, exp. 29, fol. 626. Courtesy of the Archivo General de la Nación, Mexico.

The Inquisition consulted Juan Antonio de Oviedo, the cosmopolitan Jesuit scholar, preacher, and administrator (and a noted promoter of devotion to miraculous images) about the print and its foreign language captions, which the inquisitors presumed were written in English and French. Oviedo translated the French caption (which a native-speaking fellow Jesuit reviewed for him) and consulted another Jesuit brother in the capital who was fluent in English. But the presumed English text turned out to be Dutch, so another brother who knew Dutch was asked to translate that passage. The translators were in agreement that both passages could be rendered as "Even though there are only two of us, we are of one lineage; we do not dress as they do, but they do as we do." In Oviedo's opinion, this was, indeed, a subversive image in light of the earlier Tzeltal rebellion in which Satan persuaded the Indians to revere the Indian Virgin of Cancuc and cast off the yoke of Spanish rule. In his view, the caption could be interpreted as follows: "their Nation is strong and they are all of one lineage alludes to a new uprising; and 'they do as we do' means, I fear, that in adoring the young Indian woman or her image on the print the Indians will be doing the same as Christians do when they venerate sacred images." These proceedings in Mexico City and Chiapas took place during the War of Austrian Succession, one of those eighteenth-century European wars with American theaters. There were British and Spanish naval engagements in the Caribbean from 1739 to 1742, which may explain why the inquisitors presumed that the caption was in English. Oviedo was convinced that heretical Dutchmen made and distributed the prints in Chiapas and Tabasco to move the Indians to worship the Virgin of Cancuc and rise up once again against the Spaniards. In his opinion the best course of action was to immediately send word to parish priests and the Inquisition's commissaries, especially those in Chiapas and Tabasco, to do everything possible to recover all the prints they could find. And that is what the Inquisition did the following month, while cautioning pastors and commissaries to proceed "gently, kindly, and with the greatest care."[91]

Our Lady of Light

A historian would ask of any object, what is it and in what contexts of time and place can it be understood best? Who made it? Where has it been? Is location an important aspect of its meaning? How was it regarded and used? Often we have something to say about what and when, but not much more. This essay reaches for more, but in the case of Our Lady of Light I am unable to go much beyond what is represented in the original painting and how the representation of this advocation of Mary changed, changed again, and was promoted. Reception and uses are particularly elusive here. Still, the late colonial history of this image, including the arguments over how it should be represented, provides some tantalizing material for reflecting on the popularity and power of images.

According to the tradition recounted in a long devotional text published in Italy in 1733 and republished in Mexico in Spanish translation in 1737 when the devotion to the image was spreading there, the original painting had been made in Palermo, Sicily, around 1722 for an Italian Jesuit, Antonio Genovesi, in need of a new image of Mary that would inspire devotion among Italian Catholics whose faith had cooled.[92] He asked a nun known for her visionary gifts to seek direction from the Blessed Mary. Mary visited the nun, radiant in her beauty, just as she wanted to be represented, and gave detailed instructions for a tableau, including the graphic depiction of a sinner being rescued as he was about to fall into the yawning mouth of a toothy, fire-breathing monster representing Hell.[93] On the second try, a painting was completed to the Blessed Mary's satisfaction and used by Father Genovesi in his itinerant, wonder-working mission. This painting was brought to Mexico in 1732 with a long burst of interest.[94] Various Jesuit houses vied to receive it; lots were drawn and the honor went to the new hospice in the Villa de León, Guanajuato. Soon, copies were commissioned, first in Mexico City, where an altar was dedicated to her in the church of Porta Coeli that year.[95] In 1734 the Dominicans commissioned a large painting of Our Lady of Light for their church, and sumptuous altars to the image and advocation were installed in several Jesuit churches and colleges there, in 1735 and 1739.

The devotion spread rapidly thereafter, mainly to places in central, western, and northern New Spain where Jesuits and Franciscans were active in revival movements. Other than the images in León and Mexico City, celebrated images and altars were placed in the Jesuit church of the city of Zacatecas in 1750, in several churches of Puebla by the 1750s, in Santa Fe, New Mexico's Castrense Chapel (1761), and at Salvatierra, Guanajuato, in 1785.[96] Elsewhere confraternities were established in her honor, several university theses were dedicated to her in the 1740s and 1760s, and at least twenty-one publications promoting the devotion were published in Mexico City and Puebla between 1732 and 1821, with a clustering in the 1760s and

1770s. Then the presses were silent until 1790, after which at least seven more devotional publications appeared before 1821.[97] The Santa Fe and Salvatierra paintings were famously associated with great favors to devotees and souls in Purgatory. Missions and altars dedicated to Our Lady of Light became a feature of Franciscan frontier evangelization in the eighteenth century, from Texas (1756) to the Sierra Gorda of Querétaro (1760s), Chihuahua, and Alta California (1770s). In Mexico today, Our Lady of Light remains the patroness of the city of León and a popular devotion in other places. Since 1898, when Mexico City's ophthalmology hospital was dedicated to Our Lady of Light, she has come to be regarded as the guardian of sight.

The standard representation in New Spain from 1732 to the 1750s was faithful to the painting sent to the Villa de León. The Blessed Mary, with her left knee bent as if about to step out of the frame, holds the Christ child in her left arm. He has taken two flaming hearts, meant to represent penitential souls, from a basket brimming with other such hearts, held up to him by a kneeling angel. Baby angels surround Mary, beneath her feet and above; two of them in a sunburst around her head hold up a starry golden crown. With her right hand, Mary grasps the arm of a soul in danger of falling into the fiery abyss of Leviathan's gaping mouth. Most of the early paintings for churches were larger than life size, accentuating the drama of the scene. Our Lady of Light is directly related to the longstanding devotional interest in souls trapped in Purgatory (*las ánimas en purgatorio*), for which there were confraternities in many Mexican communities by the eighteenth century. But the name "Our Lady of *Light*" draws attention back to Christ, who is also an agent in this image. The usual explanation of the name was that light stood for Christ—"I am the light of the world."[98]

In the years just before the expulsion of the Jesuits from New Spain in 1767 a controversy arose over the image of Our Lady of Light. The objection to the image was that it seemed to suggest one could receive salvation directly from the Virgin, or naïve or disingenuous devotees might conclude that the Mother of God would pull devotees out of Hell's fire no matter what their transgressions, rather than leading them toward a more virtuous life and thereby lessening the likelihood of eternal damnation. Evidently this was a serious controversy, and some paintings of the time omitted the fire-breathing Leviathan. At the Fourth Synod of Mexican prelates in 1771, the case against graphic depictions of Hell in images of Our Lady of Light was discussed. The issue, as it was framed for

Fig. 1.11. *Our Lady of Light* by Miguel Cabrera (d. 1768), n.d. (1760s?). Responding to the new ecclesiastical policy, Cabrera replaced the gaping mouth of Leviathan in the lower left corner with a faint glow on a dark horizon to suggest the fires of Hell awaiting sinners. Otherwise he followed the standard representation. Courtesy of the Patronato del Colegio de San Ignacio de Loyola, Vizcaínas, Mexico City.

the synod, was whether to "erase the dragon in order to avoid the error of thinking that the Most Holy Virgin pulled condemned sinners from Hell."[99] On the archbishop's strong recommendation, the synod agreed to prohibit further paintings of the image and to "secretly" blot out the "dragon" in existing works, although the proposed decrees of the synod were not confirmed by the papacy.[100] Prints showing the fiery jaws of Hell evidently were destroyed and at least some existing paintings were removed or Leviathan was painted out. In the painting of Our Lady of Light that still hangs in the former Jesuit church of La Profesa in Mexico City, the dragon has been covered over with black paint.[101]

Apparently this advocation of Mary was not promoted by the diocesan clergy in the years after the expulsion of the Jesuits in 1767, but a counter campaign responding to popular sentiment was mounted in the late 1780s, with a Franciscan friar, José Antonio Alcozer, in the lead. In his treatise on Our Lady of Light published in 1790 with the approval of the viceroy and various church dignitaries, Alcozer defended the devotion and the original representation.[102] The Blessed Mary, herself, devised the original painting, he noted. For good measure, he argued that the image clearly shows the Virgin preventing the soul from falling into the inferno, not pulling him out. There was no doctrinal error in this at all, he concluded. The iconography of the painting brought from Italy in 1732 had won the day by the 1790s, and most images made or displayed thereafter show the fire-breathing monster of Hell in graphic detail.[103]

Conclusion

The subject of images and immanence leads to intriguing resonances between empire and colony. In some ways, the culture of immanence in New Spain is strikingly similar to Spain (and much of Catholic Europe, for that matter) at the time. A "culture of visions" was common to both,[104] and sensuous devotion featuring images followed a similar historical trajectory. By the late sixteenth century, images were the main bridge to the power and blessings of divine presence in Spain. Apparitions and relics were not forgotten, but images came to the fore, at least in the written record, with reports of animation and favors bestowed in their presence. The images most celebrated in Spain and New Spain from the late sixteenth century were of Mary and Christ, and many of these images both in Spain and New Spain were found in natural settings, "mediat[ing] between the

Fig. 1.12. Engraved image of Our Lady of Light by Tomás de Suría, 1790, included in Alcozer's *Carta apologética*. The fire-breathing monster is back in the lower left corner, as it was before the late 1760s. From author's copy.

local society and the forces of nature."[105] Special signs of the numinous that are described in origin stories also are similar: a finder is drawn to the site by celestial music, intense light, and sweet smells; or a mule carrying the image cannot be budged from a particular spot; or the image grows impossibly heavy there; or rain falls all around, but not on the image as it is carried to its destination. Devotional practices and the politics of miracles also invite comparison. To hope to gain transparency with God in the presence of images, they had to be approached in the right state of mind, in a posture of supplication, focused on love and contrition, and bearing an offering. Some of the offerings appear to be identical—candles, little metal body parts, and, by the eighteenth century, ex-voto paintings.

It is tempting to see the many similarities as the result of practices and things transported and little changed by their transatlantic migration.[106] But a range of differences in both practice and meaning remind us that the culture of visions, effigies, and omens that developed in New Spain had its roots in precolonial Mesoamerica as well as in Spain. While most images were mute on both sides of the Spanish Atlantic, the planting of image shrines in New Spain was more often associated with an apparition giving verbal instructions to a seer, as with Tlaxcala's San Miguel del Milagro shrine, Our Lady of Guadalupe at Tepeyac, and Our Lady of Tulantongo. And while there was a shift in the history of immanence from apparitions to images in the metropole and the colony, it happened later and lasted longer in the colony. William Christian places the Spanish golden age of miraculous images in a long seventeenth century, from about 1590 to 1720.[107] For New Spain it would be from about 1621 (when the first devotional history to a miraculous image was published in Mexico City) to about 1850. Christian suggests that skepticism about miraculous images in seventeenth-century Spain hindered further development of communitywide and regional devotions then, and any increase in the number of rural shrines in Castile seems to have been modest, at least in the Diocese of Cuenca between 1583 and 1645.[108] For New Spain, skepticism was less apparent, and most of the several hundred shrines to miraculous images with more than local fame were founded in the seventeenth century.

Devotion to images of Christ, and reports of their activation increased in Spain during the seventeenth century, as they did in New Spain, and in both places their followings usually were local rather than regional or supraregional, but, again, there were differences. In Spain, their appeal during the seventeenth century seems to represent a sharper turn in religious practice, reflecting the rising popularity of Holy Week and its sponsoring lay confraternities supervised by priests. Holy Week and confraternities associated with it were important in New Spain, too, but crosses were symbols of fertility in Mesoamerica long before Europeans arrived, both the cross and crucifix had been central features of the sixteenth-century evangelization, and several—including the stone cross of Querétaro, the great wooden cross of Tlaxcala, the cross of Huatulco, and the Christ of Totolapa—were already important cult objects before the seventeenth-century founding of most shrines to Christ and Mary. Images were providentially discovered in natural settings on both sides of the Atlantic; but in Spain most were figures of Mary while in Mesoamerica, more were figures of Christ. In Mesoamerica, many of the found images were *of* nature, as well as in nature—typically encased in a tree trunk or its limbs, which bled when an unsuspecting woodsman chopped at them. The main message conveyed by the infant Jesus or the crucified Christ in early modern Spain also seems different. The Spanish images carried "a warning of judgment and a model of penance. Both the cross and the child were ultimately references to the plague."[109] Such apocalyptic messages were not absent in New Spain, but figures of Christ as a child and crucified God were more than bearers of a message of doom.[110] They were brought forward in the many colonial epidemics as protective, healing intermediaries, and they were often treated as benign protectors who were vital to community well-being as much as representations of suffering and transcendence.

Among the image shrines in New Spain, there are examples of nearly all the types of founding stories of immanence in early modern Europe, but with a different concentration. Of the three basic episodes of immanence described for early modern European image shrines by Philip Soergel[111]— holiness tried and triumphant; holiness lost and found; and holiness suddenly revealed in apparitions, activations, and other miracles—one was considerably more important in New Spain. In the first type, an image or sacred material resisted desecration and destruction. Infidels or apostates tried to destroy an image or the consecrated Host and were unable to do so. This was a characteristic founding miracle in Soergel's regional study of Bavaria, where the examples centered on the integrity of the Host—Jews and other deniers of Christ tried and failed to destroy the consecrated wafer, although sometimes they made it bleed. The examples of holiness tried and triumphant are rare for New Spain. They include the cross of Huatulco, Our Lady of La Bala, and Our Lady of La Macana. The second type fits a familiar Spanish pattern described by William Christian: images of Mary hidden by Christians in the countryside during the Muslim conquest of Iberia were discovered thanks to supernatural signs of intense light and celestial music, or a semidomesticated animal like a bull or mule was drawn to the place where the image was then discovered by a shepherd. Again, there are found objects among the founding miracles for New Spain, but they were less common and rarely hidden or abandoned by Christians on the defensive. And many more of the found objects in New Spain were figures of Christ. The third type, of holiness suddenly revealed, is overwhelmingly the most common in New Spain. In these founding stories, images already in place or arriving in mysterious circumstances showed signs of life or spontaneously began to work miracles. The founding stories of divine presence associated with images both in Spain and New Spain are about place as much as about the image, but the cases in New Spain are less often about conquest, warrior Virgins, and threats to the faith.

Images were necessary, but dangerous objects, supplied and promoted by church leaders to potentially volatile and fissive new Christians in Mesoamerica. Colonial decrees and judicial records from the sixteenth century on document many attempts by colonial authorities to impose and police what images meant, how they were used, and which ones were respectable in the face of exuberant devotees with other ideas about these matters. They help to account for similarities, but often the authorities' moves with regard to religious images were flexible in ways that made them collaborators in the remarkable resilience and peculiarities of the many shrines to miraculous images founded in seventeenth-century New Spain. Few of those shrines have withered away from economic dislocations in the region, natural disasters, social and political upheavals, the occasional antagonism of politicians, or popular indifference. Is their later development and persistence mainly the sort of delayed and prolonged response that we might expect in colonial outliers? I can't say for sure, any more than I have a novel sociological explanation to offer for why some miracle shrines grew into regional powerhouses.[112] But if we view this kind of persistence not as untroubled continuity, but as "a process through which change is structured by the cultural dispositions of the groups and individuals whose creative actions bring such changes into being,"[113] the eager reception of news of miracles by people from all social groups in New Spain and their participation in the cult of images as an avenue to material and spiritual well-being becomes a key consideration.[114] Even the long history of intermittent efforts to regulate the use of images and investigate cases of disrespect toward images were, on both sides, as much about a lasting sense of enchantment in the world as they were signs of uneasy distance between official religion and popular practice. Priests and lay devotees collaborated in the rise of miraculous images and shrines in part because, as the Tulantongo example suggests, images were less problematic for authorities than apparitions. Seers of apparitions were potential rivals to priests in their claim to privileged access to the word of God, while images were silent for the most part and turned the spotlight away from the seer. Tulantongo began with a seer who was something of a free agent and developed into an image devotion that reduced him to a humble Indian facilitator.

Efforts to prescribe and enforce religious practices in such a large, dispersed population were bound to be incomplete and their consequences sometimes unintended. And there were acts of resistance, defiance, and subversion. But they were uncommon and rarely challenged Christianity or the social and political order. The tension between official policies and local practices was plain to see in the late colonial period as representatives of the church and state repeatedly announced their determination to eliminate inopportune enthusiasm for miracles and celebrations. Even shared understandings such as the sense of beauty measured by reception could stir disagreements over the appropriateness of particular images. Still, many ecclesiastical and royal judges, as well as parish priests, were well aware of the risks of exalted adherence to the letter of the law in policing cultural practices. They participated in the popularity of miraculous images not only with their own devotion to images, but by often turning a blind eye to local tastes that offended their own sensibilities and condoning, if not embracing, their flock's eager interest in reports of miraculous events associated with images.[115] As Saint Augustine advised long before there was a Spain, much less a New Spain, "What we teach is one thing, what we tolerate another."[116]

Fig. 2.1. The text of the authoritative devotional history of the Cristo Renovado by Alfonso Alberto de Velasco, *Exaltación de la divina misericordia* . . . , was not revised in its various editions, but prints of images of the miraculous crucified Christ tipped into different editions did change. The Christ in this first edition of 1698 hangs heavy on the cross, with the ravaged torso accentuated and the figure blending into a busy, textured background set off by two lighted candles and other decorations. Courtesy of the Bancroft Library, University of California, Berkeley.

2

Two Shrines of the Cristo Renovado
Religion and Peasant Politics

WHETHER IN HAGIOGRAPHICAL LITERATURE OR SCHOLARSHIP, the Virgin Mary appears to dominate Mexico's devotional landscape, especially in the guise of Our Lady of Guadalupe. "Mexico can pride itself on the glorious title of 'Marian land,'" wrote Father Rubén Vargas Ugarte in his monumental survey of the Virgin Mary in Latin America.[1] To Victor and Edith Turner, the Virgin of Guadalupe is Mexico's "dominant symbol" presiding over "the total symbolic system"—situated at the apex of pilgrimage routes and a hierarchy of shrines and images.[2] It is a surprise, then, to find a murmur of dissent in the last pages of Francisco Javier Lazcano's 1760 biography of his fellow Jesuit and Marian devotee, Juan Antonio de Oviedo. After praising Oviedo's extensive revision and publication in 1755 of Francisco de Florencia's forgotten manuscript, *Zodíaco mariano*—the first survey of Marian shrines in Mexico, Lazcano remarked:

> May Heaven one day awaken a pen equal to that of Father Oviedo so that another great work of history worthy of the Christian World's acclamation will describe in detail the prodigious crosses and miraculous images of Jesus Christ, Our Lord, that make this kingdom famous in innumerable magnificent shrines throughout its vast dioceses. This kingdom is no less favored by the Son

of God, Jesus Christ, Our Lord, in his infinite mercy than by the most beloved Mother of a God who is her son.[3]

I am not the one to write Lazcano's imagined chronicle, but, like him, I have noticed that local and regional devotion to particular images of Christ often exceeded the popularity of celebrated images of the Virgin Mary during the colonial period (of course, the two are often intimately related and complementary, as in the Madonna and Child, or Our Lady of Sorrows and the Crucifixion) and wondered what drew devotees to them. Of about 480 Mexican shrines to miraculous images that have attracted followers from beyond their immediate vicinity since the sixteenth century, 219 are dedicated to images of the Virgin Mary and 261 to images of Christ.[4] True, the Christs are more likely than the Marys to have become famous during the nineteenth and twentieth centuries, but at least 156 of the shrines to images of Christ developed during the colonial period.[5] Most of them were confined to district-wide or regional followings, but the Lord of Chalma, the Cristo Renovado of Santa Teresa, the Stone Cross of Querétaro, Guatemala's Lord of Esquípulas, and a dozen others were more widely venerated.

Christocentric devotion in New Spain (the colonial administrative territory that encompassed modern Mexico plus much of Central America and the Spanish borderlands now part of the United States) was closely related to European practices at the time, and rooted in medieval traditions. It came to the fore in the late sixteenth and early seventeenth centuries with Catholic reforms following the Council of Trent's promotion of the liturgy of the Eucharist, commemoration of Christ's Passion during Holy Week, and the feasts of the Holy Cross and Corpus Christi. Two-thirds or more of the colonial Mexican Christ shrines were dedicated to crucifixes.[6] As in Europe, some crucifixes famously showed signs of life—sweating, bleeding, and groaning—in ways that recalled Christ's suffering, sacrifice, and promise of eternal life. Some images of Mary showed signs of life, too, but less often. Both in Europe and Mexico, dilapidated images of Christ spontaneously restored themselves to fine condition, recalling Christ's resurrection and the promise of eternal salvation of the soul, while Marian images were more often said to have remained in preternaturally fine condition when they should have decomposed or been damaged, in the spirit of Mary's perpetual virginity.[7]

In short, in New Spain and the future Mexico there was not just one dominant symbol presiding over a hierarchy of sacred places and images;

nor did images of Mary overshadow others. While the image of the Virgin of Guadalupe became the most widely known object of faith in New Spain by the late eighteenth century, before the mid-nineteenth century Tepeyac—the legendary site of the Virgin Mary's apparitions to Juan Diego in 1531 and her miraculous image—was not much more appealing beyond its vicinity than were eight or nine shrines to other miraculous images, not to mention the hundreds of shrines to yet other images of Mary and Christ that were regarded as essential to the well-being of people living nearby. Little in the way of an interlocking system of pilgrimage routes ending at Tepeyac developed, even with the advent of railroads in the late nineteenth century, when great streams of visitors to the shrine began to arrive, and there were about as many shrines to miraculous images in 1900 as in 1700. With so many shrines and images in play, the subject reaches far beyond Our Lady of Guadalupe and a Wal-Mart style history in which other shrines fell away in the face of irresistible attraction and relentless promotion for one dominant symbol.[8]

A self-restoring crucifix in central Mexico that stirred interest in two separate shrines during the eighteenth century offers an opportunity to reach beyond the idea of a hierarchy of shrines and the claim that written records generated by colonial institutions yield little more than the intentions of colonial elites and the operation of those institutions, to study Christocentric devotion in particular places and consider what Michel de Certeau called "the secondary production hidden in the process of utilization."[9] The story in this essay revolves around a loss later remembered by rural devotees in ways that made the place of the miracle of self-restoration more important than the relic itself. More broadly, it is about the politics of faith in two places through the direction and redirection of an official story, and about how historians might reckon with elusive questions of religion and the negotiation of colonial circumstances by Indian villagers. "Indian" here means the descendants of indigenous Americans who recognized themselves by, among other names, this one that Spanish authorities applied to them, but the other India also has a place in my reckoning with the bi-local developments at hand, as readers will see in the last section of the essay.

One Image, Two Shrines: The Cristo Renovado of Santa Teresa

Until recently I knew the story of the Cristo Renovado only from various editions of a small book with a long title, *Exaltación de la divina misericordia en la milagrosa renovación de la soberana imagen de Christo Señor Nuestro Crucificado. . . .*[10] It amounts to the providential biography of a celebrated crucifix in Mexico City, presented in an omniscient narrator's voice, published first in the late seventeenth century to encourage devotion and sanctify a struggling convent of Discalced Carmelite nuns founded a few years before the crucifix was brought to them. It is a story of God's grace in the world from the pen of Dr. Alfonso Alberto de Velasco, a learned metropolitan priest who served as chaplain to these nuns—a finished, official story that might well be said to colonize knowledge and silence or marginalize other voices. By itself, Velasco's text could not bring me close to devotees and other possible histories of the image. But now I have three clusters of eighteenth-century records and a sprinkling of other references that complicate Father Velasco's seamless, linear story. The host Carmelite nuns remain offstage both in Velasco's text and the administrative record of the shrine in Mexico City, and there is little to say about their devotion to the crucifix. This isn't surprising. They did not directly administer the shrine and, with their emphasis on silent prayer, individual work, poverty, privacy, and the solitude of the cell, the reformed Carmelites called for an unusual measure of austerity and discipline that kept these nuns largely out of the public record. Theirs eventually became the most prestigious convent in Mexico City, attracting local women from white, elite families to a particularly arduous, self-abnegating life, but even their assistance to the needy is little documented and they seem to have escaped the kinds of troubles that could bring the activities of cloistered life into view for strangers.[11]

First, the view from Mexico City through Father Velasco's story of the image, and a sketch of the devotion there during the colonial period. Known variously as the Señor de Santa Teresa, the Cristo Renovado de Ixmiquilpan, the Cristo de El Cardonal, or simply the Cristo Renovado, it is a nearly life-size crucifix that was removed to Mexico City in 1623 from the small mining community of Mapethé just north of El Cardonal in the western hills of modern Hidalgo state.[12] Velasco wrote in the 1680s that the crucifix had been brought to Mapethé by a Spanish miner in 1545 and housed in a modest chapel, attracting more attention from hungry insects than devotees. In 1615 the image was so dilapidated that the archbishop ordered it broken apart and buried with the next adult to die in the parish. But then for nearly six years no one died, and mysterious groans and celestial music drifted from the chapel late at night. In 1621 the image began to perspire and twitch on the cross and, during a fierce storm, it floated free and was restored to fine condition before becoming reattached. The image continued to show signs of life, occasionally opening its eyes, perspiring, and spurting blood. Marvelous healings of local people and an abundant crop of maize ensued. Later that year the archbishop ordered the image brought to Mexico City for safekeeping since the miner's chapel had virtually collapsed. Velasco mentioned that local Indians and Spaniards struggled against the removal of their now prodigious image before it was taken to the capital for safekeeping; it was received in Mexico City with great rejoicing.

I know of just one earlier reference to the image and devotion. Gil González Dávila's survey of the history of the Archdiocese of Mexico from a European perspective, published in Madrid in 1649, mentioned that the image sweated, trembled, and performed other miracles in 1621 and was moved to the Carmelite convent in Mexico City on orders of the archbishop, who wanted it rescued from its precarious location near the Chichimec frontier.[13] González Dávila did not mention the act of self-renovation that is central to Velasco's story; nor did he mention the crumbling chapel. He offered the classic *furta sacra* story of relics rescued from danger and neglect that was familiar in medieval European hagiography.[14] The shrine of the Cristo Renovado in Mexico City apparently did not become important until the end of the seventeenth century since Fr. Isidro de la Asunción, the Spanish Carmelite inspector who resided in central Mexico from 1673–1678, did not mention it in the chapter on shrines in his *Itinerario a Indias*.[15]

The first version of Velasco's account of the image, published in 1688 as *Renovación por sí misma* . . . , reads like a digest of one of the extended legal reports called *informaciones jurídicas* that were prepared for episcopal courts in seventeenth- and eighteenth-century Mexico to evaluate cases for beatification of a holy person or recognition of a miraculous image.[16] Composed for a campaign to establish the authenticity of miracles associated with the image, it bristles with testimony and references to various documents, witnesses, and experts, and is organized into a long series of numbered paragraphs rather than chapters that develop a story line. The year after *Renovación por sí misma* appeared, Archbishop Francisco Aguiar y Seijas examined a full set of depositions supporting the tradition of supernatural restoration and declared it to be an authentic miracle.[17] It is not clear whether the archbishop fully supported Velasco's dramatic extension of the origin story told by González Dávila, who may have garbled or radically simplified the tradition that reached him from Mexico.

With the archbishop's official endorsement of a miraculous restoration and a buzz of public excitement after the image was believed to have brought relief to the city from an epidemic in 1697, the devotion took off. That year Italian visitor Juan Gemelli Carreri called the chapel of the Cristo Renovado one of the Valley of Mexico's three great shrines (among more than sixty celebrated miraculous images by my count). The first edition of Velasco's hagiographical book, revised for a general readership from his 1688 publication, appeared in 1699 along with a printed program of prayers and other devotions for an annual novena in the church of Santa Teresa. A second novena booklet appeared in 1715, followed in 1724 by a reprinting of Velasco's 1699 text and a new book for devotees of the image by the Jesuit Domingo de Quiroga. Then in 1731 a lengthy sermon inspired by the image was delivered and published by one of the capital's leading preachers, Manuel Folgar. In all, there have been twelve editions of Velasco's devotional history, published without revisions to his text. They were printed in four clusters: 1699 and 1724; 1776, 1790, 1807, 1810, and 1820; 1845 and 1858; and facsimiles in 1945, 1951, and 1996. The silence between 1858 and the facsimile editions coincided with a long decline in popular and official interest in the image in Mexico City. The gaps in publication during the eighteenth and early nineteenth centuries seem to have less to do with declining interest than with the history of promotion by archiepiscopal authorities.[18] Publications and descriptions of popular devotion to the Cristo Renovado were less conspicuous during the period of concerted official promotion of Our Lady of Guadalupe in the 1740s and 1750s, but in the 1760s and 1770s chroniclers continued to single out this crucifix as one of the great miraculous images favoring New Spain, and private bequests were accumulating.[19] Between 1724 and 1776 there is ample evidence of growing devotion in Mexico City. Enthusiasm for the Cristo Renovado as a processional image and "celestial physician" (*celestial médico*) in times of illness seems to have taken firm hold during the great epidemic of 1737, when many thousands of people accompanied the image to Mexico City's cathedral and crowded in for a novena of public prayers and Masses.[20] It would be taken in procession to the cathedral for novenas during other epidemics in 1761, 1779, 1784, 1797, and 1833.[21]

Paintings of the celebrated crucifix made for devotees in Mexico City and the provincial city of Querétaro during the eighteenth century trace a similar pattern of promotion and devotion. Most were painted in Mexico City during the 1730s when the Cristo Renovado was featured in penitential

Fig. 2.2. This 1807 print from the 1807 edition of Velasco's *Exaltación de la divina misericordia* . . . is very similar to others that appeared in editions of the *Exaltación* after 1776. Here Christ's body is less tortured and seems to float on the cross. The background is plainer than that shown in Fig. 2.1 and begins to recede. Courtesy of the Bancroft Library, University of California, Berkeley.

IMAGES AND SHRINES

V.R. DE LA MILAG. IMAG. DEL SSMO. CHRISTO. RENOV. DE SANTA TERE[...]
[...] concedidos 180. dias de Indulgencias á todas las pe[r]sonas que rezaren un Credo por las nesecid[ades]
de Nuestra S. Madre la Yglecia.
Larrea, Grabó y Dedico á [...]

Fig. 2.3. This 1820 print accentuates the full-bodied figure of Christ and extends neoclassical motifs of dignified simplicity and Christ's perfection in its large but spare, fluted base, the unobtrusive background, and the refinement of the body. It is more about the figure of Christ, but less about his agony. If the differences among these three figures are signs of changing religious sensibilities, there is little to suggest that devotees of the shrine at Mapethé had caught the new spirit. Print from the 1820 edition of Velasco's *Exaltación de la divina misericordia* . . . . Courtesy of the Nettie Lee Benson Library, University of Texas at Austin.

processions.²² At least three were done by José de Ibarra, an especially popular Mexico City painter of the time, and several found their way to Spain. One that advertised itself as having "touched the original" went to a Carmelite convent in Málaga, Spain, in the 1740s, attracting an ardent following among the nuns there. They eventually received from the Mexico City shrine two of the original nails from the cross of the Cristo Renovado in exchange for three gold-plated, diamond-studded replacements.²³ These eighteenth-century paintings and publications kept the focus on the image and Mexico City as especially favored by the original miracle of self-restoration, and devotional fervor to the Cristo Renovado intensified during times of crisis, as the surge of interest during epidemics suggests.

The years immediately before and during the independence period (1810–1821), when a new and grander chapel for the Cristo Renovado was under construction in the Carmelite church, represent the period of greatest official promotion, wealth, and popularity of this shrine after the 1690s. In April 1809 the image was taken to the cathedral for a novena to appeal for the safety of the King of Spain and defeat of "French heretics"—apparently the first time the image had left the convent church of Santa Teresa except for penitential processions during epidemics. In his late 1810 diatribe against the insurrection led by Miguel Hidalgo and plea for "union and brotherhood" across New Spain's regions and social classes, Agustín Pomposo Fernández de San Salvador invoked the "Cristo de Santa Teresa la Antigua" along with the Virgin of Guadalupe and the Virgin of Los Remedios as the symbols of national unity.²⁴ A wealthy confraternity dedicated to the Cristo Renovado was active at the shrine then, and in 1814 the shrine's treasury boasted bequests and chaplaincies that produced about twenty thousand pesos in annual interest.²⁵ This sum was augmented by the usual alms collections and, in 1813, a popular raffle was instituted (the Lotería del Ssmo Cristo de Santa Teresa la Antigua) during the final months of construction of the new chapel. The raffle netted the shrine 894 pesos on gross ticket sales of 2,340 pesos during its first thirty-two months.²⁶

Although the popularity of the raffle had run its course by 1823, the shrine's stock of capital continued to produce a steady income,²⁷ and devotion peaked again during the cholera epidemic of 1833 with another procession and novena in the cathedral.²⁸ Carlos María Bustamante celebrated the image's continuing power and popularity when he wrote in the early 1840s:

This surprising rejuvenation of the Lord of Santa Teresa has not only been a matter of belief by all Mexicans up to the present, but it has been confirmed in singular marvels, including its exalted protection in every public calamity, most recently in the terrible cholera epidemic which began to recede as soon as the image was displayed in a magnificent procession.[29]

The new chapel collapsed in an earthquake in 1845, shattering the image. There was enough money in the shrine's treasury and interest among devotees both to print updated editions of Velasco's *Exaltación de la divina misericordia* for promotional purposes in 1845 and 1858 and a new novena booklet in 1849, and to rebuild the chapel and artfully remake the image. Perhaps the remade image was not perceived as "the same." In any case, the Cristo Renovado de Santa Teresa never regained its old popularity after Mexico's reform period in the 1850s and 1860s.[30] In 1916, during the Mexican Revolution, the church of Santa Teresa la Antigua was closed by the government and the image moved to the cathedral. In 1950 it was moved to the church of the Carmelite friars in Tacubaya and finally returned to the Carmelite nuns, now residing in Colonia Tlacopac, San Angel, in 1959. Today few people in Mexico City, much less elsewhere, know about the miraculous image of the Cristo Renovado, and the nuns have not succeeded in reviving much interest in it. Their facsimile edition in 1996 of an early edition of Velasco's book marking the 375th anniversary of the miracle of renovation attracted some antiquarian interest, but few new devotees.[31]

One Image, Two Shrines: The Cristo Renovado of Ixmiquilpan-Mapethé

What went on in the place where the great miracle of rejuvenation was said to have happened back in 1621? Had people there been telling themselves the miracle story Velasco eventually published? Were they drawn to the shrine in Mexico City after the image was taken from them? Was Velasco's text known to them? If so, how did they understand it? We may never know what stories local people told about the place and image during the sixteenth and seventeenth centuries. On the other hand, nothing yet known from the seventeenth century suggests that they organized pilgrimages to visit the lost image in Mexico City or honored the site of the miracle of renovation before Velasco's devotional history appeared in 1699.

The chapel at Mapethé remained in ruins until the 1720s; then, soon after the second edition of Velasco's book appeared, the situation changed. From the 1720s to the early 1800s, bursts of record making and building tell of considerable regional interest in the site. The 1728 license to rebuild the chapel noted that many people—identified as non-Indians as well as Indians—were visiting Mapethé as a place of miracles.[32] By the late 1730s several Otomí Indian leaders from the district of Ixmiquilpan vied for control over the project.[33] At the center of this first dispute was don Agustín Morales, an Otomí *cacique* (hereditary leader) and painter by trade from El Cardonal who was described by his followers as "the first founder" of the tradition. In the late 1720s he reportedly crafted two crucifixes similar to the Cristo Renovado, started to build a church on the site of the original chapel, sponsored an annual novena there during Lent, and secured licenses from ecclesiastical and royal authorities to collect alms for the building project.

While no one denied that the shrine was Morales's idea and the first phase of construction was undertaken largely at his expense, by 1737 he was entangled in litigation over who should be in charge of the project and the site.[34] He sought and received an order from the high court in Mexico City for the parish priest of El Cardonal and other colonial authorities and Indian governors throughout the area to recognize his authority—"quasi possession," the legal record calls it—and not interfere with his collection of donations and management of the building project. But his authority at the sacred site was always in dispute. In 1738, 1739, and 1742 he petitioned for confirmation of his 1737 possession and an order for the officials of El Cardonal not to interfere with his collections and administration of the project. Then in 1743 he was imprisoned on orders of the priest and charged with stealing three hundred pesos from the collection box. His principal alms collectors and fellow Indian notables, Diego Joseph and Pedro Martín Bello, seized his crucifixes and claimed to be the rightful administrators of the burgeoning devotion. Morales spent more than a year in jail until he rendered what were regarded as adequate accounts of the alms collections. Royal revenue agents and district governors got involved, accusing all of the Indian leaders of embezzling funds and complaining that the shrine was creating a vagrancy problem and depriving them of tax revenue and labor for the mines of the El Cardonal district. The protracted litigation drew in dozens of witnesses who incidentally attested to a territory of devotees and conscripted construction workers that included various Otomí towns

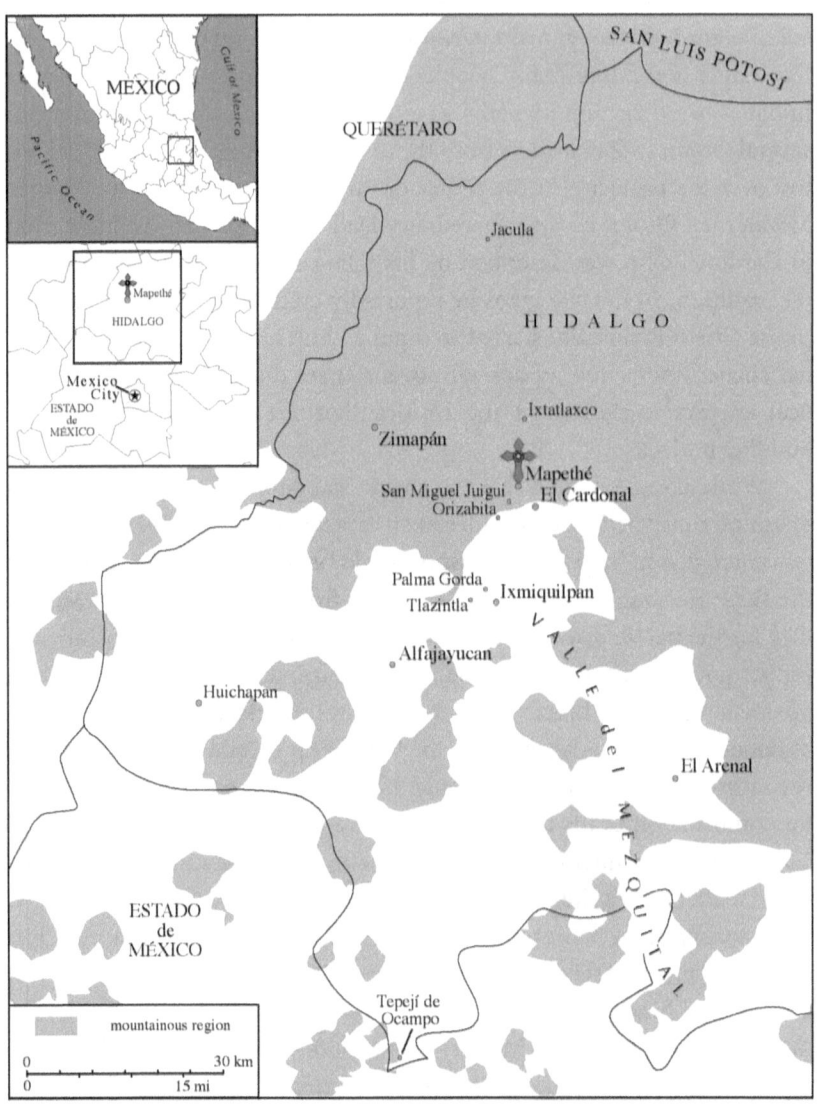

Fig. 2.4. Map of the Shrine of Mapethé and surroundings. Prepared in the Department of Geography, University of California, Berkeley, by Christine Eduok.

and hamlets in western Hidalgo. They testified that most devotees went to the holy site for the festivities Morales promoted during Lent, taking their village and family crucifixes with them, as if to charge them with sacred energy at the place of the miraculous renovation.

Bello served as *mayordomo* or administrator of the emerging shrine for two years from 1746 to 1748 and oversaw about a third of the construction completed by this date, but the job was still far from done and he, too, was brought down by accusations of withholding alms for his own use and not submitting full financial reports. Morales and his followers continued to lay claim to the project and gained a decisive legal victory over Bello and other rivals in 1748, as colonial officials pushed for completion of the shrine and regular administration by a parish priest and a single mayordomo. Bello spent that year and part of the next in jail while he and eight more self-styled "founders" of the shrine continued to appeal the verdict against his claim as rightful administrator. Morales and his followers responded with the usual vigor. The judges finally threw up their hands on December 20, 1748, and remitted the case to the archbishop's court for further consideration. There Morales was quickly confirmed as the mayordomo. Morales recovered his crucifixes—the one described as "the green cross" was given a place of honor in the temporary shrine at Mapethé—and new alms collectors resumed their rounds, but his triumph was shortlived. By the fall he had died and the church was still unfinished.

This summary of bitter, costly legal claims and counterclaims barely touches the complex, shifting webs of local interests and factions behind them. Morales, Diego Joseph, and Bello were all Otomí leaders from the vicinity of El Cardonal,[35] but the collective leadership of El Cardonal opposed Morales in the early years of this dispute, then supported him later. His most consistent supporters seem to have been people identified as Indians from the large settlements of Tlazintla and Palma Gorda, near the district capital of Ixmiquilpan. The pastors and royal governors of El Cardonal and Ixmiquilpan were suspicious of any Indian administration of this district-wide project that shifted patronage and control of finances from their offices, yet they wanted it to go forward. At one time or another they became allies or adversaries of the several Indian partisans, while struggling with each other over jurisdiction and administration of funds. District officials and the high court in Mexico City found the mounting record of dispute and shifting divisions among Indian leaders and settlements as tangled as the would-be historian does. As early as January 1744, the *alcalde mayor* (district governor) of Ixmiquilpan marveled at "the many orders and injunctions issued in this case, some in favor of Agustín Morales and others for Diego Joseph, . . . and the endless complaints of both parties."³⁶ The Otomí side of the case seemed endless because it had less to do with clear-cut legal issues that could be resolved by compromise or the final authority of a colonial court than with unremitting tetchiness over subordination to authority outside the local community. And even the apparent local communities were dispersed and often fractious.

Situated several miles north of the settlement of El Cardonal, the unfinished shrine was described in late 1748 as very large—roughly 150 feet long and more than fifty feet high, with walls nearly six feet thick and a beautiful bell tower modeled on the cathedral in Mexico City. The structure was valued at just over ten thousand pesos, and it was estimated that two years and another fourteen thousand pesos were needed to finish the job. But the way to a finished shrine and settled administrative and devotional practices still was not clear. In 1755 Archbishop Manuel Rubio y Salinas's pastoral visit report sharply criticized the shrine's administrators and alms collectors for not completing the building and keeping inadequate records of "the copious donations that are collected daily."³⁷ Yet another church official seemed convinced that the alms collectors were skimming money from the collection boxes.

This first burst of records has the hallmarks of a shrine and devotion in its early stages of development. Alms-collecting missions began then, and their purpose was to pay for construction of the first substantial church at the site. Construction was the center of activity, and weekly labor receipts for late 1748 and early 1749 show a crew of twelve Indian day laborers at work under the supervision of four skilled masons. Don Agustín Morales's two crucifixes circulated with the alms collectors and were sometimes housed at the building site, but no particular image was yet regarded as the Señor de Mapethé. The principal feast day during the week before Palm Sunday does not seem to have been well established yet.³⁸

Velasco's story of the miracle of renovation and the transfer of the image to Mexico City may well have become local knowledge in western Hidalgo at this time, with a selective, provocative twist. According to Salvador González, a mestizo from Ixmiquilpan who testified before the district governor in 1743, local people knew the story of the self-renovating crucifix "as it is described in the printed book about this astonishing portent."³⁹ And in 1748 Indians from three communities in the district⁴⁰ boldly asserted that the image in Mexico City ought to be returned to Mapethé once their church was completed—a possibility implied by Velasco, who had described how when the archbishop's deputies came to take the image away, it grew heavy and began to bleed and blink its eyes. When local people resisted its removal, their parish priest promised them he would request the return of the image "God willing, if it is not properly cared for in Mexico City," but pointed out that "at present, we have no church; it is in ruins."[41] At least some local devotees in the 1740s and later seem to have taken this passage from Velasco's book to mean that if they built a fine church for the image, it should be returned.[42]

The unfinished shrine became a parish seat in 1751, and its first pastor, Bachiller Antonio Fuentes de León, actively promoted the cult during his tenure of more than twenty years, enlarging and strengthening the building, and furnishing it with fine altars and paintings. The present building has the gilded altars from Father Fuentes's time—the main altar carries a 1765 date[43]—and an antique wooden crucifix about 3 feet high known as the Señor de Mapethé (perhaps one of the portable images Morales made in the 1720s; more likely a later crucifix commissioned by the people of Palma Gorda). On the side walls hang an undated oil painting of the Cristo Renovado bringing rain after seven years of drought and a set of four paintings dated 1773 that depict the miraculous renovation of the image in 1621. The last painting in the set shows Father Fuentes in the posture of a devout donor. If I did not know about Agustín Morales, Diego Joseph, Pedro Martín Bello, and the others, it would be tempting to conclude that the shrine and devotions at Mapethé began with, and largely depended on, the efforts of the assiduous Father Fuentes. In word and image, don Agustín and his rivals are absent from the material remains of the shrine at Mapethé. But they are there in deed.

The second long burst of written record, from 1783 to 1795, mainly concerned the Zimapán area north of Mapethé, and it establishes that interest in the shrine remained strong after Father Fuentes died and spread to the north and west, mainly among Otomí people.[44] By then, the fifth Friday of Lent, just before Palm Sunday, had become the day for the annual gathering of crucifixes from throughout the region. Participants spoke of this event as ancient practice—"*de tiempo inmemorial*"—as if it had always been so.[45] By then one or more images displayed at the shrine were recognized as the Lord of Mapethé, although not without some controversy. Many Indians were making the one-day walk from the district of Zimapán,[46] where the most productive silver mines in the region were located at that time. Indians of Zimapán, many of them transient or recently settled, reportedly left their work in the mines to visit the shrine at least once a year, confessed and took communion at Mapethé rather than at home, and sometimes hid from the local tax collector and the labor bosses when they returned. The royal officials of Zimapán were not about to lose their grip on Indian labor and local taxes without a contest in the courtroom. The result is an ample record of sharp dispute over this thirteen-year period and more testimony about the shrine.

If the conflicts of the 1730s and 1740s involving the shrine at Mapethé crosscut local society in more directions than I can describe in a few pages, those of the 1780s and early 1790s are even more complex and less localized. Three kinds of conflict appear in this new documentation: (1) between Indians of the Zimapán area and their alcalde mayor and parish priest over fees, taxes, and where their political loyalties belonged; (2) between Zimapán's Indian governors and the Indian mayordomo who organized the annual nine-day pilgrimage to Mapethé over collection of expense money[47]; and (3) between the alcalde mayor and parish priest of Ixmiquilpan on one side and the alcalde mayor and parish priest of Zimapán on the other over how and where Indians of the district of Zimapán should spend their money and receive communion. Despite the divisions, when it came time for the annual journey to Mapethé with the local crucifixes, the various Otomí rivals seem to have joined in, including the Indian governors who had complained of the mayordomo. Nor did higher colonial authorities interfere. Perhaps because devotees could show that they were not gone long and did not engage in unruly activity, the litigation of the 1790s did not lead to orders from the archbishop or the viceroy to suspend the processions or discourage the devotion in other ways.[48] This tacit acceptance is surprising, since official policy at the time discouraged most alms collections and large Indian gatherings, and district officials were concerned about "Indians" in El Cardonal harboring suspicions that "the Spaniards" meant to destroy them.[49] Mexico City authorities may not have interfered with the Mapethé shrine because they did not want to chance disturbances over devotional practices in a place uncomfortably close to the Sierra de Tututepec, where an Indian millenarian movement during the 1760s was still well remembered.[50] The appeal of the Mapethé shrine does not seem to have been growing much in the late eighteenth century, but it would not have been easy to suppress if colonial authorities had been inclined to try. When the alcalde mayor of Zimapán did forbid the annual visit to Mapethé in 1792 (before the dispute was appealed to Mexico City), local people ignored his order and went to the shrine anyway.[51]

The third burst of political drama and record making, lasting for most of nine years, followed the creation of a town at the shrine, known as Pueblo Nuevo (El Santuario on modern maps). About two hundred people, most of them Otomí Indians, had taken up residence near the shrine by 1776 without being formally constituted as a town until a viceregal decree to that effect was issued in 1795. Creating a formal town meant loss of jurisdiction, and in this case also loss of population and labor service, by the head town of El Cardonal, since most members of Pueblo Nuevo came from its Guigui and Cardonalito *barrios* (a Spanish term for neighborhood, here applied to dispersed, extended-family settlements that were the common Otomí residential pattern in the area). The most contentious and enduring issue, however, was land rights. El Cardonal ceded the new settlement its townsite, a square about 550 yards on a side, but the access its residents would have to farmlands, pastures, and woodlands was unresolved. Most of the original two hundred settlers in 1776 had ancestral lands nearby; many of the roughly four hundred inhabitants in 1804 did not.[52] From 1799 to 1804 the people of Pueblo Nuevo were in constant, sometimes violent dispute over woodlands with neighboring rancheros and the Otomí town of Orizaba.[53]

A separate, indirectly related dispute came to a head at the time of these land struggles.[54] In late 1799 Palma Gorda, a subordinate settlement of Orizaba, in the parish of Ixmiquilpan (the parish seat and district head town for Pueblo Nuevo was the smaller El Cardonal), complained to the alcalde mayor of Ixmiquilpan and to the archbishop's court in Mexico City that a crucifix donated by their community, which had long occupied the place of honor on the main altar of the shrine, had been replaced with a new image belonging to Pueblo Nuevo. The attorney for Pueblo Nuevo responded that malcontents from Ixmiquilpan with unspecified ulterior motives were behind this complaint. A flurry of charges and countercharges followed, leaving the archbishop's legal adviser to make sense in April 1800 of "the confusing writings of the Indians of Palma Gorda," and to separate fact from fulmination. After three years of dispute, the archbishop's adviser counted heads and recognized that the old image was "the object of particular devotion, visited by people from throughout the area." He recommended that the old image be restored to the main altar, and it was.[55]

The original image of the Cristo Renovado was never repatriated from Mexico City, but a report on resources and conditions in the district in 1792 remarked on the well-furnished church at Mapethé, ready to welcome the original image, as promised in Velasco's account, "when the famous dispute over where it belongs is resolved."[56] Even in the 1860s, the animated Cristo Renovado was vividly recalled by a local chronicler who assured his readers that sighs, groans, sobs, and the tolling of phantom bells could still be heard at Mapethé, just as Velasco had described them for the years leading up to 1621. Interest in the original image among western Hidalgo's Otomí people has increased since the 1950s as some local families and unmarried men and women migrated to Mexico City or were exposed to government programs encouraging speakers of native languages to reclaim their history while becoming educated Mexicans. In the late 1970s, Pedro Martín Godínez Salas, an Otomí speaker from the Ixmiquilpan area, completed a master's thesis project in ethnolinguistics on the impact of land reform in the area of Mapethé. In the course of his research Godínez Salas came upon Velasco's text and began to delve into the story of the shrine at Mapethé as an example of Christian values betrayed, with Indians as the victims. His thesis quoted liberally from Velasco as an important part of an otherwise unwritten history of his region that few local people had read for themselves. Like some local readers in the eighteenth century, Godínez Salas noticed Velasco's passing comment that seemed to promise eventual return of the original image to Mapethé. Otomíes from the Mapethé area who moved to the capital from 1940 to 1970 traveled back to the shrine for the annual spring procession of the crosses when they could. They also discovered in the early 1960s that the original image of the Cristo Renovado had lately been moved to the convent church of the Discalced Carmelite nuns in San Angel. Some of them began to organize group visits to the image and press officials of the Archdiocese of Mexico for its return to Mapethé. When archdiocesan leaders responded by sending Mapethé a "replica" of the Lord of Santa Teresa, as they called it, local people were less than satisfied, according to one of Godínez's informants:

> This image was sent to placate the people who live here, to replace the image that was taken away. But when I went to the Carmelite convent we noticed that the miraculous image and the image in the shrine of Mapethé don't look at all alike. While I spoke to the Carmelite nuns, they said they guard the image day and night so

that it won't disappear. Clearly these [fears] are myths, and we don't know whether they have a basis in reality, but these people who guard the image are deeply suspicious of our interest. Just to see it we had to say that we were from a place called the "the Poor Lead Mines" [Real de Minas de Plomo Pobre], and even then they demanded identification before letting us in.[57]

Popular devotion to the Cristo Renovado hardly exists in Mexico City any longer, while the shrine at Mapethé continues to attract a regional following and recently underwent restoration under the supervision of the Instituto Nacional de Antropología e Historia's Escuela Nacional de Conservación, Restauración y Museografía—thanks in part to Velasco's sunlit account of providential beginnings for what he represented as a major urban shrine. But there is not a straight line, happily-ever-after story of growth and Otomí or Indian solidarity for the rural Mapethé shrine, either. We have the eighteenth-century records that carry the history of the Cristo Renovado beyond Velasco's Mexico City story because of perennial struggles in the district of Ixmiquilpan and Zimapán, most of them struggles among Otomí groups. The main celebration at the shrine still falls on the fifth Friday of Lent, but it is overshadowed by the crowds and commerce on the same day in the nearby town of El Arenal. There in El Arenal another miracle-working crucifix is honored, perhaps one of those that paid its respects at Mapethé in the eighteenth century.[58]

The history of the miraculous Cristo Renovado connects a remote rural place to the capital city without establishing a pilgrimage route or authority and subordination between them. And many other local histories in Mexico bear comparison to it. Some shrines were more popular than others, but there were no great pilgrimage routes through a landscape of secondary shrines like those to Rome or Compostela. Before the great organized pilgrimages to Tepeyac developed in the late nineteenth century, large numbers of devotees of all social ranks were going to several hundred shrines all over Mexico. They still go. Most seventeenth- and eighteenth-century visitors to shrines did not travel far or linger over the journey as a prolonged penitential quest, and many who revered a renowned image never visited its shrine. Mapethé is an unusual case of holy theft, but in shifting the story away from distant travels, Marian devotion, official chroniclers, and a hierarchy of shrines, it strikes the dominant chord.

Contexts and Connections

I have framed this presentation of the Cristo Renovado around two shrines with different historical trajectories that can suggest how rural Indian subjects might interrupt and refashion the logic of a printed text produced in Mexico City from a metropolitan viewpoint and the logic of the wider social order to meet their expectations and circumstances. Here local knowledge seems to have taken its cue from Velasco's book, but made the place where a moldering crucifix was said to have restored itself to fine condition more important than the absent relic.[59] These two histories of one Cristo Renovado are more than self-contained stories running on parallel tracks. In the eighteenth century they converged most immediately for colonial authorities in Mexico City, Ixmiquilpan, and El Cardonal who presided over the long-running litigation and administrative affairs of the Mapethé shrine. But they also converge in the history of growing Christocentric devotion in Spain and Spanish America during the seventeenth and eighteenth centuries.

Most of the important Spanish and Mexican shrines to miraculous images of Christ began early in the seventeenth century, and some of them—especially in Mexico—attracted even greater interest in the eighteenth and nineteenth centuries. This trajectory of formation and growth, punctuated by ebbs and flows of interest, was also true of many Marian shrines in Europe. William Christian and others find that the new importance of image shrines in Spain and much of Western Europe from the sixteenth century is related to declining interest in relics and sacred sites in the countryside.[60] The Mexican case was bound to be somewhat different. Saints' relics were never as important in the Americas. America had few saints of its own before John Paul II's papacy, and minor European saints' relics were imported but rarely caught on as objects of popular devotion.[61] To the extent that the interest in miraculous images in Mexico was orchestrated by church leaders during the seventeenth century, it has less to do with deflecting attention from relics than with muffling stories of apparitions reported by Indian neophytes, stories that sixteenth-century Franciscans in particular had encouraged and celebrated in their American chronicles.[62] The growing importance of urban sites of marvels and image shrines was shared with Europe, but without overshadowing the countryside. The found or animated images of Christ in Mexico during the seventeenth and eighteenth centuries were mostly reported from rural places and small settlements.

To approach the emergence of the Mapethé shrine in the eighteenth century as more than a local story in isolation calls especially for attention to the nature and reach of Otomí devotion to this cristo renovado and the cross as a sacred symbol. The shrine's reach was not limited to the immediate vicinity of Mapethé or the district of Ixmiquilpan where it was centered.[63] The parish priest based at Mapethé in 1793 testified that the annual fiesta and procession of crucifixes during Lent were sponsored by the Indian pueblos of Jacala, Zimapán, Yxtatlaxco, and Tepejí (del Río), as well as Ixmiquilpan. These places form a band through western Hidalgo approximately thirty miles long from north to south, none of them more than a two-day walk from the shrine. This was the main catchment area of visitors. A larger territory of interest in the shrine can be traced in the reports submitted by alms collectors in 1748 and 1749. This area of donors reached further west, into southern Querétaro and Guanajuato. Collectors reported in from San Juan del Río and La Cañada near the city of Querétaro; from Irapuato (Guanajuato); from settlements around Hacienda Saus near Silao (Guanajuato); and from the city of Guanajuato and vicinity. All of them were sending back to the shrine substantial sums of twenty to eighty silver pesos every month or six weeks (see Figs. 2.2 and 2.5).

The travels and settlement sites of Otomí people may hold a key to this greater spiritual geography of the Mapethé shrine and growing devotion to images of Christ in Hidalgo and the Bajío. Before Spanish colonization, Otomí-speakers occupied much of modern Querétaro and Hidalgo, with pockets of settlement and migration reaching into San Luis Potosí, Michoacán, Guanajuato, México, Puebla, and Tlaxcala. Unlike the Tlaxcalans or the Tenocha-Mexica, precolonial Otomíes did not constitute a proper "kingdom," and their most important center, Xilotepec (in Hidalgo), was not an urban capital like Tenochtitlan or Tlaxcala. Rather, Otomíes evidently had many smaller, scattered pockets of settlement and authority, mirroring the organization of their local communities, in which most people lived dispersed in extended family clusters. Beyond modern Hidalgo's Mezquital Valley, their ancestral lands were high, dry, and stony, and during the colonial period they could rarely make a living from maize farming and horticulture the way their ancestors may have done, and as other groups in central Mexico continued to do. In addition to farming and gathering food, family members had long made charcoal and produced *pulque* (fermented juice of a native agave plant) and pottery vessels in which to carry it to consumers. Other Otomíes were recruited by more

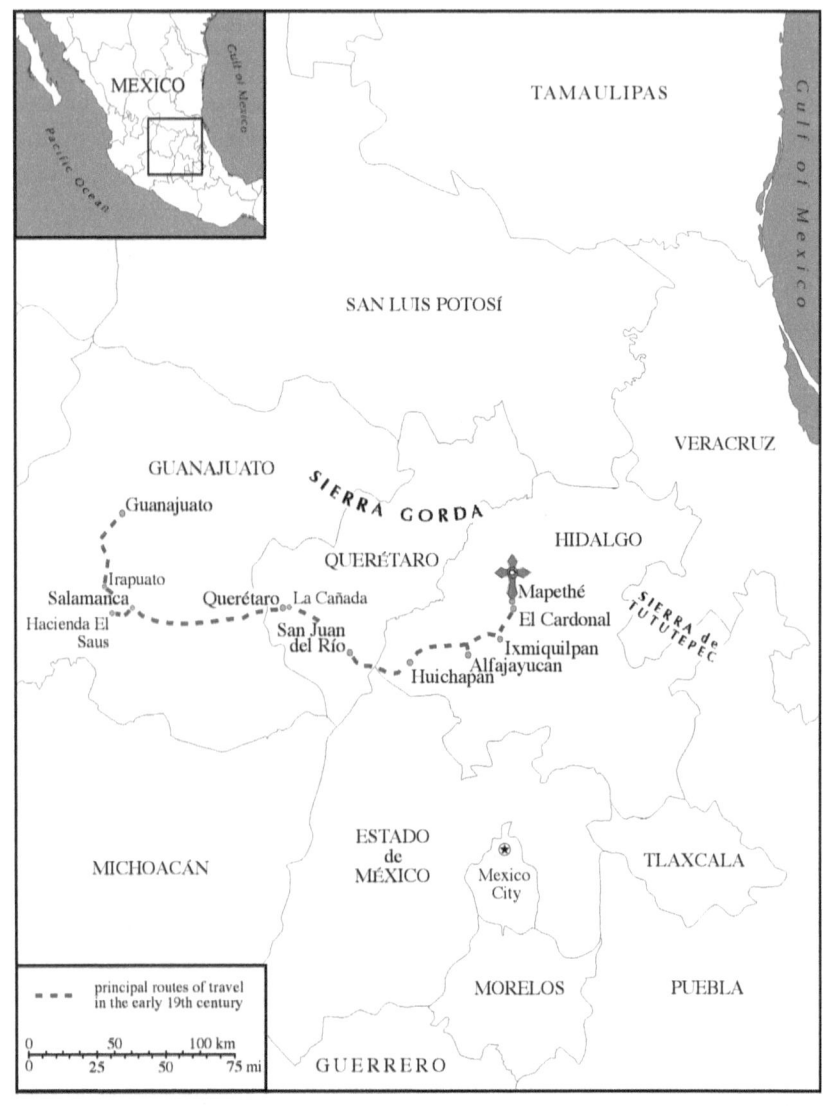

Fig. 2.5 Map showing the reach of Otomí alms collectors for the Cristo Renovado. Prepared in the Department of Geography, University of California, Berkeley, by Christine Eduok.

organized states—including, later, the Spanish colonial regime—as warriors and laborers.[64]

The Otomí presence during the colonial period extended into more of modern Hidalgo, Querétaro, and Guanajuato, even as their population shrank. Herding sheep by both Otomíes and non-Indians beginning in the sixteenth century contributed to this dispersion and reinforced the old pattern of scattered settlements of extended families. While communities associated with the shrine at Mapethé mainly were located in the hotter, drier northern portion of the Mezquital Valley where ranching did not predominate, the new pastoralism undermined traditional agriculture throughout Hidalgo—reduced to small pockets of irrigated fields by overgrazing, erosion, and lower water tables.[65] In the sixteenth and seventeenth centuries some Otomí groups also were resettled in townships near Spanish settlements or on frontier missions intended as buffers against hostile "Chichimecs." In the eighteenth century, more Otomíes migrated for work within this core territory—especially to the colonial mines, haciendas, and towns of Guanajuato and Querétaro as day laborers, or to Zimapán and other mining settlements of northern Hidalgo. Aggressive expansion of non-Indian ranches and growing numbers of landless Otomíes made them more vulnerable to coercive labor practices, contributed to this late colonial migration, and strained labor relations in the mines of Zimapán and El Cardonal.[66]

Otomíes also began to spill beyond old limits of settlement in the early colonial missions of the Sierra Gorda—the "land of war" with hostile "Chichimecs" in northern Hidalgo, Querétaro, and San Luis Potosí. Zimapán itself had once been one of these frontier missions, but in 1703 its Dominican mission of Santa María de los Dolores was moved deeper into the Sierra Gorda in order to isolate and overcome Indians then in rebellion. From the beginning of the eighteenth century the mountains of the Sierra Gorda and eastern Hidalgo were volatile areas of "Chichimec" (and sometimes Otomí) resistance, of military expeditions during the 1740s, secularization of missions from the 1740s to the 1770s, and millenarian uprisings at Xichú in 1768 and the Sierra de Tututepec in 1769.[67]

Colonial Otomí Christianity drew on local traditions and organization in ways that emphasized the cross and Christ crucified. Early chroniclers mentioned their unusual attachment to festivals of the Cross, and the practice of bringing local saints and crosses to great processions of the Cross in Querétaro, Chalma, and San Miguel Allende, among other places, was established before the end of the colonial period.[68] Otomíes from Querétaro and Hidalgo were drawn to the famous miracle-working stone cross of the Franciscans in the city of Querétaro, and to the Christ of Chalma, near Malinalco in the Estado de México. At both sites, they took part in great processions of portable crosses brought from their home communities.[69] Miraculous crosses, sometimes green in color (suggesting both fertility and life everlasting), abounded in Otomí communities. Following a brief rebellion of Otomí people in the district of Amanalco, Hidalgo, against their parish priest in 1792, the Archbishop of Mexico ordered Indians in the area to turn over to the parish priest all the crosses that dotted the hilltops and other places "in order to give them proper veneration and avoid superstitions, abuses, inappropriate observances, and perhaps worse."[70] An unusual number of Otomí men were baptized with the name of the cross (such as "Juan de la Cruz"), and the many stone sanctuaries that served as Otomí family chapels in rural Hidalgo from the late colonial period and the nineteenth century had special associations with the cross, ancestors, and shamanic healing. Although most of the family chapels in the northern Mezquital Valley have been put to other uses or neglected in recent years, many are still active in mountain communities of Querétaro and Hidalgo. Even if the family has a patron saint, his or her image usually cedes center stage to a cross or crucifix. Other, smaller crosses are found there, too, along with paper cutouts and other objects for healing and fertility ceremonies that one would not find in the parish church.[71]

Otomí veneration of the cross amounted to more than the crucified Christ as distant, terrifying symbol of suffering and punishment or as the embodiment of their own suffering under Spanish and Mexican rule.[72] Their colonial Franciscan and Augustinian mentors presented the cross as a symbol of life, both temporal and eternal, and protection against Satan's wiles; and Otomí attachment to stories of self-renovating crucifixes may well stem from an Augustinian predilection.[73] Local meanings are especially associated with protection, propitiation, fertility, veneration of ancestors, and sacred movement in the outdoors. The script of a play about Emperor Constantine's veneration of the cross composed in 1714 for Otomí Indians of Santa Cruz Cozcaquauhatlauhticpac, Tlaxcala, presents the cross as the tree of life and protector. In this play Constantine comes to discover the true faith in the sign of the cross; and the cross, in turn, is treated as a gift from God with which to conquer his enemies. This is the familiar story of his conversion and providential conquests as a Christian emperor, but the play ends with a local, protective twist. All the actors kneel before the cross and Constantine's mother, Saint Helene, speaks at length about the "adorable cross, truly the tree of life," saying "the land is blessed by the divine cross."[74]

Recent ethnographic accounts add suggestively to the colonial-period record of Otomí understandings of the cross and other local practices that colonial authorities regarded as superstitions (or worse) and rarely recorded. Studies of Otomí rituals and family chapels suggest that crosses have been so prominent because they comprised a bundle of meanings for social and personal well-being. The numerous crosses inside Otomí family chapels have especially to do with ancestor veneration. The principal cross on the altar represents "the first common ancestor," and smaller crosses represent the souls of other ancestors.[75] Inside these sanctuaries, images of the patron saints also are placed, along with paper cutouts representing other divine beings in nature that are used by local shamans in curing and fertility ceremonies.[76]

Otomí oral traditions and prayers place the cross and Christ crucified at the center of their cultural landscape as a protective, healing gift from God and the promise of renewal and continuity, including personal redemption.[77] Prayers invoke the souls of ancestors and the cross in the same breath, "May they help us and accompany us." The cross as "master of life, master of health" is invoked for "a good path, my good entry way."[78] When in danger, make a cross with your fingers and say, "Cruz, cruz, cruz, que se vaya el Diablo y venga Jesús" (Cross, cross, cross, may Jesus come and banish the devil).[79] But crosses, especially household crosses, can be "bad." In the spirit of Durkheim's notion of "contagiousness of the sacred," they are invested with harmful as well as beneficent powers and need to be approached properly and propitiated so that they do not spill out in undesirable ways.[80]

The placement and movement of crosses throughout the landscape—near caves, rock outcroppings, springs, on hilltops, and especially along pathways and at thresholds—is a longstanding practice.[81] In Huizquilucan on the edge of the Valley of Mexico, H. R. Harvey found that crosses on hilltops are taken to embody the Otomí rain divinity or, in one case, Makata, the Otomí divine essence and lord of the mountains. The cross associated with Makata is carried in procession through much of the district during early May, at the time of the feast of the Holy Cross. Otomíes from Chimalpa el Grande, Tlaxcala, evidently regard their shrine on the summit of Cerro de la Malinche as the birthplace of the Lord of Chalma, who departed long ago for his cave near Malinalco in the Estado de México.[82]

Little is known about Otomíes' role as carriers of enthusiasm for particular crucifixes and other images during the colonial period. The shrine of the Christ of Chalma, near Malinalco, Estado de México, which may have attracted many devotees from more distant places than any other late colonial shrine to an image of Christ, was a favorite destination of scattered Otomí communities. Juan Carlos Ruiz Guadalajara recently described a dense web of devotion to the black Christ of Salamanca (state of Guanajuato) and at least three other renowned crucifixes that connected Otomíes residing in towns and cities of the Bajío during the eighteenth century.[83] And Otomí fiestas to the Holy Cross often end with a group of local people traveling with their portable crosses and saints to a major shrine such as the shrines of the Lord of Chalma, the Virgin of Guadalupe, or Our Lady of San Juan de los Lagos. But Otomí devotion to sacred images is less about interest in a few distant images of Christ or the Virgin than veneration of favorite local images, usually of Christ. The travels of these images and of people to their shrines meant to broadcast sacred energy from its dwelling places as well as concentrate it there. Judging by the recent circulation of images and their devotees in the districts of Ixmiquilpan and El Cardonal, these travels could have served as a diplomatic counterweight to highly localized affiliations—promoting alliances and political peace among neighboring communities. Especially the more celebrated images of neighboring communities are invited to the feast day celebrations of other communities and received with a great show of respect. The host community is expected to reciprocate by sending its own miracle-working images to the neighbors' celebrations.[84]

The Mapethé shrine acquired a place in the wider webs of dispersed Otomí settlement, migration, and portable devotion during the eighteenth century. The spiritual territory of this shrine reached west from its home districts of Ixmiquilpan, Zimapán, Alfajayuca, and Tepejí in a distinctive pattern: the main sites of alms collection during the 1740s were located along a route south and west from Ixmiquilpan into the Bajío—through southern Querétaro, then north to the mines of Guanajuato, where some groups of Otomí people had lived for many generations and others had recently settled as mineworkers and ranchhands.[85] What did this larger area of donations mean for a history of affiliation that centered on the Mapethé shrine? There is little to go on. The alms records do not establish whether the contributors had ever visited the shrine or would do so in the future, but the court records that document the processions at Mapethé in the late eighteenth century mention no participants from outside the primary catchment area. Unless the traveling collectors were gifted salesmen, able to persuade strangers to the story of the Cristo Renovado that they should support a new source of divine protection, we should assume that Otomí contacts through the area had already established a reservoir of interest.[86]

Conclusion

Thinking about these developments at Mapethé and Mexico City in terms of how power worked and how people's actions reiterate and change their situations brought to mind a generation of South Asian writings on colonialism that have intrigued me since reading Ashis Nandy's *The Intimate Enemy: Loss and Recovery of Self Under Colonialism* twenty years ago.[87] Students of Latin American history lately have been drawn especially to the work of the South Asian Subaltern Studies Collective for its attention to human intentionality, the politics of concerted resistance to elites by peasants and other marginalized people, and a healthy skepticism about Western modernity and its forms of knowledge.[88] I have found the writings of this group good to think with as they have unfolded since the early 1980s, but the guiding concepts in them have not provided a model for understanding the complexities of Spanish American colonialism, at least not in Mexico. While Ranajit Guha does not claim to speak for the group, and some of his colleagues no longer share his exclusive enthusiasm for the political or categories of dominance and subordination, domination and collaboration, domination and resistance, and other sharp distinctions, his emphasis on violent resistance, the fragmentary, and "the contribution made by the people *on their own* [sic], that is independently of the elite" remain fundamental to the approach: the people united as freestanding agents versus the elite.[89] And the Subaltern Studies scholarship has been inclined to leave aside the religious faith—beliefs and practices—of peasant actors either as false consciousness or beside the point of their politics.[90]

Devotion and politics at Mapethé in the eighteenth century do bring to mind disruptive "fragments" of subaltern activity—unquiet episodes of faith and affiliation that reworked Father Velasco's official story of a sacred treasure rescued from danger and neglect at the periphery followed by steady growth in popularity and marvelous benefits for devotees under the watchful eyes of the proper authorities in its new, central location. But these episodes of struggle, separation, and growing faith were not so clearly a rejection of the colonizers' logic and authority as a Subaltern Studies perspective might imagine, with its two-fold emphasis on resistance and collaboration.

Nandy, a noted political psychologist and public intellectual, has attracted less attention from historians—no doubt his sharp criticism of historians' truth claims has something to do with this[91]—but he has a way of thinking about colonial experience that comes closer to the overlapping lines and connections in the episodes at Mapethé. Or so it seems to a Latin Americanist in search of a more synoptic approach to "Indians" under colonial rule in Mesoamerica (the area of densely settled, precolonial state societies in modern central and southern Mexico and Central American highlands). By "synoptic approach" I mean keeping in mind and under study as many of the actors, dimensions, and primary sources of an episode or structure as I can manage, without claiming that there will be a sum total, a Braudelian *histoire totale*, or very definite conclusions. I still find great merit in the aim of early *Annales* historians—going back to Marc Bloch and Lucien Febvre—to combine material, documentary, and theoretical approaches to the past.[92] By reckoning with many contexts, relationships, and sources one can hope to recognize which were salient in a particular situation, but context does not have to mean wholeness.[93]

Nandy writes of counterplayers, nonplayers, and players.[94] These are gross, heuristic categories—no individual or group is simply one of them, once and for all. Players in one situation may be nonplayers or counterplayers in another. Players are not always compliant collaborators, and being a nonplayer does not just mean deflecting colonial domination. In particular circumstances, players may be as rebellious as counterplayers or as remote from particular colonial demands and truth claims as nonplayers. Yet even while blurring at the edges, these categories point toward patterned tendencies in different colonial histories that reach beyond the resistance and collaboration pairing of Subaltern Studies.[95] Counterplayers—the focus of much attention by Subaltern Studies scholars—reject the logic and authority of the colonizers and confront them openly, violently. Nandy regards colonial India's counterplayers as heroic losers, comparatively few in number and soon eliminated.[96] Nonplayers—who are Nandy's favorite subjects—do not adopt the colonizers' logic, either, but they succeed, as Michel de Certeau put it, in "subvert[ing] from within the colonizers' 'success' in imposing their own culture."⁹⁷ They use the colonizers' laws and truth claims instrumentally, resist them nonviolently, or succeed in bypassing them rather than making a frontal assault. Mohandas Gandhi is only the most famous of the nonplayers who made a place for themselves at the margins of colonial thought in ways that allowed them to "resist the loving embrace of the West's dominant self," as Nandy puts it, and in the long run to succeed in outlasting, if not colonizing, the colonizers.⁹⁸ Nandy's nonplayers range beyond his particular interest in intellectuals and political leaders to, among others, Indian cricket players and their audiences who reinvented a sport in ways that became only incidentally British.⁹⁹ In this sense—and in contrast to counterplaying—becoming westernized is a way of being Indian. Finally, players learn the logic of the colonial regime and its institutions and live within this logic, language, and authority more than nonplayers and counterplayers do. Like nonplayers, they are survivors, but they live *by* colonial rules and values as much as *with* them, sometimes turning them to advantage for local, often personal, interests.

Pierre Bourdieu's discussion of "heretical discourse" sets out the counterplayer position more specifically: exploiting "the possibility of changing the social world . . . by counterpoising a paradoxical pre-vision, a utopia, a project or programme, to the ordinary vision [here, colonial vision] which apprehends the social world as a natural world."¹⁰⁰ Colonial authorities of New Spain feared a contagion of heretical discourse and Indian uprisings in places near the edges of settled colonial life like western Hidalgo (occasionally for good reason), but if Velasco's book and promotion of the shrine in Mexico City represent the "ordinary vision," the founding of Mapethé's shrine and the activities of its devotees show little opposing "pre-vision." The counterplaying possibilities in Mapethé as a telluric site that recharged visiting crosses with sacred, protective energy remained latent except in intermittent calls for return of the miraculous image from Mexico City. Devotees of the Cristo Renovado in western Hidalgo did not publicly proclaim a break with the ordinary order or set themselves on a collision course with the colonial church. In their way, they remained loyal, accountable Catholics, fulfilling prescribed Christian duties and respecting the authority of priests.¹⁰¹ Otomíes as counterplayers fought in 1811 near Ixmiquilpan, El Cardonal, and Alfajayuca behind insurgent leader Julián Villagrán during the early years of Mexico's war of independence, and did not come to terms with royalist authorities until 1814 or 1815. Who they were and where they came from is not certain, but judging by their negotiations with the royalists, their pre-vision was local—the right to bear arms and govern their own communities—and some proceeded to fight against insurgents in 1816.[102]

Michel de Certeau had something like Nandy's nonplayers in mind when he referred to Mesoamerican Indians under Spanish colonial rule in his study of the practice of everyday life:

> Submissive, and even consenting to their subjection, the Indians nevertheless often *made of* the situations, representations, and laws imposed on them something quite different from what their conquerors had in mind; they subverted them not by rejecting or altering them, but by using them with respect to ends and references foreign to the system they had no choice but to accept. They were *other* within the very colonization that outwardly assimilated them; their use of the dominant social order deflected its power, which they lacked the means to challenge; they escaped it without leaving it [emphasis in original].[103]

Mapethé's shrine to the miracle of the absent, self-restoring crucifix and the annual convention of crosses brought by pilgrims from much of western Hidalgo who did not make pilgrimages to the image in Mexico City does express "something in daily life that is marginal to the discourse of the dominant rationality," as de Certeau and Jesús Martín Barbero would understand it.[104] Mapethé was not conceived or accepted by its founders or later devotees as a satellite of the shrine in Mexico City; nor did they accept Velasco's furta sacra story that the sacred energy contained in the miracle resided only in the image, any more than Indians laboring in the mines of Zimapán heeded the objections of their employers or the injunction by the district governor not to abandon their work when it was time to visit Mapethé.[105] The visitors from Zimapán apparently thought of their trip to Mapethé during Lent not as a pilgrimage to a fixed destination, but as participation in what they called "the procession of crucifixes,"[106] sanctifying movement in which they entered a landscape of their own making, a little heaven on earth in the vicinity of the shrine.

But there is also more to this story than local or Otomí solidarity. Otomí devotees of the Cristo Renovado miracle were nonplayers and perhaps sometimes counterplayers, but they were always players, too. The nonplayer features and counterplayer possibilities were continually crosscut by personal, factional, and intercommunity rivalries pursued for more than seventy years in every colonial court available, the higher the better. Asking how the devotees of Mapethé could be both players and nonplayers is a way to recognize that "embracing the fragment," as Subaltern Studies scholars have recommended, may mean reaching beyond the idea of freestanding, autonomous subjects in colonial histories to how and why they acted as *colonial* subjects.[107] The case for keeping subaltern "fragments" and the imagination of the state in view at the same time is even more compelling for Mesoamerican Indians than for South Asia. While they were still the numerical majority at the end of the eighteenth century, the four million or so Mesoamerican Indians were far fewer in number and occupied a smaller territory than rural South Asians, and they had a more extensive, arguably deeper, experience of European colonial institutions and culture, however intermittent and attenuated it may have been.

Sherry Ortner expressed the challenge of writing more synoptic histories with multiple agencies under colonialism as "a problematic of the dynamics of power ... : processes of legitimation, 'residence' and resistance, contestation, accommodation; relations between elites and commoners, bosses and workers, ... colonial authorities and colonial subjects."[108] On the Otomí side, devotees of the Cristo Renovado understood themselves in various terms—as members or allies of competing extended families, as men and women with gendered duties and loyalties, as residents of a dispersed settlement within a township, as fellow devotees, and as Catholics and subjects of the Spanish king under the sign of the cross. Most also knew themselves to be Otomíes, an identity that may well have become stronger in a colonial setting that marginalized their communities economically yet established routes of migration that put them in touch with far-flung relatives and Otomí speakers. And they knew themselves as "Indians" when they fulfilled Indian duties and made use of Indian prerogatives in their repeated dealings with state authorities, miners, priests, and ranchers. But recognizing themselves as Otomíes and Indians under colonial law did not translate into a strong sense of common cause with Indian strangers except for a time in the early years of Mexico's independence struggle. Even then, the distinctive subaltern logic they defended was local and evidently not attached to the miraculous cristo renovado. The eighteenth-century devotees of Mapethé did not propose to replace the colonial regime or withdraw from its authority and patronage. On the contrary, their struggles from within the Spanish colonial state expressed both their local affiliations and categories of corporate (more than individual) enfranchisement fostered by colonial laws and institutions. Their resistance to outside authority was likely to be directed at a rival faction or leader in or near the local community, at employers, landlords, or, less often, at the parish priest, district governor, and Spanish colonialism. The more popular the shrine of Mapethé became and the more its leaders prospered, the more they were checked by district authorities of the crown and the local interests and suspicions of their neighbors.

My thanks to the University of Chicago Press for permission to revise and republish this essay, originally published in *The American Historical Review* 110:4 (October 2005), 945–74 (© 2005).

PART II

Our Lady of Guadalupe
Toward a History of Devotion

Mexico's Virgin of Guadalupe in the Seventeenth Century
Hagiography and Beyond

> I find the history [of the image and miracles of Our Lady of los Remedios] most difficult, not at all like a well full of stones that I could remove little by little. Rather, I find myself again and again on land that is filled with crags and barrens. It is a difficult thing to finally reach the water of truth there.
> —Luis de Cisneros, *Historia de El Principio*[1]

CATHOLIC HAGIOGRAPHY AS SACRED BIOGRAPHY REACHES BEYOND the lives of saints and other holy people to include the "lives" of images, relics, and places of a saint or Christ renowned as sites of divine presence and favor. This branch of hagiography for miraculous images, signs, and apparitions was especially important in colonial Spanish America. The New World of the sixteenth, seventeenth, and eighteenth centuries had very few saints of its own and was comparatively poor in certified relics of Old World saints. Not surprisingly, many of the most popular hagiographical and devotional texts that began to appear in New Spain in the 1620s concerned miraculous images and apparitions, especially of the Virgin Mary or Christ. Of the various images and shrines celebrated and promoted in printed hagiographies, sermons, and novena booklets, Our Lady of Guadalupe at Tepeyac eventually came to occupy a preeminent place in the devotional history and literature of Mexico. As Jeannette Rodríguez writes, "To be of Mexican descent is to recognize the image of Our Lady of Guadalupe."[2]

But were the early hagiographers of miraculous images, especially of Our Lady of Guadalupe, largely inventing a tradition in their texts, or were they mainly faithful scribes recording the tradition? Did they make memory or mainly capture and codify it? This is no small matter to historians of the Mexican Guadalupe because the first published hagiographies appeared more than a century after the events they purport to recount, and no manuscript versions of the tradition that definitely predate the published texts seem to have survived. If the published hagiographies of the mid-seventeenth century basically invented the tradition of Marian apparitions to a humble Indian at Tepeyac in 1531—as a main current of recent scholarship suggests—then the spotlight falls on the learned clerical inventors and their precocious seventeenth-century protonationalism. If the hagiographers were trying to catch up with and promote an already deep popular devotion, attention shifts to an older and more anonymous current of piety, perhaps all the way back to the 1530s.

In earlier work, I tracked part of a history of devotion to Our Lady of Guadalupe during the eighteenth century with help from serial evidence of several kinds—baptismal records, published periodicals and journals, sermons, and some key figures and events, especially during the years 1731–1754.[3] I have come to regard those years as central to the broad appeal of guadalupanismo later on. The sixteenth and seventeenth centuries remain more elusive, particularly the sixteenth century with its long silences and few, glancing references that have been made to carry so much weight in later efforts to validate or dismiss an official story.[4]

Clearly, important changes occurred at the shrine of Our Lady of Guadalupe during the seventeenth century. A 1608 inspection of the municipal lands of Mexico City located a northern boundary at the "hermita [chapel, hermitage] de Nuestra Señora de Guadalupe" and planted the boundary marker on top of Tepeyac hill. No important settlement was described, only a "tiny pueblo" (*pueblecillo*) called Sancta Ysabel was said to be nearby, "*antes de la subida del cerro de Tepeaquilla.*" In a similar inspection of 1690–1691 that marked the municipal boundary on top of Tepeyac again, a more significant shrine and settlement had taken shape: "el santuario y hermita de Nuestra Señora de Guadalupe de el pueblo de Peaquilla."[5]

The story of Our Lady of Guadalupe first comes into bold relief in the mid-seventeenth century, in a cluster of studied little books by priest-devotees printed between 1648 and 1688: Miguel Sánchez's *Imagen de la Virgen María de Dios de Guadalupe* (1648); Luis Lasso de la Vega's *Huei tlamahuiçoltica* (1649); Luis Becerra Tanco's, *Felicidad de México* (1675); and Francisco de Florencia's *La estrella del norte de México* (1688).[6] Not much is known about the history of the tradition during the seventeenth century beyond what scholars and devotees have inferred from these texts, several paintings and prints, building activity early and late in the century, and a set of testimonies about the tradition recorded in 1666. Hagiography effectively has passed as the seventeenth-century history of guadalupanismo, whether it is taken to validate a sixteenth-century story of early devotion or to express values and intentions of seventeenth-century authors.[7]

I mean "studied little books" in the double sense of self-conscious narratives that aspire to official standing and texts that are repeatedly combed and cited by students of guadalupanismo seeking or debunking a kind of biblical certainty about beginnings. With this double meaning of "studied" in mind, Francisco de la Maza playfully but astutely called the authors of these seventeenth-century hagiographies the "four evangelists," as if they succeeded in composing texts that were similar in aim and reception to the Gospels of the New Testament. They, along with Mateo de la Cruz's extract of Sánchez's book, were the first printed texts to tell the story of apparitions of the Virgin Mary at Tepeyac in 1531 as it has been retold countless times since:

> On Saturday, December 9, Juan Diego, an Indian from Cuauhtitlán was on his way to attend Mass at the Franciscan convent of Tlatelolco. Passing the hill of Tepeyac he heard celestial music and climbed up to encounter a resplendent Lady who instructed him to tell the bishop in Mexico City that she wished a church to be built there. The bishop received Juan Diego cordially, but did not promise to build the church. Juan Diego returned disconsolate to Tepeyac with this news, but the Lady instructed him to visit the bishop again with the same request. He did so on Sunday with a similar result—the bishop required a sign that Juan Diego was not speaking only for himself. When he returned to Tepeyac, the Lady appeared a third time, instructing him to go to his village saying she would provide a sign. Back in Cuauhtitlán he spent Monday looking after his uncle, Juan Bernardino, who had fallen gravely ill.

Early Tuesday morning, December 12, Juan Diego hurried toward Tlatelolco in search of a confessor for his uncle. He skirted the hill of Tepeyac to the east, but the Lady came down to him, calling him. Wanting to be on his way, he explained his urgent mission. The Lady responded that his uncle had already recovered from his illness and that Juan Diego should climb the hill and gather summer roses on this near-winter day as a sign to the bishop. Where the Lady appeared to him this fourth time a small spring of healing fresh water emerged. When Juan Diego spread the roses before the bishop, the image of the Lady—the Virgin Mary—was revealed on his cloak. The astonished bishop moved quickly to erect a church at Tepeyac and placed the image there shortly before his departure for Spain. Juan Diego and his uncle thenceforth devoted their lives to serving the Virgin Mary and practiced a vow of chastity. He received one last visit from Mary in 1548, informing him of his impending death, which would precede the bishop's by a short time. Thanks to the intercession of Our Lady, both the bishop and Juan Diego would receive their reward in Heaven.[8]

Each of the four "evangelists" approached the subject somewhat differently. Miguel Sánchez wrote for the learned, especially for fellow priests in Mexico City, as Florencia noticed when he wrote that Sánchez's book was "para hombres doctos."[9] Sánchez sprinkled his account of the apparitions and history of the image with providential biblical analogies and Latin phrases and gave special attention to Mary's protection of the capital city. Mateo de la Cruz's extract of *Imagen de la Virgen María*, published first in Puebla in 1660, was intended to bring the story to a wider audience.[10] Lasso de la Vega's Nahuatl text does not have the learned references or many of the providential asides and downplays the Mexico City connection. It lovingly elaborates on the apparition stories in ways that associate them with Indian believers.[11] His text, in contrast to Sánchez's, was evidently directed more toward priests in pastoral service among Nahuatl-speakers of central Mexico and perhaps a Nahua lay elite. Becerra Tanco gave more attention to the floods of 1629–1634 as a sign and a benchmark of devotion, while Florencia offered a longer, survey treatment for a general audience, citing Sánchez and Becerra Tanco as his first sources for the tradition and omitting the learned references. Florencia added some history of the culto[12] up to his own time, enlarged the standard list of miracles, and gave special emphasis to the incorruptibility of the image itself. His *La estrella del norte de México* amounts to a more elaborate, historical, and accessible version of Sánchez's text.

Despite their differences, the four "evangelists" feature the apparition stories at Tepeyac and the culminating miracle of the image on December 12 in similar accounts. All four give special attention to Juan Diego and his uncle in the apparitions, a core set of miracles that favored both Spaniards and Indians, and Spaniards of Mexico City, as the great benefactors of the shrine. All were written by American-born Spanish priests who expressed pride in "Mexico" (the vicinity of Mexico City) and America as places especially favored by the Virgin Mary. Sánchez, for example, referred to this image as *nuestra soberana criolla*, "our sovereign American Lady."[13]

The fact that no securely dated text for the Guadalupan tradition precedes those of the four "evangelists" from 1648–1688[14] has led most recent scholars to a creole nationalist interpretation of the tradition. This interpretation holds that the four seventeenth-century hagiographies amount to the invention of the tradition as an expression of "creole consciousness"—expressing their love of their American homeland and pressing for the religious autonomy of their American *reino* (kingdom).[15] In this interpretation, the story of apparitions and miraculous origin of the image amounts to a creole Spanish appropriation of a secondary, nearly moribund shrine in the mid-seventeenth century. Indian devotees are left out of the picture except as objects of a new evangelization, and the culto is assumed to have blossomed into a widespread, protonational devotion shortly after the publication of Sánchez's book. Sánchez and Lasso de la Vega, of course, firmly rejected such an interpretation, claiming that they were, as Lasso de la Vega put it, no more than "sleeping Adams" who had awakened to faithfully record a well-established tradition.

The seventeenth-century hagiographies give us the apparition stories, two Indian men of the Valley of Mexico as central to the tradition, and the makings of a December 12 feast day. But were their authors leading or mainly following an upward curve of devotion? And was it a single, steep curve? Did they essentially invent the tradition or were they, as they claimed, simply publishing what was already widely known to the faithful? When was the tradition of apparitions known, celebrated, promoted, and widely accepted? Was there much Indian devotion to Our Lady of Guadalupe in the seventeenth century? Did the hagiographers want what other devotees wanted? We are left to wonder. The four "evangelists" themselves do not provide many answers.

Beyond Hagiography

Other seventeenth-century sources of recorded memory about Our Lady of Guadalupe and the history of veneration of the image are more prosaic and dispersed than these four hagiographies. No books of miracles or donations have come to light for this shrine—no long lists of donors or reported marvels recorded sequentially over many years, as one sometimes finds in Europe[16]; and no long series of ex-voto paintings for the seventeenth and eighteenth centuries like the eye-catching collections for the late nineteenth and twentieth centuries. There is no long run of gacetas (periodicals) for the seventeenth century, as there is for much of the eighteenth century, but we do have Gregorio Guijo's and Antonio de Robles's *efemérides* (unofficial journals of public events from a Mexico City perspective) for the second half of the century,[17] and the minutes of the colonial *ayuntamiento* of Mexico City and the *cabildo eclesiástico* of the cathedral. Tepeyac appears in the sixteenth-century and early seventeenth-century minutes of the ayuntamiento mainly as a principal point of entry into Mexico City, with a heavily traveled road to be maintained. By 1586 Tepeyac was established as the resting place for new viceroys on their way from Veracruz to Mexico City. The viceroy lingered there for a day or two while the city government prepared his grand procession to the viceregal palace and offices on the main square. The shrine itself and the image of Our Lady of Guadalupe are not mentioned in the early references to these processions, but by the 1620s *casas de novenarios* (lodgings for visitors who came for a nine-day round of devotions) there doubled as the viceroy's quarters, as needed, although they were reported to be in poor condition in 1624 and the site of the viceroy's rest and grand entrance was moved to Chapultepec.[18] The shrine and image of Mary at Tepeyac are rarely mentioned in the ayuntamiento minutes before 1648, even during the period of the great flood from 1629–1634,[19] which some scholars and witnesses in the 1666 inquiry into the Guadalupan tradition have regarded as a pivotal date. Entries in the Guijo and Robles efemérides for 1648–1703 also have remarkably little to say about veneration of the image of Guadalupe. But, like the ayuntamiento minutes, they frequently mention another famous image and shrine in the Valley of Mexico, that of Our Lady of los Remedios.

The financial records prepared for official inspections (visitas) of the shrine at Tepeyac by delegates of the archbishop offer some additional information about seventeenth-century guadalupanismo that can be set alongside the four famous seventeenth-century texts. They amount to more than two thousand manuscript pages, including summary accounts and descriptions, and many individual receipts for expenditures and income, dating from 1634, 1648–1651, 1653, 1664–1669, and 1693–1698.[20] It would be wonderful to have a continuous run of such records for the seventeenth century and beyond, but these four clusters come at convenient, even predictable intervals. Not surprisingly, they appear at pivotal points in the history of promotion and regulation of guadalupanismo by the cathedral and chaplains of the shrine, if not necessarily pivotal points in popular devotion.[21]

Mainly, there have been two views about the history of guadalupanismo up to 1648. One, expressed first by Miguel Sánchez himself, sees a progressive series of steps culminating in a fully elaborated, widespread guadalupanismo in the 1650s. Jacques Lafaye pursued this idea in his book, *Quetzalcóatl and Guadalupe*,[22] underscoring 1629—the year the great flood began in the Valley of Mexico—as a step near the top of this stairway. Serge Gruzinski has disagreed in a way that led him to place even more emphasis than do most creole nationalism interpreters on 1648 and the publication of Sánchez's text as the turning point of guadalupanismo. His intriguing hypothesis is that Sánchez and Lasso de la Vega were trying to rescue a devotion that had fallen on hard times and was about to disappear.[23] In place of Sánchez's and Lafaye's ascending stairway, Gruzinski would give us a sinking ship, not much more than a row boat. David Brading also takes the publication of Sánchez's book to signal "the sudden efflorescence" of the tradition and popular devotion.[24] Stafford Poole's recent *Our Lady of Guadalupe: The Origins and Sources of a Mexican National Symbol, 1531–1797*, joins others in highlighting 1648, but he thinks that a culto had hardly developed by that time, especially among Indians, so there was little to revive. For Poole, the content of the tradition we associate with the Mexican Guadalupe was more or less invented by Sánchez and Lasso de la Vega.[25]

The half-century or so after the first two "evangelists" published in 1648 and 1649 has been associated mainly with the efforts of Miguel Sánchez, Luis Becerra Tanco, and the Mexico City cathedral chapter to promote the culto and the shrine at Tepeyac. Those efforts culminated in appeals to Rome for recognition of the tradition, an official investigation for this purpose in 1666, Becerra Tanco's text, *Felicidad de México* (revised for publication in 1675 from his 1666 report), the various writings of the Jesuit Marian devotee Francisco de Florencia in the 1680s and 1690s—"the great orchestrator," as Gruzinski aptly calls him—the first cluster of published sermons, churches dedicated to the Virgin of Guadalupe in Querétaro, San Luis Potosí, and Mexico City, and the construction of a grand, new shrine to house the precious image, largely underwritten by Mexico City patrons.

In speaking of a history of guadalupanismo in the half centuries or so before and after Sánchez's and Lasso's books were published, I want to touch on two historical issues in particular about which there has not been much agreement or really much known. First is the tradition of apparitions occurring in 1531. Miguel Sánchez was the first to publish on this subject, but when was the tradition known and by whom? When was it widely accepted? How was it expressed, and promoted? What, then, is the place of the 1648–1649 publications and the 1666 investigations in establishing and shaping the apparition story and the culto? Second is the question of Indian devotion to Our Lady of Guadalupe in the seventeenth century. Here the literature is divided more than silent or muffled. Poole infers that there was little Indian devotion to speak of before Sánchez and Lasso de la Vega published. Octavio Paz, Francisco de la Maza, and Lafaye, among others, think it was mainly a popular, Indian devotion until learned creoles began to catch up in the mid-seventeenth century, but offer little support for their conclusion. Those who have ventured into these two issues have been inclined to slight the special importance of Mexico City to the early history of devotion to Our Lady of Guadalupe.[26]

The decades before 1648 were a formative period for the development of regional miracle shrines in many parts of New Spain, including Izamal (Yucatán), Ocotlán (Tlaxcala), San Miguel del Milagro (Tlaxcala), Chalma (Estado de México), Tecaxic (Valley of Toluca, Estado de México), Cosamaloapa (Veracruz), Zapopan (Jalisco), San Juan de los Lagos (Jalisco), and los Remedios (Valley of Mexico), among others. The early years of the seventeenth century may well have been a formative time for Tepeyac and the Guadalupe story, too, but with a concentration of interest in Mexico City and among Indians in and near the Valley of Mexico, without yet becoming the widespread devotion and shared understanding that can be traced in considerable detail from the 1730s.[27]

Was the shrine of Guadalupe at Tepeyac on the verge of collapse at the time Miguel Sánchez's hagiography was published? The financial records of 1634 and 1648–1653 suggest not, but neither do they support the teleological enthusiasm of Sánchez and nine other distinguished priests who spoke in 1666 of unbroken and widespread devotion since 1531. The 1634 financial records note that before the floods began in 1629 people, including many priests, frequented the shrine at Tepeyac on Sundays, and that alms of about five silver pesos were collected on an average Sunday. During the flood years, from 1629–1634, when the image was removed from the shrine and taken to the cathedral in Mexico City, the Sunday collections dropped to less than half a peso. No wonder the shrine was said in 1633 to be "very poor."[28] Yet a new church had been completed in 1622 and the thoroughfare from Tepeyac to the city was enlarged under the sponsorship of Archbishop Juan Pérez de la Serna between 1613 and 1622[29]; at least one substantial bequest was received from a Spanish resident of the city[30]; the 1634 financial records note that casas de novenarios were under construction at the shrine before the floods, and, by 1637, the shrine would gain a sumptuous new altarpiece donated by Doña Magdalena Pérez de Viveros of Mexico City that Sánchez, reaching for a suitably fulsome appreciation, called "precious, rich, splendid, magnificent, singular, rare, excellent, exquisite."[31] Unless the casas de novenarios were just a retreat house for devotees from the nearby capital or mainly maintained in anticipation of the arrival of a future viceroy, these lodgings suggest that visitors to the shrine were coming, or were encouraged to come, from more distant places.[32] This set of 1634 accounts also notes that during the flood years only "*indios de la sierra*" came to the shrine, and that the pastor there preached "*en las dos lenguas*" (Spanish and Nahuatl). So, some Indian devotion beyond the city and valley is apparent in 1634, but just where Indian devotees were from and how many travelled to Tepeyac and when is not clear. The meager alms collections suggest small numbers, especially during the flood years.

The real estate belonging to the shrine in 1634 was limited to its compound. No properties in Mexico City were listed, no precious objects of silver and gold were acquired that year, and no collections by demanda were reported (that is, no one was licensed by the archbishop and viceroy to go out on alms-gathering missions).[33] The property of the shrine amounted to the building and grounds, some religious art and furnishings, and seven thousand pesos in capital.

The 1634 accounts refer to important Semana Santa celebrations and a "fiesta de la cassa" that year, but they do not say when the fiesta took place. Was it December 12? The absence of a date here raises the question of when December 12 became the important feast day for the shrine. That would be

Fig. 3.1 Annual Income Tabulated from the Visita Records, 1634–1698

	1634	1648–1650	1651–1653	1664	1693–1698
Income-producing property	None listed	1,239p (11 houses, 15 censos)	1,312p (10 houses, 1 hacienda)	Information missing	1937p (10 houses, 6 tiendas, 11 censos)
Alms at the shrine	34p[a]	303p6rr[b]	475p6rr[b]	Information missing	581p6rr
Demandas	—	Ca. 1,400p	Ca. 1,050p	Information missing	Less than 240p
Other income	867p[c]	1,406p (4,218p7rr total)[d]	1,200p[e]	Information missing	223p4rr[d]
Total	**901p**	**4,351p6rr**	**3,237p6rr**	**—**	**2,982p2rr**

Note: p = peso; rr = reales.
[a] 220–260p/year in the years immediately before the floods of 1629–1634.
[b] Includes the alms box at the shrine and collections during the fiestas principales.
[c] Gifts of cash and kind.
[d] Includes wills, cash, sales of wax and oil.
[e] Money owed by Lic. Muñoz.

solid evidence of when the apparition story as Sánchez, Lasso de la Vega, Becerra Tanco, and Florencia told it was widely known and celebrated. The fact that the image was moved to Mexico City during the floods of 1629–1634 suggests that the tradition of its supernatural origin was not yet firmly in place. The image was not yet too precious to move. The absence of a centennial celebration in 1631, or any mention of December 12 or the Virgin of Guadalupe among the December religious events in Mexico City's actas de cabildo before 1648, also suggest that the apparition story as we know it had not yet become established, at least not officially.[34]

In 1634 substantial sums were spent at the shrine. In fact, the 1634 expenditures were exceeded only by 1648–1650 in these seventeenth-century financial records. The outlays that year were mainly for construction of casas de novenarios and repairs of damage caused by the floods.

The next set of accounts and receipts, from 1648–1653, indicate that this was the period of highest annual income for the shrine during the seventeenth century, as well as a time of substantial expenditures on precious furnishings. With the peak of income and expenditures coming at midcentury, there was no continuous increase in income and property throughout

Fig. 3.2 Annual Expenditures Tabulated from the Visita Records, 1634–1698

	1634	1648–1650	1651–1653	1664–1669	1693–1698
Salaries	400p[a]	679p6rr[b]	600p[c]	600p[c]	781p[d]
Upkeep & improvements	3,265p	964p2rr	Information missing	500p (3,002p2rr total)	513p6rr[e]
Upkeep on rentals	—	—	577p (1,729p5rr total)	185p1r	Information missing
Ornamentos & vestments	—	2,862p (8,587p total)	1,145p (3,435p total)	942p (5,651p total)	485p (2,912p total)
Liturgical costs	250p (semana santa)	Ca. 196p (semana santa)	—	—	—
Legal fees	—	52p2rr[f]	114r5rr	—	Ca. 45p
Other	—	80p[g]	137p	51p[h]	—
Total	3,915p	4,834p	2,583p5rr	2,278p1r	1,825p

Note: p = peso; rr = reales.
[a] For vicario and sacristán.
[b] For vicario, mayordomo, sacristán, and procurador.
[c] For vicario, mayordomo, and sacristán.
[d] For vicario, mayordomo, sacristán, and ayudante de sacristán.
[e] Incomplete. Only "gasto de esclavo" listed.
[f] Plus 438p legal fees concerning an *obra pía* (pious work) attached to the shrine.
[g] Accountant's fee.
[h] Includes 216p paid for printing a novena booklet.

the century, either from 1629 or 1648 onward, as one might expect, and apparently no great crescendo of popular devotion beyond Mexico City in the second half of the seventeenth century that a reading of the evangelists would anticipate.

The growing expenditures evident in the 1648–1653 accounts largely followed publication of Sánchez's book, but the growth in income preceded his book, which suggests that 1634–1648 was an active and successful period for the promotion of the culto, and a time of growing popular devotion in Mexico City after the return of the image from the cathedral to the shrine as the flood waters receded in 1633–1634. By 1648 the shrine already had acquired most of the income-producing real estate it possessed during the seventeenth century. All of those properties were in Mexico City and most of them were situated in the neighborhood of the Plaza de Santo Domingo.

There was an increase in capital from wills and cash gifts around 1648; and in the years immediately following 1648, five demandantes collected for the shrine in various parts of the Archdiocese of Mexico. So, 1648–1653 stands out in the seventeenth-century financial records as a very active period of spending and getting (see Figs. 3.1 and 3.2), but it did not all follow publication of Sánchez's book, as one line of interpretation would imagine. The activity in 1653 was more the extension of a trend of promotion, devotion, and accumulation than a departure from the immediate past.[35]

The floods of 1629–1634 were important to the history of guadalupanismo from 1634 to 1648, but not quite in the linear way that Lafaye and Sánchez imagined. (Lafaye was thinking of Guadalupe's sudden fame in protecting against floods, literally and figuratively, which clerical witnesses mentioned in the 1666 investigation.) Those years between 1629 and 1634 were, I think, a time of crisis for the shrine, if not for the reputation of the image in Mexico City. The new church of 1622, the casas de novenarios project, and the income of the shrine all suffered during the flood years. Alms collections at the shrine, and other donations, shriveled once the image was taken to Mexico City and the physical plant deteriorated ("The buildings were crumbling," reports the 1634 account record[36]). Then in 1634 there were substantial expenditures from the existing capital of seven thousand pesos, and the 1648 records indicate mounting donations for the shrine by Mexico City patrons in the preceding years, before Sánchez's book was published. Sánchez's emphasis on the apparitions and the supernatural origin of the image served as a powerful reason for keeping the image where it was and thereby securing the income of the shrine. This permanent residence of the image at Tepeyac after 1634 protected the shrine of Guadalupe from the erratic income cycles of the shrine of los Remedios, which were a result of that image's extended absences in Mexico City.

The financial records after 1649 shed some additional light on the history of the apparition tradition and popular devotion. Those from the 1660s and 1690s, in particular, yield a somewhat different story than the extraordinary devotion suggested by the 1666 testimonies and the writings of the third and fourth evangelists, Luis Becerra Tanco and Francisco de Florencia. The 1660s records unfortunately do not include income, but they register substantial payments for improvements to the buildings and purchase of expensive silver and gold furnishings to dignify the culto. These expenditures were almost as much as those of 1634. By contrast, the income and expenditure figures for the early 1690s are surprisingly modest. The alms-collecting initiatives produced much less in the 1690s than they had at midcentury—less than 240 pesos a year, compared to about twelve hundred pesos a year from 1648–1653. The total income of the shrine in 1693 was about twenty-four hundred pesos compared to between thirty-two hundred and four thousand pesos annually from 1648 to 1653. And little new real estate had been acquired by the shrine between 1653 and 1693.

Although the financial records for the 1690s showed mediocre returns rather than the expected surge of income, property, and popular devotion, other developments since the 1660s anticipated the guadalupanismo of later times. The image had not been moved beyond its precinct; construction of a new and much grander church was planned by 1694; and December 12 had become a significant holiday at the shrine, although the popularity of this holiday seems to have come late in the century and was less important than would be expected from Florencia's emphasis on it in *La estrella del norte de México* (1688).[37] The 1660s may well be when December 12 was introduced into the calendar of feast days.[38] The Capilla del Cerrito, at the site where Juan Diego was believed to have gathered the roses in his cloak, was dedicated in 1667,[39] and the 1666 investigation was meant to win papal approval of the apparition story and a December 12 feast day. The pace of activity in Mexico City supporting the apparition story and the shrine quickened in the 1670s. Reconstruction of the thoroughfare from the shrine to the city, with fifteen imposing monuments to the mysteries of Mary, was begun in 1675 and completed in August 1676.[40] A few sermons about the apparitions began to appear in print; in 1676 Antonio de Robles's journal recorded for the first time a celebration of the apparitions, on the night of December 11; and the archbishop ordered in 1677 that the glass case protecting the image should no longer be opened for the faithful to kiss and touch the cloth.[41] Then in 1679 doña Teresa de Aguirre of Mexico City established an endowment for an annual December 12 fiesta at the Capilla del Cerrito.[42] In 1682, papal bulls were published that permitted Masses at the main altar of the shrine and granted indulgences to those who visited the shrine and prayed there.[43]

December 12 was an annual celebration by the 1690s, but the financial records of that time connect the celebration only to the Capilla del Cerrito and they indicate that this date had not yet displaced what was called the *fiesta principal del santuario*, which was celebrated during a two week period in November: one week for Spaniards and castas, and one week for Indians. While Robles had mentioned a celebration of the apparition in

1676, he did not mention it again as a significant event until 1703 when he wrote, "the fiesta of Nuestra Señora de Guadalupe" had been celebrated on December 12 "with great solemnity."[44]

Why was the seventeenth-century Guadalupan fiesta principal in November? The financial records do not say, but it could have been to honor Mary as Nuestra Señora del Patrocinio (Our Lady of Intercession), a generic devotion, much as the Virgin Mary in all her various representations was also called Queen of the Angels (la Reina de los Ángeles). The feast of this advocation of Mary as Nuestra Señora del Patrocinio falls on the second Sunday in November and it was observed in Mexico City (and elsewhere in New Spain) during the seventeenth century.[45] This fiesta principal in November for the shrine of Guadalupe is highlighted in the 1651–1652 financial accounts. In 1651 the November fiestas represented fully half of the income of the shrine that year. In 1693 they still produced nearly twice the annual sum collected in alms at the shrine. The 1693 financial accounts unfortunately do not separate out the income from the December 12 events at the Capilla del Cerrito, but the monthly receipts from the alms boxes at the shrine show only a slight increase in donations during December.

These account records raise doubts about whether the story of Marian apparitions to a humble Indian at Tepeyac in 1531 was as widely known and celebrated as the seventeenth-century hagiographies seem to suggest. But neither do the account files support an emphatic creole nationalism interpretation that regards the hagiographers as inventors of the tradition and leaves Indian devotees out of the picture or only vaguely present until the second half of the century. By themselves, these financial records help to problematize the history of devotion to Our Lady of Guadalupe in the seventeenth century, but they offer only tantalizing suggestions of a deeper history of devotion.

Several more familiar seventeenth-century sources may contribute something new to historical study of guadalupanismo if they are approached with the financial records in mind. The best known of these sources are the depositions by nineteen elderly men and one woman in 1666 (eight Indian elders from Cuauhtitlán, one descendant of Moctezuma from Mexico City, and eleven distinguished senior priests based in the capital, including Miguel Sánchez). They were recorded in support of the appeal by the councils of the archdiocese and the city of Mexico for papal recognition of the culto. Most of the witnesses said they recalled from their childhoods in the late sixteenth century stories of apparitions of the Virgin

Mary to Juan Diego, the miraculous origin of her image on his cloak in 1531, and Indian devotion at Tepeyac.[46] And in the published version of his lengthy report to the 1666 commission, Luis Becerra Tanco claimed that he had witnessed Indian dances of a kind performed before the 1629 flood in which Indian elders sang of Juan Diego, the apparitions of Mary, and the miraculous image.[47]

Taken on their own, the 1666 testimonies may be doubted as pious hearsay and hindsight—expressing the ardent devotion of witnesses who were caught up in a high tide of promotion of the culto by cathedral dignitaries and priests attached to the shrine, without direct, personal knowledge of the sixteenth-century events of which they spoke.[48] But the 1666 testimonies should not be so easily dismissed as evidence only of the 1660s, rather than an earlier time. Most of the witnesses were testifying to practices and beliefs and conversations that they might well have witnessed or experienced long before Sánchez's book was published in 1648, if not from the sixteenth century. After all, Chimalpahin, the early seventeenth-century Nahua chronicler and longtime resident of Mexico City, testified to a tradition of apparition when he wrote that Our Lady of Guadalupe had "revealed herself" on top of Tepeyac in 1556.[49] An artifact from the early seventeenth century that would seem to corroborate the 1666 witnesses' claims about an earlier belief in the miraculous origin of the image and Marian apparitions is the oldest signed and dated copy of the image, painted by Baltasar de Echave Orio in 1606. The painting depicts not only the image of the Mexican Virgin of Guadalupe, but also the cloth on which the image appears, as if the cloth were as much the object of veneration as the image.[50] Echave Orio, a peninsular Spaniard, was the most celebrated artist in Mexico City at the time, and this painting would have been an important commission.[51]

But who commissioned Echave Orio's painting? Where was it displayed? What did such a painting of the cloth and image of Mary signify to its patron and viewers? Miguel Sánchez offered a possible clue, albeit third hand, in his testimony for the 1666 inquiry. He testified to having heard Lic. Bartholomé García (who served as chaplain of the shrine at Tepeyac from 1624–1646) say that Alonso Muñoz, dean of the cathedral chapter in Mexico City, had seen Archbishop Fr. García de Mendoza (1601–1606) "reading with singular tenderness the legal records concerning the aforementioned apparition."[52] Was Archbishop García de Mendoza, in fact, the patron and owner of Echave Orio's 1606 painting of the image and cloth?

Did it hang in the archiepiscopal palace? If so, who beyond Juan Pérez de la Serna (archbishop from 1613 to 1625, responsible for completing the new church and thoroughfare and promoting donations with prints of an image of Guadalupe as miracle worker, known as the Stradanus engraving) shared García de Mendoza's enthusiasm for the image? Even if Sánchez's hearsay testimony can be trusted and the Echave Orio painting was commissioned by Archbishop García de Mendoza, who the devotees were and what they understood remains uncertain, even for high clergymen of the early seventeenth century. An undated note apparently written by or for García de Mendoza between 1603 and 1606, recalled a flood in the city the previous year but made no mention of appeals to Our Lady of Guadalupe for relief.[53] One sermon delivered at the Tepeyac shrine was published in 1622, but it did not concern Our Lady of Guadalupe directly. Only in the 1670s did sermons come to be published on Guadalupe and the apparitions theme. And the extant university theses abstracts from the colonial period that so often were dedicated to a patron saint or special advocation of Mary or Christ, do not register dedications to the Virgin of Guadalupe until the 1650s.[54]

Conclusion

The years during and immediately after the publication of Sánchez's and Lasso de la Vega's hagiographies of Our Lady of Guadalupe (1648–1653) were, indeed, a pivotal point in this history of faith, but there was not a sudden and definitive beginning then for the apparition tradition or Indian devotion, as creole nationalism hypotheses often suggest. Nor were the developments of 1648–1653 only the culmination of a swelling wave of popular devotion going back to 1531 as Sánchez claimed, though it is likely that Sánchez was building directly on developments in the 1620s and 1630s, and a still older tradition of miracles and apparition. Sánchez both built on a devotion in the making and actively promoted it in a way that eventually ensured the exceptional importance of the shrine at Tepeyac, the tradition of the apparitions to Juan Diego, and the December 12 feast. Sánchez, Lasso, and the other "evangelists" brought together two devotional streams—an "Indian" apparitionist stream that remains something of a mystery in its details and devotees, and a "Spanish" stream situated mainly in Mexico City that was, in part, an expression of creole protonationalism (although peninsular devotees were prominent throughout the seventeenth and eighteenth centuries, too). Ritually, the two streams remained separate in their annual fiestas and much else, but the story of apparitions, as Sánchez and Lasso wrote it, would come to be shared by all devotees.[55] Sánchez's book and those of the other "evangelists" were significant events in a story of devotion that had some momentum of its own and was actively promoted from the cathedral in Mexico City and priests at the shrine itself, both creoles and peninsulars. These printed texts were artifacts of an increasing devotion, but this momentum at midcentury did not quickly make December 12 and the apparition stories into the widespread culto we can trace from the 1730s.

The visita financial records and other sources that reach beyond the hagiographies into a more ample history of devotion do not reveal a wholly different seventeenth-century experience of guadalupanismo. However, they do suggest leads that place the famous texts of Sánchez, Lasso de la Vega, Mateo de la Cruz, Becerra Tanco, the 1666 testimonies, and Florencia into a process of devotion and promotion, rather than as the first or last words, standing in splendid isolation for a changeless past and present, or as largely irrelevant to that past except as manifestations of the aims and piety of their authors. Sánchez and Lasso de la Vega meant to order and publicize the tradition, and their books represent a kind of consolidation and elaboration—in retrospect, a codification—of an apparition story, but it was not yet the consolidation of a widespread tradition. An apparition tradition circulated from the late sixteenth century in some colonial Indian communities of central Mexico and among some leaders of the archdiocese in Mexico City. The Echave Orio painting, Chimalpahin's notation for 1556, and Sánchez's and Becerra Tanco's testimony in 1666 suggest as much. Just what that older tradition was (if, in fact, there was just one) is not clear. Judging by the silence about a December 12 feast day before the 1660s, and Chimalpahin's and the anonymous annals's reference to a Marian apparition at Tepeyac only in the 1550s, none of the traditions may have been as specific to apparitions during four days in December 1531 as the "evangelists" suggest.[56]

These glimpses of a history of devotion in the seventeenth-century financial records and other sources suggest that the familiar tradition and practice were not firmly in place even at the end of the seventeenth century. The books of the "evangelists" had not suddenly spread the word and awakened mass devotion. Florencia was still working on that project in his *La estrella del norte de México* of 1688. A transition toward the familiar tradition and practice comes into view in the 1690s financial records and the cluster of sermons published in Mexico City between 1695 and 1720, but it would take another concerted effort at promotion in the 1720s, the bicentennial in 1731, the great epidemic of 1737, Archbishop-Viceroy Vizarrón's active sponsorship, and the papal decree of 1754 to firmly establish the tradition and December 12 as the day of Our Lady of Guadalupe, and open a new era of popular devotion and promotion. The fiesta principal of Our Lady of Guadalupe in November is forgotten today, but it did not disappear even with the eighteenth-century surge of guadalupanismo and the by-then official story of the seventeenth-century hagiographers. Even in the mid-nineteenth century the popular calendars published by Galván Rivera listed the fourth Sunday of November as the "fiesta de los naturales en Guadalupe."[57]

In this essay I have attempted to go to and a little beyond the "evangelists" hagiographies for a history of recorded memory about, and devotion to, Our Lady of Guadalupe in the seventeenth century. That memory appears rather fluid in the seventeenth century, despite the "evangelists" best efforts to capture and contain it. Projecting back to 1531 a timeless tradition of widespread belief and Indian devotion to an image of miraculous origin associated with apparitions of the Virgin Mary—whether it is Miguel Sánchez writing in 1648, Octavio Paz writing in the 1970s, Beverly Donofrio writing in 2000, or a pilgrim who will make the long trek to Tepeyac this December[58]—is likely to tell us more about memory and faith than about experience in the sixteenth and seventeenth centuries. The guadalupanismo glimpsed in the seventeenth-century financial records seems more incipient and open to substantial change later in the colonial period, but it was not just the invention of Sánchez and Lasso de la Vega, either.

History, says Richard White, is the enemy of memory. "Memory lives within us and cannot be separated from us without becoming something else. Memory constantly rearranges the past to make sense of the present."[59] Historians cannot eliminate or isolate memory and tradition as if they were simply untrue or irrelevant, or just more social facts to historicize. To do so would be to ignore or trivialize a vital part of human experience, *the* vital part a devotee would say. Traditions like December 9–12, 1531, as the dates of Marian apparitions to Juan Diego cannot simply be explained away with the wave of a sheaf of documents that show no December 12 feast day before the late seventeenth century, any more than other kinds of convictions that give meaning to life can be easily suppressed with circumstantial evidence.⁶⁰ Such traditions have a life of their own. But they can be engaged in conversation with past experience and as past experience, and their differences from documented traces of experience and their connections to the history we write can be made clearer. In Carl Schorske's words, we can think with history, as well as think about history.⁶¹ Or as White suggests, the limits of our reckonings with the past, as well as the limits of memory, need to be made clear. The limits of historical knowledge about the "lives" of sacred images are obvious enough, as Luis de Cisneros's distant words of 1616 about the barren, rocky plain of history remind us, though knowledge about them, like memory, is open to revision and, hopefully, to enlargement.

My thanks to Taylor & Francis for permission to revise and republish this essay, which first appeared in Allan Greer and Jodi Bilinkoff, eds., *Colonial Saints: Discovering the Holy in the Americas, 1500–1800* (New York: Routledge, 2003), 277–98.

Places of Our Lady of Guadalupe in Eighteenth-Century Mexico

THE MAIN STORY OF GUADALUPANISMO IN MEXICO DURING THE eighteenth century is one of vigorous promotion and widespread devotion in which the 1730s, 1740s, and 1750s were the watershed. Early in the great epidemic of 1737 peninsular Archbishop-Viceroy Juan Antonio de Vizarrón y Eguiarreta, already a devotee, proclaimed Our Lady of Guadalupe patroness of Mexico City and New Spain and renewed the campaign for papal recognition of the apparition story.[1] His initiatives were well received at home and abroad, culminating in a papal bull of 1754 in which Pope Benedict XIV officially announced the miracle and recognized Mary of Guadalupe as patroness of New Spain, borrowing the words of Psalm 147, "*Non fecit taliter omni nationi*" (He [God] has favored no other people in this way).[2] A closer consideration of how the devotion grew in the eighteenth century, especially how it grew without Tepeyac yet becoming a magnet for pilgrims from distant places, is the aim of this essay. In order to highlight the main points, most of the primary sources that substantiate them are left in the notes, usually with examples rather than an exhaustive listing of cases.

Promotion and Growth

By just about any measure a historian can summon, the devotion seems to have grown as never before after 1754. Great celebrations of thanksgiving were ordered and undertaken in the cities of the viceroyalty after the bull was published in America in 1756. Soon every diocesan capital had a shrine to Our Lady of Guadalupe, and many other towns and occupational groups received licenses to construct their own church or resplendent altar to Guadalupe.[3] Holders of the winning tickets in the Gran Sorteo Piadoso de Nuestra Señora de Guadalupe, the blockbuster raffle to benefit the shrine in 1800, came from distant Durango, Veracruz, and Valladolid, as well as Mexico City.[4] Some towns turned to Guadalupe instead of the saints they had traditionally favored[5]; a veritable flood of devotional literature was published[6]; prints and painted copies of the image dating from 1740 to 1810 survive in far greater numbers in churches, archives, and private collections than from the seventeenth and early eighteenth centuries, and more are recorded in church inventories and wills of all classes of people in the late eighteenth century.[7] Thousands of houses, probably tens or hundreds of thousands, boasted a painting or cheap print of the image over a home altar. Young scholars at the university in Mexico City dedicated their academic theses to Our Lady of Guadalupe in unprecedented numbers after 1754. More places were named or renamed for her; Guadalupe became a widely popular baptismal name for the first time[8]; and her presence was reported more often in events regarded as miracles, including healings, rescues, and sightings of the image in nature from the 1750s forward.[9] One of these miraculous events, in 1783, put the spotlight on the shrine at Tepeyac. That year a hot spring suddenly welled up from behind the main altar, bringing forth a fine oil as well as water.[10] Growing attention to the site of the original apparitions is indicated also by the rebuilding of the Capilla del Cerrito in 1749; groundbreaking for a new *camarín* (dressing room) in 1778[11]; provision for repairs and maintenance of the original sixteenth-century chapel in 1784[12]; construction of a Capuchin convent next to the church from 1781–1787; and the exquisite Capilla del Pocito, begun in 1777 and completed in 1791.

As Guadalupe became more widely known and celebrated she was invoked for protection in new circumstances reaching far beyond her traditional role in turning back floodwaters. Throughout the eighteenth century, but especially after 1760, she was celebrated in New Spain as one of God's chosen captains in Spain's international wars.[13] She guarded against fire and illness, and she protected miners and helped them find rich veins of ore.[14] One sermonizer thought that her downcast eyes made her a natural protector against earthquakes. By midcentury she had become an all-purpose protector. In his sermon of 1741 Nicolás de Segura recommended her favor to the people of New Spain "in all their ailments" (*en todas sus dolencias*), and in his 1756 sermon Juan José de Eguiara y Eguren declared that her embrace was all-encompassing—"She has freed us from everything, she brings peace, [and] favors us all."[15]

The most telling signs of familiarity and spreading devotion were the quotidian ones that begin to dot the written record, especially in the late eighteenth century: people routinely invoking Our Lady of Guadalupe in their petitions to colonial officials; prisoners asking for pardon in her name; mission Indians in Sonora said to observe her feast day on December 12; and disputes among family members over a coveted home altar image in central Mexican villages.[16] For a parade of pupils from the primary school run by the Franciscan missionary college in Pachuca, Hidalgo, on August 12, 1797, nearly all the little boys reportedly were dressed up as Guadalupe's Indian protégé, Juan Diego. And at his trial for robbery in 1804 a mestizo muleteer from Tequila, Jalisco, in western Mexico complained that he had been arrested without cause because he was a humble man without influential friends: "They are going to punish me... because I don't have a pretty woman, or children, except for the Virgin of Guadalupe."[17]

The mounting written record in which the Virgin of Guadalupe is mentioned suggests both popular enthusiasm and a denser, more prescribed and institutionalized web of regulations and observances. The December 12 celebrations, popular in various cities and towns after the first oaths of allegiance (*juras*) ordered by Archbishop-Viceroy Vizarrón in 1737 acquired new layers of commemorative meaning as the century unfolded. The oaths were repeated in 1747 to mark the tenth anniversary and remember with gratitude both the providential apparition in 1531 and Mary's efficacious intervention in the epidemic in 1737.[18] Still grander acts of thanksgiving took place in 1756–1757 to celebrate the papal bull recognizing the authenticity of the apparitions. The veritable symphony of December 12 fiestas after 1757 commemorated both the apparition and the papal proclamation.[19] In other institutional developments, lay confraternities dedicated to Our Lady of Guadalupe grew in number from the 1740s. In the 1760s and 1770s wealthy occupational groups, including leading *hacendados* of central Mexico and the Real Colegio de Abogados of Mexico City, began sponsoring annual novenas at the shrine and publishing the keynote sermon they commissioned for it.[20] In the eighteenth century licenses were required to collect alms for a shrine, and by the 1780s they were usually restricted to short periods and small areas, if not denied altogether. Our Lady of Guadalupe was the exception to these tighter restrictions on alms collectors. Licenses to collect for Guadalupe were granted routinely and often without limits, especially after 1756.[21] Even during the late eighteenth-century reforms in the name of oversight and efficiency, itinerant and local collectors for the annual Indian fiesta at Tepeyac were waved through with two-year licenses on the grounds that it was a "time immemorial" custom.

Other formal acts meant to encourage the devotion and underwrite the cult at Tepeyac include a 1756 royal decree requiring all future wills to include a provision for the shrine[22]; circulars by the bishops encouraging devotions to Guadalupe on the twelfth of every month; and an array of promotional publications including novena booklets, sermons, leaflets and single sheets of special prayers and poems; testimonial texts, including Miguel Cabrera's *Maravilla Americana y conjunto de raras maravillas* (1756); and the first booklet designed expressly for religious tourists to Tepeyac, published in 1794.[23]

From the 1730s the search was on for Guadalupan relics and fresh evidence to authenticate the miracles of apparition. Italian savant Lorenzo Boturini was caught up in this groundswell of guadalupanismo when he arrived in Mexico City in 1736, just as the great epidemic was about to strike. Over the next seven years he acquired an extraordinary collection of manuscripts relating to pre-Columbian Mesoamerica and the apparitions and shrine at Tepeyac, before his arrest and deportation to Spain in 1744.[24] Mariano Fernández de Echeverría y Veytia, a young creole attorney who represented his father's legal affairs in Europe from 1738–1750 took Boturini into his home in Madrid for nearly two years (1744–1746) and became fascinated by his Mexican studies. For the rest of his life Echeverría y Veytia devoted spare hours to his own studies of pre-Columbian civilizations, the history of his hometown, Puebla, and a manuscript he called *Baluartes de México*, a providential history of the Virgin Mary in New Spain that focused on Our Lady of Guadalupe and Mexico City.[25] He recounted in *Baluartes* a trip in 1746 to Valladolid, Spain, hometown of Juan de Zumárraga, the bishop to whom Juan Diego reportedly revealed the miracles, but who left no trace of the encounters or his devotion. Entering the cathedral church there Echeverría y Veytia glimpsed a large painting of Mexico's Virgin of Guadalupe next to the altar railing of the main chapel, and his heart skipped a beat. Here, he thought, was the long sought evidence of Zumárraga's personal connection to the apparition story. He hurried forward only to be disappointed. The painting could not have been the gift of Zumárraga himself or a contemporary for it was dated 1667, at the time of the first wave of petitions to Rome for recognition of the apparitions.[26] In the same spirit of eager anticipation, a reconstruction project at the shrine in 1751 included an unsuccessful search for the bones of Juan Diego.[27]

But there are twists in this story of promotion and continuous development of guadalupanismo from the 1730s. Take the role usually assigned to Archbishop-Viceroy Vizarrón as architect of the watershed events from 1737–1754. He certainly proved himself an enthusiastic guadalupano before the epidemic of 1737 and was a determined and skillful promoter until death overtook him in 1747.[28] From the time he arrived as archbishop-elect in late 1731 he organized and attended ceremonies at the shrine, including the bicentennial of the apparition and the groundbreaking for a convent on site in November and December 1731, donated an exquisite Italian vestment embroidered with gold thread in 1735, and pushed for formal recognition of the settlement at Tepeyac as a pueblo and a villa.[29] Then during the epidemic he declared Our Lady of Guadalupe patroness of the city and the viceroyalty, and afterwards reignited the campaign for papal recognition and pursued the elevation of the shrine as a collegiate church. But it was the city government rather than the archbishop-viceroy that first pushed for recognition of Our Lady of Guadalupe as official patroness during the early weeks of the epidemic in January 1737, and Vizarrón firmly resisted the city councilors' plea for the image to be brought from the shrine to the cathedral, as had been done during the great flood of 1629–1634.[30]

Above all, the record of guadalupanismo in Mexico before Vizarrón arrived suggests that his efforts to promote the devotion depended on initiatives and momentum that had been building strongly for more than thirty years. Antonio Margil de Jesús, the great Franciscan proselytizer and Guadalupan devotee spread the image and devotion north from Zacatecas all the way to Texas in the first years of the eighteenth century, as did missionaries from the Apostolic College of Our Lady of Guadalupe he founded at Zacatecas in 1706.[31] Completion of the great temple at Tepeyac in 1709 brought on a burst of enthusiasm, donations, and new construction. Santuarios to Guadalupe were already established or under construction then in the provincial cities of Valladolid, Zacatecas, Antequera, and Pachuca, and more of the Guadalupan sermons being published in the early eighteenth century than before were originally delivered in provincial churches. The planning for a college of ecclesiastical dignitaries (*colegiata*) at Tepeyac—one of Vizarrón's pet projects—dates back to the completion of the new church there, and petitions for licenses to found the college met with success from the crown and papacy in 1717 and 1725, long before he arrived. The college was not in operation until 1750, after Vizarrón's death, because the site lacked the required settlement and infrastructure to qualify as a villa. The bicentennial celebrations and founding of a Capuchin convent at the shrine also were planned before Vizarrón's arrival and point to a new interest in commemorative events that added to the popularity of the image and the apparition story before 1737. As a run up to the bicentennial of the apparition in 1731 (there had been no centennial celebration in 1631), the great church at Tepeyac was lavishly rededicated in May 1722 and the cathedral dignitaries undertook a second inquiry into the authenticity of the apparition story as part of a new petition to Rome.[32] In the early 1720s Pope Innocent XIII (May 1721–March 1724) signaled his interest in the case of Guadalupe and gave the Spanish crown good reason to look after the well-being of the shrine at Tepeyac shrine by granting the crown a 6 percent share of its annual income.[33]

A string of commemorations before the great epidemic and declaration of the Virgin of Guadalupe as patroness followed. On December 12, 1728, the 197th anniversary of the apparition was celebrated in Mexico City; in 1729 the centennial of the beginning of the flood that marked Guadalupe's first great public miracle was observed, along with the 198th anniversary of the apparition. Then came the bicentennial celebrations in 1731, the centennial of flood relief in 1634, and the fiftieth anniversary of the confraternity to Guadalupe at Tepeyac in 1735.[34] In Mexico City, at least, Our Lady of Guadalupe seemed like a natural point of reference by then even in other kinds of solemn celebrations. When the Carmelite friars of the capital thought to celebrate the canonization of St. John of the Cross in 1730 with a tableau for public viewing in their main patio, Tepeyac and Guadalupe were the miniaturized setting they chose. The raised platform offered a natural landscape that, in the Carmelites' description, sounds like an exquisite model railroad layout complete with flora and fauna, and a shimmering, tinsel river. It featured an intricate representation of the hill of Tepeyac, complete with rock outcroppings, caves, and a variety of other details, topped with a church to the Virgin of Guadalupe and a fine copy of the image. On the road leading to the shrine, figures of St. John and St. Theresa of Avila were placed, dressed as pilgrims. There at Tepeyac,

Mary's most renowned home in New Spain, Spain's favorite mystic saints found an American place.[35]

While a flowering of Guadalupan devotion and sponsorship from 1737 to the end of the eighteenth century is abundantly documented, the story becomes more complicated and fluid when particular situations—places, people, and times—are considered. For example, the history of confraternities dedicated to Guadalupe does not follow a smooth upward trajectory everywhere. For the Archdiocese of Mexico, the pastoral visit of 1683–1685 found five confraternities dedicated to Guadalupe in the ninety or so parishes visited outside the Valley of Mexico, four of them in or near the Valley of Toluca; the visit in 1717 found eleven Guadalupan confraternities, but only two of them near Toluca and most of the new ones concentrated in parishes of the modern states of Morelos and Querétaro situated close to the Valley of Mexico; and the pastoral visits of 1752–1758 found fifteen, with a yet different regional distribution. By then, only one was still active around Toluca, but nine new ones appeared in the modern state of Hidalgo.[36] So, these formal institutions of lay devotion to Guadalupe rose and fell in popularity, if they were present at all, and, in a few cases, rural communities actively resisted the promotion of guadalupanismo in their parishes.[37] Even the shrine at Tepeyac experienced periods of disappointing revenue and had to resort to special collections and raffles to meet expenses despite several sponsoring cofradías, the royal order of 1756 that all testaments in New Spain include a provision for Guadalupe, and the blanket licenses for alms collections.[38] No place, except perhaps Mexico City or the city of San Luis Potosí and its hinterland, fits the pattern of steady growth to a tee, not even the community that grew up around the shrine at Tepeyac in the seventeenth and eighteenth centuries.[39] Developments there during the eighteenth century appear to be more the result of promotion by authorities in Mexico City and opportunities for employment in construction than from waves of ardent devotees moving to the holy site as if it were a New World Varanasi.[40]

How much of this growth in Guadalupan devotion was promotion by elite devotees and how much was self-generated popular fervor? What was guided by authorities? And what was spontaneous and inner-directed? The answers no doubt vary by place and time, and depend on evidence of coercion or direct resistance. By the eighteenth century, the image of Guadalupe was so familiar that promotion and devotion can hardly be separated. One promotional campaign that clearly took root and initiated a new habit in devotional practice was the custom of dedicating the twelfth of every month to special veneration of the Virgin Mary "in her admirable and prodigious image of Guadalupe." Beginning in 1755, distinguished priests including Juan José de Eguiara y Eguren wrote and published booklets of prayers and devotional exercises for these monthly occasions. Entitled, with variations, *Día doce de cada mes consagrado a Nuestra Madre y Señora María Santísima de Guadalupe, en veneración de su maravillosa aparición*, these booklets were printed and reprinted at least thirteen times by 1807, ten of them between 1782 and 1807. Most were printed in Mexico City, but Puebla printshops published editions in 1773 and 1782, and the March 18, 1796, issue of *Gazeta de México* reported that the monthly veneration was being actively promoted in Guanajuato:

> With the purpose of propagating throughout all of our America the monthly demonstration of love and gratitude to our singular Patroness Most Holy Mary of Guadalupe, it has been considered opportune for this city [of Guanajuato] to participate, following the example of Mexico City; and so, new devotions to the Lady have begun on the twelfth of every month, displaying her holy images in windows and illuminating them with candles part of the night.[41]

Precisely who practiced the monthly devotions, and where, probably is beyond the reach of historians, but the frequent reprintings and evidence of enthusiasm for the practice in Puebla and Guanajuato suggest considerable popularity, and not only in Mexico City.

The promotional campaigns can be charted in detail, but the reception and local practices they may have inspired are not so clearly documented. It was rarely a simple matter of promotion followed by devotion, but whether leading or following, the official promotion seems to have been well received for the most part across classes and regions. Well received, but often taken in directions not intended or always welcomed by official promoters. Images of Guadalupe and materials associated with them circulated well beyond the reach of the carriers who represented them officially, into the hands, homes, and chapels of individuals, families, and landed estates, and into churches that were visited by a priest perhaps once a year.[42] Local enthusiasm spilled beyond the official even in Mexico City where neighborhoods and occupational groups like the street vendors of the Zócalo and the honey merchants of the Calle de la Azequia celebrated their own Guadalupan fiestas and Rosary processions on the twelfth of every month and organized themselves into semiformal brotherhoods without official license or close supervision.[43] Unlicensed, reportedly unruly Guadalupan processions were particularly worrisome to officials in the capital and elsewhere, as lengthy cases from Toluca in 1751 and the Barrio del Hornillo and Santo Domingo neighborhood in Mexico City in 1772–1773 and 1776 show.[44]

The growing association of Our Lady of Guadalupe with Indians and Indian devotion suggests some of the difficulties of trying to untangle promotion and devotion. Guadalupanismo is still commonly regarded as first and foremost an Indian devotion, and it is assumed to have been wildly popular from the first years of Spanish colonization, with church officials hurrying in to direct it. Octavio Paz is only the most famous writer to suppose that this devotion began with Indians in central Mexico, turning to this image of the Virgin Mary for consolation in their "spiritual orphanhood" in the aftermath of conquest.[45] Recent scholarship, based largely on writings by distinguished priests of the period, has taken the opposite tack, positing that early Indian devotion is a myth, that guadalupanismo was born and raised by urban and creole Spaniards. It was not primarily an Indian devotion, but clearly there were many Indian devotees of Our Lady of Guadalupe from Tlatelolco, the Valley of Mexico, and surrounding highland communities who visited the shrine at Tepeyac by the early seventeenth century. The celebration at that time of separate fiesta seasons at the shrine for Indians and Spaniards is hard to account for otherwise. And there is considerable, widely scattered evidence of Indian interest in Our Lady of Guadalupe during the eighteenth century, especially in central Mexico.[46] However, the growing prominence of Indians in the record of guadalupanismo during the eighteenth century may well owe more to promotion by leading creole and peninsular churchmen and artists than to spontaneous Indian devotion. It is from evangelizing priests working on spiritual revival among the laity that we have most of the sweeping testimonials to an Indian essence of the cult in the late colonial period and the growing interest in Juan Diego. The earliest sermon I know of that describes Guadalupe as appearing in the guise of an Indian is Jesuit Nicolás de Segura's sermon *Plática de la milagrosa imagen de Nuestra Señora de Guadalupe de México*, delivered in 1741 and printed in 1742:

> Who would deny that this most benign Mother appeared with the avowed intention of resembling in every way the natives of

the country, valuing the Indian so highly that she seems to have affected their appearance in every way: in the Tilma or cloak of Juan Diego on which her image was painted; in her humble and shy posture and the tilt of her head; in the pleasing separation of her hair, which is black and thick; and in the distinct olive-colored complexion of the face and hands; in the full-length tunic from her neck and shoulders to her feet, and the flowing robe from head to foot in the manner of a shawl—all of these signs and indications in which she shows her wish to have appeared in every way like Indian nobles of this America.[47]

Segura and later eighteenth-century preachers and pastors invited Indians to regard Our Lady of Guadalupe as their special spiritual mother, and to identify with her Indian seer, Juan Diego.[48] For example, in 1769 Ignacio José Hugo de Omerick, an elderly diocesan pastor in a central Mexican parish exhorted young pastors in Indian parishes to make judicious use of the Guadalupe story and Juan Diego's place in it:

With our image of Guadalupe [the Indians] live exceedingly proud, and with good reason: any kind of copy of the image furnished to them is gratefully received and kept; and when they hear that that most fortunate Indian, Juan Diego, was worthy of receiving the apparitions of Our Lady when he was on his way to catechism lessons, they become very emotional and are moved to venerate her.[49]

It is probably more than coincidental that Hugo de Omerick wrote during the term of Mexico's high profile Archbishop Francisco Antonio Lorenzana (1766–1771), himself an ardent Guadalupan devotee, who actively encouraged the devotion among Indians. During his pastoral visit in 1766–1767, he stopped for prayers at Tepeyac on his way out of the capital and proceeded to commend Guadalupe to Indian parishioners he met. In pastoral letters, sermons, and other writings he spoke of Guadalupe as *morena*—dark-skinned, like the most celebrated images of Mary in Spain; "the dark color adds charm to the image," he once wrote—and exhorted everyone, but especially Indians, to embrace her special gift to New Spain: "May all the Indians come; may the Indian women come fervently to pay homage to this Lady; may their children come, and may the Indian women believe."[50] Elsewhere he asked, rhetorically, "Who does she resemble most, a Spanish woman or an Indian noblewoman? . . . [She is] dressed in their clothing, in the manner of this country in order to attract the recently conquered."[51] The prominence of Juan Diego in these Guadalupan tracts from the mid-eighteenth century is paralleled by new pictorial representations of him. Paintings of Guadalupe with small depictions of the four apparitions to Juan Diego in the corners began in the late seventeenth century, but became more common during the second half of the eighteenth century. And Miguel Cabrera, among other artists, painted Juan Diego alone—heavily bearded and looking more like one of the apostles than a native commoner—claiming that these were "true portraits."[52]

At the same time, from the 1740s to 1800s, devotion to Guadalupe did become more evident in Indian communities, especially in the center, west, and north-center. New images, altars, and chapels to Guadalupe appeared in their churches; more Indian children received Guadalupe as their baptismal name; and she was mentioned more often in their wills and property disputes. Indian communities honored her in other ways, such as the practice in Sultepec (Estado de México) of naming the sponsors of various local saints on December 12, the date associated with the first apparition.[53] Special pleas in the name our Our Lady of Guadalupe—such as "For the love of God and the Virgin of Guadalupe"—in Indian legal and political records were especially common in the last decades of the colonial period.[54] And Indian communities in the Valley of Mexico that could claim some association with the miracle stories of Juan Diego and his uncle, Juan Bernardino, sought to benefit from the burgeoning popular devotion as well as to express their own devotion to the image of Guadalupe. From Tolpetlac (district of Ecatepec on the edge of the Valley of Mexico) in 1789 came a petition seeking permission to build a chapel on the site where it was believed Our Lady of Guadalupe appeared to Juan Bernardino and cured him of a grave illness.[55] Then in December 1803 a woman from Cuauhtitlán, Juan Diego's presumed birthplace, claimed to have found a 1559 will of his aunt, Gregoria María, that referred to the apparitions. She sought to complete a chapel on the site of Juan Diego's house in the Tlayac neighborhood licensed by Viceroy d. Félix Berenguer de Marquina (who served from April 1800 to the first days of January 1803).[56] The idea was to collect alms to support the project and acquire an image of Guadalupe to display there. In 1784 a special sodality of Indians dedicated to Our Lady of Guadalupe was established to keep the original chapel from the sixteenth century in good condition and to build an inn for Indian visitors.

The constitution required that Indians from anywhere in the viceroyalty who wished to join could be enrolled as long as they paid an initiation fee and weekly contribution of one-half real. Whether or not this sodality was an Indian initiative, it became an Indian institution.[57] Italian Franciscan Ilarione da Bergamo, who lived in Mexico City in the 1760s, was almost rapturous in his description of the popular, Indian devotion to Guadalupe: "What an immense pleasure to view every morning the many carriages heading to this sanctuary from Mexico City and, even more, the people on foot reciting the rosary aloud along the route.... The concourse of Indian folk, especially, is so immense that it is a source of wonderment."[58] Were these indications of popular devotion to the Virgin of Guadalupe the result of some particular promotional activity? Perhaps so, but the lack of evidence for the relationship in the written record suggests that it was more likely indirect, or at least not simply managed by the promoter.

The kind of independent vernacular use of Guadalupan devotion that probably worried official promoters and ecclesiastical judges in the cities most comes out in the case of an Indian visionary brought before the Archbishop of Mexico's court in 1728, nearly a decade before Archbishop-Viceroy Vizarrón launched his campaign for universal Guadalupan patronage, and three years before he became the archbishop. Charges of sacrilegious deception were brought that year against Francisco Diego, an Indian tributary of San Mateo Atenco in the parish of Metepec (Estado de México), whom witnesses considered a *"buen hombre,"* respectable in his habits and customs until he let it be known that Our Lady of Guadalupe had spoken to him through a copy of the image. Her message was that she would provide five silver pesos for him to buy adobe bricks and build her a chapel; then she would give him one hundred pesos so that he could buy two reales (one-fourth of a silver peso) worth of fruit to give to the poorest people. He also claimed she had given him a supply of heavenly incense and a staff of authority so that he could become *gobernador* of the community. The case summary states that once Francisco Diego made his apparition story public, many people—Indians and non-Indians alike—were drawn to his house, eager to meet the seer, gather sacred souvenirs, and find out more for themselves. There he showed them a gourd bowl of water with a marigold floating on top. He told them the flower was a precious relic since he had used it to wipe beads of perspiration from the image after the apparition. Confronted with the testimony against him and the court's attempt to coax him into admitting deception, Francisco remained steadfast in his story. The only part of the testimony that was false, he said, was the rumor that he had cured an Indian's infected leg by drawing a worm with horns from the wound. Juan Francisco was sentenced to twenty-five lashes, court costs (which amounted to a sentence of penal servitude since he had no savings), and an elaborate, prolonged public display of repentance and abject submission to church authority. It included an auto da fé—a ceremonial "act of faith"—in the parish church, with the condemned standing in a cage wearing a cone-shaped hat, a noose around his neck, a green candle in one hand, and a sign that described his crime. Left standing during the Mass up to the Sanctus, the verdict was read aloud to him, followed by a "grave but brief" exhortation in the parishioners' native language by the local pastor, pointing out the seriousness of the offense. Then he was whipped and ordered to attend every religious function in the community for two years. On Sundays during Mass he was to stand in a designated place so that everyone could witness his humiliation and repentance. He was also to confess at least every three months for a year, and to sweep the church every Saturday.[59] Such an apparition story with an Indian seer in a Juan Diego-like role may be unique in the eighteenth-century written record, but, like many other events, it suggests that devotional enthusiasm could be encouraged and shaped by promotion, but was not simply contained by it.

The main point to be made about promotion and devotion during the eighteenth century is that there was plenty of both, and that promotion and devotion rarely moved along entirely separate tracks or followed one causal line. Simultaneously there was more institutionalization of the devotion *and* more unauthorized or at least unsupervised contagion and enthusiasm; more promotion of a special Indian connection and abundant evidence that Guadalupe was regarded as a providential sign of the sacred for everyone, across class, ethnicity, and region. A paradox contained in this history of Guadalupan devotion and promotion that further complicates the main story of dramatic growth is that while the devotion was spreading throughout the viceroyalty there was not a corresponding movement of devout visitors to Tepeyac from distant places.

Popularity and Pilgrimage

Thinking about the medieval and early modern European tradition of pilgrimage, I expected to find pilgrims and a pilgrimage literature for

Guadalupan devotion in colonial Mexico, especially in the eighteenth century. Guidebooks, books of miracles, and scores of personal accounts of pilgrimage circulated in Europe during the Middle Ages, and there are other records in the form of certificates of pilgrimage and papal indulgences for those who completed the journeys to Rome, Jerusalem, and Compostela. Few Christians undertook those great journeys, or perhaps even went to a less remote regional shrine, but the idea of the long-distance journey of hardship, penance, spiritual cleansing, and reward was familiar to all and desired by many. Sacred journeys have an important place in pre-Columbian Mexican lore, too, so I was surprised to find no guide books or accounts of long-distance pilgrimage to Tepeyac, no network of shrines and sacred routes leading there during the colonial period, especially during the eighteenth century when guadalupanismo was so obviously expanding.

The literature on Mexican guadalupanismo imagines otherwise. To Victor and Edith Turner, for example, the Virgin of Guadalupe was Mexico's "dominant symbol" presiding over what they called "the total symbolic system"—situated at the apex of pilgrimage routes, above an orderly hierarchy of shrines and images. The Turners were persuaded that what they took to be a European tradition of Christian pilgrimage had moved to America. They wrote, "The medieval mode of Catholic pilgrimage was given a new lease on life in the overseas empires of Spain, Portugal, and France. . . . Foremost among the shrines of the major pilgrimage systems are those dedicated to the Mother of God. . . . All are subordinate in fame and catchment scope to the cultus of the Virgin of Guadalupe. . . . The system ensures the constant crisscrossing of pilgrimage ways, as in medieval Europe."[60] But Our Lady of Guadalupe and Tepeyac did not predominate in this way. Hundreds of shrines attracted devotees from beyond the immediate vicinity. While the image of the Virgin of Guadalupe became the most widely known object of faith in New Spain by the late eighteenth century, there is little to suggest that the legendary site of the Virgin Mary's apparitions to Juan Diego was much more popular as a destination for sacred travel beyond its vicinity than were half a dozen shrines to other miraculous images, not to mention the hundreds of other shrines that were regarded as essential to the well-being of people living closer by. Little in the way of an interlocking system of pilgrimage routes developed (even with the advent of railroads in the late nineteenth century, when great streams of visitors began to travel there), and there were about as many shrines to miraculous images in Mexico 1850 or 2000 as in 1700. Few were displaced by Guadalupe and Tepeyac.[61]

How could people be so attracted to the image of Guadalupe without being equally interested in Tepeyac, where the image had appeared on the cloak of a humble Indian and was still displayed? I am emphasizing attachment to place, but there are other considerations, too. Few people could afford to go unless they regarded it as the final journey, and the broken terrain, great distances, and dangers of the road also discouraged long-distance travels. Another consideration is the lack of official encouragement, if not active discouragement, for European-style great pilgrimages on the grounds that pilgrims would contribute to vagrancy, social disorder, and economic dislocations. Long penitential sojourns to a shrine were part of the mental world of hispanized subjects in New Spain, but indulgences for actual pilgrimages were not issued by colonial bishops, and when a creole Spanish woman from Monterrey in northern Mexico promised to go to Tepeyac if she recovered from a grave illness in 1758, the Bishop of Guadalajara was quick to excuse her from the vow.[62] When Christianity broke in on America is part of an explanation. The new politics of religion in Europe during the sixteenth century also worked against holy wanderers and travel to remote destinations.[63] Border crossings became riskier, and in Protestant regions religious pilgrimages were virtually eliminated. In Catholic areas they were regulated more closely, if not discouraged, and sacred travel often was channeled toward shorter journeys to regional shrines that reinforced the importance of dioceses and state territories.[64] Nevertheless, there remained more long-distance travel to sacred places in Europe than in the viceroyalty.

Another piece of the puzzle of limited pilgrimage may be found in the notion of beauty and the significance of copies of religious images in early modern Catholic culture, before the age of mechanical reproduction. Most of the painted copies that found their way into parish churches and regional shrines were the same size as the image at Tepeyac and executed with the greatest care to replicate it as faithfully as humanly possible. If we take the viewpoint of the consumers and makers of these many images, something more complex was going on than slavish imitation emptied of spiritual content. The standard of beauty for religious images had to do with reception, more than originality—if a representation of Christ or Mary or another saint evoked feelings of intense love and contrition from devotees and thereby was pleasing to God and invited His presence and favor, it could be considered beautiful.⁶⁵ The effects—including miracles—were the proof. Accurate, painstaking representation of the form and spirit of the subject was understood to be especially pleasing to God. The more a copy resembled the matrix image, the more it, too, invited Mary's presence and inspired a sense of awe. If a particular image was thought to be of great beauty, thanks especially to its association with miracles, what could be better than a nearly perfect copy, especially if the two had touched? This was a conception of beauty that could value replication as the real thing.⁶⁶ With a fine copy of the image in a church within reach, or even a cheap print on a home altar, there was less reason, rather than more, to go to Tepeyac on pilgrimage. Guadalupe was already with you, if approached in the right way.

If few devotees of Guadalupe were going to Tepeyac from great distances, were they going somewhere else? Yes, they were going to local and regional sites, usually on foot, or they were finding Guadalupe at home. Even as concentration of the sacred in one place was being promoted by viceregal and archiepiscopal officials and spreading out from there after 1737, decentralization was at work. Mexico City and its officials always had difficulty convincing the viceroyalty's thousands of outlying settlements that *they* were not the navel of the universe. Local copies of the Virgin of Guadalupe were said to come alive—sweating, crying, bleeding, changing expression—all signs of divine presence that beckoned to devotees.⁶⁷ For example, at Temamatla, near Chalco in the Valley of Mexico, local people announced in 1737 that their copy of Our Lady of Guadalupe sweated and spoke to them—Mary was fully present right there, in their image.⁶⁸ And a millenarian movement at Tututepec in the Sierra of Meztitlán (Hidalgo) in 1769 made even stronger claims for the Virgin's presence. The old man said to be the New Savior was paired with a young woman who was reputed to be the incarnation of Our Lady of Guadalupe. She had come to Tututepec in the flesh, said one witness, because "Our Lady of Guadalupe, the one who appeared in Mexico City, fell from her greatness there."⁶⁹ In less provocative ways, most devotees living beyond the Valley of Mexico were satisfied with the likeness of Guadalupe that was close at hand, set among the other revered images in their local church or on a home altar, or in a regional capital. Few seem to have felt themselves powerfully "drawn to the image" at Tepeyac from great distances, as so many devotees do today.

The articulation of space and place is a key to this paradox of shrines with little long-distance pilgrimage. Often expressed by scholars in terms of space *versus* place, it is an ongoing conundrum that has engaged and sometimes riled geographers in the United States for many years. Yi-fu Tuan and other "humanistic" geographers and anthropologists have given primacy to place and intersections of activity in conceptualizing location for many world cultures, while the more calibrated approaches of "scientific" geographers tend to emphasize space and mathematical modeling. Philosopher-phenomenologist-intellectual historian Edward Casey has given the humanistic geographers' perspective a more polemical and historical edge with his project of "recovering" place as the most fundamental form of embodied experience (where self, space, and time blend), arguing against the idea of space as having an a priori existence as a void to be filled in. Casey regards the a priori existence of space as a distinctly western and modern concept, epitomized by Newton and Descartes's view of places as compartmentalized parts of space.[70]

Newtonian and Cartesian space is the common sense of our time and culture, but place was more immediately apprehended by earlier Europeans and has been fundamental to at least some nonwestern cultures. In Mexico, the Catholic Church and other Spanish colonial institutions introduced some new and larger bounded spaces—dioceses and high court districts among them—and standard units of measurement, including the *vara* (about 33 inches long) and the *estancia de ganado mayor* grazing allotment (5,000 varas x 5,000 varas), but notions of greater distance were still not yet measured and fixed. Beyond a town's limits or the dimensions of a land grant, distance was still relational. A league was commonly understood to be the distance a mule could travel in one hour *over local terrain*; and territories like dioceses and audiencias were defined by the settlements located within them rather than by hypothetical boundary lines traced on the ground.

I am less interested in debates over the conceptual primacy of space or place than in trying to find ways of thinking about them in relational terms that highlight colonial people's experiences of devotion and their surroundings. Place *making* and *circulation* of people, things, ideas, and sacred energy that are not necessarily marked by buildings and other visible boundaries have become important to my approach to shrines. I am inclined to follow J. B. Jackson in speaking about place in rather fluid terms as existential space, where intersections and interactions among people and locations stand out more than fixed boundaries.[71] Places get *made* when people occupy them—physically, but also mentally and spiritually—when they become "inside." Space, place, and other ideas about location and territory are not neutral, objective concepts. They have to do with how people perceive and encounter terrain and territory. Take burial places. Whether located within or beyond a residential community, burial places express remembrance, continuity, and the idea of home. During the colonial period the settlements and burial sites of rural central and southern Mexico were part of a symbolic landscape of social, moral, and cosmic order. The saints, like the dead, *occupied* this place. The late sixteenth-century Indian resettlement program in central and southern Mexico had mixed results in large part because people would not lightly abandon such dwelling places of their ancestors and patrons, even for better farmlands.

As a way to think in-between place and space, and to sidestep center-periphery dichotomies and a nested hierarchy of places, I have been considering devotional *landscapes*. J. B. Jackson characterizes landscapes as "the various ways humans had come to terms with their environment, specifically how we created landscapes as places where we could live and work and celebrate together."[72] Speaking of landscapes invites a view of place that is marked by *movement* and allows me to look beyond a fixed point without jumping into the void of space.

Lee Hoinacki, a former Benedictine monk turned professor of political science and subsistence farmer, experienced landscape in this way during his month-long walk along the pilgrimage trail to Santiago de Compostela in 1993. He wrote in his journal:

> After several hours, I begin to feel something new, something never before experienced. I strongly sense with my whole self that I am moving from one place to another. Puzzled, I nevertheless clearly realize that I have never tasted anything like this, never known about this. I am not passing *through* space, as one does in a car or airplane. This is a radically different sensation. I feel I am in a place; actually in an infinite number of places. I am not in an undifferentiated space—what one feels in many modern places that, really, are non-places; they are simply repetitions of concepts—the concept of hospital space, shopping mall space, highway space, suburb space, and so on. Here, with each step, I am always in place, in some place, going to the next place.[73]

The sensory experience of surroundings conferred by pedestrian travel seems to be a key to past place-centered European experiences of location, and walking was the common means of conveyance in Mexico until the twentieth century. Walking was virtually the only means of travel over land before the arrival of European draft animals, and it was fundamental to much colonial-era movement and place making. I think of colonial land grant ceremonies in which the judge and interested parties walked the boundaries of the property, pulling up grass and tossing stones in the air as they went, and the circumambulations and other religious processions that both marked the liturgical year and traced physical boundaries.

The experiences of sacred place and territory in New Spain seem to me to be less about fixed location than about circulation, dwelling, proximity, comings, and goings. A shrine implies territory, "a small sovereignty," wrote Jackson,[74] but that is sometimes true in more ways than I had imagined. Territory in devotional terms was rarely an unbroken, undifferentiated area, and, other than the shrine compound, it often had to be remade and re-marked through all the senses and kinesthetic experiences of encompassing, arriving, seeing, touching, hearing, smelling, tasting, speaking, and making music. In short, landscapes were restless.

Shrines also are located in space by proximate directions. Vistas (in Mesoamerica they were often marked by sacred mountains), entrances and exits, and routes of procession and circumambulation come to mind. Shrines often have prominent natural features nearby, but their boundaries are traced by human movement and perception that made them into devotional landscapes. This movement, again, usually was on foot—a slow, tactile experience of surroundings. Processions and journeys to a shrine by groups of devout visitors from a nearby community, often in the company of sacred images, were place making, inspiriting pedestrian activities that were repeated with some regularity. Within this kind of landscape the world could become ordered and complete, while what remained outside was unfinished, wild, and, in a sense, off the spiritual map.

My main leads into this more fluid, kinetic sense of place come from the importance of pedestrian travel in the history of New Spain and from a distinction made in seventeenth- and eighteenth-century Spanish sources that is muffled by the English word pilgrimage. Today the Spanish terms *peregrinación* and *romería* serve more or less interchangeably as equivalents of the English word pilgrimage, but they used to carry more distinct meanings. As early eighteenth-century Spanish savant and Benedictine monk Benito Jerónimo Feijóo explained, peregrinación meant what we would generally mean by the word pilgrimage—to leave one's land or region on a journey to a distant place of miraculous events and things, in search of transcendence. For Feijóo, the long, arduous, penitential journeys to Jerusalem, Rome, and Santiago de Compostela were model pilgrimages.[75] Romerías were sacred journeys, too, but to sites closer to home; they were more like an extended procession than a pilgrimage. If pilgrimage was an ideal and a compelling way to think about mundane and spiritual life, romería was the common practice. Romerías were not long journeys, but neither were they short parades around the church grounds. They were often journeys of a day or two, or prolonged processions, long in duration if not in distance, moving to the edges of homeland, marking a local landscape that centered on the shrine building and reached beyond it. The annual procession of parishioners of Nativitas on the south side of Mexico City with their cherished statue of Mary Immaculate every September, moving slowly, together, through the streets that trace the parish limits, is one example; delegations of villagers from the Valley of Toluca accompanying their saints on a two- or three-day journey on foot to the shrine of the Christ of Chalma for a special blessing is another.

At the close of Part I of Cervantes's *Don Quixote*, the good don once more detects a lady in distress when he happens upon a procession of white-clad penitents carrying a statue of the Virgin Mary draped in mourning to a hillside shrine to appeal for rain. Don Quixote had stumbled upon something characteristic, yet another kind of romería. Restless landscapes have New World and local features, but they are not uniquely American. As Eamon Duffy insists in a good-natured rant against the emphasis on long-distance pilgrimage and the attention lavished by English scholars on the voluble Margery Kempe, most sacred journeys in medieval and early modern Europe were little more than romerías.[76] Yet Duffy also recognizes that the idea of the great pilgrimage remained a compelling point of reference and that those who undertook such a journey were regarded with respect, even awe. In Mexico, the idea may have been compelling in the abstract, but practitioners, beyond the occasional hermit residing near a shrine, went largely unnoticed in the written record.

Conclusion

The flowering of guadalupanismo across classes and the Mexican landscape in the eighteenth century, then, leads back to many sacred places other than Mexico City and Tepeyac more than it undercut their importance.

Long-distance pilgrimages themselves were rare, in part because distant places were not imagined as more central than one's own, except for a particular purpose. While some shrines were better known and more visited than others, devotees did not act as if there were a hierarchy of shrines or a single dominant symbol. For example, the Indians of Huejutla on the edge of the Valley of Mexico preferred to go with their musicians to the district headtown of Texcoco to honor Our Lady of Guadalupe on December 12 in the 1770s rather than either making the day-long trek to Tepeyac or staying home and worshipping at the altar to Guadalupe in their village church.[77]

This lure of the local in Mexican guadalupanismo has not disappeared with the rise of Tepeyac as a great pilgrimage destination since the advent of rapid transit. In conversation with a Huichol man from the mountains of southwestern Zacatecas who had visited Tepeyac, historian Thomas Calvo recently brushed up against one of those transforming acts of possession in which distance and time collapse, and circulation of people and objects comes to rest in place, as it did for Tututepec's Guadalupe-in-the-flesh in 1769. Calvo writes,

> In one of my trips to Huichol communities, a man who had visited Mexico City and the shrine of Guadalupe showed me a *tuki* temple with its altar displaying votive offerings and other symbols, among them two pictures of the Virgin of Guadalupe. I made a point of asking my Huichol informant if that "Virgin" wasn't the famous "Mexican" one, since it was just like the one he had seen in Mexico City. To my insistent questions he replied without wavering that "No, the Virgin of Guadalupe is not Mexican, she is Huichol." I tried to make him see that it was a symbol taken from Mexico City, even if the Huicholes identify it with the goddess tanana. Finally he replied, "I have already told you that the Virgin of Guadalupe is ours, is Huichol; the vecinos [Mexicans] stole it from us some time ago."[78]

As the fame of Our Lady of Guadalupe reached into remote corners of the future Mexico, the image was on the way to becoming a dominant symbol. But it was a peculiar kind of dominant symbol, one that tended to reinforce the importance of many localities and many images more than ordering a vast spiritual geography. Territories of recognition and devotion were much larger than territories of sacred travel; as important as alms collectors, missionaries, pastoral visitors, and other official carriers may have been to the territorial reach of particular images and shrines, much of the dissemination occurred in secondary ways, from provincial places and unofficial sources rather than from the main shrine. The painstakingly executed eighteenth-century copies of Our Lady of Guadalupe were likely to take on lives of their own rather than propel the viewer to Tepeyac. To many Guadalupan devotees, Mary was as present in an admired copy or a found object that resembled the Virgin of Guadalupe[79] as she was in the matrix image.

This conception of immanence is more than a historical curiosity. It continues to be expressed now and far from home. In addition to the paintings and mechanical reproductions of the image that they own or visit, people find Mary-as-Guadalupe in the shadows cast on the bark of a tree in Watsonville, California; in a pool of spilled ice cream on a sidewalk in Houston, Texas; in a water stain on a bedroom wall in Holly, Colorado; on the glass sheathing of an office building in Clearwater, Florida; and on the back of a highway sign in Yakima, Washington. People go to these places "to be with her," they say. Even in our time, then, when Tepeyac has become the most visited of Catholic shrines, in one of the world's largest cities, it is not just a center and periphery story. It was even less so in the colonial period, when pious wayfarers sought less for individual salvation in faraway places than for divine presence and favor in the landscape of home.

5

Guadalupe, Remedios, and Cultural Politics of the Independence Period

DURING THE STRUGGLES OF THE INDEPENDENCE PERIOD ALL sides deployed an arsenal of metaphors, imperatives, and images borrowed from three centuries of Christian culture and political discourse. The image of Our Lady of Guadalupe had a special place in the sentiments of the time, associated especially with the quest for independence and justice in Mexico.[1] Father Hidalgo's Grito de Dolores appealed to Our Lady of Guadalupe as patroness and shield, and the image of Guadalupe became a popular insurgent logo, present in countersigns and battle cries as well as published propaganda and banners that expressed a more complex political theology.[2] In December 1810, the insurgent periodical *El despertador americano* resoundingly declared "We count on the avowed support of the Holy Mother of Guadalupe, Tutelary Spirit of this Empire, and sworn Captain of our Legions"[3]; and a few months later a startled royalist officer sent to suppress a rebellion at Tlalpuxajua brushed up against this claim to divine inspiration and protection when "a clamor of voices commenced, shouting 'now is the time, long live Our Lady of Guadalupe and death to all of them,' and at that moment a hail of rocks rained down upon us."[4] José María Morelos's personal devotion to Guadalupe, his use of the image as patroness and inspiration for the armed struggle—with image and nation virtually equated—became widely known as he led his forces into western and southern Mexico from 1811 to 1815.[5]

Since independence, la Guadalupana has come to be regarded as *the* Marian symbol of the insurgency, uniting creoles and Indians, rich and poor in common cause to forge the Mexican nation, in opposition to Our Lady of los Remedios and several other images that stood for Spanish and imperial rule on Mexican soil.[6] Mid-nineteenth-century Liberals like Ignacio Manuel Altamirano recognized the political culture of their Mexico in these terms even as they sought to separate religion from politics and reduce its popularity. Guadalupe, averred Altamirano, is the "symbol of the hopes of the nation."[7] Mexican heads of state have acknowledged the appeal of la Guadalupana ever since, and shown a personal attachment in some way. Agustín de Iturbide was the first, adopting Our Lady of Guadalupe and the eagle of Anáhuac as symbols of the nation, establishing the Order of Guadalupe as the most exalted recognition of Mexican patriotism, and calling upon royalists to beg her pardon for opposing the cause of independence.[8] His successors in the first Mexican republic proclaimed the December 12 feast of Our Lady of Guadalupe to be one of the three national religious holidays.[9] And this was just the beginning.

But was the image of the Virgin of Guadalupe the touchstone of insurgency and emergent nationalism? Did the popularity and political significance of her image change substantially during the struggle or as a result of the struggle? Was Our Lady of los Remedios regarded as a rival image at the time? Whose voices are we hearing? Do we exaggerate by placing these two images of the Blessed Mary near the center of partisan politics?[10]

Our Lady of Guadalupe's *Visita sin despedida*

The century leading up to the independence struggle was eventful, even momentous, for the cult of Our Lady of Guadalupe. And it was a time of almost unrelieved growth in popularity and institution building. The second third of the century, especially 1737–1754, was a watershed in this history, including official promotion of the image and shrine at Tepeyac as providential sign and patroness of the capital city and the whole viceroyalty, and papal recognition of the apparition miracles and the December 12 feast day with its own special rites in 1754. But the devotion was building in just about every way imaginable from the beginning of the century. In the process, Guadalupe's protection came to have new meanings that reached far beyond its traditional role dating from the early seventeenth century as the guardian against floods. A martial role was one of these added meanings for creole and *peninsular* patriots, as well as colonial officials. The eighteenth century witnessed a series of European wars with American theaters in which Guadalupe became a favorite line of defense. One of the inevitable enemies after 1740 was Protestant Great Britain, and Mary as Guadalupe became God's chosen captain and avenger. Preachers, colonial dignitaries, and the city fathers of the capital entrusted Guadalupe with defense of the Kingdom of New Spain and all the Spanish kingdoms during the War of Spanish Succession at the beginning of the century (1700–1713), during the War of Austrian Succession (1739–1746), during the Seven Years' War (1756–1763), and wars against Britain and France in the 1790s and first years of the nineteenth century.[11]

As the preceding essay, Chapter 4, suggested, guadalupanismo was both vigorously promoted and well received for the most part by laity in many parts of Mexico during the eighteenth century. Popular devotion could spill well beyond the bounds intended by the high clergy and government, but the devotion crossed lines of class, region, gender, and age like no other. A paradox in this history of Guadalupan devotion and promotion that complicates the main story of dramatic growth and bears on the meaning of guadalupanismo in the independence period is that while the devotion was spreading throughout the viceroyalty there was no corresponding movement of devout visitors to Tepeyac from distant places. The eighteenth-century urban shrines in diocesan capitals attest to the intention of building a network of shrines that at least symbolically converged at Tepeyac, but Our Lady of Guadalupe and Tepeyac did not predominate in this way. Hundreds of shrines attracted devotees from beyond the immediate vicinity. While the image of the Virgin of Guadalupe became the most widely known object of faith in New Spain by the late eighteenth century, there is little to suggest that the legendary site of the Virgin Mary's apparitions to Juan Diego was much more popular as a destination for sacred travel beyond its vicinity than were half a dozen shrines to other miraculous images, not to mention the hundreds of other shrines that were regarded as essential to the well-being of people living closer by. Little in the way of an interlocking system of pilgrimage routes developed (even with the advent of railroads in the late nineteenth century, when great streams of visitors began to travel there), and there were about as many shrines to miraculous images in Mexico in 1850 or 2000 as in 1700. This is not a history in which other shrines fell away in the face of irresistible attraction and relentless promotion of Our Lady of Guadalupe at Tepeyac.[12] Few devotees from distant places seem to have felt powerfully drawn to Tepeyac during the eighteenth century, as so many devotees do today.

The flowering of guadalupanismo in the eighteenth century, then, leads back to many sacred places other than Mexico City and Tepeyac more than it undercut their importance. Long-distance pilgrimages themselves were rare, in part because distant places were not imagined as more central than one's own, except for a particular purpose. While some shrines were better known and more visited than others, devotees did not act as if there was a hierarchy of shrines or a single dominant symbol. For the viceroyalty's cultural center, Mexico City, David Brading noticed a change in elite interest in Guadalupe during the second half of the eighteenth century—from "exultant confidence of the 1750s" to "audacious criticism." But Enlightenment skepticism had not simply replaced ardent devotion, belief in the apparitions and the miracle of her image on cloth, and prophetic expectation. The sermon by Mexican Jesuit Francisco Javier Carranza in 1748 predicting that Our Lady of Guadalupe would make New Spain the new land of Christian destiny at the end of the world reverberated into the independence period. It was remembered then especially by royalists, but was well suited to the new nationalism of the 1820s, too. The venerable Zúñiga y Ontiveros publishing house reprinted it in 1821 during the Iturbide regime.[13]

Given the successful promotion of the Virgin of Guadalupe as patroness and providential sign for New Spain after the papal recognition of 1754, and the wide appeal of the image in many parts of the viceroyalty by 1810, it is not surprising to find that she would come up often as advocate and defender during the years of armed struggle—by insurgents, royalists, and bystanders alike. Whether this devotion moved many people to rise up in arms is a different matter. Recent scholarship suggests that appeals to Guadalupe had little to do with inciting rural people or anyone else to rebel.[14] How rural people responded to calls to arms invoking the name and protection of Guadalupe requires more study in many places. Perhaps the tipping point for some of the many early insurgents in the Bajío or San Luis Potosí and Zacatecas connected faith in Guadalupe to their sense of outrage against the political and social order as they knew it. And the Zacualtipan district of the Sierra de Meztitlán, Hidalgo, did become a pocket of Indian rebellions during the insurgency that consciously invoked "the law of Our

Lady of Guadalupe."[15] But the Sierra de Meztitlán was an unusual place, home to a rare millenarian movement in 1769 that claimed Guadalupe's presence and patronage. It is one of the few places in rural Mexico during the early nineteenth century where politics and faith coalesced so specifically, where a call to action in the name of Guadalupe was understood as more than an appeal for protection. The strength of localized meanings of devotion to the image of Guadalupe in the eighteenth century would have made the appeal of a call to arms in her name by outsiders less than automatic in provincial towns and rural areas. Campesinos might join, but their reasons for doing so were more complex.

And royalists were not about to allow the Virgin of Guadalupe and declarations of faith to be monopolized for political purposes by their insurgent adversaries. On the contrary, royalists declared insurgents to be traitors to God and religion, as well as the patria.[16] The connection between royalists and Guadalupe often is left out of histories of the independence period and deserves a little elaboration here for that reason. The first, and lasting, response of royalists to insurgent appeals to Guadalupe was a combination of indignation and the customary call to unity of all the subjects of the Spanish crown under her sign, which colonial leaders had actively promoted since 1754. For example, a viceregal decree of September 28, 1810, denouncing the insurgents for claiming the protection of la Guadalupana was quickly followed by Agustín Pomposo de San Salvador's royalist tract *Memoria cristiano-política sobre lo mucho que la Nueva España debe temer de su disunion en partidos, y las grandes ventaja que puede esperar de su unión y confraternidad*, which warned against the dangers of disunion and rebellion. Invoking Guadalupe as "tender Mother of Americans" (*Madre tierna de los Americanos*), Remedios as "this prodigious simulacrum of the Mother of God" (*este otro prodigioso simulacro de la Madre de Dios*), and the Cristo Renovado de Santa Teresa as "that other most loving and consoling wonder" (*ese otro amorísimo y consolante portento*), Pomposo de San Salvador called for social and political solidarity among all good Catholic subjects of the Spanish king's New Spain—"we are all children of Jesus and Mary.... We are united indissolubly either as relatives or as cobeneficiaries."[17]

Some famously sacrilegious acts against prints of Our Lady of Guadalupe by royalist soldiers have been regarded as evidence of royalist opposition to Guadalupe, if not contempt for devotion to her. At least one case of royalists shooting an image of Guadalupe was reported, and, most notoriously, Mariano Matamoros supposedly joined José María Morelos in the struggle against Spanish rule when he learned from his housekeeper that a royalist soldier stationed in his parish had used a print of Our Lady of Guadalupe as toilet paper.[18] Given the abundant evidence of royalist invocations of Guadalupe as their patroness, royalist propagandists' appeals for unity of all the king's subjects under her protective cloak, and their indignation over insurgent appropriation of the image, a more plausible reading of these scandalous acts would seem to be that the royalists were taunting their enemies with evidence that the Virgin of Guadalupe would not come to their aid even if provoked in these outrageous ways. Still, the lack of evidence of similar provocations by insurgents who raised the standard of Guadalupe suggests that guadalupanismo was closer to the core of how they identified themselves.

Royalist Mexico City retained control over the shrines and images of Guadalupe and Remedios throughout the independence period, which gave the city's leaders and populace direct access to these holy places and divine images. Both were used to stage the customary celebrations on feast days and to fuel their providentialist propaganda. But the expected sharp lines of loyalty and affiliation pitting royalist Spaniards against Indians and patriotic creoles blur on closer inspection—the political uncertainties and dangers did not rally all royalists or insurgents to common cause under the sign of Guadalupe. The same old tensions continued among church administrators, and between civil officials and priests at the shrine. For example, in 1814 the abbot at Tepeyac lodged a judicial complaint against the priest responsible for collecting alms for the shrine of Guadalupe, accusing him of keeping inadequate records and skimming money from the collection boxes,[19] and the next year the royalist *subdelegado* and commander of San Cristóbal Ecatepec complained that the abbot was not showing him and royal authority proper respect.[20]

Another line of cultural division and alliance that blurs on closer inspection is the idea that Indian villagers usually sided with insurgents rather than royalists thanks to their attachment to the Virgin of Guadalupe. Royalist propagandists and cultural leaders certainly made direct appeals to Indian devotion to Guadalupe and through her to solidarity with the royalist cause. A play written by José de la Cruz in 1816 for the annual December 12 fiesta can serve as an example. Four characters have speaking parts: the Virgin, Juan Diego, the archbishop, and the archbishop's porter. The play highlights Juan Diego being rebuffed at the archbishop's palace (including brusque treatment of him by the porter), then winning everyone over with his steadfast faith and the image that mysteriously appeared on his cloak. In two of her utterances, the Virgin says "Indians, I wish to live in your company" (de los indios quiero vivir en compañía vuestra) and "I come looking for the Indians, and I wish to remain among them until I ascend with them all to my rightful place in my Celestial Court" (a buscar vengo a los yndios y quiero quedar entre ellos hasta que con todos suba a aquel mi devido asiento de mi Corte Celestial).[21] Did the propagandists succeed in such appeals to Indians? Again, the question has to be answered locally before it can be answered generally. Indians—presumably from in and near the Valley of Mexico—continued to visit Tepeyac under royalist control during the years of insurgency, whether or not they were committed to the royalist cause. In the 1814 dispute over alms collection, the abbot of the shrine admitted that collections were rising not because the collector was turning over more alms from his collection tours, but because many Indians came for the *fiesta general de yndios* and left a few coins behind.[22] And Indians at Zacapoaxtla, Puebla, who rallied to the royalist cause in 1810–1811, attributed their successes to the Virgin of Guadalupe.[23]

In sum, the Virgin of Guadalupe was a shared symbol, widely known and much revered before and during the independence wars, but not yet tied to the same nationalizing purposes, with the same meaning; not yet "the temple of the national religion."[24] The image was revered in many copies throughout Mexico in the early nineteenth century, and the story of Mary's apparitions to Juan Diego enjoyed increasing fame, but local meanings of the image often spilled beyond the reach of official interpreters and promoters in Mexico City and the other cathedral cities. Most devotees had never been to Tepeyac; and where Guadalupe became a popular devotion, local meanings had more to do with Mary's presence and favor through a copy close at hand than with the mystique of Tepeyac or the authority of a published text like Miguel Sánchez's *Imagen de la Virgin María* or Francisco de Florencia's *La estrella del norte de México*.[25] Those meanings sometimes were openly localocentric, as in San Mateo Atenco in 1728 and the Sierra de Meztitlán in 1769. And distinct, local meanings lived on, well beyond the independence struggles. They still do.

Nonetheless, guadalupanismo was deeply intertwined with the political crises of the early nineteenth century. Some changes in the nature and popularity of the devotion that were evident in the late eighteenth century intensified, were redirected, or took on new political significance after 1808 and 1810, with new participants, in new ceremonial and martial circumstances, with a sense of the *"nación"* as embodied by the people, not just the monarch. In a written *"demostración de fidelidad"* (show of loyalty) of July 1808 in support of the absent young monarch Fernando VII and resistance to the French invasion of Spain, the city council of Campeche proclaimed that "the nación [in which the Spanish 'kingdoms' were united] must be free and independent" (*la nación ha de ser libre e independiente*).[26] To other town councils of the future Mexico in 1808 this independent nación or patria was expressed in the defense of "our sacred religion" (*nuestra sagrada religión*), above all. In elaborating on this militant coupling of religion and patria, the thoughts of the city fathers of Sombrerete and Tlaxcala in 1808 turned to the Virgin of Guadalupe, "that divine simulacrum" (*ese divino simulacro*), "universal patroness of America" (*la universal patrona de la América*).[27] Who the people of the patria might be was deeply confused by the partisan struggles of the war, but it became clear that this patria was no longer simply the transatlantic Spanish "nación." In the crucible of war and the enshrining of Miguel Hidalgo and José María Morelos as fathers of a new patria during the 1820s, possibilities for shared identity through Guadalupe that had been latent or broadcast from viceregal offices and cathedral towers, became part of the new politics of the church, liberalism, and republican institutions. In the era of weak, unstable central governments that followed, the results of the new politics reinforced locality more than nationality, but the ongoing counterpoints among locality, province, and nationality would make Guadalupe a universal emblem of Mexicanness, however variously and incompletely.

Nuestra Señora de los Remedios: Another Face of the Blessed Virgin in Wartime

In independence-period lore, Nuestra Señora de los Remedios has become the Spaniards' Virgin, the politicized patroness of royalists in their struggles against Guadalupan insurgents.[28] There is a kernel of truth in this, but like most kernels of truth, it is also a source of misunderstanding. The misunderstanding here stems from treating the independence struggle from the vantage point of Mexico City sources when much of the action occurred elsewhere, and from dichotomizing lines of division and affiliation that in practice blurred and separated more than they converged or collided as an opposing pair.

Remedios and Guadalupe, the two most important sites of Marian devotion in the Valley of Mexico, were often mentioned in the same breath and revered by many of the same colonial sponsors, public figures, and authors during the seventeenth and eighteenth centuries. And their benefactions were understood in complementary ways, especially when it came to that fickle necessity, water. Our Lady of los Remedios was the special advocate in times of drought; Our Lady of Guadalupe became the special advocate in times of flood, most famously in the prolonged flood of 1629–1634 when the image made its only recorded trip beyond the sanctuary precinct, to take up residence in the cathedral until the waters receded.

Yet there were striking differences, especially in the popularity and reach of the two shrines during the eighteenth century. Whereas Guadalupe was regarded as an image of supernatural origin associated with apparitions and special favor to Indians, copied and revered in different ways in many places, several distinct images of Nuestra Señora de los Remedios were celebrated in regional pockets. In addition to the statuette we think of as the royalists' Virgin, with its shrine on the hill of Totoltepec near Naucalpan in the Valley of Mexico, other images known as Nuestra Señora de los Remedios had their own shrines elsewhere, including Cholula (Puebla) and Zitácuaro (Michoacán). These different images and cultos of Nuestra Señora de los Remedios—a devotion that was so familiar in the spiritual landscape of Spain during the fifteenth and sixteenth centuries—were introduced into New Spain by early colonists. Devotion to Our Lady of Guadalupe had a regional concentration in and near the Valley of Mexico, too, but by the eighteenth century it also had a far-reaching and diverse following thanks to a concerted promotional campaign and the many copies that were revered in shrines, chapels, altars, and homes throughout much of the viceroyalty. Devotion to the best-known images of Remedios was more confined geographically. This was true of the Remedios shrine at Totoltepec, with its strong Mexico City association.

The link between the Totoltepec Remedios and Mexico City was shaped by the city government's right of patronato over the shrine. This circumstance of an urban corporation, rather than the crown and its highest colonial officials, exercising patronato powers dated from a royal concession in 1574. In exchange for the privilege of appointing the chaplains, overseeing shrine affairs, and exercising some authority over uses of the image, the city council (*ayuntamiento*) agreed to underwrite the cost of construction and maintenance of a new and larger chapel on the site, and otherwise promote the devotion. Serving also as officers of the culto's *archicofradía*, the alcaldes and *regidores* of the ayuntamiento promoted the image's reputation for providential protection of the city by sponsoring the annual fiesta at the shrine and periodic *"venidas"*—visits to the cathedral— for novenas of prayer and thanksgiving. Transporting a famously miraculous image—rather than a surrogate "peregrina" or traveling copy—from its shrine was unusual, and the practice continued for nearly three hundred years in the case of the Totoltepec Remedios.[29] First undertaken during the catastrophic epidemic of 1576, these venidas, as well as the romerías (processions of the faithful from nearby communities) of devotees and annual fiestas at the shrine, marked the rhythm of devotion to Remedios in the Valley of Mexico into the mid-nineteenth century.

But the festive venidas were more than just a regular feature of the longstanding association of the image with the city. They punctuated an erratic history of intense politicking, divided loyalties, and changing fortunes for the shrine and the devotion. For more than a century after 1574, the venidas were infrequent and reserved for local crises, especially droughts that threatened widespread famine and illness. Few venidas then did not mean the shrine enjoyed little fame or wealth; just the opposite. A petition to the ayuntamiento in 1621 claimed that "one finds in this shrine more devotion and feeling than in any other,"[30] and early inventories and descriptions recorded an impressive store of large silver lamps and other treasure.[31] Indeed, absence was understood to make the heart grow even fonder. After describing the solemn pageantry and benefits of the third venida in 1616, in which many Indians and more than a thousand Spaniards joined the solemn procession in Mexico City and some forty thousand people accompanied the image on its return to the shrine, Remedios's first chronicler, Luis de Cisneros, warned in 1621 that frequent visits to the city could undercut the devotion.[32]

By 1685 there had been only twelve venidas—roughly one every nine years—and they were limited to the period of a novena of Masses and prayers in the cathedral. The following forty-four years witnessed eleven more venidas (one every four years), and by the late eighteenth century Remedios was being brought to the city nearly every year, sometimes several times a year.[33] But there were also two decades of few venidas in the eighteenth century, from 1738 to the late 1750s, when Our Lady of Guadalupe was actively promoted in and beyond its locality, at the expense of other miraculous images in the city and Valley of Mexico. In retrospect, those years marked the onset of a more contested spiritual geography for Remedios. They also marked the first time that expenses outstripped revenues over more than a few years. Revenues increased again by the late 1750s, thanks mainly to a renewed enchantment with Remedios in Mexico City that was both popular and actively encouraged by viceregal officials, the city fathers, and peninsular merchants.[34] But even with a return to a favorable balance sheet, the shrine and culto of Remedios were never the same. The santuario and outbuildings were often described from the 1760s to the 1820s as "in a deplorable state." Major maintenance and most building projects were deferred in order to reduce expenses, leaving shrine administrators to respond to one emergency repair after another. Neglect during the 1810s and 1820s was especially hard on the physical plant.[35]

The year 1685 marked more than the beginning of frequent visits to the city. For several decades thereafter the culto generated more income, accumulated more wealth, and enjoyed more active promotion than ever before. Arguably, this was the devotion's golden age.[36] The timing was not accidental. It followed in the wake of a protracted challenge to the ayuntamiento's patronato privilege by the archbishop-viceroy. From 1671 to 1684 Archbishop-Viceroy Payo Enríquez de Rivera laid claim to the privileges of the patronato at the shrine, insisting on his right to appoint the chaplain and to make official inspections, sending the archdiocese's chief judge and administrator (*provisor*) to inventory and evaluate the shrine's possessions. During those years of dispute, the physical plant deteriorated and Enríquez de Rivera denied the ayuntamiento permission to bring the image to the city. Eventually, in 1683, the crown reconfirmed the ayuntamiento's patronato rights, and chronicler Antonio Robles recorded the last formality on May 29, 1684: "the city [fathers] went out in carriages to take possession of the shrine of Our Lady of los Remedios."[37] This unsuccessful attempt by the viceroy-archbishop to wrest administrative authority over the shrine and image from the city government followed many years of other challenges by rivals. The alcalde mayor of Tacuba, in whose district the shrine was located, claimed jurisdiction at one point in the seventeenth century, and private landowners in the district lobbied for venidas at their convenience.[38] At intervals, Franciscans, Mercedarians, Dominicans, and Augustinians expressed interest in serving at the shrine, which would have undermined the city's administrative control. All were firmly rebuffed by the ayuntamiento,[39] but the high politics of the venidas continued in the eighteenth century, with viceroys, archbishops, and peninsular merchants often taking the initiative and the ayuntamiento officers following their lead and covering costs.

The venidas became longer in the eighteenth century, as well as more frequent, sometimes because the shrine was in disrepair, but more often for reasons of state or because various urban devotees clamored for an extended visit. The customary nine-day visit was first broken in 1685. After the image arrived on May 2 that year, the viceroy called for it to remain in the city through the Corpus Christi feast, and it was returned to the shrine only on July 7. During the intervening two months, various nunneries were allowed to take the statue to their churches for a few days. In subsequent venidas, convents also appealed to the authorities to let the image stay with them for a *triduo* or three-day round of prayers, and this became a common practice. From the second half of the seventeenth century several viceroys and their wives took the lead in promoting the culto and extending the venidas.[40] Apparently because Viceroy Conde de Galve and his wife were ardent devotees, when the image was transferred to Mexico City for a novena in May 1692 to appeal for rain, it stayed until 1695.[41] Another venida of about two months occurred in 1696, with the image arriving on August 29 for prayers for the safe return of the fleet to Spain and staying on for another novena beginning on November 9 for the well-being of the monarchy (*por los buenos sucesos de la monarquía*).[42] The image was back in the city for a year and a half in 1713–1714, and was not returned promptly after novena visits in 1716, 1718, and 1719 on the grounds that the fleet had not yet returned safely to Spain or the Manila Galleon had not yet reached Acapulco.[43] In January 1737 the image was brought to the city to ward off a worsening epidemic and did not return to the shrine until long after the contagion ended in order to satisfy the viceroy's desire for a special appeal to Mary for safe passage of the fleet back to Spain.[44] At other times, viceroys vetoed the ayuntamiento's or archbishop's proposal to bring the image to the city, usually on the grounds that the danger was not yet serious enough.[45] Some very long absences from the shrine followed: first, during most of the 1740s while Spain was drawn into the War of Austrian Succession[46]; then during the independence period, from late 1810 to 1821. Before the city's trusteeship expired with the formal separation of church and state during the Reforma and the República Restaurada, the image was long absent from the shrine once more, from 1844 to 1856.

The official reasons for bringing the image to Mexico City changed with the new patterns of frequency and duration. Appeals for the rainy season to begin and stave off impending drought and disease (and by analogy the sickness of the soul) were always a leitmotif of the venidas; but defending the empire in dangerous times became important from the 1690s, centering on the monarchy and the prolonged European wars that drew in Spain and America, including the War of Spanish Succession (1701–1713), the War of Austrian Succession (1739–1748), the Seven Years' war (1756–1763), and the fitful battles among France, Spain, and Britain during the 1790s and 1800s.[47] Increasingly, venidas were undertaken for the health of the king or queen, the birth of a prince, to beseech or thank the Virgin for victory on the battlefields of Europe, to celebrate a treaty, or to appeal for safe passage of the ships crossing the Atlantic with trade goods and royal treasure.

The Virgin Mary's martial side—for Remedios, but also for Guadalupe—became evident long before the War of Independence, especially during the great European wars that drew in Spain and America, and Remedios's reputation as "La Conquistadora," the image that protected the Spanish survivors of the Noche Triste, received new emphasis. During the War of Spanish Succession, sermonizers invoked both Remedios and Guadalupe as military commanders. For example, Bartolomé Navarro de San Antonio, O.P., referred to the Virgin of Guadalupe as La Capitana in his sermon for the novena in 1702, while fellow sermonizers began to refer to Remedios as La Generala, as well as La Conquistadora and La Capitana. In his 1728 sermon of thanks to Remedios for the safe passage of the fleet to Spain, Juan Domingo de Leoz spoke of her as the "Real Capitana," and added that she was "so loving toward the crown of Spain and the Spaniards."[48] Remedios's unofficial fame in Mexico City as La Generala was given a boost by the Napoleonic invasion of Spain in 1808. Carlos María Bustamante's booklet about devotions to Remedios published at the end of a three-month venida from May 13 to August 10, 1810, describes how, when the image was taken to the convent of San Gerónimo, the nuns adorned it with "a general's sash and staff of office, and the Child with a saber."[49] Better known as an ardent guadalupano, Bustamante here called upon the ayuntamiento, as patron of the shrine, to "apply all of your influence and support so that Our Lady of los Remedios may be declared Commanding General of all our armies and civilian corps."[50]

The frequent and prolonged absences of the image from the shrine during the late colonial period brought to the surface a mounting tension that was built into the spiritual geography of the culto from the time of the patronato concession in 1574. The counterpoint of a beloved image shared by a rural shrine with its regional, mainly Indian constituency, and the capital city with a large, diverse constituency and active promoters among colonial authorities at the highest levels worked quite smoothly for many years, as long as the venidas were not too frequent and the image was returned after the customary novena. Popular enthusiasm in the city intensified during those visits, drawing tens of thousands of people into the streets and the cathedral's aisles for processions, Masses, and prayers, generating thousands of pesos in revenue from donations and sales of medals, *medidas*, prints, scapularies, and other sacred memorabilia. The overhead costs for a short visit were comparatively modest and there were corporate sponsors for the liturgical events, so a good portion of the proceeds—sometimes 30 or 40 percent—went directly to the archicofradía to support the culto and improvements at the shrine.[51] And the shrine was not without its sacred image for long, so the rhythm of devotions, fiestas, visitors, and collections there went on with little interruption.

But when the image was absent often or for months and years at a time, the balance that kept the revenues flowing and expenses in check in the city and at the shrine was disturbed. Long visits to Mexico City may have pleased viceroys, nuns, and peninsular merchants, but they strained the finances of the culto in the city and contributed to the deterioration of the shrine. The intensity of popular enthusiasm in the city for the Virgin's presence waned during the longer visits, and the donations and sales tapered off. Yet certain fixed expenses for the image to remain in Mexico City continued. The revenues from venidas literally went up in smoke. The cost of wax for candles to keep the image properly illuminated could be staggering. During the first six years of the image's extended stay in the 1740s, the cost of candle wax paid by the archicofradía was 16,761 pesos five reales, exceeding all revenues by nearly three thousand pesos.[52] As early as 1743, the ayuntamiento resolved to consult the viceroy about returning the image to the shrine, "in light of the long time absent and the shrine lacking its alms and the disappointment of those who go there on pilgrimages."[53] There were immediate consequences of extended venidas for the shrine, too. Without the image, the annual fiestas at Totoltepec attracted smaller crowds, fewer romerías arrived at other times, alms declined sharply, and major repairs were neglected. The long absences were beginning to look like furta sacra (holy theft) to rural devotees. The image was less and less available to them at the shrine.

The old devotional and political counterpoints were turning into double polarities of city and shrine, and governing officials and "la gente" that verged on estrangement by 1810, with the ayuntamiento caught in the middle. When thirty lancers were sent by the viceroy to escort the image to Mexico City for safekeeping on the morning of October 30, 1810, Indians of Naucalpan, Tacuba, and other nearby pueblos wept and spread the word that they were being robbed. According to the royalist propagandist and doctor of theology Juan Bautista Díaz Calvillo, a crowd of local people converged on Naucalpan, released the mules pulling the carriage, and could not be dissuaded from pushing it back toward the shrine. Only when Doña Josefa Montes de Oca of Naucalpan, a local benefactor of the shrine, showed the Indian leaders a paper signed by two priests and the senior councilman of the city promising to return the image "shortly" (*después de poco tiempo*) did they relent.[54] An empty promise, as it happened.

After independence, the estrangement became profound. In the 1830 venida residents of communities near the shrine reportedly created a "disturbance" (*desorden*) when the image was removed from the shrine, wailing over its departure, and clamoring to kiss it and touch their rosaries to it. According to Mexico City authorities this was the third year in a row of such disturbances. Their solution was to send an armed escort "to contain the riots of the people."[55] Appeals, complaints, and disturbances over venidas punctuated the 1840s. In 1840 the *regente* (mayor) of the city, with the consent of the ayuntamiento, undertook a secret "transfer" (*traslación*) in order to prevent a "rebuff" (*desaire*) that, instead, elicited an immediate and urgent chorus of appeals from Naucalpan and its pueblos for the return of the image.[56] Their fears that it might never return were not unfounded, given the growing perception in the city that the image belonged there. On July 26, 1843, the ayuntamiento voted to allow the image to be taken to the shrine for a novena, as if the old relationship between city and shrine had been reversed.[57] After the novena was over and the image was taken back to Mexico City, people living near the shrine sent an emotional letter to the regente in which they decried the "collapse of the culto at her Holy Temple" (*pérdida del culto de su Santo Templo*) and their impoverishment. They were worried that no date had been set for return of the image and asked for its immediate return. Thirty local men signed the petition, including the local pastor, Primo Sánchez.[58] Then in August 1845 residents of the shrine pleaded for the return of the image after it made the rounds of the convents that customarily hosted it following a novena in the cathedral. The ayuntamiento demurred, saying that the image could not be returned until repairs had been made to the shrine's altar and difficulties with the foreign war were resolved, noting that there "countless petitions from citizens of the capital" for Our Lady of los Remedios to remain in the city.[59] And in June 1852 thirty-nine "residents of the shrine" (most of them "principal residents" of Naucalpan) sent another petition lamenting the effects of the loss of the image, including decline of pious customs and people leaving the area.[60] Only when the image was returned to the shrine for good in the 1860s did these laments and "*alborotos*" (uprisings) end.

During the independence period, Our Lady of los Remedios was less *the* royalist, *gachupín* Virgin than might be supposed, even in Mexico City.[61] Royalist partisans were as likely to invoke Our Lady of Guadalupe or a renowned regional avatar of Mary such as Our Lady of El Pueblito or Our Lady of Guanajuato as they were to call upon Remedios.[62] Even Díaz Calvillo's 1812 text, "Noticias para la historia de Nuestra Señora de los Remedios desde el año de 1808," which is often cited for the providentialist association of royalists and Remedios in the war, claimed that "Mary freed us," not any particular advocation of Mary. And nowhere in his lengthy "Noticias" does he pose a rivalry between Remedios and Guadalupe.[63] Viceroy Francisco Xavier Venegas apparently was of two minds about featuring the Virgin of los Remedios in the royalist cause: placing his staff of office at the feet of the Virgin of Remedios on October 31, 1810,[64] but declining to formally declare her General of the royalist troops. On the other hand, some wealthy peninsulares in the city did lobby for Remedios to be recognized as the special patroness of the royalist cause, linking this image back to the origin story recounted by Luis de Cisneros in 1621 and Spain's conquest of Mexico in the sixteenth century.

The most public and persistent promoter of Remedios as warrior-patroness of the royalists was doña Ana María de Yraeta, widow of don Cosmé de Mier y Trespalacios, the former regent of the Audiencia de México. Early in 1811, following a great procession on February 21 in which the city's militia forces and royalist troops "by superior order paid this holy Image the military honors corresponding to the rank of Captain General,"[65] she urged the ayuntamiento to support her two-fold petition to the viceroy that (1) October 30 be declared a perpetual holiday to memorialize the victory at Monte de las Cruces and the royalist soldiers who died there, and (2) that Nuestra Señora de los Remedios be officially proclaimed la Generala. The ayuntamiento respectfully declined to sponsor her petition on the grounds that an assembly of generals would need to be consulted about whether such a designation was advisable, and that a consultation of this kind would have to wait for an interlude of peace.⁶⁶ After Yraeta objected to the ayuntamiento's tepid response, the city fathers forwarded her petition to the viceroy without their endorsement. The matter apparently rested there. Yraeta renewed her proposal to name Nuestra Señora de los Remedios Generala de las Armas in 1817, this time with the support of the Jeronymites in Mexico City and an old ally, Dr. Agustín Pomposo Fernández. She built her case around the claim that the victory over Hidalgo at Monte de las Cruces resulted from divine intervention by Nuestra Señora de los Remedios when the image reentered Mexico City for safekeeping on the very day of the victory, October 30, 1810. This time the ayuntamiento was supportive, submitting her thick dossier of supporting materials to the viceroy with its endorsement. The viceroy's chief legal adviser was skeptical. After reviewing the proposal in January 1818, he declared his personal devotion to Remedios, but concluded that while Hidalgo's retreat in 1810 was a wonderful event, it was not a miracle. His ecclesiastical advisers, Dr. Fr. Luis Carrasco, O.P., and Mercedarian Fr. Manuel Mercadillo, concurred, observing that the Virgin Mary in different guises protected Mexico City in all directions, not just as Nuestra Señora de los Remedios.⁶⁷

That Ana María de Yraeta, a leading peninsular devotee in Mexico City as early as 1806 and enthusiastic royalist promoter of the devotion during the war,⁶⁸ remained a prominent sponsor of the culto in 1822 points to complexities in the devotion to Remedios and the narrow scope of political and social transformation in Mexico City in the immediate aftermath of the independence wars.⁶⁹ Remedios had not suddenly become a pariah, the defeated Virgin. She still had her devotees in the city, including the remaining peninsulares and ayuntamiento officials who had been her most conspicuous sponsors before and during the war, and in the villages and towns near her shrine in the northwestern portion of the valley. The venidas to the city continued every year but one between 1821 and 1835.⁷⁰

In retrospect, however, independence marked a watershed for the shrine and the place of the Virgin of los Remedios in Mexican history and culture. From 1821 to 1867 the shrine suffered declining revenues, deferred maintenance, haphazard administration, and, ultimately, a long, slow decline of *capitalino* interest in the image and shrine. The ayuntamiento officers who directed the archicofradía were less active as a group during the

1820s, 1830s, and 1840s—perhaps a sign of declining public interest and certainly related to their own preoccupations with the unsettling political events swirling about them. Their meetings to deliberate on shrine matters became infrequent and often failed to muster a quorum of members.[71] And with the expulsion of Spaniards in 1828 the culto required an ideological makeover. In 1829 the ayuntamiento instructed the chaplain to secretly destroy any remaining prints that hinted at Remedios's earlier fame as a Spanish *conquistadora*, including prints of Hernán Cortés and Spanish nobles kneeling before the image. Remedios was repackaged then as the "celestial watchtower of the Mexicans" in a little publication called "Salutación a la Virgen de los Remedios," printed for the venida that year.[72]

There were short periods of renewed sponsorship and repairs, especially in the early 1830s, but the end of the city government's patronato authority at the beginning of the República Restaurada in 1867 was the final blow more than a sudden transformation. To answer the Who are we/Who are they questions, nationalism calls for heroes and anti-heroes. As the unwanted reputation as Royalist Virgin clung to Our Lady of los Remedios and the culto receded from Mexico City after independence (despite the efforts of some dedicated and wealthy devotees in the capital), the villagers and small-town *vecinos* of the northeast fringe of the Valley of Mexico and neighboring districts sought to reclaim their cherished image of the Virgin Mary. Even as the buildings at the shrine deteriorated, revenues declined, and robberies of silverware and jewels were reported, they guarded the possessions of the shrine as best they could. And the shrine and image continued to attract devotees from surrounding pueblos in the Valley and nearby states. Some three thousand to four thousand people from close to fifty pueblos reportedly attended the annual feast day celebrations in 1843.[73] Only in the late nineteenth century was the shrine virtually stripped of its wealth by self-serving administrators.[74]

The culto of Nuestra Señora de los Remedios of Totoltepec and Mexico City was always more than a political symbol, but it made two turns during the eighteenth and early nineteenth centuries that drew it more directly into the high politics of the time. Like other colonial shrines, its reach was primarily local and regional, but the association with the capital city and its ayuntamiento placed it in an unusual position, with other possibilities. First, it was lifted onto the stage of imperial politics as a martial figure, guardian against the empire's international enemies, first during the War of Spanish Succession, and especially during the Napoleonic invasion after 1808. Then during the independence struggles it was enlisted by royalist leaders in the capital as a heavenly patron, among others, against the new political enemies within. It was still essentially a local devotion, but now with partisan more than universal associations that would threaten the bond with the city when efforts at nation building by Mexican-born elites moved decisively in 1828 to exclude Spaniards from the country's future. The story of contraction of the Remedios culto after independence was part of the stormy political history of the time, in which the political elite of Mexico City became less interested in the shrine, but this decline was not the product of secularized culture and disenchantment. The towns and villages in and near the district of Naucalpan remained ardently loyal to Our Lady of los Remedios although they and more distant devotees always had other favorite providential images that also were vital to their personal and collective well-being.

Conclusion

Three months after Father Hidalgo's Grito, the royalist vicar of Tamasulapan in the Mixteca Alta of northern Oaxaca staged a spectacle featuring the Virgin of Guadalupe that was laced with political symbols of solidarity and defense of the patria.[75] Learning on December 24 that emissaries from Mexico City were about to arrive with ceremonial lances from Viceroy Venegas in honor of twelve nearby Indian parishes for their "patriotism, loyalty, and obedience," the local pastor immediately sent word to the district governor (*subdelegado*) of Teposcolula asking him to invite leaders in the parish seats and villages of the district to attend the presentation ceremony he would host on December 27. Early on the 27th the lances and a portrait of Fernando VII were taken to a chapel on the outskirts of town where the parish's copy of Our Lady of Guadalupe had been placed the day before. Shortly after sunrise, to the tolling of church bells, the subdelegado, priests from neighboring parishes, Indian governors, "other distinguished residents," local militia troops, and a crowd of spectators assembled at the parish church and walked nearly a kilometer to the chapel where the lances and paintings were displayed next to the altar. Inside the chapel the dignitaries took their seats and the emissaries, holding the lances, stood in front by the king's portrait. Slowly and clearly, the pastor read aloud both the letter the Indians of the twelve parishes had sent to the viceroy on November 29 with their donations in support of the royalist cause and the viceroy's reply. Then he congratulated the parishioners on the high honor bestowed by the viceroy for their loyalty and patriotism and instructed them to keep their commemorative lances safe as further inspiration to defend "our sacred religion, the rights of our Catholic monarch, and those of the fatherland without allowing in seductive enemies of God and humanity" and to obey "the legitimate powers."[76]

After the subdelegado presented the lances to the Indian governors, the assembled dignitaries processed back to the parish church in a line that stretched for nearly two blocks in a noisy display of hierarchical order and discipline led by the cross and the providential couple—the king and the Virgin. Bearers of the parish cross led the way, followed "at a fitting distance" by the portrait of the king, accompanied by a group of musicians; then "at a suitable distance" came the image of Our Lady of Guadalupe on the shoulders of several Indians, with an honor guard of four soldiers and others carrying the lances; then the pastor of Tecomatlan in full regalia, assisted by the pastor of Chalcatongo and a curate of Tamasulapa; then the subdelegado accompanied by distinguished citizens, including Indian governors and alcaldes; and, finally, the militia troops and more musicians. As the portraits of Fernando VII and Our Lady of Guadalupe left the chapel, rockets were launched and guns fired. Church bells rang and more rockets resounded as the procession entered the parish church, where the paintings were placed on either side of the altar and the subdelegado, priests, and Indian governors took their seats in the place of honor. The pastor of Tecomatlán celebrated a high Mass, and another Mass followed for the troops and spectators who were waiting outside. After these ceremonies, the troops reformed under their captain in the atrium of the church and marched with the lances and the portrait of Fernando VII to the town offices as the crowd trailed along. The portrait was set up with the lances on either side and remained there under guard all day, punctuated by "cheers directed to our religion, the purity of most holy Mary, our Catholic sovereign, the government, the patria, the legitimate authorities," and "to the peace and union among all communities."[77] The troops shot off their firearms and more rockets in the patio of the town offices as a final salute. Tchaikovsky would have enjoyed this solemn New World thunder.

"To our religion, the purity of Most Holy Mary, our Catholic sovereign, the government, the patria, the legitimate authorities," and "to the peace and union among all communities." Except for toasting the king, here was a litany of values widely shared across firing lines of the independence struggles. This was a war widely understood to protect religion, control territory, and settle scores, not to secularize society or separate church from state. But who were the true "seductive enemies of God and humanity"? Answers varied in ways that separated Catholic from Catholic and region from region more than the godless from the God-fearing. While images of the Virgin were adorned with swords and proclaimed generals, issues of church and religion were dividing as much as unifying Mexican society in spite of the deep reservoir of popular piety and growing deployment of the Virgin of Guadalupe across classes and communities.

Political theater of the kind practiced in Tamasulapa in 1810—calling on remote communities to recognize their place in a greater polity, whether of empire, nation, or province—played out with new and partisan vigor in the years beginning with the Napoleonic invasion of Spain in 1808. After September 1810 similar ceremonies would have been staged by insurgents in villages and parishes that supported them and their aspirations to win a future Mexico free of colonial rule.[78] No image or name of divine sanction and protection for these contradictory aspirations was more available than that of the Virgin of Guadalupe, thanks to its remarkable dissemination during the eighteenth century. Even in northern Oaxaca, which was not much known for guadalupanismo at the time, there was a copy of the image in the parish church ready for the pastor's civics lesson.

But were such ceremonial uses of Guadalupe—soon to be layered with other symbols and memories of Fathers Hidalgo and Morelos, among the martyred heroes to the cause of nationhood—vectors of a more broadly Mexican "imagined community" in the 1810s? We need to know more about how such images and spectacles were received, not just where they appeared and how they were promoted. What did the villagers who assembled at Tamasulapa see in the ceremony of December 27, 1810? Did it contribute to a new and larger vision of themselves in community? We have only the priest's account of the festivities, but other events in the area during the independence period suggest that symbols of membership in an imagined Mexico would have had an intermittent appeal, usually trumped by local interests and a localized sense of the sacred. Old animosities often overrode new solidarities. Many villages in Oaxaca carried on their perennial litigation against their neighbors throughout the independence period, approaching whatever courts were in session.[79] Their association with insurgents or royalists was fluid and had more to do with local grievances than new solidarities and greater loyalties. In July 1812, for example, the royalist subdelegado of Villa Alta reported that the town of Jalahuy was now in rebellion (*insurgentado*) because its people were angered by the royal government's failure to act in their land dispute with the neighboring town of Yahuive. The subdelegado's solution was to assign the disputed lands to the people of Yahuive on the condition that they would make war on the "insurgent robbers" of Jalahuy.[80] Royalist officials in Oaxaca City took the initiative in 1811 to settle land litigation for Santos Reyes de Sola in order to gain their support against insurgents in the area.[81] And at Nochistlán, a few miles down the road from Tamasulapan, people apparently had been little moved by the patriotic pageantry of December 27, 1810. They supported insurgents during 1811, but then asked the alcalde mayor of Teocuicuilco in February 1812 for reconciliation with the royal government and reinstatement of their cura. Their petition was immediately granted.[82]

These Oaxaca cases, along with the pronounced pattern of localized Guadalupan devotion in the eighteenth century, rather than a vast pilgrimage network focused on Tepeyac, suggest that the image and name of Guadalupe during the independence period expressed participation in a still largely *un*imagined, albeit more imaginable, national community. Guadalupe as national symbol would continue to be crosscut by local attachments and other hierophanies long after 1821. Religious pilgrimages to distant shrines did emerge as a vital cultural expression of wider affiliations soon after independence, but they were more provincial than national in scope. The idea of long, penitential journeys to the shrine of Guadalupe at Tepeyac as the most sacred center of Mexico had been expressed by educated creoles after 1754, and as early as 1840 a small group of Ópata women and men from southern Sonora journeyed there on foot,[83] but the greater pilgrimages between the 1820s and 1860s took devotees to regional shrines like San Juan de los Lagos and Talpa in Jalisco, to the burgeoning new shrine of Plateros in Zacatecas, to Izamal in Yucatán, Juquila in Oaxaca, and Chalma and Amecameca in the Estado de México, as much as to Tepeyac.[84] The development of Tepeyac as Mexico's universally acclaimed epicenter of the sacred would come later.

My thanks to the Instituto de Investigaciones Históricas of the Universidad Nacional Autónoma de México for permission to publish this essay, which first appeared in Spanish in Alicia Mayer and Juan Ramón de la Fuente, eds., *México en tres momentos: 1810-1910-2010. Hacia la conmemoración del bicentenario de la Independencia y el centenario de la Revolución Mexicana. Retos y perspectivas* (Mexico: Universidad Nacional Autónoma de México/Instituto de Investigaciones Históricas, 2008), II:211-38.

PART III

Beyond the Colonial Period

6

Shrines and Marvels in the Wake of Mexican Independence

HISTORIES OF DEVOTIONAL PRACTICES ARE BOUND TO BE elusive and incomplete, but Solange Alberro recently threw up her hands at even the prospect for nineteenth-century Mexico. Popular religiosity then, more than at other times, is lost to historians she suggested, "hid[den] among individual, family, or regional practices" that escape documentation and memory.[1] True, there is little scholarship on the subject for the first forty years or so of Mexico's national history and the written record and other artifacts that might help are sparse, but more is possible without just filling the silence with scattered examples and inferences from earlier or recent times.[2] This chapter is a halting attempt to say what that more might be. I have noticed several patterns of devotion, but following their tracks toward devotional sensibilities is mainly what I can offer. Most of the questions we would want to ask about actual practices and experience of divine "presence"[3] go unanswered here, and establishing how representative or momentous a change might have been at the time is always a problem. I address two of the ways a history of devotional practices during the first half of the nineteenth century might be approached—shrines and news of miracles—both of which draw attention to the importance of images in Catholic devotion generally and Mexican devotion in particular. The chapter highlights surprising growth of old and new shrines at the time, and signs of greater laicization of faith, with "the conditions that render ritual effective" more often managed by local laity who regarded themselves as faithful members of the universal church.[4] Prominent among them in the early nineteenth century were the members of sodalities who constituted communities of faith within their parishes, participating in the celebrations, financial affairs, and spiritual well-being of the group and their devotion to a particular saint or feast day; other men's and women's devotional and charitable organizations; the caretakers of churches and their belongings; those who maintained and used family chapels and home altars; the makers and guardians of religious images and increasingly popular ex-voto paintings; healers and occasional visionaries; pilgrims; consumers of the growing religious literature that was being printed; alms collectors; and the devout who prayed, brought flowers, and lit candles to Christ and the saints at sacred places.

Highlighting shrines and laicization in the history of devotion draws attention to rural settlements and their head towns, and leaves the national capital and provincial cities more to the side. There is a cost to this less than comprehensive approach. Most nineteenth-century Mexicans were from rural towns, villages, haciendas, and *rancherías*, but the cities and their citizens have a vital place in the history of religion in Mexico that is just now coming into its own as an area of study. New directions in religious life with an institutional focus and a paper trail usually began, or at least incubated, in the cities. There, especially, one might be able to study how currents of "reformed piety" in the late eighteenth century that centered on more contemplative, more restrained, and private practices reached a wider audience then and after independence. The burgeoning Escuelas de Cristo of Mexico City and several provincial cities, emphasizing collective self-discipline and including artisans and manual laborers as well as social elites (though their membership was limited to ethnic Spaniards and capped at seventy-two each, including twenty-four priests), are intriguing evidence of devotional practices across class.[5] But what happened to them after independence and what was their wider impact? Some European theological currents circulated in print for the first time in Mexico after independence. How did the changing religious discourse after independence that brought spiritual writers like St. Alphonsus Ligouri into currency play out in practice among elites whose religious sensibilities are often now described as Jansenist?[6] How did it ripple through society? Did Ligouri's "prudent" criticism of Jansen's predestinarian views and vision of humanity as radically corrupt, and the mission of his Redemptorist congregation to preach and teach in urban slums, move Mexican pastors to follow his example and stir local spiritual revivals? If so, when (was it mainly after Ligouri's canonization in 1839?) and to what effect? And when and where did circulation of writings by and about St. Vincent de Paul and the activist organizations associated with him that undertook missions of charitable relief in rural areas, prisons, and hospitals take hold and what impact did they have on lay devotions? They may have been considerable. The Vincentian Sisters of Charity were the only new religious order in Mexico during the nineteenth century, but their charitable work and that of the auxiliary Ladies of Charity and Daughters of Charity seems to have been a post-1850 story. Were the Sisters of Charity and their lay followers evidence of widespread "feminization of piety" then?[7] And did their influence reach deeper into popular practice through the Daughters of Charity sodalities of young laywomen affiliated with houses of the Sisters of Charity that were popular in Catholic Europe? Again, this would have been a later nineteenth-century development, arising from widespread enthusiasm for, and papal endorsement in 1847 of, the story of the apparition of the Virgin Mary of the Miraculous Medal to Catherine Labouré, a French Sisters of Charity novice, in 1830. Within this current of spiritual revival, prophetic vision, and activist mission, the teachings of Vincentians and Liguori converged long before 1850 or the dogma of the Immaculate Conception in 1854 in a wholehearted enthusiasm for Mariology, as did nineteenth-century Catholicism in Europe and Latin America more generally. Deep Marian devotion was hardly new in Mexico, but there seems to have been an important shift in ideas about devotion and model femininity underway that would help to account for more recent, sometimes timeless, claims that Marian devotion is the essence of Mexican Catholicism.

Whatever the approach to devotional practices across Mexico in the nineteenth century, the challenge remains to find better ways to address processes and paradoxes of change and continuity, moving into and through familiar categories of domination and resistance, elite and popular, official and unofficial, orthodox and heterodox, private and public, enchantment and disenchantment, appearance and disappearance, rural and urban, secular society vs. confessional society, modern vs. traditional, and science vs. religion. An accumulation of particular places over time and well-documented episodes and individuals situated in their place and time may be the historian's best chance to break through convenient categories and glimpse how people "experienced the Word as they hear it; . . . the actualities of believing."[8] It will take patience and more time than I could give it.

Church and State Leaders Reckon with the Popular

The weakness of the institutional church coupled with abundant signs of faith in action, both public and private, is one of the paradoxes of the nineteenth century for students of religious institutions and popular religiosity in Mexico. The church was embattled and in retreat, its clergy diminished and their role in public life questioned. *Capellanía* endowments, cofradía treasuries, lands dedicated to the sponsoring devotions, and other sources of income for the church and its ministers were in decline[9]; various dioceses were without a resident bishop; fewer priests were in pastoral service, and those who were found themselves embroiled in politically charged local disputes; fewer young men were training for the priesthood, and they were less well educated on average and with little chance of a comfortable living; sacrilegious provocations became more common, or at least more notorious[10]; and the more politicized church during and after the independence period was a perennial source of controversy. Yet the power of faith in many places seems to have been undiminished; if anything it was stronger in emotional intensity. The growth of shrines with broad appeal is described later in this chapter, but the new popularity of particular devotions, perhaps especially to the infant Jesus and the Sacred Heart of Jesus,[11] also is noteworthy.

The growth of the Penitente brotherhoods in Hispanic villages (that is, the non-Pueblo Indian communities) of northern New Mexico during and immediately after the independence period is a striking case of laicization. The Penitentes are thought to have been offshoots of lay confraternities established under Franciscan direction in the last quarter of the eighteenth century and associated with the distinctive *santero* art and spiritual meetinghouses (*moradas*) of the area.[12] With the gradual removal of Franciscan pastors from New Mexican settlements in the late colonial period, and their separation from pastoral service altogether in New Mexico in the early 1830s, most rural communities were left without a resident or visiting priest. Most men in these communities came to participate in rites of penitential discipline and, during the "autonomous period" after about 1830, they became exemplars of fervent devotion and shapers of local faith.[13] In his pastoral visits to the province of New Mexico in 1833 and 1845 the bishop of Durango ordered the suppression of the Penitentes, but their organizations continued and grew, with little oversight, throughout the nineteenth century. Withdrawal of the clergy from pastoral work in other parts of rural Mexico after 1810 also gave rise to more independent local lay leaders and some distinctive devotional practices. When Franciscans returned to their missions among the Huicholes and Coras in the mountains of Zacatecas in 1843 after an absence of thirty-two years, they complained of a return to idolatrous rites, being performed in "little pagan temples" under the direction of native shamans.[14]

Meanwhile, ideas about proper devotional practices by Mexico's new national and state governments and some church leaders in the 1820s and 1830s continued Bourbon attempts at reform more than they broke from them. The big, contentious issues of (1) which activities and institutions fell within the exclusive jurisdiction of the church and which were subject to state authority, and (2) what was private and what was public and proper continued to stir debate and action both within the church and between church and state. Late Bourbon initiatives to reduce the number of religious holidays and make the observances less lavish and raucous, to restrict the alms-collecting tours for particular devotions, to promote a more austere, neoclassical style of architectural design and decoration in place of teeming baroque exuberance, to limit the use of religious images in processions and pilgrimages outside their hometowns, to reduce the wealth and independence of confraternities, and to instill a Jansenist sobriety were renewed and extended after 1821. Public displays of faith were to be reined in and those fiestas and processions that continued were to be more tasteful and restrained in their spirituality, and less costly.

An old tension within the Catholic community over church officials demanding the transfer of religious images in private hands to the parish church when they gained public notoriety attracted the interest of state authorities in the 1820s, especially in Mexico City. Asserting their authority over the use of images and casting doubt on the political loyalties of local Indians, the alcalde and ayuntamiento of Azcapotzalco, with tacit support of the governor of the Distrito Federal, removed celebrated images from family chapels and placed them in the parish church and, in 1826, tried to remove two crucifixes in the *tecpan* (native government palace) chapels there on the grounds that a tecpan was a municipal building where worldly business was transacted, not a church.[15] In a policy initiative that was as much about public order as putting religious activities in their proper place, the government of the Distrito Federal acted in 1824 to remove religious images from outdoor locations in the city, beginning with statues of the Santo Ecce Homo and Mary Immaculate from their niches in the Portal de Mercaderes on the Zócalo, and a statue of Our Lady El Refugio in the calle de los Tlapaleros. The decrees for removal noted that these were public places of commerce frequented by disreputable people whose very presence profaned the sacred images and were an offense to piety, decency, and good order. Keeping suspicious people from gathering in the streets at night seems to have been the more pressing reason for the city government's interest in dignifying the cult in this way. Other outdoor chapels were closed and their images moved indoors in 1828 and 1831; and the landmark, but dilapidated, Talabarteros chapel next to the cathedral was demolished in 1824 because its dark corners were said to have become a meeting place for criminals and a public nuisance.[16] At the national level, Mexican representatives to Rome fulfilled a mission dear to the hearts of Bourbon reformers by securing a papal proclamation in 1839 that reduced the number of obligatory religious holidays to Sundays and the feasts of the Circumcision, Epiphany, Ascencion, Corpus Christi, Christmas, the Immaculate Conception, Our Lady of Guadalupe, St. Peter and St. Paul, All Saints, and the birth of St. John the Baptist.[17]

Despite these moves to restrict devotion in public places, the early years of Mexico's national history saw less than full enforcement and no apparent decline of popular religious enthusiasm and improvisation. Even the Mexico City initiatives against public display of religious images were not a resounding success. Facing determined neighborhood opposition, the order to remove the image of El Refugio from its street corner niche still had not been implemented in 1844; that year the governor of the Distrito Federal rebuffed the latest attempt to relocate the image to the chapel of the nearby Santo Domingo convent.[18] And the 1826 Azcapotzalco case raised jurisdictional doubts and such strong opposition in the ensuing months from Indian officials who were acknowledged to be pious and respected leaders of the community that the municipal alcalde first, and then the governor of the Distrito Federal, were forced to reconsider their decision to expropriate the tecpan crucifixes.[19] On the advice of the alcalde of neighboring Tacuba that a comparison of this case to the statues in the Portal de Mercaderes was misguided since the tecpan chapels were separated from mundane activities and maintained in a most decorous way, the alcalde of Azcapotzalco recommended to the ayuntamiento that the images be returned to the Indian chapels. The parish priest of Azcapotzalco was also instructed to report on the matter. He was understandably reluctant to do so, wanting to maintain good relations with the ayuntamiento and his parishioners, most of whom were Indians who visited the tecpan chapels and wanted the images to stay there. Nervously bowing in all directions, with praise for the intentions of the ayuntamiento in issuing the original order of expropriation and noting that the local Indians were not pro-Spanish and that they did keep their chapels in good condition and practiced their faith in a decorous way, he, too, finally recommended that the images be returned.

The governor of the Distrito Federal was torn between the controversy this removal of images was causing and his authority to order their removal in the interest of decorous religious practice and public order. The case record ends with the governor retreating from his bold exercise of state *patronato* rights and passing the matter to the archbishop for his advice. Discretion had long been the better part of valor when church and state authorities intervened in local uses of religious images. In responding to a decree of Charles III in 1767 against the abuse of religious images, especially their use for profane purposes (for example on buttons and kitchen utensils), a parish priest from Coxutepeque in the Archdiocese of Guatemala asked the archbishop if this meant that he should confiscate all "imperfect" religious images. If so, he said, the parish church would be emptied of its images since all of them were unseemly—crude, decrepit, or strangely attired. They inspired "much mockery and neither devotion nor edification for the faithful," but he was sure that removing them would cause a great clamor for their return, if not a rebellion. The archbishop's terse response was to avoid "inciting any kind of uprising."[20]

It may not be possible to establish with much certainty whether or not veneration of images was growing in popularity after independence, but the passionate contests over images from the 1820s to the 1850s look very similar to those from the late colonial period. There was the perennial concern of officials not to leave unchecked the belief in unproven miracles that spread among "la gente rústica,"[21] but images as pathways to divine favor were still regarded as vital to well-being, and rights to them were sought and vigorously defended with an open purse, especially in times of rampant illness and political crisis. For example, in 1850 members of the confraternity of Nuestro Señor del Socorro in Mexico City's Santa Catarina parish wanted their patron image removed temporarily from the convent church of Santa Ynés so it could be brought to their neighbor to ward off the spread of sickness. The nuns of Santa Ynés opposed the move and litigation began.[22] That year, in another twist on the tension over indispensable images, don Tomás Tirado, resident of Yztayopan in the district of Xochimilco, complained that he had been compelled to lend the community an image of Nuestra Señora de la Soledad during an epidemic in the 1830s and it had not been returned.[23] As usual, the case for who had rights in the image was more tangled than the parties to the dispute conceded. Although no final verdict is recorded in this file, the case was moving in the usual direction of declaring the chapel that housed the image to be public, thus removing Tirado from his personal claims as the administrator.

Miracles

Reports of miracles—those events in human affairs that seem to defy natural explanation and are regarded as direct interventions of divine goodness or retribution—abounded in Mexico during the nineteenth century and were received with enthusiasm, much as they had been during the colonial period.[24] The continuity is obvious and widespread, though not universal, and the timing and scale of changes it is likely to cloak are not obvious, largely because the written record, again, is spotty. Yet the turmoil in many facets of public life in Mexico and the dramatic changes in the history of miracles in Europe at the time would seem to anticipate important, perhaps decisive, changes in Mexico, too. Was there a comparable demystification of sudden recovery from grave illness with advances in medical science and growth of the medical profession? If not, why not? Especially for Germany and France, European historians have posited a veritable eruption of faith and time of miracles centered on new shrines visited by great numbers of faithful in the 1850s, after decades of "disenchantment" and decline in church influence and public witnessing of Christian faith.[25] Mexico was not untouched by the European developments, especially the great fame of the shrine at Lourdes, but new apparitions do not seem to have been widely noted and celebrated by Mexicans, as they apparently were in the new age of miracles in some of Western Europe.[26]

Apparitions of the Virgin Mary, which returned so resoundingly in Europe during the mid-nineteenth century to stir mass followings, were less evident and elaborated in nineteenth-century Mexico. The famous European apparitions, such as Lourdes, La Salette, and the Miraculous Medal, spoke to their visionaries, often with messages of foreboding.

Reported Mexican apparitions and signs of divine animation in the world, on the other hand, usually were mute and did not gain the same notoriety. Soon after terrifying earthquakes struck Ocotlán, Jalisco, in October 1847, a luminous cloud appeared in the northwest sky in the shape of Christ crucified and was taken as a sign from heaven—a call to repentance and renewed devotion that seemed to echo the European divine messages.[27] More common were reports of statues or paintings of saints and Christ silently bleeding, perspiring, or otherwise showing signs of life and bringing the hope of protection to the faithful, as they had for centuries. If there was a message from the Virgin, with premonitions, warnings, and signs in the manner of the day in Europe, as there was in the miracle marked by the ring of the Virgin of Guadalupe of Zacatecas in 1844, it was more parochial and less political. According to the published account of this apparition of Mary, two Franciscan nuns wrote to the guardian of the Franciscan College of Nuestra Señora de Guadalupe in Zacatecas with the news that they had received urgent instructions from the Blessed Mary to tell him that the college and its members would soon face a great test of their strength as a community, and that they should strive to obey the rule of the order as a unified group and begin an annual observance on August 25 to confess their sins and shortcomings before an image of the Virgin and vow to fulfill their religious exercises more diligently. To seal the promise, Mary wished them to celebrate a spiritual marriage with her, betokened by a ring they would give her. As proof that the message was real, she promised three signs: that they would be told of things they had been keeping secret; that the new hospice they had under construction would fall down; and that the image of San Pascual Bailón in their church would fall off its pedestal, but would not be damaged. The signs came to pass and the community fell into disputes, but they kept their promise to the Virgin and were able to come together after all.[28]

The abbreviated miracle stories circulating in print during the early nineteenth century were much like their colonial counterparts in being mostly about recovery from grave illness or accidents and escape from other fatal situations. There was bound to be some variation by place—miracles for shrines in Campeche and Veracruz, for example, were more likely to involve storms and accidents at sea; those in ranching areas of the Bajío to involve mishaps with animals. Several new kinds of miracles appear in the early nineteenth century. While they do not predominate among the known stories, they suggest changing circumstances and new fears that were experienced and expressed by different kinds of people, not just elites—surviving highway robberies for one, and military engagements and escape from execution in politically charged circumstances for another. Nineteenth-century miracle stories also seem somewhat different in their attention to divine punishment for sacrilegious acts, failure to fulfill promises to the saints, and other unchristian acts and misdeeds, perhaps reflecting a sense of the church and faith embattled.[29]

A striking change in the record of miracles produced and displayed in churches and shrines in the aftermath of the independence wars was the advent of inexpensive, usually rustic ex-voto paintings on small sheets of tin. Painted representations of a personal favor were not altogether new in Mexico, much less Europe. From the early seventeenth century, paintings of miracle events, donors, and their celestial patrons graced the walls of the shrines of Nuestra Señora de los Remedios and Nuestra Señora de Guadalupe in the Valley of Mexico, among others,[30] and this form of votive offering and witness was especially popular in Catholic Europe from the sixteenth through the eighteenth centuries. But, judging by the small number of such paintings that have been documented for New Spain, it was a much less common form of devotional art here, and their donors during the colonial period were elite men for the most part, who could afford to pay a professional artist for a fine little painting on canvas. Most votive offerings by other devotees in the colonial period were little metal or wax body parts, candles, or flowers—anonymous to all but the donor and the divine. Once inexpensive tin sheets became widely available in the 1820s, ex-voto paintings were within reach of patrons from nearly all classes as well as informally trained local artists.

These dramatic images of near-death experiences and faith are a remarkable development in popular devotion and all that this chapter aims for, but just how popular and widespread the form had become by 1850 is not clear. It is sometimes suggested in passing that the 1820s marks the important change, and that the popularity of the form increased throughout the nineteenth century. However, most of the ex-voto paintings published and studied for the nineteenth century date from after the 1860s. As with the history of religion in Mexico more generally, the early decades of this transformation of votive expression have received less attention, with the tacit assumption that the paintings either were or were not very popular before the Reforma.[31] Mario Colín's detailed description of a cache of ex-voto paintings he recovered from trunks in the sacristy of the shrine of the Señor del Huerto of Atlacomulco (Estado de México), which was built soon after the local Cristo reportedly restored itself to fine condition in 1810, suggests that these evocative painted miracles were, indeed, becoming popular in some places before 1850 in the double sense of growing production and a spectrum of donors.[32] Colín said he could only salvage a small part of what he found there, but he listed thirty-one ex-voto paintings and published twenty-six of them. Of those reproduced in his publication, twenty-two were made before 1870, ten of them before 1850. Predictably, most recounted grave illnesses and accidents for both men and women of humble as well as more privileged circumstances.

These evocative miracle paintings, mostly done before the 1960s, are not easy to interpret as historical artifacts, even with the valuable scholarly and curatorial attention they have received in recent years.[33] Hundreds of them have been published and thousands more cover the walls of Mexican shrines today, but they survive in assortments or isolated examples, not samples. Most have been lost or removed from their original context— many are no longer decipherable because they have rusted or the paint has flaked off; many more must have been disposed of or found their way into private collections and are effectively lost to scholars. It is hard to believe, for example, that only eight hundred were deposited at the shrine of Guadalupe up to 1979, hardly any of them made before 1850[34]; or that the large assortment at the shrine of Nuestra Señora de San Juan de los Lagos would include just a few that date before 1870.[35] Another challenge to understanding is that while they document particular episodes of real people, most of the paintings are quite conventional—made by a local painter of the donor's hometown or the shrine town, rather than the donor himself or herself, and usually presenting the scene in a standard, simplified way in which one grave illness or accident looks like many others, or merely shows the donor at prayer before the patron saint or image.

What can be learned about religion in the lives of Mexicans from these graphic depictions of personal faith during the early nineteenth century? Are they independent evidence of a new age of laicization, devotion, and anxious hope for miracles, or mainly another manifestation of ongoing popular faith? An abundance of votive offerings, especially of miniature wax and metal body parts, candles, and flowers is well documented for Mexican shrines and churches from the colonial period on. The miracle paintings did not replace them and probably amounted to a small portion of the total even at their peak of popularity. Does the fact that many of the paintings depict women or were donated by women indicate a "feminization of piety" in Mexico at the time? To some extent, it probably does. Women appear more often in the ex-voto paintings and other representations of miracles during the nineteenth century than they did during the colonial period, but the numbers of paintings on which to base a numerical comparison are relatively few and scattered, and the difference is not great if the paintings are compared to written accounts of miracle stories in the colonial period. Of the 578 miracle stories and ex-voto paintings I gathered from the colonial period, about 60 percent favored men and close to 40 percent favored women. While Patricia Arias and Jorge Durand speak of a "feminization" in ex-voto paintings during the nineteenth century in their study of twelve shrines and two individual artists, they recognize that less than half of their assortment—"about forty percent"—favored a particular woman and slightly more favored a man.[36] This is far fewer than the 89 percent figure for women in miracle stories in nineteenth-century France.[37] Apparently, men still predominated numerically in the Mexican ex-voto depictions and among the donors during the nineteenth century. The devotional lives of men require more attention before the scope and significance of a feminization of piety at that time can be evaluated. Arias and Durand advance the intriguing hypothesis that nineteenth-century ex-voto paintings offer a glimpse of a changing moral sensibility among women that criticized the hegemonic discourse extolling a feminine ideal of purity and self-sacrificing, suffering motherhood by depicting social violence against women and highlighting tensions in the private lives of families, but they provide only three examples, two of which date from the late nineteenth century.

Few as the published nineteenth-century ex-voto paintings are, the new occasions for miracles depicted in them may mark the 1850s as a devotional watershed. After the U.S.-Mexican war and before the wars of the Reforma some shrines had another spurt of growth.[38] It was then, with the approach of the wars of the Reforma and through the 1860s that scenes of battle, political violence, and attacks on highways became familiar themes. Shrines at just this time reported interruptions in their trade fairs, fewer pilgrims, lootings by robbers, and rumors of planned attacks by political rivals and marauding former soldiers.[39] If Arias, Durand, and Bartra are correct, the 1850s marks the production of many more ex-voto paintings to beseech or thank divine intervention for special favors in tight circumstances, and greater popularity of this form of piety among poor and rural people. This enlarged donor base would also help account for more rural settings and work-related accidents.

Shrines

Perhaps the most striking, or at least obvious, development in Mexican religious life during the early nineteenth century was the new and old shrines to miraculous images that prospered, despite the prevailing dangers of the road from prolonged warfare, separatist movements, highway robbery, the spread of firearms,[40] economic troubles, and periods of famine and epidemic disease. These catastrophes, coupled with weak national governments and a diminished institutional church, may well have abetted the development of regional shrines more than hindered it.

How and why some shrines grew in popularity and importance then needs more attention than I give it here. The later eighteenth century witnessed consolidation of many miracle shrines that began the century before, but few new shrines of more than local fame had their beginnings then. In the early nineteenth century, during and after the independence struggle, new shrines appeared, most of the older shrines survived, and some of them grew as never before, attracting large followings from across municipalities within and sometimes beyond new state lines to the annual fiesta and fair. In central, north-central, and western Mexico, at least seven became major regional shrines as few had been in the colonial period.[41]

New Shrines

Among the new shrines in the early nineteenth century, associated with a recently acquired or previously little-known image, are the Señor de la Paz in the Mixteca Baja region bordering Puebla and Oaxaca; the Señor de la Misericordia of Tepatitlán, Jalisco; the Señor del Huerto of Atlacomulco in the Toluca Valley of the Estado de Mexico; the Señor del Claustro at Tacuba in the Valley of Mexico; the Señor del Saucito at Encinillas, San Luis Potosí; and the Santo Niño de Atocha at Plateros, outside Fresnillo, Zacatecas. Of these new shrines, the Niño de Atocha at Plateros attracted the largest following. All of these new shrines (and several of the most popular older shrines—Chalma, Tepalcingo, and Amecameca) focused on a wonder-working image of Christ. Was this a result of particularly desperate times? Of an urgent desire for intimacy with God unmediated by saints that marks a significant change in devotional practices? Of a mounting sense of shared suffering and longing for salvation? Of lay leaders moving local devotion more toward natural shrines on hilltops that were associated with ancestral presence and fertility as well as Christ and Calvary? I don't know, and each of these new shrines has a different story of beginnings and development. Some appealed mainly to a particular ethnic group or began in the way miracle shrines had for several centuries—with a crucifix or picture of Mary spontaneously showing signs of life, or becoming too heavy to be moved from a particular spot, or suddenly beginning to work cures and other wonders. Some became more popular and then hit a plateau, others had periods of rapid growth and contraction, and still others grew more or less steadily without much reference to the politics and calamities of the time.

More emphatically than the others, El Señor de la Paz—also called the Cristo Negro de San Pablo Anicano, near Acatlán, Puebla—highlights political and social troubles of the time. The image was introduced between 1824 and 1830 by the local pastor in an effort to promote peace among local Mixtecs, Popolucas, Nahuas, Zapotecs, and mestizo peasants squeezed by land shortages, unemployment, and the growth of nearby haciendas. In the same vein, a more epic Mixtec story of its origins tells of sibling spirit lords of the mountains, caves, and rivers who turned against each other. A younger brother, lord of the Tizaac River, became angry with his older brother, lord of the greater Atoyac River, and began to flow in another direction. Eventually the lord of Red Mountain went to speak to the black Christ, who came to live among the spirit lords so that the brothers would help all the communities that were suffering from famine and thirst.[42]

The Santo Niño de Atocha at Plateros was the most spectacularly successful new devotion. Like the Señor de la Paz, its founding miracles reflected changing regional circumstances of postindependence society, in this case the dynamic dislocations of the near north. The Plateros shrine dates to the seventeenth century, but until the early nineteenth century statues of the crucified Christ and the Madonna and child were its main devotional images. By 1816 the Christ child was recognized as a powerful "santo" in his own right, and by 1838 he occupied the place of honor on the main altar by himself and soon was depicted in prints and paintings as an older boy in traveling garb who wore out his sandals in frequent journeys from his niche to aid the faithful. He was celebrated with his own novena booklet in 1848, and each day of his novena was associated with an early miracle, dated from 1829 to 1841. These canonical miracles and many others associated the Santo Niño with common people in trouble with the law or at work—mine workers, office workers, muleteers, housewives, murderers, and, most famously, a woman of doubtful reputation on the move, who met the Santo Niño in prison. The Santo Niño took special interest in travelers, violent assaults, and lost causes of all kinds. "He is the one who can do it all" (*Él es quien todo lo puede*), proclaimed a woman favored in one of the novena miracles. The Santo Niño's clientele made him a new kind of protector, of ordinary people in danger or in trouble with the law on Mexico's restless northern frontier. In this sense, he was something of a forerunner to Jesús Malverde and Juan Soldado, unofficial patrons of outlaws and common folk in northern Mexico and the U.S.-Mexican border zone from the mid-twentieth century. As Juan Javier Pescador points out in his study of devotion to the Santo Niño de Atocha, Fresnillo and surrounding mining towns temporarily boomed in 1830s, with an attendant arrival of all kinds of people, at a time of political turmoil for Zacatecas, precisely when the Santo Niño came into his own and ex-voto paintings began to accumulate at the shrine. The Fresnillo area was a "modernizing" social frontier that attracted newcomers who were without a dependable social patron. Many who passed through and became devotees of the Santo Niño evidently carried the devotion farther north or came from the north to trade in the fairs of Jalisco and Zacatecas. By the 1860s, altars and chapels to the Santo Niño could be found in Chihuahua, Durango, and into northern New Mexico by way of El Paso, at Española and Chimayó.[43]

Six other shrines that had been important in the late colonial period became notably more popular and more widely known in the decades after independence: Nuestra Señora de Guadalupe at Tepeyac in the Valley of Mexico; El Señor de Tepalcingo in the municipality of Jonacatepec, Morelos; Nuestra Señora de Talpa in western Jalisco; the shrine of the Sacromonte at Amecameca in the mountains between the Valley of Mexico and the temperate valleys of Morelos; Nuestra Señora del Pueblito, outside the city of Querétaro; Nuestra Señora de San Juan de los Lagos in the Altos de Jalisco; and the Señor de Chalma, near Malinalco in the Estado de México.

Our Lady of Guadalupe
Our Lady of Guadalupe was the most heavily promoted and widely revered religious image before and after independence. It was also the most politicized in the early nineteenth century. The late colonial patterns I described in the preceding chapters and summarize here continued, but they were stretched and complicated after independence.

Our Lady of Guadalupe became an especially prominent and popular devotional image during the late seventeenth and eighteenth centuries, promoted heavily in Spain, Rome, and New Spain by diocesan leaders, pastors, city fathers of the capital, and viceregal officials. Painted, sculpted, and printed copies circulated widely, especially in the center and north, and in leading towns to the south. Francisco de Florencia, the indefatigable late seventeenth-century Jesuit promoter of miraculous images in Mexico, and a particular devotee of Our Lady of Guadalupe, declared in 1688 that this miraculous image of Mary virtually saturated the viceroyalty:

> The number of images—copies of this miraculous portrait that have been made throughout this vast kingdom—is infinite, for it is to be found everywhere. There is no church, chapel, house, or hut of a Spaniard or an Indian where images of Our Lady of Guadalupe are not seen and venerated.[44]

Florencia exaggerated, but there is little doubt that, other than the crucified Christ and Mary Immaculate, Our Lady of Guadalupe was the best known religious image in New Spain by the early eighteenth century, woven into the fabric of everyday affairs for many kinds of people, not only the elite promoters. By the 1750s—after papal recognition of the apparition story and the elevation of Our Lady of Guadalupe as patroness of New Spain—the devotion spread rapidly, and the image was enlisted in all kinds of calamities. Official promotion was intense, with bishops and other colonial authorities organizing annual celebrations on December 12 in the diocesan capitals and towns in their jurisdiction, and overseeing construction or remodeling of chapels to Guadalupe; and cadres of young priests trained at seminary in Mexico City eager to carry the devotion to their pastoral assignments throughout the Archdiocese of Mexico. Booklets for novena observances at the shrine, little leaflets for special prayers on the twelfth of every month, and other devotional works were printed and reprinted after 1754. Sermons in her honor had been delivered and sometimes published in Mexico City during the seventeenth century, but after 1754 their numbers increased, and Guadalupan sermons delivered in other provincial centers were being published in Mexico City and Puebla print shops. At the same time, parish inventories in central, western, and northern Mexico recorded new altars to Guadalupe or full-size paintings of the image.

How much of this growing presence of the image was promotion by elite devotees and how much expressed popular fervor? The answers are likely to vary by place and time, and disentangling promotion and devotion is as problematic for the eighteenth century as it is for the nineteenth unless there is evidence of coercion or direct resistance. But whether leading or following, the official promotion seems to have been well received for the most part across classes and regions. The mounting evidence of devotion confirmed local identities more than focusing the attention of devotees on Tepeyac and the original artifact. Even as viceregal and archiepiscopal officials worked to concentrate the sacred at Tepeyac after 1737, decentralization with a local focus was at work. In 1737 at Temamatla, near Chalco in the Valley of Mexico, local people announced that their copy of Our Lady of Guadalupe sweated and spoke to them—Mary was fully present right there, in their image. And a millenarian movement at Tututepec in the Sierra of Meztitlán (Hidalgo) in 1769 made even stronger claims for Mary's presence (see Chapter 4). In less provocative ways, most devotees beyond the Valley of Mexico were satisfied with the likeness of Guadalupe that was close at hand, among the other revered images in place in their local church or on a home altar, or in a regional capital. Evidently few felt themselves powerfully "drawn to the image" at Tepeyac from great distances, as so many do today.

How could people be so attracted to the image of Guadalupe without being equally drawn to Tepeyac, where the image had appeared on the cloak of a humble Indian and was still displayed? Beyond the lure of the local and the hardships of travel then, an essential factor was the hesitation of ecclesiastical authorities to actively encourage European-style great pilgrimages until the late nineteenth century. Long penitential sojourns to a shrine were part of the mental world of hispanized subjects in New Spain, as they were for many Europeans, but indulgences for actual pilgrimages were not issued by colonial bishops, and when a creole Spanish woman from Monterrey in northern Mexico promised to go to Tepeyac if she recovered from a grave illness in 1758, the Bishop of Guadalajara was quick to excuse her from the vow.[45] Much of the dissemination of guadalupanismo occurred in secondary ways, from provincial places and unofficial sources rather than from the main shrine. The painstakingly accurate eighteenth-century copies of Our Lady of Guadalupe in the provinces were likely to take on lives of their own rather than propel the viewer to Tepeyac. To many Guadalupan devotees, Mary was as present in an admired copy or a found object that resembled the Virgin of Guadalupe[46] as she was in the matrix image.

As the author of an article on the Villa de Guadalupe in the venerable *Boletín de la Sociedad Mexicana de Geografía y Estadística* observed in 1859, "for Mexicans this image is the greatest treasure they can have, and so she is the Patroness of the entire Nation."[47] But the same could be said in prenational terms for the late eighteenth century, and perhaps with even greater force in the 1810s. What had changed? Further research may reveal substantial changes I have missed, but the changes seem to be mainly intensifications of established patterns more than sharp breaks from the past.[48] Serge Gruzinski had good reason to assert that "starting with the independence and for several decades thereafter, the Mexican political class seized control of the Tepeyac image: liberals and conservatives showed themselves to be equally desirous of dominating what would henceforth be considered the nation's symbol, and what had kept its absolute hold over the crowds."[49] Heads of the young Mexican state presented themselves as patrons of the devotion as well as keepers of the symbol. Emperor Agustín de Iturbide's embrace of the image and creation of the Imperial Orden de Guadalupe was only the first move.[50] Guadalupe was declared the Patrona de los Estados Unidos Mexicanos, and presidents and other political dignitaries regularly attended the solemnities on the great December 12 feast day. And stories circulated about presidents who were avid guadalupanos. Anastasio Bustamante was a frequent visitor to Tepeyac during his off-and-on presidency in the 1830s, and he expressed his faith in Guadalupe in other ways that were meant to encourage devotion to her in the provinces. When citizens of the city of San Luis Potosí grieved the loss of their celebrated seventeenth-century copy of the image that was destroyed by fire, a committee of local dignitaries began to plan how to replace the image. But when the state governor was slow to support the effort, President Bustamante personally arranged for a fine image that had touched the original at Tepeyac to be sent from Mexico City. Members of the city council of San Luis decided to cover the cost themselves, but, as the story goes, Bustamante insisted on paying for it personally.[51]

If we add civic-minded priests to the picture, the prominent promoters multiply. Preachers and orators at national holiday celebrations—in provincial cities as well as the national capital—attributed all good things political and cultural to Our Lady of Guadalupe.[52] In a grand gesture of devotional patriotism, the bishop of Guadalajara in 1837 proposed that a kind of spiritual map of the whole country be constructed at Tepeyac by placing an altar for each Mexican diocese inside the shrine flanking the hallowed image.[53] And in 1845 a sermonizer cast his eyes over the national landscape in another sweeping gesture of patriotic embrace, declaring that the December 12 feast day was for "good Mexicans, from the far coasts of California on the Pacific Ocean to the shores of Yucatán on the Atlantic, and from the banks of the Arkansas River to the borders of Guatemala."[54] On a smaller scale, when the Franciscans returned to their missions among the Huicholes of Zacatecas in the early 1850s after many years' absence, they looked to Our Lady of Guadalupe as the image of faith to combat Huichol superstitions and revive Christian devotion. In 1852, after extolling the Virgin's divine protection and aid, teaching various prayers and hymns of praise to the Virgin of Guadalupe, and celebrating the December 12 feast day at the San Sebastián mission, one of the friars put it to the local Huicholes that "if they wanted to make a gift to the Virgin of Guadalupe, they should burn the Calihuey temple."[55] And the tricentennial of the apparition in 1831 and the centennial of the viceroy-archbishop's declaration of the Virgin of Guadalupe as Patrona of New Spain in 1838 became occasions for civic celebrations as well as solemn Masses, processions, the tolling of church bells, and fireworks.[56] Funds for the 1838 festivities came from many places in central Mexico, the sum of thousands of small donations, many of them by women, rather than just from a few major donors.[57] The collections were made in *demandas*—alms-collecting missions from Mexico City. Did that mean that the collectors created the support and association more than tapping into a reservoir of enthusiastic faith in the Virgin's protection? How would one find out?

Partisan elite manipulation of Guadalupan devotion is only part of the story of what changed, and it glosses over what continued. The politicizing of the Guadalupan image and Tepeyac was apparent during the eighteenth century, too, albeit with a new intensity during the independence battles, and the politicians did not have a monopoly on control of the image's meaning and uses.[58] The Virgin of Guadalupe was a shared symbol, widely known and much revered before, during, and after the independence wars, but not simply the nationalizing emblem.[59] The image was revered in many copies throughout Mexico in the early nineteenth century, and the story of Mary's apparitions to Juan Diego enjoyed increasing fame, but local meanings of the image easily spilled beyond the reach of official interpreters and promoters in Mexico City and the other cathedral cities. Most devotees had never been to Tepeyac and, where Guadalupe became a popular devotion, local meanings had more to do with Mary's presence and favor through a copy close at hand than with the mystique of Tepeyac or the authority of a published text like Miguel Sánchez's *Imagen de la Virgin María*. Nonetheless, guadalupanismo was deeply intertwined with the political crises of the early nineteenth century. Some changes in the nature and popularity of the devotion that were evident in the late eighteenth century intensified, were redirected, or took on new political significance after 1808 and 1810, with new participants, in new ceremonial and martial circumstances, sometimes with a sense of the "nación"—traditionally Spanish, but increasingly American—as embodied by the people, not just the monarch. In the crucible of war and the enshrining of Miguel Hidalgo and José María Morelos as fathers of a new patria during the 1820s, possibilities for shared identity through Guadalupe that had been latent or broadcast from viceregal offices and cathedral pulpits became part of the new politics of the church, liberalism, and republican institutions. In the years of weak, unstable central governments that followed, the results of the new politics reinforced locality and region more than nationality, but the ongoing counterpoints among locality, province, and nationality would make Guadalupe a universal emblem of Mexicanness.

That elites of the new Mexico turned to Our Lady of Guadalupe in their efforts to move popular sentiment to their own political purposes was not just manipulation from above. The Franciscans in the Huichol missions promoted Guadalupe because they recognized that it was an aspect of Christianity Huicholes received enthusiastically. Local images of Guadalupe on home altars and in family oratorios as well as community churches in distant places were revered and sometimes showed life and worked wonders for devotees without much promotion or supervision by priests. One of these eruptions of faith and an attempt by the parish priest to manage it is documented for Zanquitlalpan (district of Tianguistengo, Estado de México) in the 1830s. In 1838 leaders of Zanquitlalpan petitioned the archiepiscopal court for permission to build a chapel to house a stone image of the Virgin of Guadalupe that had been working wonders and attracting devotees from the community and beyond. They said that "residents and natives of this pueblo" made the statue in 1779 and placed in on the stone bridge over the river from Xalatlaco y Tilapa. In 1830 they painted it and added a stone niche. Since then "the devotion has increased in enthusiasm, along with alms from the faithful," and for the past six years "numerous miracles worked by this Divine Lady have come to light." It was time to move the image to a more appropriate place. Without dismissing the new devotion, the parish priest argued against the petition and decried "that ancient inclination of the Indians to build chapels in their pueblos without taking care that they reflect the proper decorum." Better to build a side altar in the parish church and install the image there, he argued.[60]

While the extent of popular devotion to the Virgin of Guadalupe in the early nineteenth century compared to earlier or later times may be impossible to establish, ardent devotion is evident in places where it was not much documented during the colonial period, especially in the far north.[61] Establishing how many devotees visited Tepeyac and where they came from at different times is equally elusive. Long distance pilgrimages to Tepeyac were still unusual in the early nineteenth century, but examples begin to appear not long after independence, including a little group of four Ópata women and their husbands from Tuape, Sonora, who made the seven-week journey to the Valley of Mexico in 1839 in order to "know the Virgin" (*conocer a la Virgen*) of whom their Franciscan pastors spoke.[62]

With good reason Ignacio Manuel Altamirano observed in 1884 that the December 12 feast day for Our Lady of Guadalupe "is one of the major feast days of Mexican Catholicism, certainly the greatest in terms of popularity and universal observance." And he added another observation familiar to students of guadalupanismo in the colonial period that complicates our attempts to probe that "popularity" and "universality": "It is all of Mexico City that moves itself to the edge of the shrine, from morning to evening."[63] From the vantage point of Mexico's great city, the Guadalupan devotion of the late colonial and early national periods could well be called universal, and much of the commentary about the shrine's importance has come from Mexico City and its leading political and intellectual figures. But there was more to guadalupanismo than its association with the capital city, and combining those views from the center with a more comprehensive understanding remains a challenge. Whatever we make of it, Manuel Escandón provided an astonishing figure for the number of visitors to Tepeyac in his 1861 progress report on the railroad line between Mexico City and Veracruz that suggests the extraordinary appeal of the Virgin of Guadalupe in the years after independence. Up to the end of 1860 the only part of this first railroad line in Mexico that was completed ran the few miles from downtown Mexico City to Tepeyac. From the time this short section began service in July 1857 to the end of 1860, 980,650 passengers reportedly made the trip to or from Tepeyac.[64] Surely most were residents of greater Mexico City, and their frequent visits further cemented the intimate bond between the shrine and the city, but how many were pilgrims from other parts of Mexico? What did all those people have in mind when they boarded the train? Were they on a personal penitential quest? Was it an errand of entreaty and mercy in the company of relatives and neighbors? Was the novelty and thrill of a train ride the main attraction? Where would one look for answers to these questions?

Imperial Virgins Redux: El Pueblito and Remedios

Like Our Lady of Guadalupe and Tepeyac, Our Lady of El Pueblito in her shrine outside the city of Querétaro was a longstanding Marian devotion that became more prominent in the late eighteenth century, was put to partisan political uses during the independence period, and grew in popularity after 1821. But the similarities do not go much deeper. The trajectory of the El Pueblito image and shrine up to 1830 is closer to that of Our Lady of los Remedios at Totoltepec in the Valley of Mexico. Both shrines were situated in Indian pueblos not far from important colonial cities; they were closely associated with the city and with nearby pueblos; and neither had the protonational reach of the Virgin of Guadalupe. As they became more closely associated with the city, the original statuettes of both Our Lady of El Pueblito and Our Lady of Los Remedios—rather than "peregrina" (traveling) copies—were called to the center in times of crisis. These "venidas" (visits) became more frequent, even routine, in the late colonial period, strengthening the bond between the image and the city. The official reasons for bringing the image to Mexico City for a novena of prayers changed with the new patterns of frequency and duration. Appeals for the rainy season to begin and stave off impending drought and disease were always a leitmotif of the venidas; but defending the empire in dangerous times became important from the 1690s, centering on the monarchy and the prolonged European wars that drew in Spain and America, including the War of Spanish Succession (1701–1713), the War of Austrian Succession (1739–1748), the Seven Years' War (1756–1763), and the fitful warfare among France, Spain, and Britain during the 1790s and 1800s.[65] More venidas were undertaken for the health of the king or queen, the birth of a prince, to beseech or thank the Virgin for victory on the battlefields of Europe, to celebrate a treaty, or to appeal for safe passage of the ships crossing the Atlantic with trade goods and royal treasure.

As those urban visits became longer and more frequent in the eighteenth and early nineteenth centuries, resentment grew in the home pueblos, and continued to grow in the early years of independence. And the official reasons for the venidas changed.[66] Appeals for rain or to ward off epidemic disease were always an important reason for the venidas, but defending the empire in dangerous times became important, centering on the monarchy and the prolonged European wars that threatened the Spanish empire. Both images were dubbed "generals" and became closely identified with conservative elites and the royalist cause in their cities during the independence struggle.[67] Royalist partisans were almost as likely to invoke Our Lady of Los Remedios, Our Lady of El Pueblito, or Our Lady of Guanajuato as they were to call upon Guadalupe.[68] But the postindependence trajectories of the Pueblito and Remedios shrines and devotions were very different after the 1820s when both were adapting to the new and shifting politics of the time.[69]

The two main sites of devotion to Nuestra Señora del Pueblito went in different directions during the independence period, in ways that influenced postindependence developments. In the twin Indian settlements at the shrine site—largely Otomí San Francisco Galileo, and the neighborhood of more recent migrants that became known as Pueblito, situated closer to the shrine[70]—local devotions were little supervised by their pastor for several years and seem to have turned in on themselves. In 1814, the elderly Franciscan pastor of San Francisco Galileo "alias Pueblito" (conflating the two neighborhoods) was cited for long absences and failing to fulfill his sacramental duties. The archbishop's *visitador general* recommended that the pastor be dismissed and a substitute named.[71] Three years later his Franciscan replacement complained of the superstitious, if not idolatrous, practices of local Indians despite his best efforts at preaching and catechesis:

> after preaching with the greatest passion and urging the Indians to learn Christian doctrine, even taking them by the arm to church and teaching them myself, I have not been able to dispel their innumerable superstitions which are more deeply rooted than their faith in Jesus Christ. But in particular I bring to your attention as commissary of the Holy Office of the Inquisition that there is a growing superstitious cult among them to a Holy Cross that they call "the cross of justice." They hold nighttime meetings

several days a week, attended by people from various pueblos, students of this superstitious congregation founded in a chapel in Indian Patricio García's house.[72]

During the war, the image of Our Lady of El Pueblito became ever more closely tied to the political fortunes and religious identity of the city of Querétaro, beginning with the secret transfer of the image to the Franciscan church in the city in late September 1810 for a novena to implore the Virgin's protection in "the present necessities,"[73] reaffirm this advocation of Mary as the "marvelous Patroness and General" of the city, and deliver various sermons celebrating her intervention in support of "Spanish arms in Old and New Spain."[74] Eight sermons of the kind were published between 1810 and 1817, compared to thirteen sermons dedicated to this devotion for the years of late colonial expansion of the culto of El Pueblito between 1761 and 1807, and handsome new prints of the image were made in 1811 and 1814 to promote the devotion.[75]

Perhaps because devotion to Nuestra Señora del Pueblito was focused on the largely conservative city of Querétaro and its hinterland, with less of the national exposure that Mexico City brought to Nuestra Señora de los Remedios, it was easier to gloss over her association with the Royalist cause after independence from Spain, and to forget the invocation of her protection against "that satanic serpent Hidalgo" (*el serpentón Hidalgo*), as one sermonizer put it in 1817.[76] Even the ayuntamiento of Querétaro's call for a novena "to pray to God for the good government of Emperor Agustín Iturbide" in 1822 did not make the Virgin of El Pueblito politically incorrect during Mexico's turbulent birth as a republic played out in the following years.[77] On the contrary, the frequent visits of the image to the city for special novenas continued into the early 1840s. And in 1830 the congress of Querétaro decreed Nuestra Señora del Pueblito to be the state's *patrona particular*. As patrona, the Pueblito shrine and image gained new popularity in and beyond the city during the 1830s. Six new prints of the image were made and distributed in 1830 and 1831, as well as devotional literature and civic orations that further spread the fame and fortune of Our Lady of El Pueblito. Whether before or soon after the decree of 1830, devotion spread to other parts of the new state—including San Juan del Río, San Pablo Tolimán, and various haciendas and ranchos—and even to northern New Mexico.[78]

Fig. 6.1 This is the kind of print destroyed in the 1829 makeover of Our Lady of los Remedios with Fernando Cortés and Juan Rodríguez de Villafuerte. This example, made by the Mexican engraver Sylverio in 1759, was collected by Fr. Francisco de Ajofrín in the 1760s and published posthumously in *Diario del viaje que por orden de la sagrada Congregacion de Propaganda Fide hizo a la America septentrional en el siglo XVIII* (Madrid: Real Academia de la Historia, 1958–59), I:113. Courtesy of the Real Academia de la Historia, Madrid.

Fig. 6.2 Ink drawing of a proposed medal to be struck in honor of Our Lady of los Remedios and sold to devotees, suitable for postindependence use. This is a standard late colonial representation of the providential origin story in which the image was found by an Indian nobleman in a maguey plant. Archivo Histórico del Distrito Federal, "Carlos de Sigüenza y Góngora," Serie: Santuario de los Remedios, vol. 3900, exp. 14, fol. 163, 1803. Courtesy of the Archivo Histórico del Distrito Federal, México.

Independence marked a different kind of watershed for the shrine and the place of the Virgin of Los Remedios in Mexican history and culture. From 1821 to 1867 the shrine suffered declining revenues, deferred maintenance, haphazard administration, and, ultimately, a long, slow decline of capitalino interest in the image and its seat. The Mexico City ayuntamiento officers who directed the Remedios archicofradía were less active as a group during the 1820s, 1830s, and 1840s—perhaps a sign of declining public interest and certainly related to their own preoccupations with the political events swirling about them. Their meetings to deliberate on shrine matters became infrequent or failed to muster a quorum of members.[79] And with the expulsion of Spaniards in 1828 the culto required an ideological makeover. In 1829 the ayuntamiento instructed the *capellán* to secretly destroy any remaining prints that hinted at Remedios's earlier fame as a Spanish conquistadora, including prints that showed Hernán Cortés and Spanish nobles kneeling before the image. Remedios was repackaged as "the Mexicans' celestial watchtower" (*la celestial atalaya de los mexicanos*) in a little publication called "Salutación a la Virgen de los Remedios," printed for the venida that year.[80]

There were short periods of renewed sponsorship and repairs, especially in the early 1830s, but the end of the ayuntamiento's patronato authority at the beginning of the República Restaurada in 1867 was the final blow more than a sudden transformation. As the unwanted reputation as Royalist Virgin stuck to Our Lady of Los Remedios and devotion receded from Mexico City after independence, the villagers and small-town vecinos of the northeast fringe of the Valley of Mexico and neighboring districts sought to reclaim their cherished image of the Virgin Mary. Even as the buildings at the shrine deteriorated, revenues declined, and robberies of silver objects and jewels were reported, they guarded the possessions of the shrine as best they could. And the shrine and image continued to attract devotees from surrounding communities in the Valley and nearby states. Some three to four thousand people from close to fifty pueblos reportedly attended the fiesta anual in 1843.[81] Only in the late nineteenth century was the shrine virtually stripped of its wealth by self-serving administrators.[82]

Other Colonial Shrines After the Fall: Lagos, Chalma, the Sacromonte, and Talpa
In addition to Our Lady of Guadalupe at Tepeyac in the Valley of Mexico, the most renowned older shrines with far-flung followings during the early nineteenth century were those to Our Lady of San Juan de los Lagos and the Lord of Chalma. Unfortunately, there seems to be less documentation for these two shrines in the second and third quarters of the nineteenth century than there is for the late colonial period. Evidence for the scale and habits of devotion to Our Lady of San Juan de los Lagos is indirect or impressionistic, mainly in the form of information on economic activity, construction at the site, population trends, and the impressions of a few visitors. The shrine at San Juan has a large collection of ex-voto paintings, but few predate 1870.[83] The documentation on Chalma after independence is even less abundant than for Lagos, but some of it offers a glimpse of activities of ordinary devotees.

The shrine to Nuestra Señora de San Juan de los Lagos in the Altos de Jalisco, near the city of Santa María Lagos (today's Lagos de Moreno), originated in the seventeenth century and was a thriving enterprise before independence. The concentration of administrative records and viceregal decrees from 1777–1793 concerning the trade fair and principal feast of the Virgin in early December attest to its importance and vigor then.[84] The resident population in the town of San Juan in the 1790s was small—listed at 584 in 1792—but it swelled to about thirty-five thousand during the fair, where total transactions were estimated at five hundred thousand to seven hundred thousand pesos.[85] The towers of the great church were completed in 1790 and other public works were in progress. But the independence wars were a disaster for this shrine. Its fair was suspended for eleven years and many fewer visitors made their way to the shrine for the December fiestas. The local economy was also hurt by declining production in the mines of Guanajuato and an epidemic in the district from 1814–1816.[86] But recovery was swift after independence in 1821. The annual fiesta and fair blossomed again in the 1820s with the support of state licenses, and the growing town of San Juan was designated a villa in 1824. Improvements to the building and grounds were made during the 1830s, and a hospital and other public works were undertaken in the 1840s.[87] By 1837 the town represented a much larger proportion of the district population than it had in the colonial period, growing from 584 to 4,972, while the district population grew from about ten thousand to 13,038 in the same period. The fiesta and fair were said to attract about one hundred thousand visitors in the early 1840s, and they reportedly consumed eight thousand pesos worth of fruits and vegetables, 394 steers, 809 pigs, 670 sheep and lambs, and eight thousand fanegas of maize.[88] Enough visitors returned home with prints and other copies of the image of the miraculous Virgin that altars and chapels to her began to appear not only in western Mexico homes, but also in chapels dedicated to her as far away as New Mexico.[89] An 1849 article about the shrine and fair acknowledged its great popularity with a sardonic comment about officious sacristans and gullible pilgrims who clamored for relics:

> Whenever the sacristans sweep out the temple they take care to collect the accumulated trash, which they distribute as relics. The ignorance of the people is such that they believe the dirt, cigar butts and filth are a medicine which, ingested with water or as is, serves to to cure all kinds of illnesses.[90]

The town, shrine, and fair continued to grow during the 1840s, but an epidemic in 1850, contraband trade through the United States after the U.S.-Mexican War, and political struggles in 1852 added up to new setbacks for San Juan de los Lagos.[91] The fair was suspended again during the Wars of Reform and Liberal soldiers looted the shrine in 1859. The fair finally was reinstituted in 1866 and the shrine entered yet another period of growing devotion and economic activity.[92]

The documentation on Chalma, even in the eighteenth century, is sparse and disappointing for the most part, but it points quite clearly to an important regional shrine before, during, and after independence in central Mexico, especially for Indian villagers, including Otomí, Nahua, and Mazahua speakers. Why else would viceregal authorities bother to forbid pilgrimages to the shrine in the early stages of epidemics in 1807 and 1809?[93] The shrine prospered during the early nineteenth century, but without generating the wealth of financial and census records available for San Juan de los Lagos. Its remote location, far from main trade routes and political centers, and the humble means of most of its devotees perhaps explains the modest fair there and limited administrative record. Chalma only became an official pueblo in 1872 and never rivaled San Juan de los Lagos as an administrative center. The fairs during its two main religious holidays in March and June were much smaller than San Juan's. Less than one-tenth of the foodstuffs consumed at San Juan de los Lagos in the early 1840s festivities were needed for the two fiestas at Chalma in 1824.[94] But the size of the crowds at an annual fiesta and fair does not tell the whole story of a shrine's growth or importance. As the other great Indian shrine in central Mexico, it was visited throughout the year as well as during the special feast days. The frequent, incidental references in judicial records, devotional literature, wills, and household inventories to a visit to Chalma or an altar to the Chalma cristo in the local church, ex-voto paintings, and cheap prints or devotional paintings on a home altar in the early nineteenth century attest to the special appeal of the Chalma shrine, without the sharp ups and downs of activity experienced at San Juan de los Lagos.

The independence war touched Chalma at one stage, but with less of the partisanship or political repercussions that led to interruptions of the fairs and feast days at San Juan de los Lagos. In 1812 insurgent troops ventured into the settlement and shrine, but did little damage and were soon gone. According to one witness, they mainly wanted prints and medals of the miraculous image, offering to pay for them with the copper coins they used as currency.[95] Surprisingly, the Chalma shrine underwent the last phase of a major rebuilding project during and immediately after the war, between 1813 and 1830, with regular donations of labor and materials from pueblos de indios in the vicinity.[96] An 1817 record of part of an alms-collecting mission for this building project documents the reach of Chalma's appeal among Indians and workers in districts of Hidalgo, the Estado de México, the Valley of Mexico, and Tlaxcala. Among the communities visited by the alms collector between November 1816 and April 1817 were Zumpango de la Laguna, Alfajayuca, El Cardonal, Pachuca, Real del Chico, Papalota, Texcoco, Calpulalpan, and Tepetlaostoc.[97] The governor of the Estado de México made it clear in an 1828 circular to his district prefects and alcaldes that the pilgrimage to Chalma was entirely too popular, with its "numerous gathering of people of both sexes," draining vital labor from the fields, especially at Pentecost in late spring.[98] Finally, the continuing attraction of the Chalma shrine in the mid-nineteenth century is implicit in a letter dated December 26, 1850, from Francisco Cruz, an Augustinian friar at Chalma to Mariano Riva Palacio, governor of the Estado de México. The prospect of a caste war in central Mexico, like that in Yucatán, was on his mind. Writing from this center of Indian gatherings, he noted a "spirit of rebellion and extermination that others stir up among our native races" (espíritu de rebelión y exterminio que agita por otros pueblos a nuestras razas indígenas). Now, he reported, clandestine meetings were taking place, "even in the barrio churches," and rumors of plots to launch a caste war were circulating in nearby Malinalco.[99]

Like Chalma, the shrine of the Sacromonte and its image of the Santo Entierro (Christ entombed) at Amecameca is best known for its beginnings during the evangelization of native Americans in the sixteenth century and the fame of its annual fair and fiesta in the late nineteenth century, but it prospered in the early nineteenth century, too. And, like Chalma, it drew rural Indians, in this case mainly from the southern part of central Mexico near the Valley of Mexico, but also some devotees from places as far away as San Luis Potosí. Its retreat house and quarters for pilgrims date from the 1830s,[100] and a journal article from 1852 described a thriving shrine:

> The temple of our Lord is a most precious chapel, sumptuous, attractive, majestically adorned; its grandeur stands out even more thanks to the beautiful altar on which the venerable image is placed and the richness and exquisiteness of the image's adornments.... On the image's forehead is a headband studded with beautiful diamonds, and among the many vestments available to cover it there is one of such fine material and elaborate silver embroidery that it is said to be worth three thousand pesos.

During the three days of Carnaval Indians come in pilgrimages to visit the shrine from a hundred leagues away and more, from the mountains of the state of Querétaro, from San Luis Potosí and further on many families and dancers have gathered this year. Among the thousands of people of all sexes who go up to the shrine during these three days, many go up the whole way on their knees and reach the top shedding blood. Others give themselves over to more rigorous penances; and many come to confess.... In short, even though the culto of the Lord of the Sacromonte has always been great, you can be sure that it was never half as great as it in under the present priest. Promoting it is his obsession, his only thought.[101]

When the Jesuit hagiographer Francisco de Florencia chose to write about the great Marian shrines of western Mexico at the end of the seventeenth century, he focused on the Virgins of San Juan de los Lagos and Zapopan, but by 1850 Nuestra Señora del Rosario de Talpa had become the undeniable third, and copies of the image circulated and new devotees appeared as far north as New Mexico.[102] Known today as "Queen of the lowly" (*la reina de los humildes*),[103] was it the queen of the lowly as it grew in popularity during the nineteenth century? Thanks to a well-documented local history written by its mid-twentieth-century pastor, Manuel Carrillo Dueñas, and a recent sociological study, more is known about the shrine of Our Lady of Talpa in western Jalisco during the eighteenth and nineteenth centuries.[104] This was a notable shrine in the late colonial period. Developing around a story of the little Virgin's miraculous self-restoration in 1644, it was an active devotion in the late seventeenth and early eighteenth centuries when formal proceedings to document the founding miracle took place, along with later reports of marvelous healings, and a cofradía to promote the devotion, sponsor building projects, and organize the collection of alms. A novena booklet for this "amazing image" (*portentosa imagen*) was published in 1739 and reprinted in 1803 and 1804, a new church was begun in 1755, and the image was carried as far as Mascota on alms-collecting missions to pay for the construction.[105] A 1792 report spoke of "many pilgrims" gathering there for the annual feast day,[106] and Father Carrillo writes of "a notable number of pilgrims" visiting the shrine in 1800.[107] Carrillo Dueñas's history gives the impression of a colonial-era devotion that was mainly known and visited by rural and small-town devotees from the nearby mountain valleys of western Jalisco near the Pacific coast, especially the districts of Mascota and Huauchinango. Like Chalma, it was hard to reach and little more than a hamlet then. The cofradía and properties of the shrine were much diminished in the independence period, but after independence the devotion reached beyond its familiar territory, to Guadalajara and beyond. "Peregrina" images of Nuestra Señora de Talpa began to travel with alms collectors throughout the Diocese of Guadalajara and, from the 1820s, Carrillo Dueñas reports, pilgrims were taking away *brandea* (holy keepsakes) of various kinds—spent candles, flowers, medidas (colored ribbons cut to the height of the image) that had touched the image, earth from the holy well, and medals.[108] The cofradía grew again, as never before, but, like Lagos, there would be other setbacks. Throughout the 1820s and 1830s travel was especially dangerous in the district because insurgents and bandits were assaulting towns and travelers. For a time in the 1820s the fiestas and romerías to Talpa almost completely lapsed.[109] Nevertheless, the culto grew in devotees, visitors, and wealth during much of the second third of the nineteenth century. Important improvements to the shrine were undertaken in the 1830s and 1840s, and several thousand prints depicting the Virgin with a caption recounting the great miracle of renovation were printed and circulated with the bishop's permission.[110] More disorder from war, banditry, and forced conscription followed the start of the U.S.-Mexican War in 1846, but romerías to the shrine and alms-collecting expeditions continued. Most striking is the numbers of donors and members of the diocesan-wide lay hermandad of Nuestra Señora de Talpa by that time: Guadalajara, 16,445 members; La Barca 3,093; San Pedro Tlaquepaque 1,165; Santa Ana 666; Jocotepec 620, Jamay 587; Sayula 1,627; Zacoalco 1,099; Zapopan 205; Acaponeta 500; and Tecuala 485, to mention the largest contingents.[111] Participation in the romerías increased substantially at the same time, filling the church throughout the day during the February fiesta and sometimes even at night, and the modest fair turned into "a true regional fair." But the wars of la Reforma beginning in 1858 brought another notable decline, from which the shrine had recovered by 1867.[112]

Tepalcingo and Lay Politics of Devotion
The miraculous Christ of Tepalcingo (Morelos) is less often mentioned in the scholarly literature than other colonial shrines that prospered during the first half of the nineteenth century.[113] The manuscript record for the nineteenth century, as far as I know it, sheds little light on devotional practices,

but it does establish that the image and shrine remained popular then, as it had been in the eighteenth century, and with less direction from ecclesiastical authorities. The written record mainly charts disputes over who would oversee the administration of the shrine and its financial affairs. Incidentally, it documents how local "Indian" devotees claimed the santo as their own during and after the war of independence, to the dismay of most local priests and the minority of non-Indians in the community who had managed the sponsoring cofradía during most of the eighteenth century.

Little has been written about the beginnings of devotion to the wonder-working Christ of Tepalcingo beyond oral traditions that variously describe the image growing heavy when attempts were made to move it from its chosen place,[114] and a statement in the caption on a painting in the choir loft of the church that the cofradía of Jesús Nazareno was founded and approved on March 5, 1681, and that construction of the present church with its famous, ornate façade took place between 1759 and 1782.[115] Judging by a 1743 report, the new church was the fruit of a thriving popular devotion:

> In this district and town of Tepalcingo there is an image of Christ Our Lord with its shrine. Those who visit and beseech this image receive infinite rewards. Its fiesta is celebrated on the Day of the Holy Cross and on the third Friday of Lent there is a most solemn procession with such crowds that some small children suffocate in the church.... The alms collected on these occasions are copious.[116]

The 1758 construction license affirmed that a new church was needed because of "the multitude of people who gather there especially on the third Friday of Lent to venerate the aforesaid sacred image, which they can't do because the church is too small."[117] Bubbling beneath the surface of this popular eighteenth-century devotion was a bitter administrative dispute among local devotees and priests, adjudicated by the archiepiscopal court. It is mainly through a thick file of court records from 1817–1819 that the early years of the dispute are known. At that time the politics of the shrine took a new turn, during the lull in widespread political and social struggles of the independence period. Apparently the Indian founders of the cofradía in the late seventeenth century had not allowed any non-Indians (*"españoles"* or *"gente de razón"*) to become members, and they managed the resources of the shrine and its festivities in their own way. In 1722 Archbishop Lanciego intervened to reform the cofradía's organization by allowing non-Indians to join, designating "españoles" as its administrators, and reducing the participation of Indians in the affairs of the cofradía to a minority of three *diputados* on the governing board. In 1724 he canceled the annual Holy Wednesday procession because of excesses that are not specified in the summary record.[118] Indians of Tepalcingo, who outnumbered non-Indian residents by about ten to one,[119] did not accept or forget. They continued to litigate for restoration of their privileges into the 1740s, without success.[120] According to don Joseph Mijar, the *español mayordomo* of the cofradía from 1813–1816, españoles and gente de razón had been in "peaceful possession" (*quieta posesión*) of the administration from 1722 to 1816 and were responsible for the new church and the favorable balance sheet during all this time.[121] The 1758 construction license and the Indian side of the dispute in 1817 tell a more ambiguous story about "peaceful possession" and singular non-Indian patronage. In their petition for the building permit in 1758, Indians of Tepalcingo supported the project and promised to provide twenty-four workers in weekly rotations. All the parties recognized that more than religious fervor inspired the project. Indian leaders acknowledged in this petition that it was good for the local economy. They spoke of "the improvements that will come to their pueblo with the new church, which will mean greater veneration of the Holy Image and more visitors, and will result in widespread benefit to the pueblo."[122]

Popular devotion to the Christ of Tepalcingo evidently continued strong at the shrine during the independence war period. In the words of the pastor there in 1819, "the crowds of people who gather to adore the image of Jesus venerated there is immense."[123] But the war period occasioned new maneuverings over the administration of the shrine that led, first, to an attempt by Mijar to exercise more authority than the office of mayordomo allowed, and then to Indian leaders and followers taking over the shrine and its finances themselves. In the 1817–1819 records of the archiepiscopal court, Indian leaders and other Indian witnesses justified removing Mijar because he mismanaged the cofradía's considerable wealth for his own benefit and without oversight, the physical plant was deteriorating, and he had not convened a meeting of the cofradía officers since taking office in 1813. The longstanding ethnic dispute between the non-Indian minority and leaders of the Indian majority over administration of the shrine was playing out again. Indian leaders knew how the cofradía began in the seventeenth century, who its leading members had been, and who were the devotees of the Lord of Tepalcingo (an 1810 source described the people who flocked to the shrine during the third week of Lent as *"la yndiada foránea"*[124]). But larger church issues and priest-parishioner relations were at stake, too. Having secured a resident chaplain for the shrine in 1805, the Tepalcingo Indians wanted yet more independence and went to the archbishop's court in 1810 to become a separate parish. The request was not immediately granted, even though the *cura párroco* of Xonacatepec, the parish seat for Tepalcingo at that time, agreed that the difficulty of overseeing this growing population from a distance justified the separation. But the Indians of Tepalcingo did secure a resident pastor (*vicario de pie fijo*).[125] The resident pastor of Tepalcingo during the mid-1810s, Ygnacio Albares, evidently sided with Mijar and the non-Indian minority, allowing Mijar to be reelected mayordomo three times even though the constitution of the cofradía did not permit consecutive reelection. Indian witnesses in 1818 complained of Albares's tyrannical ways and his heated threats to their leaders. Pablo Bueno, chosen by the Indian faction to serve as mayordomo in place of Mijar, said the cura had grabbed the shrine keys from him and was now Bueno's "implacable enemy" (*fiera enemigo*). But one of the Indian witnesses, the church's organist, noted that when Father Albares came to the community he cared deeply for his flock, "treating them very well, but when they began to take control of the cofradía properties he joined with Mijar to abuse them."[126] The apple of discord that would seem to explain the pastor's change of heart was the cofradía treasury. The Indians were not going to take over the cofradía, shrine, and culto without a shower of litigation papers, if Mijar and Albares could help it.

The promotor fiscal summarized the several permutations of this endless dispute in his recommendation to the archbishop on November 28, 1818 (and adopted by the archbishop on January 30, 1819). The Indians, he observed, knew what they had lost. They wanted "their ancient rights as founders and proprietors restored,"[127] and they used Mijar's mismanagement of shrine properties and cofradía funds as a pretext to remove him and impose their own mayordomo. The promotor fiscal ultimately blamed the opportunism of the Indians' attorney, Mijar's "indolence," and especially the cura of Xonacatepec for stirring up old resentments and ambitions by telling the Indians that Mijar was an intruder and encouraging them to reclaim their power over the cofradía and shrine at the expense of their resident priest. The promotor found a convenient way through the immediate problem of Mijar's service as mayordomo. He noted that Mijar had broken the rules of the cofradía by holding the office four consecutive times from 1813–1816. He recommended that Mijar be removed, but that the reform of the cofradía instituted by Archbishop Lanciego in 1722 should continue in force, and that the españoles who had been "violently despoiled" of their offices by the Indians should be restored. This decision did not signal an end to the struggle over who would control the shrine and its resources. Frustrated in his attempt to take over the shrine's financial affairs, Tepalcingo's next priest, Lic. don Mariano Gonsales Escobar, claimed he was treated disrespectfully by parishioners and proposed to the archbishop in 1819 that the cofradía be disbanded altogether as a waste of funds and time, and as the source of political discord. He suggested that he should be the permanent rector of the cofradía, its finances, and other activities.[128]

The post-1821 record for Tepalcingo, as far as I know it, consists mainly of financial and administrative reports that indicate the shrine's continuing popularity and the survival—albeit unsettled—of the cofradía despite the efforts of several pastors to dismantle it once and for all. That the cofradía continued to exist is clear in the 1843 complaint by its officials to the archiepisocal court against their pastor, D. Manuel Villalobos, for taking five hundred pesos the Mesa (governing board) advanced to him to have twenty-five hundred silver medals struck for that year's fiesta and fair, and then failing to do so.[129] Judging by this order for so many medals, the fiesta and fair were still popular. The cofradía officers added that Villalobos, acting as rector of the cofradía, gathered up the alms collected during the fair and had not accounted for them or made them available for support of the culto. Their lawyer objected to Villalobos's claim that the cofradía effectively belonged to him as parish priest since it had been established for the shrine, not the parish. Once again, this thorny old issue of jurisdiction and administration was left unresolved.

Summary financial records for the Tepalcingo shrine at several points between 1807 and 1887 suggest that its following declined some in the nineteenth century, but it was still much visited, especially on the third Friday of Lent.[130] If the following summary figures are roughly accurate, the revenues (and by inference the attendance) declined by more than half from 1807 to 1818, grew again and operated in the black after independence without reaching the 1807 levels, then fell again by the 1880s. From May 15, 1806, to May 15, 1807, the shrine took in 7,565 pesos. With 1,819 pesos in expenditures, the net income to the cofradía treasury that year was 5,745 pesos. In 1818 the collections were 2,903 pesos, with expenditures of 1,876 pesos, for a net income of 1,206 pesos. In 1843, cofradía officials estimated that collections were between three thousand and four thousand pesos; and from May 25, 1886, to May 25, 1887, collections totaled 2,439 pesos against 1,826 pesos expenses for 613 pesos net income.[131] Whether this regional devotion led to many replicas of the Señor de Tepalcingo finding a place of honor in churches elsewhere is not clear. At least one replica, at Atlatlahuca, in the mountains between Tepalcingo and Mexico City, became famous in its own right, with estampas circulating in the 1840s.[132] Evidently, the fiesta and fair at Tepalcingo were still going strong in 1850. That year district officials worried that the gathering of people from so many pueblos would occasion a tax rebellion or invite an attack by gangs of robbers known to operate in the area.[133]

Conclusion

The history of the major shrines in the nineteenth century remains little known, and other leading shrines of the time such as Zapopan (Jalisco), Ocotlán (Tlaxcala), San Miguel del Milagro (Tlaxcala), Juquila (Oaxaca), Soledad (Oaxaca), and Izamal (Yucatán) ought to be included here. Also much about devotional practices is left to the imagination. Was Chalma on the annual itinerary of sacred journeys for Otomí people of San Pedro Cholula in the municipio of Ocoyoacac (Estado de México), as it is today? Did they carry their crosses and crucifixes with them? Did they stop at the same places, for the same reasons? Did they dance and sing along the way? Did they bless the four winds? Did they bring candles, flowers, and umbilical cords to leave at the shrine? Did they bring seeds to be blessed? I don't know. Nevertheless, the pattern of growing regional popularity and wealth at Tepeyac, Chalma, Talpa, San Juan de los Lagos, Plateros, and El Pueblito is clear. Tepeyac is no surprise, given the popularity and vigorous encouragement of devotion to Our Lady of Guadalupe after the 1730s, and the enthusiasm of leading politicians and priests after independence for this image as prophetic symbol of the nation, but that it did not eclipse other shrines outside the Valley of Mexico is noteworthy. The growth of these shrines was not untroubled. Some were little visited and in disrepair during the political turbulence of the independence wars, the U.S.-Mexican War, the Reforma, and the French Intervention, or because of the dangers of the road at other times, but most recovered and grew in the longer run. The independence period was a major turning point for the shrine of Our Lady of los Remedios, but barely felt at Chalma. Other shrines endured and prospered within these extremes.

Laicization—lay promotion and proactive participation in devotional practices, usually under the nominal direction of priests or at least without openly challenging church authority in spiritual matters—was a less visible development of the early nineteenth century. It was not altogether new, not apparent everywhere, and its material traces beyond the archives would have been perishable for the most part. But I find it in the growth of the Penitentes of New Mexico in the 1820s; at San Francisco Galileo, Querétaro, and Tepalcingo, Morelos, during the independence period and beyond; among the Huicholes of Zacatecas during the long absence of Franciscan missionaries; in the widening circles of devotees drawn to a favorite shrine in search of divine presence; perhaps in the growing numbers of ex-voto paintings and the enthusiasm of "Indians" from near and far (the *"indiada foránea"* of nineteenth-century reports) in life-giving, protecting images of Christ at Chalma, Tepalcingo, and the Sacromonte of Amecameca, which are still sacred territorial and temporal corners for villagers in much of central Mexico; and in the chorus of complaints by state and church officials about devotees' excesses and superstitions.

Historically, Mexican communities, large and small, have cherished the presence of Catholic priests as God's privileged mediators living among them, their sacramental and liturgical work vital to local well-being. Just about every community seemed to want a priest in residence, even when they complained of a particular pastor's demands or personal misconduct. Tepalcingo's quest for its own parish priest, or at least a resident *vicario*, is an example—appealing to the archbishop for the privilege even as local Indian leaders were moving to take control of the shrine's cofradía. Many other examples, from other places and times, could be added.[134] But after independence and up to the Porfiriato, the church in its country priests was receding from view and becoming more controversial. The response in rural Mexico to the diminished public role and presence of the clergy and the suspicion that God might be leaving with them was not the surge of sorcery, possession, and mysticism Michel de Certeau described for early modern Europe,[135] but, rather, this trend toward laicization within the church, sometimes with the encouragement of the remaining pastors. Unlike a familiar version of the modernization story, God was not disappearing or withdrawing into a private place apart from other areas of life, with a long, slow decline of public enthusiasm and display, even if political leaders in nineteenth-century Mexico who left us written records wished it so.[136]

Other changes in devotional life that may have been centered in the main towns and cities of Mexico largely elude me in this chapter. They include politicization of renowned images, feminization of piety, and a more private, interiorized piety. For less urbanized places, these directions of change are not much apparent. Mexican political leaders cloaked themselves in the legitimating aura of favorite religious images, but the overt messages of these images seem less politicized than European Marian apparitions of the time. The popularity of family altars in village homes during the nineteenth century might be taken as a kind of feminization of piety since the altars usually were maintained by women, but home altars were common in the colonial period and many were maintained by women then, too.[137] The prevalence of home altars in colonial dwellings also complicates the story of private, interiorized devotion as a new development from the late eighteenth century. Whether the modernizing outlook of state officials about a moderate and frugal (*sensato*) piety reached deep into devotional practices needs further study, keeping in mind where and how far new piety conformed to modern liberal notions of what religion is—"Autonomous, a distinct domain apart from other areas of life, private, in conformity with the causal laws of nature, reasonable, interior"[138]—which is also to ask whether emphasizing change in this direction is our teleological projection more than a reality of the time.

The new popularity of ex-voto paintings before the 1850s is hard to measure and evaluate given how rarely they survive in place in large numbers, but this mounting expression of personal devotion suggests a shift in devotional life before the Reforma: these evocative visual prayers and statements about the workings of the world and divine intervention now more than ever could amount to a calling-into-being, a "pre-diction," as Pierre Bourdieu put it. More than a private conversation or anonymous commemoration of divine favor in the form of a little silver arm or a candle,[139] the paintings could become devotional images in their own right, like a favorite statue or altar in the church that might call up the saint's presence and mediation if approached in the right way—an intimate, graphic presence for devotees in circumstances they could recognize as their own, donated by people like themselves, if not actual kin or neighbors. As stylized as they were, the ex-voto paintings have a specificity of time, place, and person that made them available to collective memory and personal faith across generations in a way that anonymous, generic votive offerings could not. They could be vernacular icons in their own right, with a symbolic language that did not simply signify something else. If I'm right,[140] this amounts to a subtle change in how faith was imbued, transmitted, and acted upon. It may have been a minor change in the scheme of things, but one that would help to explain the lasting power of belief in miracles in the face of the disappointment of unanswered prayers in troubled times and challenges from modernizing reformers among Mexico's nascent Liberals and some Conservatives.[141]

Perhaps this chapter will be taken as support for a sort of Weberian crisis thesis of popular devotion in which people facing outbreaks of war, drought, and disease respond with apocalyptic fear, a longing for miracles, and mass travels to shrines.[142] I hope not. The especially dangerous times of the independence period, the cholera epidemic of 1833, the U.S.-Mexican War, the civil wars of the Reforma, and the French intervention undoubtedly fed intense interest in the divine presence in famous images of Christ and Mary, but those dangers also disrupted the flow of visitors to the shrines. The 1830s, a calmer time politically, but shadowed by the cholera epidemic, witnessed substantial growth of miracle shrines, including San Juan de los Lagos, Plateros, and the shrine of Nuestra Señora de la Soledad in Jerez, Zacatecas.[143] These crises are not a sufficient explanation of the growth of shrines. The problem with such a periodization for the history of shrines is that political and social crisis must have seemed endemic as well as episodic in central Mexico then. Highway robbers, insurgents, separatist movements, sackings of churches and jails, food shortages, and disease were familiar dangers. And the crises that mattered most to individuals were personal more than collective—a grave illness or accident in the family, an armed attack on the way home. Sudden, early death and narrow escapes were the horizon of life for all but the most sheltered and privileged Mexicans.

There may have been great, lasting changes in devotional life during the nineteenth century that can be tracked chronologically—building on changes that date from in the mid-eighteenth century for guadalupanismo, reforms meant to desacralize the role of pastors in public life, and new gaps between elite and popular religious sensibilities; and perhaps the 1850s was a tipping point—but the more telling pattern in this early national history of religion in Mexico is change in the form of eventful continuities. Public quest for religious experience and answers continued, and reported theophanies seem to have been as frequent as ever and were shared across classes, not only among villagers and the urban poor. Regional shrines developed, but nearly all of them began in the seventeenth century and were well established before the end of the colonial period. Marian devotion intensified, especially in the second half of the nineteenth century, but this, too, was a great continuity. Devotion to the infant Jesus became more popular, and some miraculous images of Christ's Passion rose to prominence for the first time or became more popular than they had been in the colonial period, but miracle shrines dedicated to images of Christ had long been the most numerous of all in Mexico. Ex-voto paintings became more popular, too, but they were not a new form and would continue as a favorite expression of appeal and gratitude well into the twentieth century, long after they had virtually disappeared from European shrines. The localocentrism of faith that underlies the paradox of widespread reverence for Our Lady of Guadalupe throughout New Spain and Mexico without distant devotees going to Tepeyac in large numbers did not radically change. Despite all the ways provincial Mexicans were influenced by regional and global developments, nationalism or even provincialism had not displaced the conviction of many rural Mexicans that they lived "in the middle of the world rather than, as others would have it, in the middle of nowhere," as Kathleen Norris put it for another North American place.[144] Does this emphasis on eventful continuity in the first half of the nineteenth century depend on a radical separation between rural and urban or popular and elite, and an emphasis on timeless mentalities over decisive events? Shrine histories, greater changes to come, and my earlier study of priests in their parishes leads me to think not, but we know too little about the many aspects of devotional practices in the past to make sweeping claims with much confidence.

Introduction

1. *Democracy and Education: An Introduction to the Philosophy of Education*, first paperback edition (New York: The Free Press, 1966), 148.
2. Donald W. Meinig, *A Life of Learning: Charles H. Haskins Lecture*, American Council of Learned Societies occasional paper no. 19 (New York: ACLS, 1992), 18–19.
3. Thanks to conversations with Robert A. Pois at the University of Colorado, Boulder, I was introduced to the essays of Louis O. Mink early in my career. His "The Autonomy of Historical Understanding," *History & Theory* 5: no. 1 (1966): 24–47, still comes to mind when I think about my approaches to historical study and the challenge of a combined, comprehensive view. By "synoptic," Mink meant "comprehending a complex event by 'seeing things together' in a total and synoptic judgment which cannot be replaced by any analytic technique" (42).
4. *Inquietud* carries more meaning than "unease." It suggests a spirit of curiosity and action that can lead to unexpected discoveries and paradoxes in a line of inquiry. It invites travel on side roads as well as thoroughfares.
5. Lesley Byrd Simpson, *Many Mexicos* (New York: Putnam, 1941)—the first of many editions.
6. Besides Mexico itself, I have been emboldened in this undertaking not so much by writings on place theory or other histories as by J. B. Jackson's *A Sense of Place, A Sense of Time* (New Haven: Yale University Press, 1994), Yi-fu Tuan's writings on space and place, and the universe of E. B. White's small world ("I seldom went anywhere or did anything. My activities smelled of the

hearth.... Instead of being in Karachi, I was in the barn, or in the bathtub. My life was uneventful, my habits were fixed, and my thoughts to an alarming degree ranged back and forth over my small immediate affairs," *The Points of My Compass: Letters from the East, the West, the North, the South* [New York and Evanston: Harper & Row, 1962], xii). As Tuan recognizes, the challenge is to have place and space fixed and fluid in mind at the same time: "A self that is coherent and firm, yet capable of growth, would seem to call for an alternation of stillness and motion, stability, and change, place and space, the duration of each being calibrated by culture and individual temperament," *Place, Art, and Self* (Santa Fe: Center for American Places, 2004), 4.

7. *Landlord and Peasant in Colonial Oaxaca* (Stanford, CA: Stanford University Press, 1972).
8. *Drinking, Homicide, and Rebellion in Colonial Mexican Villages* (Stanford, CA: Stanford University Press, 1979).
9. *Magistrates of the Sacred: Priests and Parishioners in Eighteenth-Century Mexico* (Stanford, CA: Stanford University Press, 1996).
10. *The Second Tree from the Corner* (New York: Harper & Brothers, 1954), 173.
11. Italo Calvino, *Six Memos for the Next Millennium* (Cambridge, MA: Harvard University Press, 1988), 93–94. For a helpful discussion of material images, spoken words, and written texts as equally valued forms of knowledge and memory in the Hispanic world during the period of American colonization, see Fernando J. Bouza, *Communication, Knowledge, and Memory in Early Modern Spain* (Philadelphia: University of Pennsylvania Press, 2004).
12. In Donna Pierce, Rogelio Ruiz Gomar, and Clara Bargellini, *Painting a New World: Mexican Art and Life, 1521–1821* (Denver: Denver Art Museum, 2004), 83.
13. Jonathan Z. Smith, *Imagining Religion: From Babylon to Jonestown* (Chicago: University of Chicago Press, 1982), 52.
14. In his memorably aphoristic way, Tuan reflects on the possibilities and complexities of thinking across these fields in *Place, Art, and Self*, 3, 20, 21–22, and 44.
15. *El ogro filantrópico: Historia y política, 1971–1978* (México: Joaquín Mortiz, 1979), 49.
16. "Sólo tu fe puede guiarte a creer si fue un milagro o fue una construcción de los religiosos de ese tiempo. Sin embargo, la Virgen de Guadalupe llegó a México y fue bien recibida."
17. "Oy no se ausenta de nosotros aunque sube al Cielo," Francisco de Fuentes y Carrión, *Sermón de la Assumpción de Nuestra Señora, en su propio día: predicado en Guadalupe, con la circunstancia de su milagrossa aparición, patente el SSmo. Sacramento por aver concurrido en el último día de el jubileo circular nuevamente concedido a esta muy noble ciudad, y corte de México; y su primera vez en Guadalupe celebrado* (México: En la Imprenta de Francisco Ribera Calderón, 1707); Miguel Tadeo de Guevara, *Visita sin despedida, que hizo Maria Santísima de Guadalupe al reyno, para la estabilidad y firmeza de la Iglesia americana. Oración panegyrica, que en su insigne y real Colegiata predicó el dia de la celebridad de su aparición, 12 de diciembre del año pasado de 1780* (Mexico: Zúñiga y Ontiveros, 1781); article in the *Dallas Morning*

News, December 12, 1995, A.1, during the economic crisis that followed the Salinas de Gortari administration. "She came to stay," as "a simple Indian woman," said to Virgil Elizondo at Tepeyac, foreword to Jeannette Rodríguez, *Our Lady of Guadalupe: Faith and Empowerment Among Mexican-American Women* (Austin: University of Texas Press, 1993), xiii.
18. *Letters of E. B. White*, rev. ed. (New York: HarperCollins, 2006), 669.
19. *The History Primer* (New York: Basic Books, 1971), 80 and 207–16.
20. From McNair's talk at the Maine Historical Society, Portland, ME, June 24, 2007.

Chapter 1

1. The beginnings of the shrine at Tulantongo and the Franciscans' complaint in 1656 are documented in Archivo General de la Nación (hereafter AGN) Indios 20, exp. 200, fols. 151–53. For Archbishop Aguiar y Seijas's pastoral visit to Tulantongo, see Archivo Histórico del Arzobispado de México, filed with other pastoral visit records, fols. 39–40, November 17, 1683. Vetancurt's mention of the dedication of the new church in 1676, the Franciscan pastor in residence, and popularity of the shrine in the 1690s is in his *Teatro mexicano; descripción breve de los sucesos ejemplares, históricos y religiosos del Nuevo Mundo de las Indias. Crónica de la Provincia del Santo Evangelio de México* (México: Porrúa, 1971), facsimile of 1697 first edition, 134, par. 87. For the shrine's origin story as told in the mid-eighteenth century, see Francisco de Solano, ed., *Relaciones geográficas del Arzobispado de México. 1743* (Madrid: C.S.I.C., 1988), II:460–61, and José Antonio Villaseñor y Sánchez, *Theatro Americano: Descripción general de los reynos y provincias de la Nueva España, y sus jurisdicciones . . .* (México: Viuda de J. B. de Hogal, 1746), I, chap. 34: 156–57. The New Testament miracle story in John 9:6–7 established what a proper healing miracle of this kind, but without the image, should be like: "I am the light of the world. As he said this, he spat on the ground and made clay of the spittle and anointed the man's eyes with the clay, saying to him, 'Go, wash in the pool of Si'login' [which means sent]. So he went and washed and came back seeing."
2. AGN Cofradías y Archicofradías 14, exp. 7, fols. 199–234.
3. Antonio Flores Flores, *Zapotlán del Rey* (Zapotlán del Rey: n.p., 1995), 70.
4. Social and temporal dimensions of immanence and images deserve much fuller study than I give them here, and they open another array of questions. Was immanence understood to be more available at certain times of the year—liturgical and agricultural? At particular stages of life? In times of personal and collective calamity? What activities were involved, beyond the posture of prayer and state of contrition? And where was immanence likely to be found? Was intimacy with particular images available to all, in the same way? Were priests vital to availability, either as custodians of sacred images or as consecrators of them in the Buddhist way?

   Valuable entries into the subject of saints and images in colonial Mexico include Pierre Ragon, *Les saints et les images du Mexique (XVI–XVIII siècle)* (Paris: L'Harmattan, 2003), and Serge Gruzinski, *Images at War: Mexico*

From Columbus to Blade Runner (1492–2019) (Durham, NC: Duke University Press, 2001).

5. *Disertación crítico-theo-filosófica sobre la conservación de la santa imagen de Nuestra Señora de los Ángeles*... (México: Zúñiga y Ontiveros, 1801), 1. "Reverenciamos las Imágenes con un culto relativo por la excelencia de su original, de modo que aquell sumisión eternal con que nos presentamos delante de una Imagen sagrada, se dirige inmediatamente a ella, y en ella o por ella o por ella enderesamos nuestros respetos al Santo que nos representan; y así el afecto de la sumisión interna a solo el original se encamina. Esto enseña el santo Concilio Tridentino quando dice: Por las Imágenes que besamos, a quienes descubrimos la cabeza, y en cuya presencia nos arrodillamos, adoramos a Christo, y veneramos a los Santos cuya semejanza tienen."

In fewer words, Fr. Joseph Manuel Rodríguez summarized this position in his sermon, *El país afortunado: oración panegyrica, que en la anual solemnidad con que celebra la nobilíssma ciudad de México la maravillosa aparición de Nuestra Señora de Guadalupe*... (México: Zúñiga y Ontiveros, 1768), "What veneration do we owe to images? The same that we would give to the saints they represent." (¿Y qué reverencia es la que debemos a las imágenes?... la misma que daríamos a los Santos que representan.)

6. This was a familiar idea in Christian, soon-to-be Catholic practice before Columbus. As Patricia Lee Rubin notes for fifteenth-century Florence, spoken words and visual representations that followed established formulas were primary instruments of instruction in Christian history and doctrine, and the "ignorant" laity was understood to mean all those who were unable to read Latin and therefore lacked direct access to holy scripture (see "Art and the Imagery of Memory," in *Art, Memory, and Family in Renaissance Florence*, ed. Giovanni Ciappelli and Patricia Lee Rubin, 67–85 [New York: Cambridge University Press, 2000]).

In the broadest sense, the purpose of art has been "to 'keep' and transmit meanings," as expressed by Christian Norberg-Shulz, *Genius Loci: Towards a Phenomenology of Architecture* (New York: Rizzoli, 1980), 5. One of the witnesses in the formal investigation of miracles associated with Diego Lázaro and the shrine of San Miguel del Milagro in Tlaxcala in 1644 was his maternal grandmother. She brought in two paintings depicting the events, given to her by her grandson, who, she said, told her to keep them safe (see Francisco de Florencia, *Narración de la marabillosa aparición, que hizo el archangel San Miguel a Diego Lázaro*... [Sevilla: Impr. de las Siete Revueltas, 1692], 96–99).

7. In his unpaginated *aprobación* for a sermon by Manuel Folgar about the famous Cristo Renovado de Ixmiquilpan, *La mayor fortuna de la América, nacida de gozar un Santo Christo renovado, en vez de tenerlo aparecido* (México: F. de Rivera Calderón, 1731).

8. Ibid.

9. *Sermón panegyrico, que predicó el muy rdo. p. Antonio Paredes de la sagrada Compañía de Jesús... en la solemne acción de gracias, que el día 14. de octubre de 1759...* (México: Colegio de San Ildefonso, 1761). Paredes's words—"*son las imágenes eloquentes oradores que provocan la piedad*"—would have been inspired by the view and practice of the founder of his order, Ignatius of

Loyola, in his *Spiritual Exercises*, a program of spiritual experience in which visual images became a way to spiritual knowledge, inflaming the soul with love of its Creator, quoted in Jeffrey Chipps Smith, *Sensuous Worship: Jesuits and the Art of the Early Catholic Reformation in Germany* (Princeton, NJ: Princeton University Press, 2002), 24. Fernando Bouza rightly emphasizes that painted or printed images, written or printed words, and spoken words all were equally—if differently—valued as forms of knowing and remembering in early modern Spain (*Communication, Knowledge, and Memory in Early Modern Spain* [Philadelphia: University of Pennsylvania Press, 2004]). (Other forms of communication might be added, especially gestures, including dance.) Bouza goes a step further to suggest that people then understood "the possibility that a representation could materialize as a real presence. The idea that saying [or showing] something was not far removed from invoking whatever was being named" (21).

10. In Calvino's essay on "Visibility" in *Six Memos for the Next Millennium* (Cambridge, MA: Harvard University Press, 1988), 81–91.

11. Diana L. Eck, *Darsan: Seeing the Divine Image in India*, 2nd ed. (Chambersburg, PA: Anima Books, 1985), 6 and passim. See also Richard H. Davis, *Lives of Indian Images* (Princeton, NJ: Princeton University Press, 1999), chap. 1. The significance of images in Buddhist practices also provides a suggestive comparison. Donald K. Swearer (*Becoming the Buddha: The Ritual of Image Consecration in Thailand* [Princeton, NJ: Princeton University Press, 2004], 5, 13, 77–79, 110) shows how consecration rituals for images of the Buddha in Thailand are about "opening the eyes" of the image, instilling it with the power achieved by the Buddha at his enlightenment by instructing the image in the life story of the person the image represents. The Buddha is made present in the consecration. The image "symbolizes and *is* the Buddha." The result is not so different from the idea of immanence in Christian images discussed here, although Thai Buddhism places greater emphasis on the act of consecration.

Yi-fu Tuan noticed how sight as the main way of experiencing and knowing—seeing is believing—has cultural and historical dimensions. In *Segmented Worlds and Self: Group Life and Individual Consciousness* (Minneapolis: University of Minnesota Press, 1982), 124, he wrote that since the sixteenth century, especially with the new vogue of perspective painting in oils, "Europeans, even more than the Chinese, have moved in the direction of the visual.... The European medieval world [by contrast] was odoriferous to a high degree."

In its turn toward reception and a sprawling conception of visual culture, the field of art history has become more interested in synesthesia—a "multisensory range of experiences"—not only sight. See, for example, Deborah Cherry, ed., *Art History: Visual: Culture* (London: Blackwell, 2005).

12. Toribio de Benavente (Motolinía), *Memoriales e Historia de los indios de la Nueva España* (Biblioteca de Autores Españoles, Madrid: Atlas, 1970), 321. Motolinía also attributed the salubrious effects of St. Francis's knotted girdle to sincere faith as much as to the object itself: "yo bien creo que obra tanto la devoción que en el cordón tienen, como la virtud que en él hay." Agustín

Dávila Padilla reported in 1596 that Fray Thomas de San Juan witnessed an apparition of Our Lady of los Ángeles in his cell when "más fervor tenía en su contemplación," in *Historia de la Provincia de Santiago de México por la Orden de Predicadores, y las vidas de sus varones insignes, y cosas notables de Nueva España*, 3rd ed. (Bruselas: En casa de Francisco Vivien, 1648 [first ed., 1596]), 376–78.

13. Notions of beauty and art have become more historicized in recent scholarship as art historians reconsidered basic issues of what to study and how. The practice of an older, humanistic connoisseurship, exemplified by, say, Bernard Berenson and Kenneth Clarke, in which the expert maintains an aestheticizing distance in order to identify the great and characteristic works of art from a given time and culture, were challenged by scholars who found the standards of such experts time bound and idiosyncratic more than timeless and universal. The prevailing conception of art and beauty, along with the distinction between art and craft, they proposed, were products of eighteenth-century notions of art versus craft and a universalizing, largely secular conception of art and beauty; for example, Larry Shiner, *The Invention of Art: A Cultural History* (Chicago: University of Chicago Press, 2003), passim, but especially 34, drawing on Paul Oskar Kristeller's famous essay, "Modern System of the Arts: A Study in the History of Aesthetics," *Journal of the History of Ideas* 12, no. 4 (1951): 496–527 and 13, no. 1 (1952): 17–46. Major works in this vein are David Freedberg, *The Power of Images: Studies in the History and Theory of Response* (Chicago: University of Chicago Press, 1989), and Hans Belting, *Likeness and Presence: A History of the Image Before the Era of Art*, trans. Edmund Jephcott (Chicago: University of Chicago Press, 1994). These works challenged the secularizing connoisseurship view of art and beauty by blurring the line between fine art and craft and situating the meaning of beauty and the "power" of images in time and place by giving more attention to reception. Freedberg's book, in particular, has opened the way, but it also represents something of a new secularism in its functionalist stance, little attention to immanence, and the limits to what historians can hope to do with reception. A recent article by James I. Porter challenges Kristeller's view of a radical change in the eighteenth century, but not in a way that vindicates the older connoisseurship (see "Is Art Modern? 'Modern System of the Arts' Reconsidered," *The British Journal of Aesthetics* 49, no. 1 [2009]: 1–24).

14. "La imagen de la Señora es Hermosa a las maravillas ... causa devoción, respeto y ternura mirarle a la cara," *La casa peregrina, solar ilustre, en que nació la Reyna de los Ángeles* ... (México: Herederos de la Viuda de Bernardo Calderón, 1689), fol. 87r.

15. *Relaciones geográficas del Arzobispado de México. 1743*, I:251–52, "un hermoso y divino lienzo ... cuya bellísima imagen es tan propia y semejante a su prodigioso original que ... atrae a todos los fieles como dulce imán de sus devociones, a quienes con sus piadosos favores enriquece de celestiales dones."

16. "Perfection" often came to mind as ecclesiastical authors both in Spain and Spanish America described renowned images. An eighteenth-century Spanish text, *Aragón, reyno de Christo, y dote de María SSma: fundado sobre la columna immóbil de nuestra señora en su ciudad de Zaragoza* ..., by Roque Alberto Faci (Zaragoza: Unión Aragonesa del Libro, 1979 facsimile

of 1739 edition), wrote of perfection in terms of its emotional impact on the viewer, "Esta imagen es muy perfecta y causa gran compunción a quantos la miran" (39); "se inmute el Corazón ... se sentía el peso de aquella Magestad" (48); "los mueve a singular dolor y compasión" (67). Perfection carried the image beyond human abilities and signaled divine intervention, either guiding the artist's hand or made by angels. For example, the 1712 sermon by José Ximénez de Villaseñor, O.P., *Sermón panegírico en la célebre fiesta*... (México: Herederos de J. J. Guillena Carrascoso, 1712), described the statue of Nuestra Señora de la Plata as "no de Humana mano, sino de la Diestra de Dios."

17. For example, Florencia added to his description of the Virgin of Loreto that the image was covered in "very rich jewels of gold and precious stones, very elegant and costly garments," *La casa peregrina*, fol. 87r. Francisco de la Rosa, the Franciscan promoter of devotion to Our Lady of Intercession of Tepetlatcingo, discussed in my *Marvels and Miracles in Late Colonial Mexico: Three Texts in Context* (forthcoming, University of New Mexico Press), wanted to adorn this statue with gold, pearls, and costly garments.

18. "*Decoroso*" appears in Inquisition edicts describing appropriate images; e.g., AGN Edictos de Inquisición II, exps. 13 and 14.

19. Colonial Mexican religious images deserve closer study as "evolved objects" that accrued meaning from long use that could be read on their surfaces and in the stories about them. J. E. Ziegler coined the term "evolved objects" and began to examine some European examples in "The Medieval Virgin as Object: Art or Anthropology?," *Historical Reflections/Reflexions Historiques* 16, no. 2–3 (summer/fall 1989): 261–62. A particularly rich case of an evolved object that became a uniquely precious vessel of collective memory and continuity through use and embellishment is the Golden Stool of Ashanti rulers in West Africa. It is discussed briefly, but well, by Richard J. Parmentier, in *The Sacred Remains: Myth, History, and Polity in Belau* (Chicago: University of Chicago Press, 1987), 13.

20. For example, Cuauhtitlán in 1785–1786, AGN Clero Regular y Secular 103, exp. 11, and D. José Gómez, *Anales de México* (1776–1798), manuscript copy evidently prepared for Carlos María Bustamante, Bancroft Library, University of California, Berkeley (hereafter Bancroft), M-M 105, fol. 148r-v; and Xichú in 1768 as described by Felipe Castro Gutiérrez, "Resistencia étnica y mesianismo en Xichú, 1769," *Sierra Gorda, pasado y presente: Coloquio en homenaje a Lino Gómez Canedo 1991* (Querétaro: Fondo Editorial de Querétaro, 1994), 134–35. In his inspection of possessions in churches of Nayarit in 1884, Father Manuel María Estragues seemed bemused by the fact that a large crucifix that he judged "no longer serviceable" was still "much revered," in Eucario López, ed., *Algunos documentos de Nayarit* (Guadalajara: Librería Font, 1978), 101.

21. For example, Bancroft MSS 72/57m, box 3, folder 20, file of compliance letters from parishes in Mexico and Guatemala, 1767–1768.

22. "Los milagros de esta Imagen son vozes que la publican"; "tenemos por ciertas sólo con fe humana," *La milagrosa invención de un tesoro escondido en un campo*... (México: Viuda de Juan de Ribera, 1685), chaps. 1 and 2.

23. *Exaltación de la divina misericordia en la milagrosa renovación de la soberana imagen de Christo* . . . , 4th ed. (Mexico: Herederos del Lic. D. Joseph de Jáuregui, 1790), 1.

Countless records document the popularity across colonial society of scapularies, religious medals, printed images, prayer books, and brandea of all sorts that were associated with miraculous images. For example, in the words of Carmelite Padre Alonso, quoted in Dionisio Victoria Moreno, *Los Carmelitas Descalzos y la conquista espiritual de Mexico, 1585–1612* (México: Porrúa, 1966), 196: "En sólo el convento de México todos los meses pasa de ordinario de 100 pesos de limosna de escapularios y [hay] meses de 150 pesos y otros han llegado a 200 pesos y a más que se han más de 300 escapularios a todo género de gente y lo que más es, a muchos eclesiásticos y religiosos de otras Ordenes y monjas."

24. "The Visual Image: Its Place in Communication," in *The Essential Gombrich*, ed. Richard Woodfield, 42 (London: Phaidon Press, 1996).

25. On the human body as sacred vessel of cosmic powers in precolonial Mesoamerica, see Davíd Carrasco, *Religions of Mesoamerica: Cosmovision and Ceremonial Centers* (San Francisco: Harper & Row, 1990), 66, and Alfredo López Austin, *The Human Body and Ideology: Concepts of the Ancient Nahuas*, 2 vols. (Salt Lake City: University of Utah Press, 1988). A suggestive example is Elizabeth Boone's reading of the Mixtec Codex Vienna in which the divine figure/culture hero Nine Wind proceeds to create life on earth following "a conference" with twelve anthropomorphic stones and plants, in *Stories in Red and Black: Pictorial Histories of the Aztecs and Mixtecs* (Austin: University of Texas Press, 2000), 94.

26. Henry B. Nicholson, "Religion in Pre-Hispanic Central Mexico," in *Handbook of Middle American Indians* (Austin: University of Texas Press, 1971), 10:395–446, especially 408.

27. As Inga Clendinnen observed "maize . . . at each stage of its growth [was represented] by a human of the appropriate age and stage, while the images which represented the fruitful or more benign aspects of earth Mother, in her role as Sustenance Woman or as Jade Skirt, goddess of fresh waters, were commonly mature women. The faces are typically impassive and the images dwarfed by their regalia, most especially their vastly elaborate headdress, but they remain indubitably human for all that," in *Aztecs, An Interpretation* (Cambridge and New York: Cambridge University Press, 1991), 348, n. 61. But this is only part of the story of precolonial forms. Clendinnen also emphasizes that monumental female figures such as the great image of Coatlicue were not human effigies and had nothing human about them beyond her architectural form. "Insofar as they were women, they were bloody creative force, suffused by sacred danger" (Personal communication).

28. William B. Taylor, "Cristos de Caña," in *Oxford Encyclopedia of Mesoamerican Cultures*, ed. Davíd Carrasco, I:286–87 (New York: Oxford University Press, 2001).

29. Relics are not discussed in this essay although they would have an important place in this history of immanence. Relics for the consecration of churches and time-honored relic shrines dating from the Middle Ages were still

important in Catholic Europe in the early modern period, though they were coming to be overshadowed by other manifestations of divine presence, especially apparitions and images, or combined with them. In America, where there were no native saints until the seventeenth century and few at all before the twentieth century, relics played a different role. Jesuits, in particular, were great importers of relics for nearly two centuries, but these holy materials were more important to the orders in America—especially the women's orders—in their personal and community devotions, and in the consecration of churches, than as focal points of divine immanence in popular devotion. Like the Jesuits, Franciscans in New Spain treated the bodies of their holiest members and martyrs as virtual relics and associated them with miracles. Again, these materials seem to have been mostly popular among the friars themselves. One possible exception is splinters of the True Cross, which were displayed in several churches in central Mexico and attracted more attention, especially the one in the Franciscan college church in Pachuca.

30. In her study of a sixteenth-century text of miracle stories in Nahuatl, Louise Burkhart noted that eight of the ten stories involved the Virgin Mary, and that six of the eight Marian miracles were apparitions in which Mary came to them in a dream, or spoke to them, or appeared without speaking ("'Here is Another Marvel': Marian Miracle Narratives in a Nahuatl Manuscript," in *Spiritual Encounters: Interactions Between Christianity and Native Religions in Colonial America*, ed. Nicholas Griffiths and Fernando Cervantes, 91–115 [Lincoln: University of Nebraska Press, 1999]). For an example of an individual claiming to be God Almighty, see AGN Bienes Nacionales 1285, exp. 19, 1660, "contra un indio llamado Gregorio Juan que en el pueblo de Atohuizcuautla se hace venerar como Dios Todopoderoso, acompañado de doce apóstoles."

31. Gerónimo de Mendieta, *Historia eclesiástica indiana* (México: Consejo Nacional para la Cultura y las Artes, 1997), vol. I, chap. 49, 473–76.

32. The celebrated apparition story of the Virgin of Guadalupe was settled and enthusiastically promoted for creoles and Indians by ecclesiastical authorities in Mexico City from 1648; the apparition stories for the shrines of the *cruz de piedra* in Querétaro and San Miguel del Milagro in Tlaxcala were established even earlier; and the apparition story for the Virgin of Tulantongo was accepted and developed from the 1640s, as well. Apparition stories for the Virgin of La Salud of Pátzcuaro (Michoacán) and Dolores Soriano (Querétaro) date from the early eighteenth century.

33. Library of Congress, Henry A. Monday Collection, container 17 (reel 13 of the microfilm edition). The investigation was led by Lic. Luis Becerra Tanco, best known for his later role as a leading promoter of devotion to the image and apparition story of Our Lady of Guadalupe. Martinus Cawley emphasizes the Gospel spirit in which the investigation was carried out, "Becerra Tanco as Expert for an Apparition of 1648," unpublished manuscript.

Occasionally other apparitions by souls in Purgatory are mentioned in the colonial record. At the end of the sixteenth century, Mendieta dedicated Chapter 28 of his *Historia eclesiástica indiana* to "algunos defunctos que por divina voluntad han aparecido a personas particulares, para ser socorridos." And Mariano Fernández de Echeverría y Veytia (1718–1779), apparently writing in the 1770s, mentioned an artifact much like Pachuca's flaming hand of Purgatory. Among the venerable "relics" of the chapel of Our Lady of los Remedios in the city of Puebla were two boards branded with handprints "que se dice ser de dos mujeres cuyas almas estaban en el purgatorio y apareciéndose a otras vivas se pidieron sufragios, para salir de sus penas y por indicio de éstas estamparon las manos en aquellas tablas," *Historia de la fundación de la ciudad de la Puebla de los Ángeles en la Nueva España. Su descripción y presente estado*, posthumous publication (Puebla: Imprenta Labor, 1931).

34. Jacinto de la Serna, "Manual de ministros de indios para el conocimiento de sus idolatrías y extirpación de ellas," in *Colección de documentos inéditos para la historia de España* (Madrid: Academia de la Historia, 1893), 104:1–267; Pedro Ponce, "Breve relación de los dioses y ritos de la gentilidad," in *Tratado de las idolatrías, supersticiones, dioses, ritos, hechicerías y otras costumbres gentílicas de las razas aborígenes de México* (México: Ediciones Fuente Cultural, 1953), I:369–80. Another example is in Archivo Histórico del Arzobispado de México (hereafter AHAM), caja 1691–1769, 1691 "Diligencias contra indio idólatra de Calimaya, Domingo de San Juan por visiones diabólicas."

35. AHAM, caja for 1728, exp. 11. Francisco Diego was subjected to public humiliation, among other penalties.

36. Tulantongo is mentioned by Vetancurt, *Teatro mexicano* (Mexico: Porrúa, 1971), 134, but not as an apparition story. Franciscans and Jesuits were particularly active promoters of images and their association with miracles. Their missions of spiritual renewal would seem to be the thread that connects them in this way, often extolling the same notable images or advocations.

37. Images at home, displayed on walls and improvised altars, are frequently documented in colonial chronicles, and notarial, administrative, and judicial records, especially wills, inventories of personal possessions, and disputes within families over inheritance of images. Occasionally there are more descriptive references to early home altars. A purported 1582 inquiry into miracles associated with the image of the Virgin Mary known as La Conquistadora in Puebla, copied in 1632 and published in 1804, includes testimony that Hernán Cortés gave the image to a native cacique, don Gonzalo, in thanks for his services during the conquest of Tenochtitlan, and that don Gonzalo kept it "on a board made into a table, with many flowers and painted cloths, and there he venerated it." A 1645 criminal case mentions an "oratory in the home of the Indian choirmaster, well-swept . . . with lighted candles on the altar and framed with boughs and roses" (AGN Criminal 187, fol. 276). An especially detailed description of a home oratory is in AHAM, caja for 1754–1755, in the home of Luis Nicolás, Indian of San Nicolás Tlachialoya, district of Toluca, 1755. Descriptions of early home altars of non-Indians with images and candles are included in AGN Inquisición 471, exp. 78, 1606 Puebla, and Bancroft MSS 96/95m, box 5, item 3, 1617 Mexico City.

38. The idea of altars and images sanctifying and protecting the home was widely shared across colonial society. Consider the recent discovery of medals, coins, and palm crosses placed in a hollow stone ball atop one of the belltowers of Mexico City's cathedral in 1791 to ward off storms ("200-year-old time

capsule discovered in Mexico City Cathedral," *Catholic News Agency* [www.catholicnewsagency.com], January 17, 2008).

39. Douglas Sharon, ed., *Mesas and Cosmologies in Mesoamerica* (San Diego: Museum of Man, 2003), 143.

40. These origin stories are spread across the viceroyalty, but they concentrate in central and western Mexico. Most date from the seventeenth century or are described in eighteenth-century sources that trace the devotion back to the seventeenth century.

41. A rare case is the Cristo de las Ampollas in Mérida, Yucatán, home of the famous speaking crosses of the nineteenth century, Luis Mario Schneider, *Cristos, santos y vírgenes: Santuarios y devociones de México* (México: Grupo Planeta, 1995), 29–31. Another apparition story in the early seventeenth century is the origin story of the shrine of San Miguel del Milagro, Tlaxcala, found in Francisco de Florencia, *Narración de la marabillosa aparición que hizo el archangel San Miguel a Diego Lázaro de San Francisco* ... (Sevilla: Imprenta de las Siete Revueltas, 1692).

42. Some crosses were—and others still are—painted green, with the same symbolic meaning, I suppose. See H. R. Harvey, "Pilgrimage and Shrine: Religious Practices Among the Otomí of Huixquilucan, Estado de México," in *Pilgrimage in Latin America*, ed. N. Ross Crumrine and E. Alan Morinis, 91–108 (New York: Greenwood, 1991).

43. "En el pueblo de Tepic de la Nueva Galicia se halla aquella portentosa cruz de yervas que apostando duraciones con el tiempo siempre se conserva verde y ermosa aunque está seco del inmediato terreno y tan fecunda que apenas se corta alguna yerva para Reliquias, lo que se hace cada dia y en grande copia, al dia inmediato ya está toda entera. No para aquí la maravilla porque como media tercia de los Brazos se advierte un hoio como herida correspondiente a la de el costado de Nro Divino Dueño, lleno de tierra blanquizina tan inagotable que con ser que para Reliquias y medizina se toma mucha porción continuamente siempre se conserva lleno.... [A]unque muchas vezes se ha procurado techar la capilla dentro de cuio sitio se halla jamás se ha podido ... Pues si el lugar desde donde Christo nuestro Dios subió a su eterno Padre nunca admitió cubierta...." *Representación hecha al Rey Nro. Sr. Dn. Ferndo. Sexto por los Yndios de la Nueva Espana* (ca. 1755), Bancroft MSS 99/374m, fol. 48r. The earliest mention of this miraculous cross seems to have been 1619. See Domingo Lázaro de Arregui, *Descripción de la Nueva Galicia*, ed. François Chevalier, 93–95 (Sevilla: Escuela de Estudios Hispano-Americanos, 1946).

44. The images of Mary from Tulantongo and Xalmolonga were said to have self-restored, and the incomplete images of La Redonda and Piedad in Mexico City were finished under mysterious circumstances. Citations for Tulantongo are in note 1 above; for Xalmolonga (brought to Mexico City in 1677), see Francisco de Florencia (and Antonio de Oviedo, *Zodíaco mariano* ... (México: Colegio de San Ildefonso, 1755), 101–7; for La Redonda and La Piedad, see Florencia, *Zodíaco*, 87–90 and 82–84, and Esteban Puente Camacho, *La estrella del sur: Historia de la Santísima Virgen de la Piedad* (México: Tipografía Hispano Mexicana, 1946).

45. Examples from the *Zodíaco mariano* include Nuestra Señora de las Angustias in the Hospital de Amor de Dios (1660) and Nuestra Señora del Coro in the convent of Santa Catharina de Sena (1629), 112–13 and 117–18.
46. Jose Guadalupe Victoria, *Un pintor y su tiempo: Baltasar de Echave Orio* (Mexico: UNAM, 1994), 276. In the decrees of the Third Mexican Synod (1585) painted images were preferred: "se prohiben amuletos o cédulas supersticiosas; conviene que se pinten las imágenes, pero si fueren de escultura, hágaseles el ropaje de la misma material; no se graben o formen imágenes sagradas en los manjares, vasos, etcétera," Mariano Galván Rivera, ed., *Concilio III provincial mexicano, celebrado en México el año de 1585* . . . , 2nd ed. (Barcelona: Imprenta de Manuel Miró and D. Marsá, 1870), 332.
47. In his 1653 pastoral letter, *Carta pastoral, y dictámenes de curas* (Madrid: Diego Díaz de Carrera, impresor del reyno, 1653), Juan de Palafox y Mendoza, the great promoter of the shrine of San Miguel del Milagro, underscored the need to keep images in good repair and to expose idolatry.
48. AHAM, pastoral visit book of Archbishop Aguiar y Seijas.
49. AGN Edictos de Inquisición 1, fol. 16.
50. "obviar el abuso de poner y pintar cruces en rincones públicos y otros lugares indecentes con fin de preservarlos de las inmundicias ordinarias," AGN Edictos de Inquisición 1, exp. 15. Fiestas on the day of the Holy Cross were again forbidden in 1694 (AGN General de Parte 17, exp. 34).
51. AGN Inquisición 735, segunda parte, fol. 460, 1786 case referring to an Inquisition decree on this matter from the early 1770s. The Inquisition sent the same decree to Tixtla (Guerrero) in 1794 (AGN Inquisición 1319, exp. 17).
52. AGN Inquisición 735, segunda parte, fol. 460.
53. Archive of the Metropolitan Cathedral, Mexico City, Actas del Cabildo Eclesiástico, May 29, 1654; AGN Inquisición 735, segunda parte, fol. 460.
54. Since the court of the Inquisition did not have jurisdiction over Indians after its founding in 1571, most of the documentation on what was regarded as Indian uses and misuse of images comes from episcopal court records and reports, which are used in other parts of this essay. The episcopal courts did not pursue irreverence toward images as vigorously as the Inquisition.
55. Rather than referencing all the cases of desacato de imágenes considered here, I have included a list with the Bancroft Library's copy of this book. Another kind of irreverence toward images from the church's point of view was veneration of the images of holy people who had not yet been canonized.
56. William B. Taylor, *Magistrates of the Sacred: Priests and Parishioners in Eighteenth-Century Mexico* (Stanford, CA: Stanford University Press, 1996), 71–72.
57. Ibid., 268.
58. Policing of images was one of the concerns of Archbishop Manuel José Rubio y Salinas during his pastoral visit of 1759. See the record of this visit in AHAM. An Inquisition circular that only decorous images contributing to true piety, devotion, and reverence be allowed was reprinted on December 24 in 1760 and 1767 (AGN Edictos de Inquisición 1, and AGN Inquisición 1113, exp. 6). A 1767 royal edict against "*imágenes aplicadas a usos profanos*" led to

a circular by the Inquisition and responses from districts in modern Mexico and Guatemala (Bancroft 72/57m, box 3).

59. For example, the three cases of prints of the Virgin Mary folded up and inserted in shoes date from the late eighteenth century (AGN Inquisición 1314, exp. 25, 1798; Inquisición 1096, exp. 9, 1772; and Inquisición 928, exp. 7, 1759).

60. An example of a district governor accused of heretical propositions concerning images would be don Bernardo Madrid, the alcalde mayor's lieutenant for Teotitlán del Valle, Oaxaca, in 1788 (AGN Inquisición 1245, exp. 6, and 1356, exp. 7). An Inquisition file on Manuel Flon for doubtful utterances about images and religious doctrine before he became the intendant of Puebla is in Bancroft MS 72/57m, box 6, item 3. Examples of the growing number of robberies of religious images and jewels at the end of the colonial period include AGN Criminal 569, exp. 11, 1806 (Mexico City); Criminal 506, exp. 7, 1813 (El Pueblito, Querétaro); and Criminal 620, exp. 12, 1815 (Zacatecas).

61. AHAM Fondo Catedral Colonial, 1796, "Representacion del Yllmo. Sor. Obispo de Puebla sobre excesos in en transito de las Ymagenes de los pueblos de Indios a las cabeceras por su concurrencia en las procesiones."

62. Ibid., fols. 75–79, "las cosas santas han de ser tratadas santamente."

63. Bancroft MSS 72/57m, box 6, item 3, 1786.

64. The governor of Zacatecas and his six local reporters clearly were uneasy with local Indian religious practices in this frontier zone even though there were few Indian *pueblos*. The governor reported disorders in processions from the four villages nearby but noted that the residents of these communities were not Indians, but *gente de castas*. One of his reporters wrote emphatically about Indian "indolence, laziness, and semi-heathen ways" (*indolencia, desidia y semigentiles*), and they all roundly condemned their "exceedingly ridiculous" dances and behavior in church at fiesta time. At the same time, they acknowledged either that the practice of carrying images in procession outside the community was not practiced or that it was done inappropriately, but not irreverently. Nevertheless, they wanted the proposed prohibition on processions of images. The Bishop of Nuevo León wrote that this was not an issue in his diocese because there were few Indian pueblos there, and those few were close to the district capitals, but that in other dioceses where he had served these abuses were common, with the people going out to party more than pray.

65. AHAM Fondo Catedral Colonial, 1796, January 19, 1798, report by Archbishop of Mexico: "porque los yndios son muy tenaces en conservar sus costumbres y muy aficionados a conducir imagenes, cruces, ciriales, pendones y estandartes de partes distantes con ruido de cohetes y instrumentos."

66. Ibid., report by the Intendant of Veracruz, February 15, 1797.

67. In *Cultura popular y religión en el Anáhuac* (Mexico: Centro de Estudios Ecuménicos, 1978), chap. 6.

68. Ibid., 147–48.

69. Ibid., 147, "desde el punto de vista de los pueblerinos, son éstos [the images] y no ellos los verdaderos protagonistas de la peregrinacion. Las imágenes tienen, además, la 'obligación' de peregrinar." Images were also carried from shrines to communities in distress, especially in epidemics and droughts. Florencia

and Oviedo give the example of a statue of the Virgin Mary at Chalma that was processed to Malinalco various times for this purpose, *Zodíaco mariano*, 141. And there were the matrix images that circulated seasonally, such as the Virgen del Socorro of Zapotlán del Rey mentioned at the beginning of this essay and Our Lady of Zapopan near Guadalajara. Many shrines had "peregrina" statues—small replicas of a celebrated image—that also circulated, often on alms-collecting missions. An especially early one of Our Lady of San Juan de los Lagos in the 1640s is mentioned in *Zodíaco mariano*, 302–21. Peregrina images of Nuestra Señora de la Salud at Pátzcuaro (Michoacán) were said to circulate in the Philippines and Spain as well as throughout New Spain (*Zodíaco mariano*, 259ff).

70. AHAM Fondo Catedral Colonial, 1796, report for Michoacán, September 23: "edificando con su veneración y culto, que me ha llenado de satisfacción."

71. The districts reporting processions with images in the Diocese of Michoacán were Valladolid, Piedad, Zitácuaro, Carácuaro, Cuitzeo, Tlalpuxahua, Uruapan, Huetamo, Charo, Huango, Puruándiro, Angamacútiro, Xiquilpan, Yndaparapeo, Capula, Taretan, and Tacámbaro.

72. AHAM Fondo Catedral Colonial, 1796, report for November 29: "causa admiración ver aquel anhelo que dichos naturales tienen no sólo a la ymagen que traen sino también a las flores, velas, yncienso y adorno de ella."

73. Ibid., report for October 25: "ningún exceso, antes sí mucha devoción cantando en voz alta el Rosario en rústica tono, que aunque sin reglas no se hace desagradable al oido."

74. Ibid., report for district of "coaquai.r," October 24: "Los indios de Ostula traen a la Santísima Birgen a Maquilid a dos funciones en el año, una al fin de febrero y otra en el mes de henero; el modo de traerla es que biene el alcalde y becinos y las cargadoras que llaman eyos, salen de la Yglesia cantando letanías y quantas oraciones el cantor . . . y otro les guia por todo el camino sin siquiera ponerse los sombreros las indias por el camino, cargando a la Birgen saumándolas con grandísima seriedad y mucha reberensia y debosión. Los indios de Maquilid llevan a María Santíssima a Ostula otras dos funsiones y atraer la limosna de sus debotos. Esto lo hazen con una urbanidad los dos dichos pueblos, constándome de bista la mucha debosión y Reberensia que dichos indios frequentan sus yglesias y con todas las ymáganes, el aseo y adorno de heyas, pues en los días de fiesta que no ai misa siempre se juntan y rezan el rosario, cantan letanías y alabado, y se ban a sus casas."

75. Robert G. Ousterhout, "The Virgin of the Chora: An Image and Its Contexts," in *The Sacred Image East and West*, ed. Robert G. Ousterhout and Leslie Brubaker, 91–109, especially p. 94 (Champaign: University of Illinois Press, 1994).

76. The example of Francisco de la Rosa Figuroa's campaign to embellish the statue of Mary at Nativitas with gold and pearls is discussed by William B. Taylor, "A Pastor's Local Religion," in *Marvels and Miracles in Late Colonial Mexico: Three Texts in Context*, ed. William B. Taylor (Albuquerque: University of New Mexico Press, forthcoming).

77. However, the claim was sometimes made that any image of Our Lady of Dolores would have to be miraculous; e.g., see Francisco Antonio Navarrete, S.J., *Relación peregrina de la agua correinte, que para beber, y vivir goza la*

muy noble, leal, y florida ciudad de Santiago de Querétaro (México: Joseph Bernardo de Hogal, 1739), 18, "*qualquiera imagen de la Virgen de Dolores no puede menos que ser milagrosa.*"

78. Matrix image refers to those especially renowned images of Mary that were, themselves, copied many times over. The term "matrix image" is used here instead of "original" (even though the latter sometimes appears in the sources) to emphasize the theological point often mentioned at the time that all images of her were copies.

79. Miguel Cabrera, *Maravilla Americana y conjunto de raras maravillas* . . . [1756], facsimile ed. (México: Editorial Jus, 1977), 10.

80. José Francisco Sotomayor, *Historia del Apostólico Colegio de Nuestra Señora de Guadalupe de Zacatecas* . . . , 2nd ed. (Zacatecas: Imp. y Encuadernación de "La Rosa," 1889), 312.

81. An example from 1770 of official worries about the allure of prints and the "truth" of printed matter is in AGN Bandos 7, exp. 73, fol. 257.

82. *Likeness and Presence: A History of the Image Before the Era of Art* (Chicago: University of Chicago Press, 1994), 484.

83. Juan de Magallanes, *Novena de la santa imagen del santo Cristo, que se venera en el religioso convento, y santuario de religiosos ermitaños del orden de N. P. S. Agustín, de San Miguel de Chalma* (México: Impreso por Juan Ojeda, Escalerillas núm. 2., 1841 [1731]), unnumbered final pages. There are examples of copies, including prints, reported to show signs of life. The copy of Our Lady of Guadalupe at Temamatla, near Chalco in the Valley of Mexico, reportedly sweated and spoke in 1737 (Juan Francisco Sahagún Arévalo Ladrón de Guevara, ed., *Gazeta de México, 1728–1742*, in *Bibliografía mexicana del siglo XVIII*, ed. Nicolás León [México: Imp. de Díaz de León, 1902-8], *Boletín del Instituto Bibliográfico* 5: 722, gazeta for September 1737). And the print of Christ in the Jesuit church of Parras, Coahuila, reportedly sweated in 1748 (AGN Archivo Histórico de Hacienda, leg. 1999, exp. 5). Franciscan Friar Francisco Antonio de la Rosa Figueroa claimed that his last remaining print from the engraving of Our Lady of Intercession that he had commissioned was working wondrous healings in the 1770s, see Taylor, *Marvels and Miracles in Late Colonial Mexico*.

84. AGN Archivo Histórico de Hacienda, leg. 1999, exp. 5. The witnesses included the local artist (*escultor*) who was asked to frame the print and first noticed the drops of perspiration, and seven other local residents, including the district governor, the administrator of the *alcabala* tax, and a local merchant, all of them except the escultor identified with the honorific "don."

85. This point was reiterated in other devotional writings, such as José Francisco Valdés's *Día doce de cada mes consagrado a Nuestra Madre y Señora María Santísima de Guadalupe* (México: Imp. de la Viuda e Hijos de Murguía, 1878 [first edition listed in WorldCat: 1797]), 18: "lograremos vuestras saludables influencias en esta vida, y mereceremos ver el original de vuestra sagrada imagen cara a cara en la gloria."

86. On copies as creative work, see Barbara M. Stafford, *Visual Analogy: Consciousness as the Art of Connecting* (Cambridge, MA: MIT Press, 1999), 138 ("We do not merely illustrate or copy what is given, but give birth to

something that would not otherwise exist"); Eric Gable, "Bad Copies: The Colonial Aesthetic and the Manjaco-Portuguese Encounter," in *Images and Empires: Visuality in Colonial and Postcolonial Africa*, ed. Paul L. Landau and Deborah D. Kaspin, 294–319 (Berkeley: University of California Press, 2002); and Clara Bargellini, "Originality and Invention in the Painting of New Spain," in *Painting a New World: Mexican Art and Life, 1521–1821*, ed. Donna Pierce, Rogelio Ruiz Gomar, and Clara Bargellini, 84, 86 (Denver: Denver Art Museum [distributed by University of Texas Press], 2004).

87. AGN Bandos 7, exp. 73, fol. 257. Especially after about 1625, images of holy persons not yet canonized were highlighted as dangerous: AGN Edictos de Inquisición 1, fol. 69 (n.d., post-1625); Edictos de Inquisición 1, exp. 70, 1653; and Edictos de Inquisición 1, fol. 15, 1691.

88. For example, decree 3-21-7 of the Fourth Mexican Synod in 1771, Nicolás León and Rafael Sabás Camacho, eds., *Concilio Provincial Mexicano IV, celebrado en la ciudad de México en el año de 1771* . . . (Querétaro: Imprenta de la Escuela de Artes, 1898), 166–67, "En las pinturas de Imágenes se han introducido no menores corruptelas por los pintores contra todo el espíritu de la Yglesia, y en deshonor de los Santos, ya pintando a Nuestra Señora y a las santas con escote [low neckline] y vestiduras profanas de que nunca usaron; ya descubiertos los pechos, ya en ademanes provocativos, ya con adornos de las Mugeres del siglo; y casi el mismo abuso se nota en los escultores."

89. AGN Clero Regular y Secular 215, exp. 26, fols. 604–38.

90. For differing interpretations of this rebellion by historians, see Kevin Gosner, *Soldiers of the Virgin: The Moral Economy of a Colonial Maya Rebellion* (Tucson: University of Arizona Press, 1992) and Prudencio Moscoso Pastrana, *Rebeliones indígenas en los Altos de Chiapas* (México: UNAM, 1992).

91. AGN Inquisición 801, exp. 9, fols., 108–14.

92. *La devoción de María Madre Santísima de la Luz, distribuida en tres partes por un sacerdote de la Compañía de Jesús*, trans. Lucas Rincón, S. J., 2 vols. (México: Imprenta Real del Superior Gobierno y del Nuevo Rezado, de Doña María de Rivera, 1737–1738). A 1732 Mexico City publication first announced the new devotion (it is mentioned in *Gazeta de México*, num 52, March 1732, and cited in José Toribio Medina, *La imprenta en México: Edición facsimilar* [Mexico: UNAM, 1989], entry no. 3251.)

93. The iconography here follows scriptural references to Hell's doorstep: Job 3:8, "May those who curse days curse that day, those who are ready to rouse Leviathan"; Job 41:5 "Who can open the doors of his face?" Together they suggest that Leviathan's gaping mouth was a one-way entrance to damnation and the pit of Hell. The nightmare monster in Our Lady of Light follows medieval Christian depictions of the entrance to Hell quite closely: "The Mouth of Hell was traditionally represented as the mouth of a huge and malevolent beast, which dragged sinners into its maw. . . . Leviathan's jaws are open and flame gushes out" (Robert Hughes, *Heaven and Hell in Western Art* [London: Weidenfeld and Nicolson, 1968], 175, 178).

94. Why the Italians would have let the painting leave the country is one of many silences in the streamlined legendary account of *La devoción de María Madre Santísima de la Luz*.

95. According to an early novena booklet dedicated to Our Lady of Light, for which the title page unfortunately is missing, the cultus was growing in Mexico City, "*que el dia de oy hai en varias iglesias pinceles de ellas*." It singles out the images in the church of Porta Coeli (1732) and the Dominican monastery (1734) (Sutro Library BX 2161.5.I4 N68, exp. 4).
96. By the 1780s the devotion was evident in images and confraternities in various communities, not only where Jesuits and Franciscans were active promoters of it. I have not made a systematic search, but late colonial records and secondary works mention other paintings and sculpted images as personal possessions and in the parish of Santa María de la Redonda (Mexico City); Tepotzotlán (D.F.); the city of Guanajuato; Pachuca (Hidalgo); Yautepec and Tlaltizapán (Morelos); Tochimilco (Puebla); several parishes of the city of Puebla; the Alta California missions; Jesuit missions in Chihuahua, Sonora, and Baja California; Durango; and Mérida (Yucatán). A number of ships plying Atlantic waters were named for her in the late eighteenth century.
97. These figures for devotional publications dedicated to Our Lady of Light are based on a survey of Medina, *La imprenta en México*.
98. Matthew 5:14; John 9:6. Light is a fundamental metaphor in Christianity and, in the form of candles, the most common votive offering.
99. Bancroft M-M 69–70, vol. 1, fols. 46–47, "borrarse el dragon para evitar el error . . . de que la Ssma Virgen sacaba a los condenados del Ynfierno."
100. Bancroft M-M 69–70, vol. 1, fols. 46ff. A valuable secondary source on Our Lady of Light, Norman Neuerburg's "La Madre Santísima de la Luz," *The Journal of San Diego History* 41, no. 2 (Spring 1995) (consulted online at www.sandiegohistory.org/journa/95spring/laluz.htm), suggests that the debate in the synod ended without resolution, but does not elaborate.
101. The campaign to blot out the image of the monster continued off and on into the early 1780s. During his pastoral visit to parishes in the modern state of Morelos in 1778, Archbishop Alonso Núñez de Haro y Peralta ordered the "dragon" to be painted over in two paintings of Our Lady of Light in Yautepec and one in Tlaltizapán (AHAM L10/20 1770, fols. 191v–212r). And José Gómez recorded in his diary on August 24, 1781, that the large painting of Our Lady of Light that had been displayed in the Jesuit church of the Colegio de San Pedro y San Pedro was moved to a side altar in the Sagrario church attached to the cathedral. He noted that on August 26 of that year, the "dragon" had been removed "on higher orders" (*por superior mandato*), presumably by Archbishop Haro y Peralta (Bancroft M-M 105, fols. 170–71).
102. Alcozer, *Carta apologética a favor del título de Madre Santísima de la Luz* . . . (México: Zúñiga y Ontiveros, 1790).
103. There are exceptions. Examples of nineteenth-century paintings without the Leviathan are in the parish church of San Agustín in Tlalpan, D.F. (*Catálogo Nacional de Monumentos Históricos. Muebles: Tlapan* [México: Instituto Nacional de Antropología e Historia (hereafter INAH), Dirección de Monumentos Históricos, 1988], 48) and the shrine to Our Lady of Light in Lagos de Moreno, Jalisco (Luis Enrique Orozco, *Iconografía mariana de la Arquidiócesis de Guadalajara* [Guadalajara: Impr. de J. Vera, 1954], I:411). An undated lavishly illustrated publication from the late nineteenth century

shows Our Lady of Light with a fiery man in the lower left corner, but not as an anthropomorphized furnace of Hell (*Galería Americana: A Collection of Religious Pictures* [México: Casa de J. Michaud, n.d.], second plate).

104. William A. Christian Jr., *Apparitions in Late Medieval and Renaissance Spain* (Princeton, NJ: Princeton University Press, 1981), 80.

105. Ibid., 18.

106. As George Foster proposed in *Culture and Conquest: America's Spanish Heritage* (New York: Wenner-Gren, 1960). Foster was reacting to a powerful ahistorical current in anthropology that, in its celebration of native survival and adaptation, largely disregarded European influence.

107. William A. Christian Jr., "Images as Beings in Early Modern Spain," in *Sacred Spain: Art and Belief in the Spanish World*, ed. Ronda Kasl, 75–99 (Indianapolis: Indianapolis Museum of Art, 2009).

108. Helen Rawlins, *Church, Religion, and Society in Early Modern Spain* (New York: Palgrave, 2002), 92–93.

109. Christian, *Apparitions*, 222.

110. An exception that highlights the rule is Manuel Antonio Moxica's little book, *Tesoro escondido en el delicioso campo, ameno huerto, florida vergel, y fragrante pensil del noviciado de los frayles predicadores de esta Provincia de Santiago de México* (México: Fernández Jáuregui, 1799 reprinting). His miracles of warning and punishment had a very particular audience: they were cautionary stories directed at Dominican novices who might be tempted to abandon their vows.

111. Philip M. Soergel, *Wondrous in His Saints: Counter-Reformation Propaganda in Bavaria* (Berkeley: University of California Press, 1993), chap. 5. Based on information about 3,126 European shrines, Mary Lee and Sidney Nolan describe seven types of origin stories in *Christian Pilgrimage in Modern Western Europe* (Chapel Hill: University of North Carolina Press 1989), 216–90. Again, at least a few examples of nearly all of their types can be found in America, but the distribution was substantially different.

112. I am persuaded that these developments were specific to particular places and times more than amenable to sweeping generalization. For a discussion of several shrines that grew in the early nineteenth century, see my essay, "Shrines and Marvels in the Wake of Mexican Independence" in this volume. For the shrines of Guadalupe and Remedios, see the essays in Part III. For the Cristo Renovado de Santa Teresa and Ixmiquilpan, see "Two Shrines of the Cristo Renovado: Religion and Peasant Politics in Late Colonial Mexico," in Part I.

113. Lee Panich, "Persistence of Native Identity in Mission Santa Catalina," PhD dissertation in Anthropology, University of California, Berkeley, 2009, 15.

114. Except perhaps for Chalma and a few other cases, there was much more to the story of images of immanence in New Spain than Spanish introduction and promotion and Indian attraction or resistance.

115. A few examples of this kind of accommodation are the recommendation of the audiencia's fiscal in the case of the pastor of San Miguel Totomaloyan who was eager to reduce feast day expenses: "*como en materia de constumbres en los pueblos, no deve procederse para removerlas sin perfecto conocimiento de la causa*" (AGN Clero Regular y Secular 206, exp. 3); the archbishop of Guatemala's terse response to one of his parish priests who was eager to

enforce the king's edict against improper religious images in 1767 to "avoid inciting any kind of uprising" (Bancroft MS 72/57m, box 3, folder 20). In the discussion of blotting out the graphic representation of Hell in images of Our Lady of Light, various prelates at the Fourth Mexican Synod in 1771 cautioned prudence: "*proceder con mucho tiento en el asunto, así en lo substancial de él, como respecto al pueblo*" (Bancroft M-M 69–70, vol. 1, fol. 46–47).

116. Quoted in Eamon Duffy's review of *Flesh Made Word: Saints' Stories and the Western Imagination* by Aviad Kleinberg, London Review of Books 31, no. 2 (January 29, 2009): 31.

Chapter 2

1. *Historia del culto de María en Ibero-América y de sus imágenes y santuarios más celebrados* (Madrid: Talleres Gráficos Jura, 1956), II:163.
2. Victor Turner and Edith Turner, *Image and Pilgrimage in Christian Culture: Anthropological Perspectives* (New York: Columbia University Press, 1978), 245.
3. Francisco Javier Lazcano, *Vida exemplar y virtudes heróicas del venerable padre Juan Antonio de Oviedo de la Compañía de Jesús* (Mexico: Imprenta del Colegio de San Ildefonso, 1760), 341.
4. These figures come from tabulating individual cases documented in various manuscript and printed sources, plus several compendia, especially *Zodíaco mariano*; Luis Mario Schneider, *Cristos, santos y vírgenes: Santuarios y devociones de México* (Mexico: Editorial Planeta Mexicana, 1995); and *La ruta de los santuarios en México* (Mexico: Secretaría de Turismo/Lotería Nacional, 1994), which identifies eighty-nine Cristo shrines and seventy-eight Marian shrines.
5. For sixty-nine of the remaining 105 shrines I have no information about when they began.
6. Specifically, 104 of 157, plus twenty-one miraculous crosses. This proportion holds true for more recent times, although since the early nineteenth century some images of the infant Jesus have gained a large and loyal following.
7. On the other hand, there were several striking trans-Atlantic differences. In Spain, many miraculous images of Mary were discovered under unusual circumstances in caves, trees, or shallow burials, and on hilltops, after the Christian reconquest of an area from the Moors. In New Spain, it was mostly images of Christ that were discovered, and they were frequently *of* nature—formed in trees, marked on rocks, associated with the color green—as well as found *in* nature, and without the scent of holy war. These various associations point to Christ's resurrection and eternal life, but they are also signs of His active, protective presence on earth, a theme that may have been less common in Spain after the seventeenth century.
8. Turner and Turner, *Image and Pilgrimage*, chap. 1 and 2, and Appendix A.
9. *The Practice of Everyday Life*, trans. Steven Rendall (Berkeley: University of California Press, 1984), xiii.
10. Mexico: Viuda de Rivera, 1699; Mexico: Herederos de Rivera, 1724; Mexico: Sánchez Réciente, 1729; Mexico: Jáuregui, 1776; Mexico: Jáuregui, 1790;

Mexico: Zúñiga y Ontiveros, 1807; Mexico: Zúñiga y Ontiveros, 1860; Mexico: Valdés, 1820.

11. New Spain's Carmelite nuns have been studied by Manuel Ramos Medina in *Místicas y descalzas: Fundaciones femeninas carmelitas en la Nueva España* (Mexico: Condumex, 1997), see especially xxiii, 113–17, 197–98. Ramos Medina found only one burst of public record for this convent. In the mid-seventeenth century the nuns appealed to Spain to be removed from the jurisdiction of secular ecclesiastical authorities and placed under the supervision of Carmelite prelates (152–63).

12. The word "Mapethé" has no obvious sacred connotation in the Otomí language. Pedro Martín Godínez Salas translated it as the "place of the mineral washing basins" (*deslavaderos*) (*Abandono y recuperación de la tierra en Santuario de Mapethé, Hidalgo* [Mexico: SEP-INI, 1982], Serie Ethnolinguistica 29, 53–54).

Velasco's first publication about the Cristo Renovado reported that the image was known locally as "the Santo Cristo de Zimapán, del Cardonal, etc., and also as the Santo Cristo de las minas del Plomo pobre and de las minas de Guerrero, for its original owner, . . . but most commonly as the Santo Cristo de Yxmiquilpa, which is the head town of the district" (*Renovación por sí misma* . . . [Mexico: Viuda de Francisco Rodríguez Lupercio, 1688], fol. 6v). These various names point to tensions between shared devotion and local proprietary claims discussed later in the essay.

13. *Teatro eclesiástico de la Santa Iglesia de México* (Madrid: Díaz de la Carrera, 1649–1655), 59. The image, he wrote, had sweated three times on February 17, 1621—forty days before the death of King Philip III—and trembled on the cross five months later.

14. Patrick J. Geary, *Furta Sacra: Thefts of Relics in the Central Middle Ages* (Princeton, NJ: Princeton University Press, 1978).

15. *Itinerario a Indias (1673–1678)* (Mexico: Condumex, 1992), 103–9.

16. José Toribio Medina, the great nineteenth-century bibliographer and historian, identified the 1688 publication as "un informe historial jurídico" (a historical-juridical report) rather than a devotional history in *La imprenta en México (1539–1810)*, edición facsimilar (Mexico: UNAM, 1989), III:222–24. It may have circulated in manuscript a few years earlier, perhaps as early as 1684 when Archbishop Aguiar y Seijas blessed Mexico City's newly finished Carmelite church of Santa Teresa. In his preface to *Renovación por sí misma*, Francisco de Florencia wrote that he had read Velasco's manuscript in 1685.

17. Antonio de Robles, *Diario de sucesos notables (1665–1703)* (Mexico: Porrúa, 1946), II:72; Juan Antonio Rivera, *Diario curioso del capellán del Hospital de Jesús Nazareno de México* (Mexico: Vargas Rea, 1953), II:24 reported that on May 19, 1689, "se repicó en todas las iglesias de México por haber declarado milagrosa el Arzobispo d. Francisco Aguiar y Seijas la renovación del Señor de Santa Teresa."

18. The publication history of Velasco's text during the eighteenth and nineteenth century more often points toward promotion. The 1724 edition was sponsored by the nuns of the Santa Teresa la Antigua convent—"*a devoción de la madre priora y religiosas*"—for whom the image had been brought to Mexico City. The

1996 facsimile edition of Velasco also apparently resulted from the desire of the Discalced Carmelite nuns of Mexico City to promote the devotion. Writing in 1997, Manuel Ramos Medina noticed that "very few know its history in spite of the efforts of the nuns to promote the devotion. Recently these Carmelites commemorated the 375th anniversary of the renovation of the Christ of Ixmiquilpan and reprinted Velasco's book," *Místicas y descalzas*, 136.

19. Francisco de Ajofrín, *Diario del viaje que hizo la América en el siglo XVIII el P. Fray Francisco de Ajofrín* (Mexico: Instituto Cultural Hispano Mexicano, 1964), I:106; Agustín Francisco Esquivel y Vargas, *El fénix del amor*, facsimile edition with study and notes by Alberto Carrillo Cázares (Zamora: El Colegio de Michoacán, 1990), 109; Francisco Javier Alegre, *Historia de la Compañía de Jesús en Nueva España* (Mexico: Imprenta de J.M. Lara, 1841–1842), II:125–28; Lazcano, *Vida exemplar*, 341; Juan de Viera, *Compendiosa narración de la ciudad de México (1777)* (Mexico-Buenos Aires: Editorial Guaranía, 1952), 56. New printings of the novena booklets appeared in 1766, 1784, 1790, 1809, and 1816.

Archivo General de la Nación, Mexico (hereafter AGN) Bienes Nacionales 1210, exp. 7, *dotación de novena* by Doña María Teresa de Borja, a two thousand pesos lien on a house in Mexico City.

20. *Gazeta de México*, April 28, 1737, reported a great procession to the cathedral for prayers to restore the city to health.

21. D. José Gómez, *Anales de México (1776–1798)*, manuscript copy evidently prepared for Carlos María Bustamante, Bancroft Library, University of California, Berkeley (hereafter Bancroft), M-M, vol. 105, p. 115, December 22, 1779; M-M 105, p. 266–67, April 18, 1784; M-M 105, p. 724–25, November 17, 1796; *Gazeta de México*, November 29, 1797, note appended to an article on the 1797 procession to the cathedral.

22. Cayetano de Cabrera y Quintero, *Escudo de armas de México . . .* (Mexico: Viuda de Joseph Bernardo del Hogal, 1746), 450–56.

23. On other paintings of the Cristo Renovado, especially those by Ibarra, see Rogelio Ruiz Gomar, "José de Ibarra," in *Painting a New World: Mexican Art and Life, 1521–1821* (Denver: Denver Art Museum, 2004), 201–2.

24. *Memoria Cristiano-política sobre lo mucho que la Nueva España debe temer de su desunión en partidos, y las grandes ventajas que puede esperar de su unión y confraternidad* (Mexico: M. de Zúñiga y Ontiveros, 1810). Ignacio Carrillo y Pérez, the late-colonial hagiographer of miraculous images in the Valley of Mexico, wrote book-length devotional texts about four shrines: Our Lady of Guadalupe, Our Lady of Los Remedios, Our Lady of Los Ángeles, and the Cristo Renovado. Only the first two were published, in 1797 and 1808.

In the embattled spirit of the time and place, furta sacra was the theme of a mural painting by Rafael Ximeno y Planés commissioned for the new Mexico City chapel of the Cristo Renovado in 1813. It was destroyed in the 1845 earthquake, but a preliminary study survives in the collections of the Museo Nacional de Arte. See Jaime Cuadriello, *Catálogo comentado del acervo del Museo Nacional de Arte: Nueva España* (Mexico: Museo Nacional del Arte, 2000), I:182–86, and Xavier Moyssén, "Una maqueta de Rafael Ximeno," *Anales del Instituto de Investigaciones Estéticas* 48 (1978): 67–70. Similar in style to Goya's scenes of war in Spain during the French intervention,

1808–1814, the painting depicts the archbishop's men fighting off local people in their effort to transport the image to Mexico City. Various Indian attackers in the foreground are shirtless, and others in the distance are dressed only in loincloths, with bows drawn, in the pose of Chichimec barbarians.

25. AGN Bienes Nacionales 1864, exp. 34 (1807); AGN Bienes Nacionales 800, exp. 12 (1814).
26. AGN Bienes Nacionales 423, exp. 19, and 466, exp. 20.
27. AGN Bienes Nacionales 466, exp. 20 (1823), report of the shrine's treasurer.
28. See *Odita al contemplar que desaparece de la Metropolitana de México...* (Mexico: Imprenta de Valdés, 1833), on the occasion of the Cristo Renovado's return from the cathedral to the Santa Teresa convent church, and Carlos María Bustamante's *México religioso: Procesión del Señor de Santa Teresa de México a la iglesia cathedral con motivo de la chólera morbus* (Mexico: Imprenta de Valdés, 1833).
29. Quoted in Alegre, *Historia de la Compañía de Jesús*, II:128.
30. It did, however, appear as one of the ten Mexican shrines recommended by Archbishop Pelagio Antonio de Labastida y Dávalos in his prescription for thirty-one days of virtual spiritual travel with special prayers to the great shrines of Europe and Mexico in October 1874 (*Guía de la peregrinación que se verificara en el Arzobispado de México en el mes de octubre del presente año de 1874. Extractada del itinerario formado por el Illmo. Sr. Arzobispo...* [México: Impr. de F. Márquez, 1874]).
31. The only photograph of the Cristo Renovado de Santa Teresa published recently treats it as an art object rather than a devotional image; see Elisa Vargas Lugo, et al., *Parábola novohispana: Cristo en el arte virreinal* (Mexico: Fomento Cultural Banamex, 2000), unnumbered.
32. AGN Tierras 2155, exp. 5.
33. AGN Civil 1384, exp. 11; AGN Civil 2292, exp. 4. The alcaldía mayor district of Ixmiquilpan encompassed the two parishes of Ixmiquilpan and El Cardonal and the Indian head towns of Ixmiquilpan, El Cardonal, Orizaba, and Tlazintla, and their outliers. People widely known historically and in records from the colonial period as Otomíes usually identify themselves today as Ñähñu.
34. The following discussion of 1737–1748 developments is based on AGN Tierras 2155, exp. 5, AGN Indiferente Virreinal, caja 3405, exp. 20, and AGN Tierras 2904, exp. 2.
35. AGN Tierras 2155, exp. 5. In April 1744 both Morales and Diego Joseph were identified as *indios principales* (Indian nobles) of El Cardonal.
36. AGN Tierras 2155, exp. 5, fol. 92.
37. Archivo Histórico del Arzobispado de México (hereafter AHAM), Rubio y Salinas pastoral visit book, fols. 101v–106v, February 11, 1755.
38. Archbishop Rubio y Salinas refers to "la semana de San Lázaro" festivities in his 1755 pastoral visit report, archived in AHAM, Mexico City, caja 21, L10A/5.
39. *Relaciones geográficas del Arzobispado de México, 1743* (Madrid: C.S.I.C., 1988), I:69.
40. Tlazintla, Palma Gorda, and Ixmiquilpan (AGN Civil 1384, exp. 11, fol. 50r).

41. Alfonso Alberto de Velasco, *Exaltación de la divina misericordia en la milagrosa renovación de la soberana imagen de Christo Señor Nuestro Crucificado*... (Mexico: Jáuregui, 1790), 33. According to Velasco, when porters attempted to take the crucifix toward Mexico City, "2,000" local Indians and some Spaniards seized the image and took it to Ixmiquilpan. Healings and other signs of Christ's presence in the image happened there before it was eventually removed to Mexico City. No one in 1748 seems to have threatened a similar mass action for the return of the image.
42. AGN Civil 1384, exp. 11, ff. 50–53; Velasco, *Exaltación* (1790 edition), 33–35.
43. *Dones y promesas: 500 años de arte ofrenda (exvotos mexicanos)* (Mexico: Centro Cultural Televisa, 1996), 96.
44. AGN Civil 1111, exps. 1, 12, and 991.
45. AGN Civil 1111, exp. 12.
46. One witness testified that the trip from the town of Zimapán to Mapethé took about five hours (AGN Civil 1111, exp. 991).
47. The mayordomo had his two processional crucifixes confiscated and was charged with collecting money without a license to defray expenses, including rental of outfits for those who went armed as Roman soldiers. Even ceremonial arming of Indians was controversial in this region.

    While the Indian governors and councilmen nominally chose the mayordomo annually, one mayordomo served throughout this period, while governors and councilmen came and went. He may well have become an especially powerful figure in the community.
48. The parish priest at the shrine and the mayordomos of Zimapán assured authorities in Mexico City that the Indians behaved decorously (AGN Civil 1111, exp. 991; AGN Civil 1111, exp. 1).
49. For example, see Bancroft Library, uncatalogued 2002 acquisition, "Año de 1802, criminal contra las indios del Cardonal por tumultuarios." According to Antonio Fonseca's report of March 4, 1802, after five Indian laborers perished when the wall of a reservoir they were rebuilding caved in on them, the rumor spread that Spaniards wanted to kill Indians.

    In 1799, the archbishop did ban a larger procession of *cristos* in the city of Querétaro on Maundy Thursday involving as many as eight thousand Indians from neighboring communities (AGN Arzobispos y Obispos 2, fols. 308–15). In 1803 the archbishop also banned the Corpus Christi festivities in San Pedro de la Cañada, near the city of Querétaro because of "abominable excesses." But in general he found Querétaro a pious place (AHAM L10B/32, fol. 44r, 1803 pastoral visit).
50. A few little-known shrines in others parts of central Mexico that suddenly attracted many followers from distant places, such as the Cruz de Huaquechula in the modern state of Puebla or the Grano de Maiz, were the main targets of official suppression in the late eighteenth century.
51. So reported the parish priest of El Cardonal, Lic. Felipe de la Bárzena. He wrote that Indians came that year from Zimapán and throughout the district of El Cardonal (AGN Civil 1111, exp. 991).

52. AGN Indios 70, exp. 259, reported 97 tributaries in 1804. Using a multiplying factor of four inhabitants per tributary, the population would have been about 388.
53. AGN Tierras 2152, exp. 6; AGN Indios 70, exps. 180 and 259. In the 1740s, the head town of Orizaba with its subordinate settlements registered 945 Otomí families and eighty non-Indian families nearby, or about four thousand people in all, José Antonio de Villaseñor y Sánchez, *Theatro Americano* (Mexico: Imp. de la Viuda de J. Bernardo de Hogal, 1746), chap. 32. El Cardonal and its outliers were said to have 215 Otomí families and seventy-three non-Indian families at the time. The third important Indian town and outliers in the district of Ixmiquilpan was Tlazintla with 945 Otomí families and fifty non-Indian families.
54. The two sets of disputes pitting the people of Pueblo Nuevo against their Otomí neighbors were interlocking, at least in terms of political alliances. The people of Palma Gorda belonged to the town of Orizaba and were described as close allies. Both of these adversaries of the new pueblo belonged to the parish of Ixmiquilpan rather than El Cardonal, though all were under the spiritual direction of Augustinian pastors.
55. AGN Bienes Nacionales 1047, exp. 13.
56. Lourdes M. Romero Navarrete and Felipe I. Echenique March, eds., *Relaciones geográficas de 1792* (Mexico: Instituto Nacional de Antropología e Historia [hereafter INAH], 1995), 43.
57. Pío Sáenz, "El misterio del Cardonal oculto en la milagrosa renobación acaesida en ese pueblo...," 1865, University of Texas at Austin, Benson Library, G85. Pedro Martín Godínez Salas, *Abandono y recuperación de la tierra en Santuario de Mapethé, Hidalgo* (México: Secretaría de Educación Pública, Instituto Nacional Indigenista, 1982), especially 51–52.
58. Construction of the shrine to El Señor de las Maravillas began in 1806 and was completed in 1912, and reportedly attracted about thirty thousand visitors to its two main feast days in the late 1940s (Higinio Vásquez Santa Ana, *Cristos célebres de México* [México: n.p., 1950], entry 24).
59. Another case from the El Cardonal area of the location of a departed crucifix being venerated—the cross of El Maye—is mentioned by Jesús Salinas Pedraza in H. Russell Bernard and Jesús Salinas Pedraza, *Native Ethnography: A Mexican Indian Describes His Culture* (Newbury Park, CA: Sage Publications, 1989), 549.
60. William A. Christian Jr., *Local Religion in Sixteenth-Century Spain* (Princeton, NJ: Princeton University Press, 1981), 123–24.
61. Use of relics for healing—often said by clerical authors to be ineffectual—appears in miracle stories recounted by Francisco Javier Alegre (1729–1788) in *Historia de la Compañía de Jesús*, II:8, 42–44, 75–76. He and other chroniclers of the orders in seventeenth- and eighteenth-century New Spain mentioned the clothing and bones of especially venerable predecessors as if they were relics.
62. For example, Gerónimo de Mendieta, *Historia eclesiástica indiana*, Cien de México ed. (Mexico: Conaculta, 1997), II, chaps. 24–26; Juan de Torquemada, *Monarquía indiana*, 6th ed., 3 vols. (Mexico: Porrúa, 1986), III:179, 200, 243–50; and *The Oroz Codex*, ed. and trans. Angélico Chávez (Washington DC:

Academy of American Franciscan History, 1972), 98, 162–64, 168, 187–92, 216–17, 248–52, 255–56, 268–69, 302–6.

63. People from the town of Alfajayuca, southwest of Ixmiquilpan seem to have had an especially strong association with Mapethé. They regularly sent alms and supplied much of the stone for construction of the church in the 1740s, in addition to participating in the annual processions.

64. On Otomí settlement patterns and their diffuse, archipelago-like distribution in central and north-central Mexico, see Leonardo Manrique C., "The Otomí," in *Handbook of Middle American Indians*, vol. 8 (*Ethnology*, part two), ed. Robert Wauchope, 682–724 (Austin: University of Texas Press, 1969); Victor W. Padelford, "Otomí House Types as a Reflection of Acculturation," in *Los Otomíes: Papers from the Ixmiquilpan Field School*, ed. H. Russell Bernard, 49–54 (Pullman, WA: Washington State University Laboratory of Anthropology Report of Investigations, no. 46, 1969); and Lourdes Mondragón, Patricia Fournier-García, and Nahúm Noguera, "Arqueología histórica y etnoarqueología de la comunidad alfarera Otomí de Santa María del Pino, México," in *Approaches to the Historical Archaeology of Mexico, Central and South America*, ed. Janine L. Gasco and Greg C. Smith, 17–28 (Los Angeles: Institute of Archaeology, UCLA, 1997).

65. Elinor Melville, *A Plague of Sheep: Environmental Consequences of the Conquest of Mexico* (New York: Cambridge University Press, 1994), and "Cultural Persistence and Environmental Change: The Otomí of the Valle del Mezquital, Mexico," in *Advances in Historical Ecology*, ed. William Balée, 334–48 (New York: Columbia University Press, 1998). In spite of the great changes on the land, the district of Ixmiquilpan, which encompassed most of the communities of the northern Mezquital Valley was reported to produce three thousand *fanegas* of maize and one thousand fanegas of wheat in 1792, although the area around El Cardonal was "arid and saline, good only for mesquite and piñon pine." This area was dotted with twenty-two lead mines and "*diferentes pueblecillos de indios*." Two-thirds of the seventeen thousand inhabitants of the district at the time were said to be Indians (Lourdes M. Romero Navarrete and Felipe I. Echenique March, eds., *Relaciones geográficas de 1792* [Mexico: INAH, 1995], 112–13).

66. Manrique, "The Otomí," 682–85. Otomí migration to Zimapán in the eighteenth century was related to the periodic surges in mining activity, but it was not just the product of a free labor market. When the Conde de Regla invested in Zimapán mines in 1768 he received permission to "employ press-gangs who rounded up laborers and forced them to work in the mines. One of these men met his end as a victim of workers' rage" (Edith Boorstein Couturier, *The Silver King: The Remarkable Life of the Conde de Regla in Colonial Mexico* [Albuquerque: University of New Mexico Press, 2003], 153).

The district of Zimapán in the late sixteenth century was described as "a land of few people," with no more than four hundred "barbarous" Indians speaking Chichimeca and Otomí. The population of the three Indian pueblos in the vicinity had been increasing by resettlements since Spanish colonization ("Relación de las minas de Zimapan," in *Papeles de Nueva España*, ed. Francisco del Paso y Troncoso, VI:3 [Madrid: Est. Tipográfico "Sucesores de Rivadeneyra," 1905]). In 1743 there were said to be 6,249 Indians and

200 families of non-Indians (perhaps 800 individuals); by 1779 the non-Indian population had grown to 2,584 Spaniards, 1,113 mestizos, and 326 mulattos (Peter Gerhard, *A Guide to the Historical Geography of New Spain* [Cambridge: Cambridge University Press, 1973], 70–71). An 1803 population count for the parish of Zimapán included 1,397 Indian families (6,992 individuals), 244 mestizo and mulatto families (889 individuals), and 387 Spanish families (1,533 individuals) (AGN Bienes Nacionales 388, exp. 19). I have not been able to establish the extent to which Indians from other places mixed with Otomíes in this area.

67. Felipe Castro Gutiérrez, "Resistencia étnica y mesianismo en Xichú, 1769," in *Sierra Gorda: Pasado y presente. Coloquio en homenaje a Lino Gómez Canedo* (Querétaro: Dondo Editorial de Querétaro, 1994), 127–36; J. Jesús Solís de la Torre, *Bárbaros y ermitaños: Chichimecas y agustinos en la Sierra Gorda, siglos XVI, XVII, y XVIII (S.L.P., Hidalgo, y Querétaro)* (Querétaro: Universidad Autónoma de Querétaro, 1983); *La Sierra Gorda: Documentos para su historia* (Mexico: INAH, 1996–1997), I:345–46.

68. Sources cited in Justino Fernández, *Danzas de los concheros en San Miguel de Allende* (Mexico: El Colegio de México, 1941), 33–41. Bibiana Ugalde Mendoza, *Xitaces con sentimiento y tradición: Historia del culto a la cruz verde de Tequisquiapan en la voz de un pueblo creyente* (Querétaro: Hear Taller Gráfico, 1997), offers an especially close treatment of the dances and procession of traveling crosses at Cerro Grande from barrios of Tequisquiapan, Querétaro, and nearby Otomí villages in Hidalgo on September 13 in honor of the green cross of the San Juan barrio.

69. José Díaz de la Vega, "Memorias de México: Memorias piadosas de la nación yndiana," Bancroft M-M 240, Part III, attributed the spread of devotion to the stone cross of Querétaro to Otomíes and Tlaxcalans. For examples of visits to Chalma, see AGN Civil 2059, exp. 4, 1817, and Ruiz Guadalajara, *Dolores antes de la independencia* (Zamora: El Colegio de Michoacán, 2004), 379.

70. AHAM L10B, fol. 107r-v.

71. On early chroniclers, see Fernández, *Danzas de los concheros*, 37–41. On the distinctive and numerous Otomí household chapels, see Mondragón, Fournier-García, and Noguera, "Arqueología histórica y etnoarqueología," 25–27 (thirty-six in the small community of Pino Suárez, Hidalgo, alone); Heidi Chemín Bässler, *Las capillas oratorio otomíes de San Miguel Tolimán* (Querétaro: Gobierno del Estado de Querétaro, 1993); Alan R. Sandstrom, *Traditional Curing and Crop Fertility Rituals Among Otomí Indians of the Sierra de Puebla, Mexico: The López Manuscripts* (Bloomington: Indiana University Museum, Occasional Papers and Monographs 3, 1981); James W. Dow, "Sierra Otomí Religious Symbolism: Mankind Responding to the Natural World," in *Mesas and Cosmologies in Mesoamerica*, ed. Douglas Sharon, 28 (San Diego: San Diego Museum Papers 42, 2003); and Jacques Galinier, *The World Below: Body and Cosmos in Otomí Ritual*, trans. Phyllis Aronoff and Howard Scott (Boulder: University Press of Colorado, 2004). For an example of the naming pattern, see the population records of 1793 for Indians in the district of El Cardonal, which registered many "de la Cruz" men (AGN Bienes Nacionales 818, exp. 8).

72. Christian, *Local Religion*, 206–8, describes the distant, terrifying symbol for early modern Spain. Richard Nebel sums up a familiar view of the

meaning of Christ figures in Indian Mexico that emphasizes Marian devotion: "Traditional Catholicism centered on devotion to Jesus Christ as a self-sacrificing man of sorrows.... In this conception, the Indio sees the suffering figure of Christ as a reflection of his own tragic past and present. He seeks consolation and refuge in his mother, the Virgin Mary, and above all in the Virgin of Guadalupe," in "The Cult of Santa Maria Tonantzin, Virgin of Guadalupe in Mexico," in *Sacred Space: Shrine, City, Land*, ed. Benjamin Kedar and R. J. Zwi Werblowsky, 255 (New York: New York University Press, 1998). For a very different view of the meaning of Christ's suffering to colonial Indians, see Miles Richardson, *Being-in-Christ and Putting Death in Its Place: An Anthropologist's Account of Christian Performance in Spanish America and the American South* (Baton Rouge: Lousiana State University, 2003).

73. Jaime Cuadriello, "Tierra de prodigios: La ventura como destino," *Los pinceles de la historia: El origen del reino de la Nueva España, 1680–1750* (Mexico: Museo Nacional del Arte, 1999), 219. Another self-renovating cross in an Augustinian doctrina of the vicinity is the Señor de Tzinguilucan, said to have rejuvenated itself in 1651 and grown in 1712 (Hector H. Schenone, *Iconografía del arte colonial: Jesucristo* [Buenos Aires, Argentina: Fundación Tarea, 1992], 328). From November 1780 to November 1781 collections at this shrine were 3,001 pesos three reales, a considerable sum (AGN Bienes Nacionales, leg. 535, exp. 24).

74. Bancroft M-M 474: item 1, "Coloquio de la invención de la Santa Cruz por la virtuosa Santa Elena," 1859 copy of a 1714 text by Br. D. Manuel de los Santos y Salazar.

75. Chemín Bassler, *Las capillas*, 91ff; Sandstrom, *Traditional Curing*, 19.

76. "There are literally scores of different figurines cut, corresponding to the large number of crops grown by the Otomí. Usually the seed figures are kept throughout the year in a wooden box which is placed on the altar of an oratorio [family chapel].... Once a year they are removed and used in a ceremony dedicated to crop increase after which they are returned to the box. Throughout the year small offerings are placed in front of the box in the hope of influencing crop yield" (Sandstrom, *Traditional Curing*, 19).

77. Bernard and Salinas Pedraza, *Native Ethnography*, 548.

78. Yolanda Lastra de Suárez, *Unidad y diversidad de la lengua: Relatos otomíes* (Mexico: Universidad Nacional Autónoma de México, 2001), 221–23.

79. Margarita de la Vega Lázaro, *Crónica otomí del Estado de México: Narrativa oral tradicional* (Toluca: Gobierno del Estado de México, 1998), 48–53.

80. Chemín Bassler, *Las capillas*, 122; Galinier, *The World Below*, 121–22.

81. Bernard and Salinas Pedraza, *Native Ethnography*, 548.

82. It used to be taken to all the old shrines on nearby peaks, which now have their own crosses. H. R. Harvey, "Pilgrimage and Shrine: Religious Practices Among the Otomí of Huixquilucan, Mexico," in N. Ross Crumrine and E. Alan Morinis, *Pilgrimage in Latin America* (New York: Greenwood Press, 1991), 91–107; Angel María Garibay, *Supervivencias de cultura intelectual precolombina entre los Otomíes de Huizquilucan* (Mexico: Instituto Indigenista Interamericano, 1957), 13–17.

83. Juan Carlos Ruiz Guadalajara, *Un teatro eclesiástico novohispano: La Congregación de Nuestra Señora de los Dolores (De altar criollo a altar de la*

patria), Master's thesis, El Colegio de Michoacán, 1999, 398–413. The other three images are the Señor del Socorro, the Señor del Calvario, and the Señor del Hospital.
84. Bernard and Salinas Pedraza, *Native Ethnography*, 275, 458, 520, 527, 552.
85. Major Otomí settlements and political centers were located in Hidalgo at Xilotepec, Ixmiquilpan, and Meztitlán, but Otomíes apparently were less concentrated in one area and more migratory than other major indigenous groups of central Mexico before and especially after the beginnings of Spanish rule. See Gerhard, *Historical Geography of New Spain*, 383–86 and 224–26. By the eighteenth century there were new or larger pockets of Otomíes in the neighboring states of the Estado de México and Querétaro, in the Bajío, and north into San Luis Potosí, and smaller concentrations in eastern Michoacán, northern Puebla and Tlaxcala. When tens of thousands of people migrated to the Bajío toward the end of the eighteenth century, these pockets of settlement served as stepping stones of communication and support for Otomíes seeking employment in the mines and rural estates.
86. Otomí ethnogenesis—growing identification as Otomíes—and its political implications and possible relationship to sacred sites and images of Christ remain unstudied. Melville ("Cultural Persistence") and Galinier (*The World Below*) both posit such a historical ethnogenesis from their knowledge of the ethnographic present, but do so without direct documentation and from quite different perspectives. Melville sees Otomí ethnogenesis during the colonial period as a result of their growing marginalization from the wider society; Galinier sees it more as an act of will, a reaction against the encroachments of colonialism and modernity.
87. Ashis Nandy, *The Intimate Enemy: Loss and Recovery of Self Under Colonialism* (Delhi: Oxford University Press, 1983).
88. For example, Florencia Mallon, "The Promise and Dilemma of Subaltern Studies: A Perspective from Latin American History," *American Historical Review* 99, no. 5 (December 1994): 1491–1515; Sinclair Thomson, *We Alone Will Rule: Native Andean Politics in the Age of Insurgency* (Madison: University of Wisconsin Press, 2002); Sergio Serulnikov, *Subverting Colonial Authority: Changes to Spanish Rule in Eighteenth-Century Southern Andes* (Durham, NC: Duke University Press, 2003); and Mark Thurner and Andrés Guerrero, eds., *After Colonial Rule: Postcolonial Predicaments of the Americas* (Durham, NC: Duke University Press, 2003). In his foreword to Thurner and Guerrero's *After Colonial Rule*, xiv–xv, Shahid Amin, a member of the Subaltern Studies Collective, invites Latin Americanist readers to go light on the theory.
89. Interview with Guha about the legacy of his work, "Writing History," *Biblio: A Review of Books* (November–December 2003): 10–12. His views remain quite similar to his early position paper, "On Some Aspects of the Historiography of Colonial India," in *Subaltern Studies I: Writings on South Asian History and Society* (Delhi: Oxford University Press, 1982), 1–4.
90. In Vinay Lal's view, "secular Indian intellectuals indubitably have an immense difficulty in accepting religious faith as a valid category of knowledge" ("Subaltern Studies and Its Critics: Debates over Indian History," *History & Theory* 40, no. 1 [2001]: 135–48). Recently, Dipesh Chakrabarty, a Subaltern

Studies founder, has recognized that religious convictions need a place in more encompassing, less categorical subaltern histories because peasant politics are not pursued only in modern, secular terms (*Habitations of Modernity: Essays in the Wake of Subaltern Studies* [Chicago: University of Chicago Press, 2002], chaps. 1–2). How he and others will bring religion into subaltern historiography and the politics of difference is not yet clear.

91. Nandy questions Western rationality and what he regards as the tyranny of historical consciousness, and his interests have inclined more toward biography and leadership than subaltern episodes. See *The Intimate Enemy: Loss and Recovery of Self Under Colonialism* (Delhi: Oxford University Press, 1983), 45, 48, 59–60, 62; *Time Warps: Silent and Evasive Pasts in Indian Politics and Religion* (London: Hurst, 2002), passim; and "History's Forgotten Doubles," *History & Theory* 34 (1995): 4: "History basically keeps open only one option— that of bringing the ahistoricals into history."

92. On "the Annales school" of historical study developed by French historians in the twentieth century, see Peter Burke, *The French Historical Revolution: The Annales School, 1929–1989* (Cambridge, UK: Polity Press, 1990).

93. See Louis O. Mink, "The Autonomy of Historical Understanding," *History & Theory* 5, no. 1 (1966): 24–47, especially 42.

94. *The Intimate Enemy: Loss and Recovery of Self Under Colonialism* (Delhi: Oxford University Press, 1983), xiii–xv.

95. These categories concern people living with, if not altogether within, colonial settings. Two other possibilities for native peoples in Mesoamerica and the Andes were flight to escape colonial rule, and the kind of totalizing victimization posited by Serge Gruzinski by the end of the sixteenth century in *The Conquest of Mexico: The Incorporation of Indian Societies into the Western World, 16th–18th Centuries* (Cambridge, UK: Polity Press, 1993).

96. Nandy speaks of Indian counterplayers as "ornamental dissenters," *Intimate Enemy*, xiv.

97. *The Practice of Everyday Life*, xii.

98. *Intimate Enemy*, xiv.

99. Ashis Nandy, *The Tao of Cricket: On Games of Destiny and the Destiny of Games* (New York: Oxford University Press, 2000).

100. *Language and Symbolic Power*, trans. John B. Thompson (Cambridge, MA: Harvard University Press, 1991), 129.

101. Mapuches in Chile, "Chichimecs" of north-central Mexico, Mayas in Yucatán for a time in the sixteenth century, and the followers of the New Savior of Tututepec, Hidalgo, in 1769 come to mind as counterplayers and counterplaying subjects. Richard Trexler highlights counterplaying aspects of the history of the once Indian, later lower-class mestizo passion play of Iztapalapa on the edge of the Valley of Mexico (*Reliving Golgotha: The Passion Play of Iztapalapan* [Cambridge, MA: Harvard University Press, 2003]).

102. John Tutino, "Buscando independencias populares: Conflicto social e insurgencia agraria en el Mezquital mexicano, 1800–1815," in *Las guerras de independencia en la América Española*, ed. Marta Terán and José Antonio Serrano Ortega, 295–321 (Zamora: El Colegio de Michoacán, 2002); William B. Taylor,

Magistrates of the Sacred: Priests and Parishioners in Eighteenth-Century Mexico (Stanford, CA: Stanford University Press, 1996), 461.
103. *The Practice of Everyday Life*, xii.
104. Jesús Martín Barbero, *Communication, Culture, and Hegemony: From the Media to Mediations* (London: Sage, 1993), 82.
105. One stream of recent scholarship in colonial Mesoamerican studies has a largely nonplayer interpretation (that might well not accept "subaltern" as an appropriate term for Nahua, Mixtec, and Maya colonial subjects): James Lockhart, *The Nahuas After the Conquest: A Social and Cultural History of the Indians of Central Mexico, Sixteenth Through Eighteenth Centuries* (Stanford, CA: Stanford University Press, 1992); Matthew Restall, *The Maya World: Yucatec Culture and Society, 1550–1850* (Stanford, CA: Stanford University Press, 1997); Kevin Terraciano, *The Mixtecs of Colonial Oaxaca: Ñudzahui History, Sixteenth Through Eighteenth Centuries* (Stanford, CA: Stanford University Press, 2001).
106. AGN Civil 1111, exp. 991, petition to the Audiencia in 1793.
107. Dipesh Chakrabarty acknowledges the link when he writes, "We live in societies structured by the state," and "the subaltern who abjures the imagination of the state does not exist in a pure form in real life" (*Habitations of Modernity: Essays in the Wake of Subaltern Studies* [Chicago: University of Chicago Press, 2002], 34, 35). In *Provincializing Europe: Postcolonial Thought and Historical Difference* (Princeton, NJ: Princeton University Press, 2000), Chakrabarty takes up players, but they are mainly male, middle class, and Hindu. He has been criticized for not attending to lower-caste peasants and urban workers as players. See the review by Gyanendra Pandey in *Journal of World History* 13, no. 2 (fall 2002): 504–6.
108. Sherry B. Ortner, "Practice, Power, and the Past," *Journal of Social Archaeology* 1, no. 2 (2001): 272, 275.

Chapter 3

1. "Hallo la historia dificultosísima y no como pozo lleno de piedra, que pudiera ir apartando, sino que me he obligado acabar de nuevo en tierra llena de peñascos y tepetates; que es cosa dificultosa llegar a dar en el agua de la verdad" (*Historia de El Principio, y origen[,] progresos[,] venidas a México y milagros de la Santa Imagen de nuestra Señora de los Remedios . . .* [Mexico: Juan Blanco de Alcaçar, 1621], prologue). This was the first published hagiography of a Mexican miraculous image and its shrine.
2. *Our Lady of Guadalupe: Faith and Empowerment Among Mexican-American Women* (Austin: University of Texas Press, 1993), xxv.
3. "The Virgin of Guadalupe in New Spain: An Inquiry into the Social History of Marian Devotion," *American Ethnologist* 14, no. 1 (February 1987): 9–43.
4. Close examination of the sparse sixteenth-century record may be found in Edmundo O'Gorman, *Destierro de sombras: Luz en el origen de la imagen y culto de Nuestra Señora de Guadalupe del Tepeyac* (Mexico: Universidad Nacional Autónoma de México, 1986); Stafford Poole, *Our Lady of Guadalupe: The Origins and Sources of a Mexican National Symbol, 1531–1797* (Tucson:

University of Arizona Press, 1995); and Xavier Noguez, *Documentos guadalupanos: Un estudio sobre las fuentes de información tempranas en torno a las mariofanías en el Tepeyac* (Mexico: Fondo de Cultura Económica, 1993).

5. Bancroft Library, University of California, Berkeley (hereafter Bancroft), Mexican manuscripts, M-M 272, fols. 12r, 89r.

6. Miguel Sánchez, *Imagen de la Virgen María de Dios de Guadalupe*... (Mexico: Bernardo Calderón, 1648); Luis Lasso de la Vega's *Huei tlamahuiçoltica*... (Mexico: Imprenta de Iuan Ruyz, 1649); Luis Becerra Tanco's, *Felicidad de México en el principio, y milaroso origen*... (Mexico: Vuida de Calderón, 1675); and Francisco de Florencia's *La estrella del norte de México*... (Mexico: Viuda de Ribera, 1688).

7. Recent scholarship on the seventeenth century that begins to range beyond the texts of Sánchez, Lasso, Becerra Tanco, and Florencia includes Solange Alberro, *El águila y la cruz: Orígenes religiosos de la conciencia criolla. México, siglos XVI–XVII* (Mexico: El Colegio de México/Fondo de Cultura Económica, 1999); Serge Gruzinski, *La guerra de las imágenes, de Cristóbal Colón a "Blade Runner" (1492–2019)* (Mexico: Fondo de Cultura Económica, 1994); D. A. Brading, *Mexican Phoenix. Our Lady of Guadalupe Image and Tradition Across Five Centuries* (Cambridge, UK: Cambridge University Press, 2001); Poole, *Our Lady of Guadalupe: The Origins and Sources*; and essays by Alicia Mayer that place guadalupanismo into a Counter Reformation context of institutions, ideas, and the devotion of seventeenth-century Mexican savant, Carlos de Sigüenza y Góngora ("Las corporaciones guadalupanas: Centros de integración 'universal' del Catolicismo y fuentes de honorabilidad y prestigio," in *Formaciones religiosas en la América colonial*, ed. María Alba Pastor and Alicia Mayer, 179–201 [Mexico: Universidad Nacional Autónoma de México, 2000]; "El guadalupanismo en Carlos de Sigüenza y Góngora," in *Carlos de Sigüenza y Góngora: Homenaje, 1700–2000*, ed. Alicia Mayer, 243–72 [Mexico: Universidad Nacional Autónoma de México, 2000]; and "The Cult of Guadalupe and the Aims of the Counter-Reformation in New Spain," unpublished paper, 2001). Jaime Cuadriello breaks new ground in his studies of the iconography and style of colonial paintings of Our Lady of Guadalupe. See especially *Maravilla americana: Variantes de la iconografía guadalupana* (Guadalajara: Patrimonio Cultural del Occidente, 1989), and "La propagación de las devociones novohispanas: Las guadalupanas y otras imágenes preferentes," in *México en el mundo de las colecciones de arte*, ed. María Luis Sabau García, III:257–99 (Mexico: Secretaría de Relaciones Exteriores/Universidad Nacional Autónoma de México, 1994). These authors lean toward the creole nationalist interpretation mentioned later in this essay. Important earlier contributions include Francisco de la Maza's *El guadalupanismo mexicano* (various Mexican editions since 1953), and Efraín Castro Morales's "El santuario de Guadalupe de México en el siglo XVII," in *Retablo barroco: A la memoria de Francisco de la Maza*, ed. Diego Angulo Iñiquez, 67–77 (Mexico: Universidad Nacional Autónoma de México, 1974).

8. The "evangelists" stories of the apparitions vary slightly. Here I paraphrase Fr. Agustín de Vetancurt's summary based on Sánchez, Becerra Tanco, and Florencia, as a likely capsule version priests would have taught in the late seventeenth century. See Vetancurt, *Teatro mexicano. Descripción breve de*

los sucesos ejemplares, históricos y religiosos del nuevo mundo de las Indias (Mexico: Bonavides, 1698), pt. 4, tratado 5, chap. 3, 127–28.

9. *La estrella del norte de México*, 74.

10. Mateo de la Cruz, *Imagen de la Virgen de Guadalupe de México, sacada de la historia que compuse Br. Miguel Sánchez: Impressa en el año de 1660 . . .* (Mexico: Calle de la Palma, 1781).

11. A first English translation from the Nahuatl has recently been accomplished by Lisa Sousa, Stafford Poole, C.M., and James Lockhart: *The Story of Guadalupe: Luis Laso de la Vega's Huey tlamahuiçoltica of 1649* (Stanford and Los Angeles: Stanford University Press, 1998).

12. "Cult" in English still implies strange or sinister practices to many readers, although the primary dictionary definition is my meaning here: veneration and devotion, directed toward a particular figure or object. I use the Spanish term "culto" in these essays to stress this primary meaning.

13. *Imagen de la Virgen María* in *Testimonios históricos guadalupanos*, ed. Ernesto de la Torre Villar and Ramiro Navarro de Anda, 261 (Mexico: Fondo de Cultura Económica, 1982).

14. The hypothesis that the "Nican Mopohua" printed in Lasso de la Vega's *Huei tlamahuiçoltica* was copied from a Nahuatl text composed by Juan Valeriano in the mid-sixteenth century has been advanced and explored, but not securely established. Among other sources, see O'Gorman, *Destierro de sombras*, 48–60. In their recent translation of the *Huei tlamahuiçoltica*, Sousa, Poole, and Lockhart are persuaded that Lasso himself was the principal author, drawing mainly on Sánchez's book, perhaps with additions from oral traditions that may or may not have been written down earlier (*The Story of Guadalupe*, especially 43–47).

15. Jacques Lafaye, *Quetzalcóatl and Guadalupe: The Formation of Mexican National Consciousness, 1531–1813*, trans. Benjamin Keen (Chicago: University of Chicago Press, 1976 [1974]), 242; Stafford Poole, *Our Lady of Guadalupe: The Origins and Sources*, 217, 223; D. A. Brading, *The First America: The Spanish Monarchy, Creole Patriots, and the Liberal State, 1492–1867* (Cambridge, UK: Cambridge University Press, 1991), 3, 343–45; Richard Kagan, *Urban Images of the Hispanic World, 1493–1867* (New Haven, CT: Yale University Press, 2000), 131, 152, 162–68.

16. Pamela Sheingorn, ed., *The Book of Sainte Foy* (Philadelphia: University of Pennsylvania Press, 1995) provides a rich example of a European book of miracles in English translation.

17. Gregorio M. Guijo, *Diario, 1648–1664*, 2nd ed., 2 vols. (Mexico: Porrúa, 1986); Antonio de Robles, *Diario de sucesos notables (1665–1703)*, 3 vols. (Mexico: Porrúa, 1946).

18. *Actas de cabildo*, Mexico City, Sept. 15, 1586; Jan. 9, 1596; April 29, 1596; May 6, 1596; Sept. 18, 1624. Chapultepec became the new site in 1624, according to Gustavo Curiel, "Fiestas para un virrey. La entrada triunfal a la ciudad de México del Conde de Baños. El caso de un patrocinio oficial, 1660," in *Patrocinio, colección y circulación de las artes* (Mexico: UNAM, 1997), 166–68. In 1660, the Conde de Baños insisted on paying his respects at the Guadalupe shrine before going on to Chapultepec (167). Jorge Traslosheros's ongoing

research on guadalupanismo in the colonial period includes an examination of the colonial *actas del cabildo eclesiástico* for the Archdiocese of Mexico. We look forward to his findings on the seventeenth century from this source.

19. In the 1628–1630 actas, the Virgin of Guadalupe was not listed among the *abogados*—divine advocates—of the city. The abogados mentioned most prominently in the actas during those years were San Gregorio Thaumaturgo, San Hipólito, Santo Domingo, and Nuestra Señora de los Remedios.

20. Archivo General de la Nación (hereafter AGN), Ramo Archivo Histórico de Hacienda (hereafter AHH), vols. 1202-2, exps. 1 (1648–1651), 2 (1634), 3 (1653), 6 (1664–1668); AHH 1202-1, exps. 1, 2 (1693–1698).

21. In the early 1630s the archbishop was embroiled in litigation with the parish of Santa Catarina Mártir over who had administrative authority at the shrine, and in 1634 the image was returned to Tepeyac after its stay in Mexico City during the flood years. The 1648–1651, 1653, and 1664–1669 visitas coincide with especially active official promotion of the culto that began with publication of Sánchez's book. And the 1693–1698 financial records coincide with the period of planning and first phase of construction of the monumental church for the santuario.

22. Lafaye, *Quetzalcóatl and Guadalupe*, 256, 292.

23. Gruzinski, *La guerra de las imágenes*, 123.

24. Brading, *Mexican Phoenix*, 11.

25. *Our Lady of Guadalupe: The Origins and Source*, passim, but especially 217. By contrast, Alberro, *El águila y la cruz*, considers Sánchez's text to be a culmination more than an early peak of creole nationalism.

26. The burst of devotion following the 1629–1634 floods that Lafaye thinks may have spread throughout New Spain probably did not extend much beyond Mexico City. Juan de Torquemada noted at the beginning of the seventeenth century that Tepeyac was one of three important pilgrimage sites in precolonial times, but that the devotion had dropped off in favor of other cultos closer to home, or because of the declining Indian population or excessive labor demands on the survivors (*Monarquía indiana*, 2nd ed. [Madrid: Nicolás Rodríguez Franco, 1723], II:245–46).

27. Cisneros's early book on the shrine of Our Lady of los Remedios, which presented the providential discovery of the image there as occurring in 1540, recognized Tepeyac as having an older history. He referred to the Virgin of Guadalupe as "el más antiguo . . . casi desde que se ganó la tierra" (*Historia de El principio*, fol. 20r). Cisneros also included a miraculous cure for his protagonist, don Juan Ceteutli, that took him on a journey to Tepeyac (fol. 38r).

28. AGN Acervo 49, caja 140, folder 24, Ruiz González petition.

29. Diego de Cisneros, *Sitio, naturaleza, y propiedad de la Ciudad de México . . .* (Mexico: Iuan de Alcaçare, 1617), fol. 109r.

30. For example, in 1618, Juana Palacios, widow of Gaspar López de Bajamonde, left her house in the Barrio de la Veracruz to the shrine. It was sold at auction for eleven hundred pesos (AGN Civil 1839, exp. 7).

31. Castro Morales, "El santuario," 75.

32. Cisneros wrote in 1616 [1621] that the shrine at Tepeyac was "de gran devoción y concurso" (*Historia de El principio*, fol. 20r).

33. A request for such a license to collect in Querétaro "and other parts" had been made in 1633 (AGN Acervo 49, caja 140, folder 24).
34. For the period before 1648, actas de cabildo survive for 1524–1630 and 1635–1643.
35. Gruzinski posits that 1653 was the first year of substantial income for the shrine, as if Sánchez's book triggered prosperity, *La guerra de las imágenes*, 123–25.
36. "Iban desmoronándose los edificios." (AGN AHH 1202-2).
37. *La estrella del norte de México*, 167–76. Lafaye, *Quetzalcóatl and Guadalupe*, 233, posits that as late as 1600 the Spanish Virgin of Guadalupe's feast day (September 8) or the Nativity of the Virgin on September 10 was the principal feast at the shrine, then supplanted by December 12. Neither the September dates nor December 12 appear in the early seventeenth-century financial records.
38. A separate 1721–1723 investigation mentioned this purpose of the 1666 *informaciones* (*Informaciones sobre la milagrosa aparición de la Santísima Virgen de Guadalupe recibidas en 1666 y 1723*, ed. Br. Fortino Hipólito Vera, 193 [Amecameca: Imp. Católica, 1889]), and the title of a 1661 sermon by Joseph Vidal de Figueroa suggests that an annual December 12 feast day was being promoted then.
39. Robles, *Diario de sucesos*, I:34, dedicated in February 1667. According to O'Gorman, *Destierro de sombras*, 283, "la primera pequeñita capilla del Cerrito" was erected in 1660. He did not cite a source.
40. Robles, *Diario de sucesos*, I:189, 201.
41. The earliest published sermon about the image of Guadalupe (following Sánchez's text and the image as part of an apparition story) seems to be Joseph Vidal de Figueroa's "Theórica de la prodigiosa imagen de la Virgen Santa María de Guadalupe de México . . . el día 12 de diziembre en la fiesta annual de su milagrosa aparición en su hermita" (Mexico: Benavides, 1661). It was followed a decade later by Juan de San Miguel's "Sermón . . . a nacimiento de Nuestra Señora y dedicación de su capilla de Guadalupe . . . " (Mexico: Lupercio, 1671); José Herrera Suárez's "Sermón . . . en la solemne fiesta . . . a la aparición milagrosa de la santa imagen de Guadalupe" (Mexico: Viuda de Calderón, 1673); and Juan de Mendoza Ayala's "Sermón que en el día de la Aparición de la Imagen Santa de Guadalupe, doze de Diziembre del Año de 1672 . . . " (Mexico: Lupercio, 1673). Robles, *Diario de sucesos*, I:206, notes the December 11 celebration in 1676. AGN Acervo 49, caja 140, folder 8, has the order to keep the glass case closed.

The construction of shrines dedicated to Our Lady of Guadalupe outside the Valley of Mexico also follows the publication of the Sánchez text and gained momentum after the 1660s. The earliest distant shrine evidently was at San Luis Potosí, begun in 1654, followed by Querétaro, with a license of 1671 (under construction in 1674 and completed in 1680) (Archivo Histórico del Arzobispado de México, caja for 1674, and Chalma in 1683; José de Olivares, "Oración panegyrica . . . de la nueva capilla que se consagró a Nuestra Señora de Gvalalvpe" [Mexico: Calderón, 1683]). For the failed attempt in 1674 by a devout Indian noble of Tepemajalco (near Tenango del Valle, modern Estado de México) to obtain a license for a chapel to Our Lady of Guadalupe, see AGN Indios 25, exps. 19, 23, and 76.

42. According to the 1690s financial records, AGN AHH 1202-1.
43. Archivo Histórico del Arzobispado de México, caja for 1684, Archbishop Aguiar y Seixas granted permission in 1685 for these bulls to be published as a group.
44. Robles, *Diario de sucesos*, III:303. According to Robles, the new shrine was dedicated on December 31, 1702. *Gazeta de México*, which was published in series from 1722 to 1742, does not mention a major feast on December 12 until 1737, but the cofradía of Nuestra Señora de Guadalupe (founded in 1674) was reported to have celebrated its *fiesta titular* on December 12, 1735, and the bicentennial celebration in 1731 was held on December 12, too.
45. Guijo, *Diario*, II, 69; Robles, *Diario de sucesos*, II, 171.
46. *Informaciones sobre la milagrosa aparición* . . . , 23–133.
47. *Felicidad de México*, fol. 14r–v.
48. See, for example, Stafford Poole's view of the 1666 testimonies as "literally a case of *post hoc ergo propter hoc*," *Our Lady of Guadalupe: The Origins and Sources*, 220.
49. "12 tecpatl xihuitl 1556. Auh ça no ypan in yhuac monextitzino yn totlaçonantzin Sancta Maria Guadalope yn Tepeyacac" (Domingo Francisco de San Anton Muñon Chimalpahin Cuauhtlehuanitzin, *Die Relationen Chimalpahin's zur Geschichte Mexico's*, ed. Günter Zimmerman, II:16 [Hamburg: Cram, De Gruyter, 1963]). These annals go up to 1615. Chimalpahin may have written them between 1615 and about 1620. Silvia Rendón translated this passage into Spanish without *ypan*'s possible sense of "on top of": "También entonces ocurrió la aparición, dicho sea con respecto, de nuestra querida madre, Sancta María de Guadalupe en el Tepeyácac" (*Relaciones originales de Chalco Amaquemecan* [Mexico: Fondo de Cultura Económica, 1965], 264). James Lockhart, *The Nahuas After the Conquest* (Stanford, CA: Stanford University Press, 1992, 247), refers to this passage in Chimalpahin, and on page 551, n. 185, notes an earlier Nahuatl reference to Our Lady of Guadalupe appearing at Tepeyac (in an anonymous annals of Tenochtitlan, apparently dating from the 1560s).
50. Echave Orio's painting was first exhibited in the "Imágenes guadalupanas, cuatro siglos" show at the Centro Cultural/Arte Contemporáneo in Mexico City, November 1987–March 1988. For a color photographic reproduction, see the catalogue to the exhibition, *Imágenes guadalupanas, cuatro siglos* (Mexico: Fundación Cultural Televisa, 1987), 31. Jaime Cuadriello provides a brief discussion of the painting in *Maravilla americana*, 33.
51. Writing in about 1610, Torquemada described Echave Orio as "un español vizcaíno, . . . único en su arte" (a Basque Spaniard, unmatched in his art). Torquemada also noted that Echave Orio worked on the main altarpiece at Tlatelolco (completed in 1609). Tepeyac was located within the political jurisdiction of Tlatelolco (*Monarquía indiana*, III:215).
52. *Informaciones sobre la milagrosa aparición* . . . , 73.
53. Marqués de Montesclaros papers, Duque de Infantado Archive, Madrid. Microfilm in the DeGolyer Library, Southern Methodist University, roll 7, exp. 82. The note was written by or for the archbishop, authorizing processions in commemoration of the first anniversary of the ebbing of the flood waters. The processions were to take place on St. Anne's day, with the consecrated

host to be displayed in a few churches, as if relief from the flood were attributable to the mother of Mary and to Christ. The note is not signed or dated. Since it appears among the papers of the Marqués de Montesclaros, who served as Viceroy of New Spain from 1603–1607, it presumably dates from that period and would seem to refer to the flood described by Torquemada, which began in August 1604 and lasted a year (*Monarquía indiana*, I:728).

54. The numbers of Guadalupan sermons listed in José Toribio Medina's *La imprenta en México* picked up after 1680, with a dramatic, sustained increase after 1737. Only two university theses out of one hundred for the 1650s were dedicated to the Virgin of Guadalupe. Between 1660 and 1700, thirty-five of 607 (5.7 percent) carried Guadalupan dedications. True to form, the peak period of Guadalupan dedications for university theses was 1750–1810, with 159 dedicated out of 1,750 theses (9.1 percent). (Figures compiled from more than four thousand theses from the 1590s to 1850 listed in *Catálogo de ilustraciones* [Mexico: AGN, 1981], vols. 12 and 13.)

55. Martinus Cawley's unpublished 2002 paper, "The Four Evangelists of Guadalupe," provides a close reading of Becerra Tanco that points toward this confluence-of-two-streams interpretation of Sánchez's and Lasso's texts. He suggests that both Sánchez and Lasso drew heavily from Becerra Tanco's 1626 copy book, which, he surmises, included Valeriano's *Nican mopohua* and Becerra Tanco's own notes on Indian dramatic performances of Guadalupan apparitions.

56. Xavier Noguez's search for Indian sources of the apparition tradition in the early colonial period led him to posit that "the information that has been considered to be 'the history' of Guadalupan mariophany [as set down by the "evangelists"] begins . . . with a group of collectively created traditions brought together from various Indian contexts already acculturated to Christianity. The principal traditions studied here were elaborated over a relatively long period, from 1521 to 1688" (*Documentos guadalupanos*, 185).

57. *Calendario de Galván, para el año bisiesto de 1848. Arreglado al meridiano de Mégico* (México: Galván Rivera, 1847), se vende en la librería num. 7 del portal de mercaderes. But was the Indian fiesta different then, with different participants who understood it differently from their seventeenth-century predecessors?

58. Paz, *El ogro filantrópico: Historia y política, 1971–1978* (Mexico: J. Mortiz, 1979), 49; Donofrio, *Looking for Mary (or, the Blessed Mother and Me)* (New York: Viking Compass, 2000), 143–45.

59. Richard White, "History, the Rugrats, and World Championship Wrestling," *AHA Perspectives*, April 1999, 13.

60. As Hortensia, a devotee of the revered Niñopan—Baby Jesus—of Xochimilco put it when asked about the lack of historical evidence for the providential story of the image's origin in the sixteenth century, "Show me the document that says it isn't so" (Vania Salles and José Manuel Valenzuela, *En muchos lugares y todos los días: Vírgenes, santos y niños Dios. Mística y religiosidad popular en Xochimilco* [Mexico: El Colegio de México, 1997], interview #7).

61. Carl Schorske, *Thinking with History: Explorations in the Passage to Modernism* (Princeton, NJ: Princeton University Press, 1998), 3.

Chapter 4

1. Many other saints and advocations of Mary and Christ were invoked during the epidemic, as well. See Cayetano Cabrera y Quintero, *Escudo de armas de México* ... (Mexico: Viuda de J. A. de Hogal, 1746).
2. In a sermon delivered in the Mexico City cathedral on August 18, 1808, Archbishop Lizana y Beaumont claimed Benedict XIV was so enamored of Our Lady of Guadalupe and so convinced of the authenticity of the apparitions that when he heard Juan Francisco López, S.J., the representative to Rome from New Spain, had on shoes he wore to visit the shrine at Tepeyac, he asked for them and remarked that if he were in America he would go to the shrine on his knees, in bare feet (*Sermón que en las solemnes rogativas que se hicieron en la santa Iglesia metropolitana de México implorando el auxilio divino en las actuales ocurrencias de la monarquía española predicó* ... [Mexico: María Fernández de Jáuregui, 1808]).
3. For example, the reports from 1760–1761 by parish priests in the Diocese of Michoacán in response to a circular requesting information about their parishes and properties mention a dozen or so recently acquired images of or altars to Our Lady of Guadalupe (Oscar Mazín Gómez, ed., *El gran Michoacán: Cuatro informes del obispado de Michoacán, 1759–1769* [Zamora: El Colegio de Michoacán, 1986], 37–180, 247–431).
4. *Gazeta de México*, December 31, 1800.
5. Such as Atotonilco el Chico, mentioned in the *relación de méritos y servicios* of Manuel Cassela, ca. 1760, John Carter Brown Library, Brown University, Providence, RI (hereafter JCB), file B760A973i; and Villa de Orizaba in 1794, Archivo General de la Nación (hereafter AGN), Clero Regular y Secular 90, exp. 9.
6. While the publication of sermons, novenarios, prayer booklets, and devotional histories for Guadalupe became common from the 1680s, the great surge came after 1745. A tabulation of publications concerning shrines and miraculous images in José Toribio Medina's nearly exhaustive bibliography of works printed in Mexico during the colonial period, *La imprenta en México*, shows that 43 of 132 such publications between 1745 and 1767 concerned Guadalupe, 48 of 174 between 1768 and 1794, and 47 of 159 between 1796 and 1812.
7. Most of the many paintings of the image of Guadalupe done in the workshop of Miguel Cabrera date from the 1750s, especially after 1751. One of his paintings from 1752 was presented to the pope. In preparation for this outpouring of paintings, Cabrera had the opportunity to inspect the original image at length at least twice, in the company of Echeverría y Veytia on April 30, 1751, and April 15, 1752 (Mariano Fernández de Echeverría y Veytia, *Baluartes de México. Descripción histórica de las cuatro milagrosas imágenes de Nuestra Señora que se veneran en la ... ciudad de México* ... [Mexico: Impr. de A. Valdés, 1820], 61). On both occasions Echeverría was impressed that no dust had collected on the image, which he regarded as a "*singular prodigio*"), and in 1756 the publication of Cabrera's little book *Maravilla Americana* solidified his connection with the successful campaign for recognition of the authenticity of the image and the apparition story. Several of the thirty colonial and

nineteenth-century paintings of Guadalupe in the city of Querétaro carry Cabrera's signature or are attributed to his workshop (José Anaya Larios, *Los lienzos de la Virgen de Guadalupe en Querétaro* [Querétaro: Talleres de Litográfica Querétaro, 2001]).

8. The *Catálogo de Ilustraciones* for the AGN lists 236 theses dedicated to Guadalupe between 1651 and 1808. Of these, 203 date from 1701–1808, clustering especially in 1756–1765 (p. 42) and the 1780s (p. 36). The index to the 3,691 volumes of the AGN Tierras records few places named Guadalupe before 1691. Nearly all of the Guadalupe place names date from the eighteenth century, especially after the 1730s, with the Tenango del Valle district of the modern state of México unusually prominent. There was also a pocket of new places called Guadalupe in San Luis Potosí. The fifty-one haciendas called Guadalupe before 1750 were mainly located in the center (the Valley of Mexico and districts of the modern states of Mexico and Hidalgo) and two areas to the north where guadalupanismo became important in the seventeenth century: Querétaro and San Luis Potosí. The sixty-nine new references to haciendas called Guadalupe after 1750 continued the regional concentration in the center, but with a range that now reached into Puebla, the west (Michoacán and Jalisco), and north (the Bajío, Durango, and Nueva Vizcaya).

9. Sutro Library, San Francisco, CA, (hereafter Sutro) BT 660.G8, 1864 copy of documents dated 1755–1759, said to be in the cathedral archive of Puebla, amounting to an investigation of a reputed miracle of healing for Madre Nicolasa María Jascinta de San José, also described in Antonio de Paredes's *Sermón panegyrico que predicó . . . el la solemne acción de gracia . . .* (México: Impr. del real y más antiguo Colegio de San Ildefonso, 1761); Sutro, manuscript *efemérides* of Felipe Zúñiga y Ontiveros (1763–1773), entry for 1764 includes a description of Guadalupe's "prodigious" protection of the city against rising flood waters that year, which Fr. Francisco de Ajofrín confirmed in 1766 in his *Diario del viaje que por orden de la Sagrada Congregación de Propaganda Fide hizo a la América septentrional en el siglo XVIII* (Madrid: Real Academia de la Historia, 1958–59), I:77; in his early 1760s relación de méritos y servicios of Juan Faustino de Escobedo, he recounted how he escaped drowning in a river he was crossing on his way to a confession in the parish of Cozcatlán when he invoked the Virgin of Guadalupe (JCB B760 A973i); José Joaquín Granados y Gálvez's *Tardes americanas: gobierno géntil y católico . . .* (Mexico: Zúñiga y Ontiveros, 1778), 537–38, mentioned that a storm in the Valley of Mexico in 1678 deposited a hailstone with a perfectly formed image of Our Lady of Guadalupe.

10. D. José Gómez, *Anales de México* (1776–1798), manuscript copy evidently prepared for Carlos María Bustamante, Bancroft Library, University of California, Berkeley (hereafter Bancroft), M-M 105, 227.

11. Gómez, *Anales*, February 12, 1778, 60–61.

12. *Patente de la Cofradía de Nuestra Señora de Guadalupe, fundada por naturales, con autoridad ordinaria, en la ermita antigua* (México: Impr. de los herederos de Joseph de Jaúregui, 1784). Other construction dates in this paragraph are listed in Delfina E. López Sarrelangue, *Una villa mexicana en el siglo XVIII* (México: Imprenta Universitaria, 1957).

13. For example, during the War of Spanish Succession, Manuel de Argüello, *Acción de gracias . . . en virtud de . . . las victorias que consiguió . . . los días*

8 y 11 de diziembre del año de 1710 . . . (Mexico: Vda. de Ribera, 1711); during the War of Austrian Succession, José de Arlegui, *Sagrado paladión del americano orbe. Sermón . . . que hizo a María Sma. de Guadalupe la muy noble e ilustre ciudad de San Luis Potosí por el feliz sucesso de las cathólicas armas* . . . (Mexico: Viuda de J. A. de Hogal, 1743); during the Seven Years' War, an acta de cabildo of the Mexico City ayuntamiento, September 13, 1762, records a viceregal decree calling for a novena in honor of Our Lady of Guadalupe for "divine aid against the menace to these dominions from the English Nation" (*divino auxilio por la amenaza de la Nación inglesa a estos dominios*), and in an entry of February 20, 1765, Zúñiga y Ontiveros recorded in his efemérides (Sutro) that a Mass had been offered to Our Lady of Guadalupe as patroness of the troops (*patrona de la tropa*); and during the wars with France and Britain during the 1790s, AGN Colegios 426, exp. 16, noted on January 13, 1796, that the special novena was being celebrated at Tepeyac to appeal for victory.

14. Antonio de Ayala, *Deprecación que por los temblores de tierra, fuego, y enfermedades, a la Sagrada Imagen de Nra. Señora la Virgen María con el título de Guadalupe, . . . el dia 20 de diziembre de 1711 en el imperial Convento de n. padre san Augustín de esta ciudad de México* . . . (México: F. de Rivera Calderón, 1712); Fr. Antonio Cristóbal Muñoz de Castilblanque, *La mina de la Virgen tapada en Nazareth, y descubierta en el cerro de Guadalupe, para ser universal patrona de los americanos, y muy principal de los mineros, y por mina de oro, de los de la minería del Potosí* . . . (México: Impr. de la Bibliotheca Mexicana, 1758).

15. Nicolás de Segura, *Plática de la milagrosa imagen de Nuestra Señora de Guadalupe de México* (México: J. A. de Hogal, 1742); Juan José de Eguiara y Eguren, *María santíssima pintándose milagrosamente en su bellíssima imagen de Guadalupe de México . . . el día diez de noviembre de 1756* . . . (México: Impr. de la Bibliotheca Mexicana, 1757).

16. For example, AGN Clero Regular y Secular 68, exp. 3, fol. 296, "that for the love of God and Our Lady of Guadalupe they appeal to the present Lord Judge to put them on the schedule of fees" (*que por amor de Dios y Nuestra Señora de Guadalupe suplican al presente Sr. Juez el arancel*), petition of the town of San Agustín, 1772; *Gazeta de México*, 1784–1809, October 4, 1794, issue, Indians of the mission San Pedro de Aconchi reportedly observed the day of Our Lady of Guadalupe; AGN Tierras 2474, exp. 5, Capultitlan (Toluca jurisdiction), 1730, and AGN Tierras 2544, exp. 14, Tianguistengo (Meztitlán jurisdiction, Hidalgo), 1795, cases of villagers litigating over family images of Guadalupe. The appeals to the criminal court of the Acordada by five plebeian prisoners in 1799 are in AGN Acordada 15. The petitioners were from Mexico City and the Bajío. For an earlier appeal to Our Lady of Guadalupe under more ordinary circumstances, there is the 1709 new year's petition of Manuel del Barrio y Sedano for her help in his efforts to shed "the old trappings of indifference, laziness, and coldness and dress myself in the new clothing of fervor, love, and charity" (*las vestiduras viejas de tibieza, flojedad, y frialdad y vista las nuevas de fervor, amor, y caridad*) (AGN Inquisición 741, fols. 306r–307v).

17. *Gazeta de México*, September 2, 1797, issue, "casi todos los niños se vistieron galanamente en trage del dichoso Neófito Juan Diego"; the muleteer's lament is in Archivo Judicial de la Audiencia de la Nueva Galicia (Biblioteca Pública

del Estado, Guadalajara, Jalisco), bundle formerly labeled 1806(120), exp. 1, "que a él lo castigarían porque no tenía mujer bonita ni hijos, y que solo que fuera la Guadalupe."

18. Antonio Pompa y Pompa, in *La Voz Guadalupana*, February 12, 1947, 6–7.
19. More major anniversaries were still to come, including the 250th anniversary of the apparition in December 1780, which led to another burst of publications, student theses, and baptisms.
20. Luis Beltrán de Beltrán, *El poder sobre las aguas. . . . Sermón que en el día 23 de junio y último del novenario que . . . hicieron los caballeros hazendados . . .* (Mexico: Imprenta de la Bibliotheca Mexicana, 1765); AGN Escribanos 20, exp. 6, 1780, notes that the Real Colegio de Escribanos had sponsored an annual fiesta in honor of Our Lady of Guadalupe since 1772.
21. AGN General de Parte 41, exp. 133.
22. Issued by the Council of the Indies on September 7, 1756 ("que se sirva mandar que en los testamentos que se otorgaren en la Nueva España se exprese por manda forzosa el santuario y simulacro de aquella santa imagen," Archivo General de Indias, Audiencia de México [hereafter, AGI Mexico], legajo 2531), followed by a cédula of July 29, 1757, issued by the Marqués de las Amarillas (Tulane University, Latin American Library, Viceregal and Ecclesiastical Mexican Collection [hereafter, VEMC] 50, exp. 11).
23. José Francisco Valdés, *Salutación a María Santíssima de Guadalupe. Práctica devota para venerarla en su santuario, quando se le hace la visita* (Mexico: Zúñiga y Ontiveros, 1794); reprinted in 1808 and 1819.
24. An inventory of Boturini's Guadalupan manuscripts appears in Ernesto de la Torre Villar and Ramiro Navarro de Anda, *Testimonios históricos guadalupanos* (Mexico: Fondo de Cultura Económica, 1982), 405–12.
25. None of these works was published during his lifetime. He died in 1780.
26. Echeverría y Veytia, *Baluartes*, 37–38.
27. Ibid., 27.
28. He was archbishop from 1731 to 1747, and viceroy from 1734 to 1740. Other peninsular officials were among the ardent guadalupanistas of the late eighteenth century; for example, Archbishop Francisco Antonio de Lorenzana (1766–1772), as well as most viceroys (perhaps especially Frey Antonio María de Bucareli, who served from 1771 to 1779 and was buried at the shrine). One exception among viceroys seems to have been the second Conde de Revilla Gigedo (1789–1794), who ordered the removal of the image of Our Lady of Guadalupe from several locations on the grounds of the royal palace in Mexico City, and did not attend the December 12 festivities at the shrine in 1791 (José Gómez, *Diario curioso . . . 1789–1794* [Mexico: UNAM, 1986], 12, 14, 44 [a partial publication of Gómez, *Anales*, which is cited earlier in this essay]).
29. *Gazeta de México*, November 19, 1731; December 12, 1731; August 1735. As Vizarrón requested, the crown approved in principle the elevation of the settlement at Tepeyac as a villa (AGN Reales Cédulas Originales 42, exp. 134). The cédulas completing the process of making the settlement a villa were issued on August 21, 1748, and July 22, 1749 (AGN Reales Cédulas Originales 68, exp. 32, and 69, exp. 16).

30. Archivo Histórico del Distrito Federal (hereafter AHDF), núm. de inventario vol. 62, the acta de cabildo for January 27, 1737, records the viceroy's reply to the ayuntamiento's request for the image to be brought to the city.
31. Joseph Guerra, *Fecunda nube del cielo guadalupano, y mystica paloma del estrecho palomar de el Colegio apostólico de Nuestra Señora de Guadalupe: Relación breve de la vida exemplar del V.P.F. Antonio Margil de Jesús* . . . (México: J. A. de Hogal, 1727).
32. The investigation was carried out in 1723 (see Fortino Hipólito Vera, ed., *Informaciones sobre la milagrosa aparición de la Santísima Virgen de Guadalupe recibidas en 1666 y 1723*, 2nd ed. [Mexico: Imprenta Gallarda, 1948], 189–247).
33. AGN Bienes Nacionales 893, exp 27. The date of the grant is not clear from this financial record, beyond being the work of Innocent XIII, who served from May 1721 to March 1724.
34. 1722–1723: *Boletín del Instituto Bibliográfico Mexicano* (hereafter *BIBM*), num. 5 (1905), 995, *Gazeta de México*, May 1722; *Informaciones . . . en 1666 y 1723*, 189–247; 1728: *BIBM*, num. 4 (1903), 82, *Gazeta de México*, December 1728. 1729: *BIBM*, num. 4 (1903), 134–35, *Gazeta de México*, September 1729; 152–53, *Gazeta de México*, December 1729. 1731: *BIBM*, num. 4 (1903), 291–92, *Gazeta de México*, December 1731. 1735: *BIBM*, num. 4 (1903), 583, *Gazeta de México*, December 1735. Mention of these commemorations is also found in the actas de cabildo of Mexico City's ayuntamiento, AHDF.
35. Joaquín Ignacio Ximénez de Bonilla, *El Segundo quinze de enero de la corte mexicana. Solemnes fiestas, que a la canonización del mystico doctor san Juan de la Cruz celebró la Provincia de San Alberto de carmelitas descalzos de esta Nueva España* . . . (Mexico: J. A. de Hogal, 1730), 109. I thank Karen Melvin for bringing this passage to my attention.
36. Archivo Histórico del Arzobispado de México (hereafter, AHAM), pastoral visit books of Archbishops Aguiar y Seijas, Lanciego, and Rubio y Salinas.
37. Cases of resistance include Tejupilco 1760 (AGN Clero Regular y Secular 204, exp. 9), Tepetlaostoc 1758 (AGN Clero Regular y Secular 156, exp. 5), Acatlan (Tulancingo jurisdiction) 1817 (AGN Clero Regular y Secular 136, exp. 8). See also my *Magistrates of the Sacred: Priests and Parishioners in Eighteenth-Century Mexico* (Stanford, CA: Stanford University Press, 1996), 286, 682.
38. The Colegiata chapter complained in 1786 that little money was coming from the wills because local pastors were not bothering to enforce the royal order (VEMC 50, exp. 11). A special raffle in 1794 was needed to covers repairs to the church when individual contributions proved insufficient (AGN Colegios 21, exp. 6).
39. The set of reports on parishes and shrines in the Archdiocese of Mexico in 1743 rarely mention Our Lady of Guadalupe (Francisco de Solano, ed., *Relaciones geográficas del Arzobispado de México. 1743*, 2 vols. [Madrid: Consejo Superior in Investigaciones Científicas, 1988]). An example of the particular appeal of Our Lady of Guadalupe in the vicinity of San Luis Potosí is the request by the parish priest of San Francisco del Valle and his parishioners for permission to build a shrine to Guadalupe in 1802. In his petition, the priest recalled the shrine in the city of San Luis ("*Hago memoria de el santuario de la ciudad de*

San Luis Potosí") and said it was difficult for his parishioners to go there or to other Guadalupan shrines (AGN Civil 1806, exp. 2).

40. Support for the colegiata was never in doubt—endowments began to accumulate from influential devotees in Mexico City as early as 1708, when the new church was nearly finished; a proposal was made to the Council of the Indies in 1717 and approved in principle (AGI Mexico 2531); a papal decree authorized its establishment in 1725 (Delfina López Sarrelangue, *Una villa mexicana en el siglo XVIII* [Mexico: Imprenta Universitaria, 1957], 32); and the next year a judge on the Audiencia de México was named Protector Especial de la Colegiata in order to move the project along (*Gazeta de México*, July 1728). To complete the process of establishing a colegiata, however, it had to be located in a substantial, formal community designated as a villa. At Archbishop-Viceroy Vizarrón's request, the crown authorized the erection of a villa there in 1733, but certain physical requirements had not yet been met (AGN Reales Cédulas Originales 52, exp. 134, December 28, 1733). The audiencia followed up in 1735, authorizing first the formation of a lesser town, a pueblo de indios, although the settlement at Tepeyac did not develop the structure of a recognized pueblo until 1741 (López Sarrelangue, *Una villa*, 33, 34). Population and organization were part of the problem. In 1721 there were 918 souls dispersed among five Indian barrios in the vicinity of the shrine, without a nucleated center (AGN Bienes Nacionales 912, exp. 16). Lack of a regular water supply was part of the problem. A water grant had been made in 1679 and attempts to build an aqueduct to the site for domestic use were started in 1714 and 1727, but not completed until 1751 (López Sarrelangue, *Una villa*, 84–90). On August 21, 1748, the standing of the settlement at the shrine as a villa was affirmed by royal cédula, and in 1749 the townsite was reformed according to an approved plan (AGN Reales Cédulas Originales 68, exp. 32, and AGN Reales Cédulas Originales 69, exp. 16, July 22, 1749). Soon thereafter, in 1750, the colegiata was finally established.

By 1797 the parish of the villa of Guadalupe had grown to 2,168 souls, with the town center accounting for half of the total (1,089) (AHAM, caja 1717–1797). Surprisingly, the proportion of residents named Guadalupe had declined substantially since 1721, even in most of the outlying Indian barrios of the jurisdiction. Six percent of Santa Ysabel Tola's people were named Guadalupe in 1721, 3.8% in 1797; 10.7% of San Juan Sigualtepec's people were named Guadalupe in 1721, 2.5% in 1797; in Santiago Zacualco, 4.5% in 1721 and .65% in 1797; and in San Pedro Zacatengo, 2.6% in 1721 and 5.4% in 1797. In the villa itself only 1.1% of the residents carried the name Guadalupe, and over half of them were living on the Calle de la Caxa de Agua. In all, 2% of the residents of the parish of the Villa de Guadalupe in 1792 were named Guadalupe, compared to 4.2% in Arandas, Jalisco, another parish dedicated to Our Lady of Guadalupe.

Small numbers of Indians from other parts of the Valley of México moved to the vicinity of Tepeyac in the late sixteenth and seventeenth centuries; for example, from Zumpango de la Laguna in 1587 (AGN Tierras 2948, exp. 60). Whether the early settlers were attracted by the aura of divine presence more than by economic opportunity or dislocation the record does not say.

41. *Gazeta de México*, March 18, 1796 issue, "con el fin de que se propague a toda nuestra América la mensual demostración de amor y gratitud a nuestra singular Patrona María Santísima de Guadalupe, se ha tenido por oportuno participar que esta ciudad, a imitación de la Metrópoli México, ha comenzado a tributar nuevos cultos a la Señora en cada día doce, exponiendo sus santas imágenes en las ventanas e iluminando estas por partes de noche."
42. Most were produced in Mexico City.
43. AGN Clero Regular y Secular 27, exp. 2, 1797 *"tratantes de la plaza"*; AGN Clero Regular y Secular 27, exp. 6, 1798 *"comerciantes meleros de la calle de la azequia"*; AGN Clero Regular y Secular 151, exp. 7, Barrio San Hipólito was in trouble over its unlicensed *hermandad* and irregularly licensed Rosary processions.
44. AHAM, caja for 1751, Toluca, "It being known that a resident of the City of Toluca during the month of December goes out on a Rosary procession to Our Lady of Guadalupe for nine straight nights, which is attended by a numerous gathering of people of all classes, which results, because of the ill-timed hour as well as from the disturbance and disorder caused by the fireworks" (Haviendo entendido que un vecino de la Ciudad de Toluca por el mes de diziembre saca un rosario de Nuestra Señora de Guadalupe, por nueve noches continuas a que asiste un numeroso concurso de gente de todas clases, de que resulta así por la hora tan intempestiva, como por la turbación, y desorden que causan los fuegos); AGN Bienes Nacionales 976, exp. 5, Barrio del Hornillo, parish of Santa Cruz y Soledad; AGN Inquisición 1099, exp. 11, 1776 Ignacio Vilchiz, a barber-surgeon who lived in the portal de Santo Domingo in Mexico City reported to the Inquisition a procession with pigskins filled with pulque and covered with flowers accompanied by many horsemen who carried a sort of banner with an image of Our Lady of Guadalupe.
45. *El ogro filantrópico: Historia y política, 1971–1978* (México: J. Mortiz, 1979, 49). Jacques Lafaye endorsed this view in *Quetzalcoatl and Guadalupe: The Formation of National Consciousness, 1531–1813*, trans. Benjamin Keen (Chicago: University of Chicago Press, 1976), especially 276.
46. The baptism and census records for parishes in central and western Mexico I reviewed for the eighteenth century typically show about twice as many non-Indians as Indians named Guadalupe. In a 1987 article, "The Virgin of Guadalupe in New Spain: An Inquiry into the Social History of Marian Devotion," *American Ethnologist* 14, no. 1 (February 1987): 9–33, I discuss baptism records for six Jalisco parishes and one for the Estado de México. Recently I have added *matrículas* (lists of residents) for the districts of El Cardonal and Zimapán in the state of Hidalgo (AGN Bienes Nacionales 388, exp. 19; AGN Bienes Nacionales 403, exp. 17; and AGN Bienes Nacionales 818, exp. 8). With the exception of Arandas, Jalisco, the general pattern of more non-Indian than Indian Guadalupes holds for these places. Arandas stands apart as a community with Guadalupe as its principal patron saint.
47. Mexico: Viuda de J. A. de Hogal, 1742, "quien negará que se apareció esta benignísima Madre con apostados empeños de asemejarse en todo a los Naturales de el País, tan preciada de India, que parece lo afectó en todas sus circunstancias: en la Tilma o capa de Juan Diego, en que se pintó; en la disposición y encogimiento humilde del Cuerpo e inclinacion de la Cabeza; en

la partición complanada de el cabello, y éste negro y bien poblado; y en lo trigueño claro de el color de rostro y manos; en la túnica talar desde el cuello y hombros hasta los pies, y en lo tendido de el manto desde la cabeza a los pies, a lo de cobija: señas todas y demostraciones en que manifiesta aver querido asemejarse en todo a los Indios nobles y principales de esta América." In a similar vein, see Cristóbal de Aldana, *Crónica de la Merced de México* (México: Biblioteca Nacional, 1953), 27.

48. Other sermons and observations of this kind include Franciscan Bartolomé Felipe de Itta y Parra's *El círculo del amor formado por la América septentrional, jurando a Maria Santíssima en su imagen de Guadalupe*... (México: Viuda de J. A. de Hogal, 1747), 18, "What do we see in that most beautiful image of Mary? A beautiful and modest Indian woman. The tunic, the cloak, the dress, all of it is of her nation" (¿Qué reconocemos en essa bellíssima Imagen de María? Una hermosa modesta Indiana. La túnica, el manto, el traje es todo de su nación); Jesuit Ignacio de Paredes's *Sermón de Nuestra Gran Reyna, Poderosísima Patrona, Madre, y Señora nuestra, María Santíssima de Guadalupe*, published in his *Promptuario manual mexicano*... (México: Impr. de la Bibliotheca Mexicana, 1759), "here briefly and clearly the history of her admirable and miraculous Apparitión is recounted so that it may come to the attention of all Indians, who have been specially favored by this very Lady" (en que breve y claramente se refiere la historia de su admirable y milagrosa Aparicion, para que ésta llegue a noticia de todos los indios, por la misma Señora especialmente favorecidos); Capuchin traveler Fr. Francisco de Ajofrín remarked that the image looked like an Indian noblewoman and that almost every day many Indians visited the sanctuary with votive offerings. He was especially taken by the simplicity and tender love with which these "dear little Indians," "these poor little people," venerated "their beloved Mother and Lady of Guadalupe" (*Diario del viaje*, I:117–20); Francisco Javier Rodríguez, *Sermón de Nuestra Señora de Guadalupe*... (México: Impr. de J. A. de Hogal, 1766); Joseph Vela, *Oración que en la festividad de Nuestra Señora de Guadalupe de México*... *el dia 12 de diciembre de 1773* (México: Reimpreso por F. de Zúñiga y Ontiveros, 1786), spoke of Juan Diego in terms of "the innocent simplicity of a humble Indian" (*la inocente sencillez de un humilde indio*) and characterized the image as notable for "its modesty, grace, and composure."

49. "Con nuestra ymagen de Guadalupe viven engreidísimos, y con razón: qualesquiera especie que de ella se les acomode, la reciven con agrado y la retienen; y al oir que aquel dichosísimo yndio Juan Diego mereció las apariciones de esta Nuestra Señora a tiempo que venía a deprehender la doctrina, se inflaman y conmueven aplicándose a ella" (manuscript entitled "Conversaciones familiares de un cura a sus feligreses yndios...," Tepecuacuilco, 1769, Bancroft M-M 113).

50. "El color Moreno no asea, antes bien agracia"; "Vengan pues todos los Indios, vengan las Indias a obsequiar reverentes a esta Sra, vengan de los hijos, y crean las indias" (Francisco Antonio Lorenzana y Butrón, *Cartas pastorales y edictos* [México: J. A. de Hogal, 1770], 211, 215).

51. *Oración de Nuestra Señora de Guadalupe, compuesta por el Illmo. Señor d. Francisco Antonio de Lorenzana, arzobispo de Mexico* (Mexico: Impr. de J. A. de Hogal, 1770), 21. Other ways in which the association of Indians and

Guadalupe was promoted include the Jesuits 1753 proposal for a school for Indian girls in Mexico City dedicated to Our Lady of Guadalupe (approved by royal cédula in 1759); promotion of guadalupanismo by pastors in Indian parishes of the Archdiocese of Mexico as indicated in their professional resumés from the early 1760s (JCB file B760 A973i); and the persistent efforts from 1756 to 1770 of a distinguished Indian priest, Julián Cirilo de Castillo, to gain permission to establish a college for Indian priests at Tepeyac. Cirilo failed in this effort, but did receive permission to found such a college in Tlaxcala (AGN Reales Cédulas Originales 74, exp. 54; 76, exp. 26; 80, exp. 22; 83, exp. 19; 84, exp. 60; 86, exp. 70; 88, exp. 33; 93, exp. 121; 97, exp. 63; 97, exp. 84; and 115, exp. 77).

52. For examples, *Imágenes guadalupanas, cuatro siglos* (México: Fundación Cultural Televisa, 1987), 103 (Cabrera, 1751), and 228 (anonymous, eighteenth century). Sermons that highlight Juan Diego include Ramón Pérez de Anastaris's *Sermón que en el día de la milagrosa aparición de Nuestra Señora de Guadalupe dixo en su santuario en el mes de diciembre del año pasado de 1796 . . .* (México: Impr. de J. Fernández de Jaúregui, 1797), which described him as a "poor Indian, very tender in his faith, of few and confused religious ideas . . . representative of his entire Nation" (*pobre Indio, de fe muy tierna, de ideas religiosas muy escasas y confusas . . . representante de toda su Nación*).

53. AGN Clero Regular y Secular 206, exp. 3.

54. Examples include the 1771 petition of Indians of San Felipe del Obraxe (Ixtlahuaca district, Estado de México) in their dispute over clerical fees with the parish priest: "que por amor de Dios y Nuestra Señora de Guadalupe suplican al presente Señor juez el arancel" (AGN Clero Regular y Secular 68, exp. 3); the murder trial record involving two men of Xochimilco in 1801, in which the offender claimed that the victim grabbed him by the testicles and that "he begged him for the love of Our Lady of Guadalupe" to let go (*le suplicaba por Nuestra Señora de Guadalupe que lo dejara*) (AGN Criminal 236, fols. 138–45); and the petition of the governor and other Indian officials of San Juan Bautista Tescatepec which begins "We appeal in the name of Most Holy Mother of Guadalupe" (*Suplicamos por Madre Santíssima de Guadalupe*) (AGN Bienes Nacionales 172, exp. 45).

55. AGN Bienes Nacionales 575, exp. 11. License to build this chapel was granted on February 16 or March 10, 1789.

56. *Gazeta de México*, December 16, 1803.

57. *Patente de la Cofradía de Nuestra Señora de Guadalupe, fundada por naturales, con autoridad ordinaria, en la ermita Antigua* (México: Impr. de los herederos de Joseph de Jaúregui, 1784).

58. Robert Ryal Miller and William J. Orr, eds., *Daily Life in Colonial Mexico: The Journey of Friar Ilarione da Bergamo, 1761–1768*, trans. William J. Orr (Norman: University of Oklahoma Press, 2000), 142.

59. AHAM, caja for 1828.

60. *Image and Pilgrimage in Christian Culture: Anthropological Perspectives* (New York: Columbia University Press, 1978), 172. The eighteenth-century urban shrines in diocesan capitals would seem to express the intention of building a network.

61. The subject of faith in territorial terms is a daunting challenge for historical study. Tracking shrine visitors, migrants, and long-distance travelers, including muleteers, traders, hermits attached to shrines, missionaries, parish priests, alms collectors, and bishops on pastoral visits is one approach, but it is easier said than done. Locating images of Our Lady of Guadalupe is another.

62. Bancroft 87/190m, Mexican Miscellany, carton 2, "Sumaria ynformación en orden a la marabilla de Nuestra Señora del Nogal," 1758. The earliest long-distance pilgrimage to Tepeyac I have seen documented was made by a small group of Ópata people in early 1840 (C. Dora Tabanico, "De Tuape a la Basílica de Guadalupe," in *Memorias: IV Simposio de la Sociedad Sonorense de Historia* [Hermosillo: Instituto Sonorense de Cultura, 1991], 133–38). It would be surprising if some of the visitors to Mexico City for litigation and appeals to the viceroy or audiencia during the seventeenth and eighteenth centuries did not make the short side trip to Tepeyac, but I have not yet found mention of this in colonial records. Even when Ignacio Manuel Altamirano seemed to observe a change toward long distance pilgrimage to Tepeyac in the late nineteenth century, he noted that the visitors were mainly people from Mexico City: "It is one of the greatest feasts of Mexican Catholicism; first, certainly, in its popularity and universality.... It is the whole city of Mexico that moves on foot to the shrine, from morning until afternoon" ([Es] una de las mayores fiestas del Catolicismo mexicano, la primera seguramente por su popularidad, por su universalidad.... Es la ciudad de México entera que se traslada al pie del santuario, desde la mañana hasta la tarde) (*Paisajes y leyendas. Tradiciones y costumbres de México* [México: Porrúa (Sepan Cuantos 375), 1979], 55).

63. Ronald C. Finucane, *Miracles and Pilgrims: Popular Beliefs in Medieval England* (Totowa, NJ: Rowman and Littlefield, 1977), 217.

64. Philip M. Soergel, *Wondrous in his Saints: Counter-Reformation Propaganda in Bavaria* (Berkeley: University of California Press, 1993).

65. All were copies—"portraits," as Florencia put it. There was only one original. That was Mary herself. As the lettering on one eighteenth-century painting of the image put it, this was a "living copy of the lifelike copy of Most Holy Mary" (*viva copia de la copia viva de María Santísima*). This painting appears as the first illustration in Jaime Cuadriello and others, *Zodíaco mariano: 250 años de la declaración pontificia de María de Guadalupe como patrono de México* (Mexico: Museo de la Basílica de Guadalupe, 2004).

66. Art historian Clara Bargellini finds originality in this seemingly endless fascination with the image in eighteenth-century Mexico. In doing so she criticizes earlier generations of art historians for not regarding the Guadalupe paintings as art and for ignoring the originality of Baroque production, "Originality and Invention in the Painting of New Spain," in *Painting a New World: Mexican Art and Life, 1521–1821*, ed. Donna Pierce, 79–91 (Denver: Denver Art Museum, 2004).

67. Other Guadalupan images elsewhere were associated with miracles before the eighteenth century, including a famous image in Antequera that remained untouched by a fire in 1665 (Francisco de Florencia, *La estrella del norte de México* [1695] [Guadalajara: Imprenta de J. Cabrera, 1895], 146–49); another in the mission church of San Francisco de Conchos, Chihuahua, that sweated

for three days in 1695 (Lauro López Beltrán, *La Guadalupana que sudó tres días* [Chihuahua: Editorial Camino, 1989]); and an image or incident in Apam, Hidalgo, before 1722 mentioned by Br. José de Lizardi y Valle in his prologue to the 1722–1723 inquiry, *Informaciones sobre la milagros aparición* . . . , 203. Omitting the details, Lizardi also mentions that there were many other miracles associated with Our Lady of Guadalupe. Our Lady of Guadalupe became a prominent patron in ex-voto paintings during the eighteenth century. Several are published in Horacio Sentíes, *La Villa de Guadalupe: Historia, estampas y leyendas* (Mexico: Departamento del Distrito Federal, 1991), 104, and *Dones y promesas: 500 años de arte ofrenda (exvotos mexicanos)* (Mexico: Fundación Cultural Televisa, 1996), 55, 57.

68. *Gazeta de México* for September 1737 in BIBM, núm. 5, 722.

69. AGN Criminal 308, exp. 1, fols. 32–34, testimony of Diego Agustín, "Nuestra Señora de Guadalupe, la que apareció en México, cayó de su grandeza allá." In his summary of events, the alcalde mayor mentioned that followers brought to the Savior's "mosque" (*mezquita*) images of Our Lady of Guadalupe and San Mateo from their home churches (fol. 12v).

70. Edward S. Casey, *The Fate of Place: A Philosophical History* (Berkeley: University of California Press, 1997), passim.

71. John B. Jackson, *A Sense of Place, A Sense of Time* (New Haven: Yale University Press, 1994), and *Landscape in Sight* (New Haven: Yale University Press, 1997).

72. Quoted in Martin J. Pasqualetti, ed., *The Evolving Landscape: Homer Aschmann's Geography* (Baltimore and London: Johns Hopkins University Press, 1997), vii.

73. Lee Hoinacki, *El Camino: Walking to Santiago de Compostela* (University Park, PA: Penn State Press, 1996), 14.

74. J. B. Jackson, *Landscape in Sight: Looking at America* (New Haven: Yale University Press, 1997), 249.

75. Benito Jerónimo de Feijóo, "Peregrinaciones sagradas y romerías," in *Obras escogidas* (Madrid: Atlas [Biblioteca de Autores Españoles], 1951–61), tomo V:51–56.

76. Eamon Duffy, "The Dynamics of Pilgrimage in Late Medieval England," in *Pilgrimage: The English Experience from Becket to Bunyan*, ed. Colin Morris and Peter Roberts, 164–77 (Cambridge, UK: Cambridge University Press, 2000).

77. This practice is known because their parish priest pursued a two-pronged formal complaint: that they did not celebrate the holiday at home and that the district governor of Texcoco charged them half a real to attend the festivities there. In response, the Audiencia ordered the district governor not to collect fees for attendance, but did not address the question of where the Indians should celebrate the holiday (AGN General de Parte 59, exp. 251 [1777]). Pilgrimages to the regional shrine at San Luis Potosí are mentioned in the 1792 sermon preached there by Antonio López Murto, *El incomparable patronato mariano* . . . (Mexico: Zúñiga y Ontiveros, 1793), 19.

78. Thomas Calvo, "Prólogo," in Félix Báez Jorge, *La parentela de María: Cultos marianos, sincretismo, e identidades nacionales en Latinoamerica* (Xalapa: Universidad Veracruzana, 1994), 18. "En una de mis visitas a los huicholes, un

hombre, que había visitado la ciudad de México y el santuario de Guadalupe me enseñaba un templo tuki, donde había un altar con ofrendas votivas y otros símbolos, entre otros dos cuadros de la Virgen de Guadalupe. Yo pregunté intencionadamente a mi informante huichol si esa 'Virgen' no era 'Mexicana,' ya que era igual a la vista por él en México. Él contestaba invariablemente a mis insistentes preguntas con una frase lacónica: 'No, la Virgen de Guadalupe no es mexciana, es huichol.' Yo intentaba hacerle ver que era un 'símbolo tomado de México,' aunque ellos la identifiquen también con la diosa Tanana. Finalmente contestó: 'Ya le he dicho que la Virgen de Guadalupe es nuestra, es huichol; los vecinos [mexicanos] nos la robaron hace tiempo.'"

79. For example, La Virgen de la Piedrita of Canalejas, Estado de México, found in 1868. See Jesús García Gutiérrez, *La Virgen de la Piedrita*, 2nd ed. (Canalejas, Estado de México: n.p. 1993).

Chapter 5

1. José Manuel Villalpando César, "Virgen insurgente: Nuestra Señora de Guadalupe en la Independencia de México, 12 de diciembre de 1794 a 12 de diciembre de 1824," *Memorias de la Academia Mexicana de la Historia*, tomo XL (1997): 55–86, especially 57.

2. As Marta Terán has written, from the beginning "hubo muchas enseñas guadalupanas en campaña. En Calderón, Calleja reunió cinco banderas y dos estandartes. De los siete, cuatro—dos banderas y dos estandartes—portaban a la Virgen de Guadalupe" (there were many Guadalupan campaign banners. At the Battle of Calderón, Calleja took five flags and two standards. Of the seven, four—two flags and two standards—carried the image of the Virgin of Guadalupe) ("Un hallazgo histórico," *Reforma: Revista Cultural "El Angel,"* February 22, 2002, 2). Dra. Terán and a Spanish colleague, Luis Sorando, recently brought to light two of the earliest banderas, captured by royalists at San Miguel El Grande in late 1810. See her description and analysis of them in "Las primeras banderas del movimiento por la independencia. El patrimonio histórico de México en el Museo del Ejército Español," in *Movimientos sociales en Michoacán, siglos XIX y XX*, ed. Eduardo N. Mijangos Díaz, 17–38 (Morelia: Universidad Michoacana de San Nicolás de Hidalgo, 1999), and "La Virgen de Guadalupe contra Napoleón Bonaparte: La defensa de la religión en el Obispado de Michoacán entre 1793y 1810," *Estudios de Historia Novohispana* 19 (1999): 91–129. There and in other essays Dra. Terán examines political and theological ideas that joined the images of Guadalupe, the Mexican eagle, and San Miguel in these early expressions of insurgent patriotism on campaign banners.

3. *El despertador americano*, núm. 2, December 27, 1810, "contamos con el patrocinio declarado de la Madre Santa de Guadalupe, Numen Tutelar de este Imperio, y Capitana Jurada de nuestras Legiones."

4. *Gaceta del Gobierno de México*, tomo 2, núm. 23, 1811, "comenzó una algazara de voces gritando 'ahora es tiempo, Viva Nuestra Señora de Guadalupe y mueran todos,' y al instante descargaron sobre nosotros una lluvia inmensa de piedras."

5. Ana Carolina Ibarra González, "Excluidos pero fieles. La respuesta de los insurgentes frente a las sanciones de la Iglesia, 1810–1817," *Signos históricos* 7 (enero–junio 2002): 65. Ibarra González gives religiosity an important place in the independence period without claiming it was a war of religion.
6. For example, René Capistrán Garza, *Virgen que forja una patria: El Tepeyac, cimiento espiritual de América*, 3rd ed. (México: Bajo el Signo de Atisbos, 1957).
7. Quoted in Villalpando César, "Virgen insurgente," 57, "símbolo de las esperanzas de la patria."
8. Villalpando César, "Virgen insurgente," 79.
9. The other national religious holidays were Corpus Christi and Thursday and Friday of Holy Week (Circular of the Primera Secretaría de Estado. Sección de Gobierno: Núm. 117: Juan Guzmán, "El Ecsmo. Sr. Presidente de los Estados-Unidos Mexicanos se ha servido dirigirme el decreto que sigue... el Soberano Congreso... ha tenido a bien decretar... las fiestas religiosas nacionales quedarán en lo sucesivo reducidas a los días de jueves y viernes Santo, Corpus y festividad de Guadalupe el 12 de diciembre.").
10. Among recent works that bear on these questions, I have found the following especially helpful: Jaime Cuadriello, "El obrador trinitario o María de Guadalupe creada en idea, imagen y materia," in *El divino pintor: La creación de María de Guadalupe en el taller celestial* (Mexico: Museo de la Basílica de Guadalupe, 2002), 61–205; "Del escudo de armas al estandarte armado," in *Pinceles de la historia: De la patria criolla a la nación mexicana, 1750–1860* (Mexico: Museo Nacional de Arte [and othe sponsors], 1999), 32–49; "Los pinceles de Dios Padre," in *Maravilla americana. Variantes de la iconografía guadalupana* (Mexico: Patrimonio Cultural del Occidente, A.C., 1989), 9–129; "Zodíaco mariano: Una alegoría de Miguel Cabrera," in *Zodíaco mariano: 250 años de la declaración pontificia de María de Guadalupe como patrona de México* (Mexico: Museo de la Basílica de Guadalupe/Museo Soumaya, 2004), 19–129; and "La propagación de las devociones novohispanas: Las guadalupanas y otras imágenes preferentes," in *México en el mundo de las colecciones de arte*, vol. III, ed. María Luisa Sabau García, 257–300 (Mexico: Secretaría de Relaciones Exteriores, 1994). Also Jorge Traslosheros, "Santa María de Guadalupe: Hispánica, novohispana, y mexicana. Tres sermones y tres voces guadalupanas, 1770–1818," *Estudios de Historia Novohispana* 18 (1998): 83–103 and "Sermones manuscritos en honor de la Virgen de Guadalupe," *Estudios de Historia Novohispana* 22 (2000): 141–63; Alicia Mayer, "El culto de Guadalupe y el proyecto tridentino en la Nueva España," *Estudios de Historia Novohispana* 26 (2002): 17–49; Marta Terán, "La relación del águila mexicana con la Virgen de Guadalupe entre los siglos XVII y XIX," *Historias* 34 (abril–septiembre 1995): 51–69; D. A. Brading, *Mexican Phoenix. Our Lady of Guadalupe: Image and Tradition Across Five Centuries* (Cambridge, UK: Cambridge University Press, 2001); as well as the essays cited above by Villalpando César and Ibarra González.
11. A July 6, 1711, acta de cabildo of the Mexico City ayuntamiento ordered Masses of thanksgiving at Tepeyac, the cathedral, and Remedios for war successes; in 1742 the rector of the university entrusted the defense of the kingdom against the English to María de Guadalupe (Guadalupe Jiménez Codinach, *México, su*

tiempo de nacer, 1750–1821 [México: Fomento Cultural Banamex, 1997], 270). See also a 1742 sermon by Jose Fernández de Palos, *Triumpho obsidional que implora . . . por medio de la Virgen María . . .* (México: María de Rivera, 1743), beseeched Our Lady of Guadalupe and Our Lady of los Remedios for protection against the English; a 1743 sermon of José de Arlegui celebrated military successes against English arms and Our Lady of Guadalupe as "protectora de las armas de este Americano Imperio," *Sagrado paladión del Americano orbe . . .* (México: Viuda de J. B. de Hogal, 1743); a September 10, 1763, acta de cabildo, Mexico City ayuntamiento, which noted that the viceroy had granted permission for a novena to Our Lady of Guadalupe for "the happy progress of the Catholic forces" (*felices progresos de las armas católicas*); Archivo General de la Nación (hereafter AGN) Correspondencia de Virreyes 178, fols. 189–90, decree of January 12, 1795, calling for an artillery salute every December 12; and the 1795 sermon by Joseph María Solano y Marcha, *Sermón moral . . . para implorar los auxilios del Todo-Poderoso . . .* (México: Zúñiga y Ontiveros, 1795), which invoked the aid of Our Lady of Guadalupe and Our Lady of los Remedios and spoke of both as conquest Virgins.

12. That many shrines would persist and thrive while guadalupanismo burgeoned testifies to the strength of local and regional loyalties in Mexico then. It also expresses the devotion of believers to several saints and images. Outside Mexico City, Guadalupe was added to the repertoire of favorite saints more than she displaced them.

13. *La transmigración de la iglesia a Guadalupe. Sermon que el 12 de diciembre de 1748 años predicó en el templo de Nuestra Señora de Guadalupe de la ciudad de Santiago de Querétaro* (Mexico: Reimpreso en la oficina de M. Zúñiga y Ontiveros, 1821). Francisco Javier Conde y Oquendo reported in 1795–1796 that preachers in Mexico City were referring to Carranza's sermon, as Brading has noted. Napoleon's descent into a seemingly Godless persecution of the pope and Iberia's Catholic monarchs was taken as a sign by José Mariano Berístain de Souza (a prominent creole priest in Mexico City who had spent many years in Spain and supported the royalist cause) at the onset of the insurgency in Mexico that Carranza's prophecy was about to be realized (Brading, *Mexican Phoenix*, 232–33).

14. Eric Van Young concludes in his richly detailed study of popular action in the independence period that rural, Indian grievances reached far beyond whatever political appeal their veneration of Guadalupe may have entailed, into local and ethnic disputes and an exalted millennialism. Without these deeper grievances, "her invocation by Father Hidalgo or any other insurgent leader would doubtless have provoked a comparatively mild response from rural people" (*The Other Rebellion: Popular Violence, Ideology, and the Mexican Struggle for Independence, 1810–1821* [Stanford, CA: Stanford University Press, 2001], 317–20).

15. "La ley de Nuestra Señora de Guadalupe," Van Young, *The Other Rebellion*, 160–61, 319, mentions Indian rebellions in the Zacualtipan area associated with Our Lady of Guadalupe during the independence period.

16. For example, *Reflexiones del Dr. d. Luis Montaño sobre los alborotos acaecidos en algunos pueblos de Tierra Adentro* (Mexico: Casa de Arizpe, 1810): "El robo, la sorpresa, la crueldad, el desorden y lo que es más el insulto a la

religión y al sagrado simulacro de Nra Sra [de Guadalupe] que es nuestro más firme apoyo para con Dios" (Robbery, surprise attack, cruelty, disorder and, what is worse, disrespect for religion and the sacred image of Our Lady [of Guadalupe], which is our greatest aid from God).

17. "todos somos de Jesús y María... estamos unidos inseparablemente o como parientes... o como correspondientes... o como beneficiados." This unnumbered tract was published by Zúñiga y Ontiveros in 1810. An equally explicit appeal to Our Lady of Guadalupe was made in the unnumbered 1810 *Exhortación de un patriota Americano a los habitantes de este reyno* (Mexico: Mariano Zúñiga y Ontiveros): "el castillo fuerte, el muro más poderoso, la defensa más segura, lo diré de una vez, la protección, el amparo, la promesa de María Santísima en su portentosa imagen de Guadalupe... nuestra tierna madre y benéfica Protectora." The creole priest Beristáin de Souza echoed Pomposo's themes in later sermons of his own. See Chapter 10 in Brading's *Mexican Phoenix* for a discussion of Beristáin's sermons and other writings during the independence period. See also José de Lezama's 1811 sermon, *Exhortación de paz que, descubierta la infame revolución de tierra dentro* (México: Zúñiga y Ontiveros, 1811). For other examples of royalist tracts invoking Our Lady of Guadalupe, see J. E. Hernández y Dávalos, *Colección de documentos para la historia de la Guerra de Independencia de México de 1808 a 1821*, 6 vols. (México: Comisión Nacional para las Celebraciones del 175 Aniversario de la Independencia Nacional y 75 Aniversario de la Revolución Mexicana, 1985), reprint of 1877–1882 ed., vol. 3, núms. 85 and 86, 379–82.

18. Villalpando César, "Virgen insurgente," 65, citing Carlos María Bustamante.

19. AGN Bienes Nacionales, leg. 976, exp. 46.

20. Bancroft Library, University of California, Berkeley (hereafter Bancroft), M-M 144, núm 3, May 1815. A similar complaint had been lodged by a previous subdelegado there in 1800.

21. Bancroft M-M 1700, pt. 1, 148.

22. AGN Bienes Nacionales 976, exp. 46.

23. Jacques Lafaye, *Quetzalcoatl and Guadalupe: The Formation of Mexican National Consciousness, 1531–1813*, trans. Benjamin Keen (Chicago: University of Chicago Press, 1987), 124; William B. Taylor, *Magistrates of the Sacred: Priests and Parishioners in Eighteenth-Century Mexico* (Stanford, CA: Stanford University Press, 1996), 295.

24. Brian Connaughton, *Clerical Ideology in a Revolutionary Age: The Guadalajara Church and the Idea of the Mexican Nation, 1788–1853*, trans. Mark A. Healey (Calgary: University of Calgary Press, 2003), 16–17, suggests that Our Lady of Guadalupe had not yet become the consensus or exclusive symbol of providential destiny of the nation perhaps partly because of the association with both sides of the bloody civil struggle 1810–1821.

25. Miguel Sánchez, *Imagen de la Virgen María de Dios de Guadalupe...* (Mexico: Bernardo Calderón, 1648); Francisco de Florencia, *Estrella del norte de México...* (Viuda de Ribera, 1688).

26. Guadalupe Nava Oteo, ed., *Cabildos y ayuntamientos de la Nueva España en 1808* (México: SepSetentas, 1973), 87.

27. Nava Oteo, *Cabildos y ayuntamientos*, 61 (the cabildo of Mezquitic, August 2, 1808), 60 (the ayuntamiento of Monterrey, August 22, 1808), 78 (the *cabildo* of Sombrerete, August 1808), and 80 and 151 for the references to the Virgin of Guadalupe.
28. For example, Villalpando César, "Virgen insurgente," and Matt S. Meier, "María insurgente," *Historia Mexicana* 91 (January–March 1974): 466–82. María Cristina Camacho de la Torre posits that antagonism over devotion to one or the other image grew and festered during the eighteenth century: "[la Virgen de los Remedios], especialmente en el siglo XVIII, es constantemente comparada como la rival española de la mexicana Guadalupe" (*Fiesta de Nuestra Señora de Guadalupe: Celebración, historia y tradición mexicana* [México: Conaculta, 2001], 26).
29. Once an image became widely famous, church authorities were reluctant to allow it to leave its shrine. Our Lady of Guadalupe is an example, not traveling from its precinct at Tepeyac after its famous favor to people of the valley of Mexico in the 1630s when it was believed to have relieved the city of the catastrophic flood that inundated the city from 1629–1633. In addition to Remedios, two regionally famous images that continued to be taken to a nearby urban center are Our Lady of El Pueblito (to the city of Querétaro), and Our Lady of Zapopan (to Guadalajara).
30. Acta de cabildo, January 8, 1621, "se ha hallado en este santuario más devoción y afecto que en otro ninguno."
31. Luis de Cisneros, *Historia de el principio y origen, progressos, venidas a México, y milagrosa de la Santa Ymagen de nuestra Señora de los Remedio* . . . (México: Iuan Blanco de Alcaçar, 1621), fols. 65r–67r.
32. Cisneros, *Historia*, fol. 126v.
33. According to Jesús García Gutiérrez, *Datos históricos sobre la venerable imagen de Nuestra Señora de los Remedios*, 2nd ed. (México: Santuario de los Remedios, 1940), 49 (citing the 1907 sermon of Vicente de P. Andrade), there were seventy-five venidas from 1576 to 1922: three in the sixteenth century, thirteen in the seventeenth, forty-eight in the eighteenth, and eight in the nineteenth. There were, in fact, more than eight venidas during the nineteenth century, but the figures for those that took place during the colonial period are reliable and highlight the dramatic increase during the eighteenth century. In 1801, at the urging of leading farmers in the Valley of Mexico, the *procurador síndico* of the city government petitioned the viceroy to formalize as an annual event the recent practice of bringing the image to the cathedral at least once a year. The viceroy demurred (AGN Ayuntamientos 217, exp. 4).
34. Archivo Histórico del Distrito Federal (hereafter AHDF), número de inventario, vol. 3896.
35. For the financial records of the shrine from the 1760s to 1820s, see AHDF 3896–3902.
36. In 1678 the Carmelite visitor Fr. Isidro de la Asunción enthused that the shrine at Totoltepec "es la iglesia más suntuosa en grandeza, riqueza y aliño que la de Guadalupe, mayor asistida de clérigos y la sacristía que puede serlo de una catedral" (*Itinerario a Indias (1673–1678)*, [Mexico: Condumex, 1992], 105). Other late seventeenth-century descriptions of the shrine also highlight

its fine condition and store of treasures: Juan Francesco Gemelli Carreri, *Viaje a la Nueva España* (1697) (México: Libro-Mex, 1955), I:112; Francisco de Florencia, *La milagrosa invención de un tesoro escondido* (México: Vda. de Juan de Ribera, 1685), noted the splendor of the furnishings (cited in García Gutiérrez, *Datos históricos*, 12–13). The financial records of the shrine from 1685–1705 describe its growing wealth in more detail (AHDF 3897–98).

37. "Fue la ciudad a tomar posesión de la ermita de Nuestra Señora de los Remedios, en carrozas." The unfolding dispute between the archbishop-viceroy and the ayuntamiento is abundantly documented in Antonio Robles, *Diario de sucesos notables (1665–1703)* (México: Porrúa, 1946), I:181, AGN Inquisición 1430, exp. 18; AGN Bienes Nacionales 1076, exp. 7; and AHDF 3895 and 3898. Later archbishops would claim rights over the stone quarry adjacent to the shrine. See Archivo Histórico del Arzobispado de México, caja labeled 1759 (1759–1773). Payo Enríquez de Rivera's initiative was not altogether unprovoked. An *acta del cabildo eclesiástico* from September 1666 remarked sourly that instead of following the customary practice of seeking the archbishop's permission for a venida, the ayuntamiento was merely advising the cathedral clergy of an impending visit a few days in advance: "la poca atención con que ha procedido la ciudad, corregidor, y regidores, no dándole cuenta como trataban de la traída" (Archivo de la Catedral, acta de cabildo, September 6, 1666).

38. Actas de cabildo, April 15, 1621, and June 24, 1624; AGN Ayuntamientos 217, exp. 4, 1801.

39. The acta of the cathedral chapter of the Archdiocese of Mexico for January 8, 1621 (in the cathedral archive) noted that the Dominicans were offering to send six friars to the shrine to help administer sacraments to "la gente que en romería a él va," and mentioned a similar proposal by the Franciscans in the late sixteenth century; Cisneros, *Historia*, fol. 18v, spoke of early Mercedarian interest, and, according to García Gutiérrez, *Datos históricos*, 20, Cabrera y Quintero (1746) mentioned the Mercedarians' desire to found a *casa de recolección* at the shrine in the mid-eighteenth century. After independence, the Augustinians negotiated with the ayuntamiento to take over the shrine in an exchange of properties.

40. According to contemporary chronicler Gregorio Guijo, the viceroy and his wife in 1663 were particular devotees (*Diario (1648–1664)* [México: Porrúa, 1986], II:149, 151); and in the early 1690s the Conde de Galve and his wife were especially ardent devotees, visiting the shrine, having the image brought to the city for extended visits, and making substantial donations to the culto (see Meredith Dodge, ed., *Two Hearts, One Soul: The Correspondence of the Condesa de Galve, 1688–1696* [Albuquerque: University of New Mexico Press, 1993], and Robles, *Diario*, II:219, 230).

41. On this extended stay, see Robles, *Diario*, II:248, 260, 270, 289, and III:13.

42. Robles, *Diario*, III:49.

43. AHDF 3897.

44. Acta de cabildo, October 9, 1637, in which the ayuntamiento concluded that the fleet would have returned by then, so the image could be returned to the shrine.

45. Two examples: the viceroy scotched the ayuntamiento's plans for a venida in April 1741 because it was too early in the year to declare a famine and the illnesses in the city were not extraordinary (acta de cabildo, April 21, 1741); and in August 1809 the *gobernador de la mitra* endorsed the ayuntamiento's proposal for a novena in the city, but the viceroy decided against it because the need was not urgent and a novena at that time might be interpreted as a sign of reverses in the war against Napoleon in Spain (AGN Ayuntamientos 161, exp. 5).

46. Acta de cabildo, March 6, 1743; AGN Reales Cédulas Originales 70, exp. 31.

47. In his 1697 chronicle of the Franciscans of the Santo Evangelio province, Agustín de Vetancurt made a providential association between Remedios and the Spanish monarchy going back to Pelayo and resistance to the Muslim conquest of Iberia that was cited and echoed in promotional literature for the shrine throughout the eighteenth century (*Teatro mexicano* [Mexico: Porrúa, 1971], facsimile of first ed. [1697], 128–32).

48. *Sermón, que en acción de gracias, por la acertada detención en la Habana de esta última flota* ... (Mexico: Hogal, 1728), "tan amante de la corona de España y de los españoles." Remedios was brought to Mexico City "por la presente guerra" in December 1794, among other times, during the prolonged episodes of war between Spain and Britain after the beginning of the French Revolution (Bancroft M-M 105, diario of José Gómez, 666–67, December 14, 1794). The next month, officers from "todos los regimientos" converged on the shrine of Guadalupe to celebrate "el buen éxito de la Guerra" (Bancroft M-M 105, 669–70, January 25, 1795).

49. *Memoria principal de la piedad y lealtead del pueblo de México en los solemnes cultos de Nuestra Señora de los Remedios, desde su llegada hasta su regreso al santuario de Totoltepec*, 18–19, "una banda de Generala y un bastón, y al Niño un sable." Bustamante's booklet was published in August 1810 and advertised in the *Gaceta del Gobierno de México*, vol. 1, num 57 (August 1810), 738. The visit in May was extended beyond the stipulated novena because lightning struck the shrine on May 14, damaging the bell tower and some of the church, at which point various convents and parishes requested a visit by the image, and the officials agreed, anticipating more alms as a result. The nuns of the San Gerónimo convent completed their gift of a military outfit for Remedios on October 30, 1811, the first anniversary of the Monte de las Cruces battle, with a fine "túnico y manto que tienen por toda su orla el bordado de capitán general" (Juan Bautista Díaz Calvillo, "Noticias para la historia de Nuestra Señora de los Remedios desde el año de 1808 hasta el corriente de 1812," in his *Sermón que en el aniversario solemne de gracias a María Santísima de los Remedios* ... [Mexico: Arizpe, 1811], republished in Juan E. Hernández y Dávalos, *Colección de documentos para la historia de la Guerra de independencia de México de 1808 a 1821* [Mexico: J. M. Sandoval, 1882], III:621).

50. "aplicar todo su influxo y valimiento para que se declare y jure a nuestra Señora de los Remedios Generalísima de nuestros exércitos por todos los cuerpos civiles y militares" (Bustamante, *Memoria principal*, 18–19).

51. Late colonial records of income and expenses during the longer venidas indicate that by far the most money was collected and net income generated during the first few days and the last two days of a novena visit; for example, the collections recorded during the image's stay in Mexico City from July 16 to December

4, 1714 (AHDF 3897). Cheap prints of the image had long been distributed to donors during the venidas, but after 1790 the sale of medals became an important source of income during these same periods. During the 1793 novena period, alms plus the sale of gold, silver, and tin medals generated 1,397 pesos in income against expenses of 281 pesos. The two novena periods in 1794 yielded 2,939 pesos and 1,813 pesos respectively from alms and the sale of medals, medidas, and prints (AHDF 3901). Sales of sacred memorabilia during the novena visit in 1807 were particularly impressive: 3,471 medals of all kinds sold for 1,914 pesos (sixteen gold medals at sixteen pesos each; 1,275 silver medals at one peso each; 880 "Roman" medals at two reales each; and thirteen hundred tin medals at one real each); 12,610 medidas, for 1,133 pesos; and 14,024 prints for 915 pesos; 955 novena booklets at one real each; 3,590 rosaries (not evaluated); and 1,560 *escapularios* (not evaluated) (AHDF 3902).

52. AHDF 3896, 1741–1746. This figure apparently does not include the accumulated cost of sacramental wine, oil, consecrated wafers, and incense. The revenues during this period amounted to 13,925 pesos.
53. Acta de cabildo, March 6, 1743, "atendiendo al mucho tiempo y el santuario careciendo de sus limosnas y desconsuelo de los que ocurren a sus peregrinaciones." The ayuntamiento may well have been prompted to act because of complaints of long absence received from Indians living near the shrine (AGN Reales Cédulas Originales 70, exp. 31). An occasional viceroy recognized the costs of long venidas and would insist on stays no longer than eleven days (see, e.g., AGN Reales Cédulas Originales 70, exp. 31, for 1750 and 1755).
54. Díaz Calvillo, "Noticias para la historia," 116.
55. AHDF 3904, exp. 136, "para contener los alborotos de la gente." More disturbances were reported at Naucalpan in 1834 at the time of another venida (AHDF 3904, exp. 125).
56. AHDF 3908, exp. 168.
57. Ibid., exp. 176.
58. Ibid. exp. 176, fol. 32.
59. Ibid., exp. 185, "sin fin de peticiones de ciudadanos de la capital."
60. AHDF 3909, exp. 224.
61. On elites promoting Remedios as the royalist Virgin in late 1810 and then veering away from the association, see Brading, *Mexican Phoenix*, 230.
62. For Nuestra Señora de El Pueblito as the royalist generala protecting Querétaro, see Manuel Agustín Gutiérrez, *Discurso que en la solemne función que hacen anualmente a María Santísima en su Imagen del Pueblito* . . . (Mexico: Oficina de A. Valdés, 1817).
63. Hernández y Dávalos, *Colección de documentos*, III:586–677, especially 590. Díaz Calvillo did associate the defeat of Hidalgo with providential intervention of the Virgin Mary in the figure of Remedios, "Noticias para la historia," 617–18.
64. Jiménez Codinach, *México, su tiempo de nacer*, 173.
65. García Gutiérrez, *Datos Históricos*, 54–55, quoting Díaz Calvillo, "por orden superior hicieron a la santa Imagen los honores militares correspondientes al rango de Capitán General."

66. AHDF 3903, exp. 74. Yraeta was probably the guiding light behind the organization of a women's auxiliary in Mexico City in 1811—the "leva sagrada de patriotas marianas"—organized to pray and otherwise support the cause "baxo el mando de María Santísima de los Remedios... esa generala, la Generala de los cielos" (Hernández y Dávalos, *Colección de documentos*, III, núm. 130, 566–68). According to Díaz Calvillo, "Noticias," 151, some twenty-five hundred women joined in for the purpose, standing guard before the image in forty-five minute shifts, and praying the rosary together from 6:00 a.m. to noon, and from 3:00–5:00 in the afternoon. Yraeta appears again in the account books for the archicofradía of Our Lady of los Remedios in 1812, having donated 557 pesos three reales for "prendas con que obsequió a las tropas" (AHDF 3895, exp. 2).
67. AHDF 3903, exp. 73, and Bancroft mf1232.D33, fols. 1–28, 30–45.
68. In that year her energetic promotion of this image as Conquistadora del Reyno came to the attention of the Inquisition. At that time she was proposing to supplement the ayuntamiento's modest sponsorship of the shrine and whip up devotion by establishing at the shrine a "convento o colegio de misioneros apostólicos de Franciscanos descalzos." She planned for twenty to forty Franciscan "soldados de Cristo" from the college at Pachuca to reside there as a base for their "excursiones evangélicas," and that she would pay for the first twenty (AGN Inquisición 1430, exp. 18). She was back with a new proposal in 1808 to establish a school at the shrine for the local residents (AHDF 3902, exp. 64). Her wartime activities at the shrine and on behalf of the image in Mexico are also documented for 1815–1816 in AHDF 3903, exps. 87, 111.
69. In 1822 Yraeta renewed her proposal to found a convent of Capuchin Franciscans at the shrine (AHDF 3903, exp. 111).
70. The venidas in the 1820s and 1830s are documented in AHDF 3906 and 3904, respectively.
71. The deterioration of the shrine and infrequent meetings of the archicofradía during the 1820s, 1830s, and 1840s are documented in AHDF 3904–8.
72. "Celestial atalalaya de los mexicanos." Administrative records for the burning of politically incorrect prints and inspection of possibly offensive paintings and statues in 1829 are in AHDF 3904, exp. 129, and AHDF 3905, exp. 130, and the acta de cabildo deliberations on June 20. The *Salutación a la Virgen de los Remedios. ¡Salve Esther compasiva! Celestial atalaya de los mexicanos...* was published in Mexico City by R. Núñez in 1829. The venida of 1829 is documented in AHDF 3904, exp. 125.
73. AHDF 3907.
74. García Gutiérrez, *Datos Históricos*, 51–52.
75. *Gaceta del Gobierno de México*, tomo 2, parte 1 (1811), 188–92.
76. "Nuestra sagrada religión, los derechos de nuestro católico monarca, [y] los de la patria, sin dar entrada a los seductores enemigos de Dios y de la humanidad"; "las legítimas potestades."
77. "vivas dirigidas a nuestra religión, a la pureza de María Santísima, a nuestro católico soberano, al gobierno, a la patria, a las authoridades legítimas," and "a la paz y unión entre los pueblos."

78. Dorothy Tanck de Estrada, *Pueblos de indios y educación en México colonial, 1750–1821* (México: El Colegio de México, 1999), 544.
79. Such as Tlacochahuaya in the Valley of Oaxaca, which had been well known for its land disputes with neighboring villages during the eighteenth century (Archivo del Estado de Oaxaca [hereafter AEO], Juzgados, bundle labeled 1812).
80. Ibid.
81. AEO, Juzgados, bundle labeled 1810: 1811 oficios de órdenes y corespondencia, fol. 35v.
82. AEO, Juzgados, bundle labeled 1812: February 27, 1812, letter of José Cerute, alcalde mayor of Teocuicuilco.
83. C. Dora Tabanico, "De Tuape a la Basílica de Guadalupe," in *Memorias: IV Simposio de la Sociedad Sonorense de Historia* (Hermosillo: Instituto Sonorense de Cultura, 1993), 133–38. One of the pilgrims gave birth to a son on the return trip to Tuape and named him Juan Diego.
84. For the development of Talpa and Plateros as regional pilgrimage centers in the mid-nineteenth century, see Manuel Carrillo, Dueñas, *Historia de Nuestra Señora del Rosario de Talpa*, 3rd ed. (Talpa de Allende: M. Carrillo Dueñas, 1962), and Juan Javier Pescador, "Seeking the Holy Child of Tierra Adentro: The Historical Origins of the Santo Niño de Atocha, 1704–1848," in *Saints and Their Cults in the Atlantic World*, ed. Margaret Cormack, 68–89 (Columbia: University of South Carolina Press, 2007).

Chapter 6

1. "Retablos and Popular Religion in Nineteenth-Century Mexico," in *Art and Faith in Mexico*, ed. Elizabeth Netto Calil Zarur and Charles M. Lovell, 65–66 (Albuquerque: University of New Mexico Press, 2001).
2. Yet upstreaming from recent times and downstreaming from precolonial times often are the only ways available to reckon with devotional practices in rural Mexico that reach into the indigenous past and present. These approaches arch over historical time and can lead to doubtful assumptions about continuities and pristine survivals of indigenous practices and beliefs, but ignoring recent ethnographic studies and the rich descriptive and analytical literature about precolonial rituals impoverishes historical study of the subject. For devotional practices, a particularly ambitious recent ethnographic project undertaken by teams of Mexican anthropologists and sociologists working on different regions produced the four volumes of *Diálogos con el territorio*, under the direction of Alicia Barabas (Mexico: Instituto National de Antropología e Historia, 2003–2004). The chapters in these volumes have much to say about the importance of sacred travel to natural shrines not far from home, especially mountains, caves, and springs as places of origin and nourishment where divine "fuerza" is to be found. See also the informative essays in Mario Humberto Ruz, coord., *De la mano de lo sacro. Santos y demonios en el mundo maya* (México: UNAM, 2006).

    Davíd Carrasco offers a challenging way through the temptations of timeless continuity in his call for a synoptic, "borderlands" approach to "hybrid-thinking spaces, contact zones, and cultural creativity" in which European, African, Asian, and native American cultural streams meet and transform ("Borderlands and the 'Biblical Hurricane': Images and Stories of Latin Amercan Rhythms of Life," *Harvard Theological Review* 101, no. 3–4 [July–October 2008]: 353–76). The trick is to find purchase points—Carrasco's contextualized "stories" from particular places and times—for what Inga Clendinnen calls "exact imagining" in historical study.

3. For a lively discussion about a place for "presence" in historiography, see Robert A. Orsi's "Abundant History: Marian Apparitions as Alternative Modernity," and his respondents in *Historically Speaking: The Bulletin of the Historical Society*, IX, no. 7 (September/October 2008).

4. Pierre Bourdieu's phrasing in *Language and Symbolic Power* (Cambridge, MA: Harvard University Press, 1999), 115.

5. See Matthew O'Hara's suggestive, well-documented paper on Escuelas de Cristo in late eighteenth-century central Mexico, "The Supple Whip: Tradition and Innovation in Colonial Mexican Catholicism," unpublished paper, 2008; O'Hara's "The Orthodox Underworld of Colonial Mexico," *Colonial Latin American Review* 17, no. 2 (Dec. 2008): 233–50, puts lay practices and orthodoxy into conversation for late colonial Mexico City in a detailed episode. His reflections on devout simulation move beyond a domination/resistance model. For another significant contribution to the study of religious organizations in the cities during the later colonial period, see Karen Melvin, "Urban Religions: Mendicant Orders in New Spain's Cities, 1570–1800," PhD diss., University of California, Berkeley, 2005.

6. Brian Connaughton has done the pioneering work on religious discourse in the early nineteenth century, with its audience and public ramifications in mind. It is a much richer topic for the history of public life in Mexico—with many surprises—than the idea of a reactionary, ultramontane church would anticipate. See his *Ideología y sociedad en Guadalajara (1788–1853)* (México: UNAM y CONACULTA [Colección Regiones], 1992) and the many deeply researched essays that have followed, especially "1856–1857: Conciencia religiosa y controversia ciudadana. La conciencia como poder politico en 'un pueblo eminentemente católico,'" in *Cultura política y poder en México, siglo XIX*, coord. Brian Connaughton, 395–464 (México: UAM/Juan Pablos, 2008), and "Los curas y la feligresía ciudadana en México, siglo XIX," in *Nuevas naciones: España y México, 1808–1850*, coord. Jaime E. Rodríguez O., 241–72 (Madrid: Fundación Mapfre, 2008).

This is not the place for an adequate discussion of how scholars have used the somewhat misleading term "Jansenist" to describe religious reforms in eighteenth- and nineteenth-century Latin America. American "Jansenists" were not much concerned with Cornelius Jansen's famous treatise on grace, his bleak view of human nature and denial of free will, and his deep theological differences with the Jesuits. As David Brading suggests, American "Jansenism" was mainly a "current of opinion" shared by an otherwise disparate array of priests and lay elites "united by a repudiation of the spiritual and intellectual culture of Baroque, post-Tridentine Catholicism" and prevailing popular piety in Mexico, in favor of a simpler interior faith (*The First America: The Spanish Monarchy, Creole Patriots, and the Liberal State,*

1492-1867 [Cambridge, UK: Cambridge University Press, 1991], 500). But Jansenism has also come to stand for one side of the acrimonious political struggles within Catholic states during the eighteenth and nineteenth centuries that pitted "ultramontane" international interests of Rome and a certain relativism in some doctrinal matters known as *probabilismo*—which the Jesuits came to symbolize in America—against a decentralizing, austere, moralistic, national Catholicism favored at the Spanish court and promoted in the colonies.

7. Silvia Arrom, *The Women of Mexico City, 1790-1857* (Stanford, CA: Stanford University Press, 1985), 47-49. In a recent article, Arrom warns against interpreting the popularity of the Ladies of Charity as unambiguous evidence of a feminization of piety ("Mexican Laywomen Spearhead a Catholic Revival: The Ladies of Charity, 1863-1910," in *Religious Culture in Modern Mexico*, ed. Martin Nesvig, 50-77 [Lanham, MD: Rowman & Littlefield, 2007]). Margaret Chowning, in "La feminización de la piedad en México: Género y piedad en las cofradías de españoles. Tendencias coloniales y poscoloniales en los arzobispados de Michoacán y Guadalajara," in *Religión, política e identidad en la Independencia de México*, ed. Brian Connaughton, 475-514 (Mexico: Universidad Autónoma Metropolitana, 2010), explores another way of documenting the role of women in religion during the nineteenth century. John Tutino also posits a more prominent role for women in lay religiosity in "Conflicto cultural en el valle de México. Liberalismo y religión popular después de la independencia," in *La reindianización de América, siglo XIX*, coord. Leticia Reina, 358-82 (México: Siglo XXI, 1997).

8. Greg Dening, interviewed by the Australian Broadcasting Co. in 2008, at http://www.abc.net.au/sundaynights/stories/Greg_Dening_m1325409.Mp3 (accessed on December 4, 2008).

9. On the decline of capellanías and loss of lands, see Francisco Javier Cervantes Bello, "El declive del crédito eclesiástico en la región de Puebla, 1800-1847," in *Iglesia, estado, y economía, siglos XVI a XIX*, coord. María del Pilar López-Cano, 131-47 (México: UNAM, 1995), and Margarita Loera, "Una historia de larga duración en el valle de Toluca. La lucha por el origen étnico, la territorialidad y la autonomía política en Calimaya y sus pueblos sujetos," *Historias* 63 (enero-abril 2007): 37-60. A case of sharp decline in cofradía properties and visitors to a regional shrine by 1850 is the long-famous Santísimo Cristo de San Román in Campeche (Archivo General de la Nación [hereafter AGN] Bienes Nacionales 19, exp. 48). Disruptions from the Guerra de Castas were regarded as a principal cause.

10. I do not know of a systematic study of sacrilege in early national Mexico. It appears that loose talk by Bourbon administrators in the late eighteenth century (e.g., Manuel Flon, who rose to the position of Intendant of Puebla and served as a royalist general during the independence period) is one of many examples. See the Inquisition dossier on Flon in Bancroft Library, University of California, Berkeley [hereafter Bancroft], MSS 72/57m, box 6, item 3, 1786– and occasional, dramatic iconoclasm of royalist district governors during the independence war contributed to a new climate of provocation. For example, the subdelegado of Tlaxomulco, Jalisco, in 1815 reportedly mocked the parish priest, did not attend Mass, and led a group into the cemetery to destroy the

cross there (Archivo Judicial de la Audiencia de la Nueva Galicia, Biblioteca Pública del Estado de Jalisco, formerly in a bundle of civil records labeled "1800–1809 leg. 3 [109]," case brought by Dr. Joseph Francisco Dávila); and the parish priest of Xonacatepec, Morelos, complained to the provisor of the Archdiocese of Mexico in August 1816 that many of his parishioners no longer fulfilled the Easter Duty, even after he brought in Fernandine friars for a revival mission. The reason, he judged, was "la libertad de la tropa, sus repetidos excesos, el despotismo y abritrariedad de sus comandantes... todos están sin cumplir con la iglesia" (AGN Acervo 49, caja 146, report by Br. José Manuel de Sotomayor). Robberies of church furnishings were reported more frequently after independence.

11. Leonor Correa Etchegaray, "El rescate de una devoción jesuítica: El Sagrado Corazón de Jesús en la primera mitad del siglo xix," in *Coloquio Historia de la Iglesia en el siglo XIX*, coord. Manuel Ramos Media, 369–80 (Chimalistac, México, D.F.: Centro de Estudios de Historia de México, Condumex, 1998).

12. Martha Weigle, *Brothers of Light, Brothers of Blood: The Penitentes of the Southwest* (Albuquerque: University of New Mexico Press, 1976), chap. 1.

13. E. Boyd, *The New Mexico Santero* (Santa Fe: Museum of New Mexico Press, 1969), 8–15; E. Boyd, *Popular Arts of Spanish New Mexico* (Santa Fe: Museum of New Mexico Press, 1974), 327–86; Larry Frank, *New Kingdom of the Saints: Religious Art of New Mexico, 1780–1907* (Santa Fe: Red Crane Books, 1992), especially chapters 1–5; Michael P. Carroll, *The Penitente Brotherhood: Patriarchy and Hispano-Catholicism in New Mexico* (Baltimore: The Johns Hopkins Press, 2002), 161, 173, 175. At about the same time a miracle shrine began at Chimayó, New Mexico, dedicated to the Lord of Esquípulas and later to the Santo Niño de Atocha. The founder, Bernardo Abeyta, was also a Penitente leader in the early years.

14. Beatriz Rojas, coord., *Los Huicholes: Documentos históricos* (México: INI-CIESAS, 1992), especially 123–88.

15. AGN Bienes Nacionales 1172, exp. 2.

16. Jaime Cuadriello, "Preámbulo," *Los pinceles de la historia (De la patria criolla a la nación mexicana, 1750–1860)*, vol. 2 of *Los Pinceles de la historia* (México: Museo Nacional de Arte, et al., 2000), 25; México, D.F., Archivo Histórico del Distrito Federal (hereafter AHDF) 2256, "Historia en general, 1824–1832," exps. 155, 156, 167, 184; and Anne Staples, *"Policía y Buen Gobierno:* Municipal Efforts to Regulate Public Behavior, 1821–1857," in *Rituals of Rule, Rituals of Resistance: Public Celebrations and Popular Culture in Mexico*, ed. William H. Beezley, Cheryl E. Martin, and William E. French, 115–26 (Wilmington, DE: SR Books, 1994). Preparation for the Talabarteros demolition is recorded in AHDF 494, exp. 3, "cansados de observar los excesos que se cometen a la sombra de la capilla." Further study probably would reveal similar efforts to sedate exuberant religious celebration in other places. One example is the Governor of the Estado de México's circular of September 13, 1828, to his district prefects and alcaldes to discourage journeys to Chalma, most especially the costly and unseemly fiestas and dances there. I thank Kinga Novak for sharing her transcription of this circular from the municipal archive of Capulhuac, caja 1, Presidencia, exp. 5, courtesy of Pilar Gonzalbo Aizpuru.

17. *Breve pontificio sobre diminución de días festivos en la República Mexicana* (México: Imprenta del Aguila, 1839). The feast of St. Joseph was recognized, too, but not as a day of rest; and feasts of local patron saints were to be moved to the preceding Sunday.
18. AHDF 2256, exp. 156.
19. AGN Bienes Nacionales 1172, exp. 2. An 1827 instance, also in Mexico City, where an image of the child Jesus as Divino Pastor was transferred from the parish church of Santa Cruz Acatlán to the care of the congregación of butchers on la calle Real del Rastro to be placed in the church of their choice is documented in AGN Bienes Nacionales 1172, exp. 4.
20. "mucha irrisión y ninguna devoción ni edificación a los fieles"; "[no] exponer essos pueblos a algún levantamiento" (Bancroft MSS 72/57m, box 3, folder 20, file of compliance letters from parishes in Mexico and Guatemala, 1767–1768).
21. Examples of strife between parish priests or higher ecclesiastical officials and individuals over control of particular images are included in William B. Taylor, *Magistrates of the Sacred: Priests and Parishioners in Eighteenth-Century Mexico* (Stanford, CA: Stanford University Press, 1996), chaps. 11 and 14. They are found in records of the independence war and early national period, too. For example, AGN Civil 2059, exp. 2, 1817 (image of the infant Jesus of San Bartolomé Huipustla); Archivo Histórico del Arzobispado de México (hereafter AHAM), caja for 1827, "Bases sobre las cuales puede transigirse el negocio que sigue el cura de Yxmiquilpan Br. Dn Celedonio Salgado sobre el patronato de la capilla de Nuestra Señora del Carmen ubicada en el mismo pueblo con Lorenzo Ramos," 1822–1826; and AHAM, caja for 1849, Hilaria Fuentes contra el cura de Tlalnepantla sobre una imagen.
22. AGN Bienes Nacionales 1050, exp. 3, 1850, don Cleto Salcedo, tesorero de la Congregación de Nuestro Señor del Socorro "pide no les prohivan las Señoras Religosas de Sta Ynés sacar la imagen." In addition to disputes within families and between communities and the state and church over possession of a revered image, there are cases of neighboring rural communities contesting ownership. For example, in 1831 the state governor's report for Guanajuato mentions as a notable disturbance to public tranquility an 1830 "*tumulto*" at Yuririapúndaro over ownership of an image of Christ between the towns of Yuririapúndaro and Uriángato (*Memoria de la administración pública del estado de Guanajuato correspondiente al año de 1831* . . . [México: n.p., 1832], report by vice-governor Manuel Gómez de Linares, 11–12).
23. AGN Bienes Nacionales 1524, exp. 10.
24. For example, the coadjutor of Tezontepec, Hidalgo, reported in December 1841 that news of a painting of the Lord of Chalma sweating, bleeding, and restoring itself to fine condition on a neighboring hacienda was so eagerly received that almost the entire route of a penitential procession bringing it to the parish church was packed with onlookers. The cura of Tizayuca who was appointed to gather information on the reported miracle noted the "suma devoción y singular reverencia" of the witnesses he deposed (AHAM, caja for 1842, "Sobre el sudor que en la casa de D. Ramón Lucio y pueblo de Tezontepec se observó a una ymagen del Señor de Chalma.")

25. Jonathan Sperber, *Popular Catholicism in Nineteenth-Century Germany* (Princeton, NJ: Princeton University Press, 1984), 277; Thomas Kselman, *Miracles and Prophecies in Nineteenth-Century France* (New Brunswick, NJ: Rutgers University Press, 1983).
26. William A. Christian Jr. kindly advises me that Spain, like Mexico, did not see the apparition activity or enthusiasm of France and Germany until late in the nineteenth century.
27. Margarito Ortega, *El prodigio de Ocotlán. Recopilación de documentos históricos relativos a la aparición de Señor de la Misericordia, que tuvo lugar en Ocotlán, Jalisco, México el día 3 de octubre de 1847* (Guadalajara: n.p., 1945), based on an *información testimonial* taken in 1897 on the fiftieth anniversary of the apparition.
28. Pascual Ruiz, *El anillo de la Virgen de Guadalupe de Zacatecas en su primer centenario* (Zacatecas: Gráfica, 1944).
29. For example, *Suceso notable y edificante* (México: Impr. de Luis Abadiano y Valdés, 1839). The "notable and edifying event" here paired a model Christian of Mexico City whose manner of death was a sign of his salvation with a notorious blasphemer whose manner of death was a warning to others. Another kind of defensive discourse of the time not examined in this chapter is the various publications by public figures like Carlos María Bustamante, José Miguel Guridi y Alcocer, and José María Tornel y Mendívil rebutting doubts about the apparitions and other miracles of the Virgin of Guadalupe at Tepeyac.
30. Luis de Cisneros, *Historia de el principio y origen progressos venidas a México y Milagros de la Santa Ymagen de nuestra Señora de los Remedios . . .* (México: Iuan Blanco de Alcaçar, 1621).
31. Marianne Bélard and Philippe Verrier considered just nine examples prior to 1880 in a sample of 126 nineteenth-century ex-votos for their valuable study of ex-votos in western Mexico (*Religión y cultura: Los exvotos del occidente de México* [México: El Colegio de Michoacán and Centre Français D'études Mexicaines et Centraméricaines, 1996]). The indispensable exhibition catalog of early ex-voto paintings, *Dones y promesas: 500 años de arte ofrenda* (México: Fundación Cultural Televisa, 1996), includes twenty-seven scattered examples for the years 1821–1869, only four of them before 1840. *El arte de dar gracias: Selección de exvotos pictóricos del Museo de la Basílica de Guadalupe* (México: Universidad Iberoamericana/Casa Lamm, 2003), speaks of eight hundred ex-votos in the collection dating between 1818 and 1979 but nearly all of those classified date from after 1870.
32. The earliest ones, before the 1830s, were painted on canvas rather than tin. Colín, *Retablos del Señor del Huerto, Atlacomulco de Fabela* (Toluca: Gobierno del Estado de México, 1981). This unusual collection/cache of retablos in Atlacomulco also points to the vagaries of locating material evidence of popular devotion in any particular place. The ex-voto paintings survived in their cajones, but Colín could find no written records about the shrine, and very few of the family oratorios that dotted the town and nearby hamlets in the nineteenth century survive (*Los retablos*, 10). Another lesser shrine that reported ex-voto paintings in the early nineteenth century is Malinaltenango's

Señor del Calvario: "su capilla está adornada de gran número de retablos y su nicho de otros tantos Milagros de plata" (AHAM, caja for 1820, "Sobre que se le conceda licencia para colectar limosnas a favor del culto de la soberana ymagen del Señor del Calvario, 1820").

33. Gloria Giffords's *Mexican Folk Retablos: Masterpieces on Tin* (Tucson: University of Arizona Press, 1974) remains a touchstone for the ex-voto paintings. Recent works that contribute to the subject for the nineteenth century include Bélard and Verrier, *Religión y cultura*; Patricia Arias and Jorge Durand, *La enferma eterna: Mujer y exvoto en México, siglos XIX y XX* (México: Universidad de Guadalajara/Colegio de San Luis, 2002); the essays in Elizabeth Netto Calil Zarur and Charles M. Lovell, *Art and Faith in Mexico: The Nineteenth-Century Retablo Tradition* (Albuquerque: University of New Mexico Press, 2001); Eli Bartra, "Fe y género. La imaginería popular en los exvotos pintados," in *México en el imaginario*, ed. Carmen Nava and Mario Alejandro Carrillo, 71–90 (México: UAM-Xochimilco, 1995); Rosa María Sánchez Lara, *Los retablos populares exvotos pintados* (México: UNAM, 1990); Jorge Durand and Douglas S. Massey, *Miracles on the Border: Retablos of Mexican Migrants to the United States* (Tucson: University of Arizona Press, 1995); and Sherry Fields, *Pestilence and Head Colds: Encountering Illness in Colonial Mexico* (New York: Columbia University Press e-book, 2008). Some publications that reproduce early ex-votos are mentioned in other notes.

34. The collection now is said to include more than two thousand examples, again nearly all from the late nineteenth and twentieth centuries (Alma Guadalupe Olguín Castro, "Dos ex-votos, testimonios de fe con valor artístico e histórico," *Boletín Guadalupano*, November 2005, n.p.).

35. Elin Luque Agraz and Mary Michele Beltrán, *El arte de dar gracias: Selección de exvotos pictóricos del Museo de la Basílica de Guadalupe* (México: Universidad Iberoamericana/Casa Lamm, 2003); *México en un espejo. Los exvotos de San Juan de los Lagos* (1870–1945), coord. Sylviane Levy Amselle (México: Dirección General de Servicios de Cómputo Académico, CEMCA, and others, 2001), compact disk.

36. *La enferma eterna*, 45. They do not say when this shift was accomplished, and few of their cases antedate 1850. A more striking difference between the colonial assortment and Arias and Durand's retablos is the number in their assortment that involved groups of people rather than an individual— for example, a whole family attacked by highway robbers or a building that toppled down on a family, or a carriage that overturned with several people in it. Perhaps this points to a mounting sense of threat to families and other groups, but it could also come from a difference in the form of presentation. Most of the colonial accounts are written rather than pictorial—very short, simplified accounts by priests, and perhaps more likely to focus on an individual when an event involved several people. The retablos leave more room for elaboration, albeit ambiguously.

37. Kselman, *Miracles and Prophecies*, 55, for the Lourdes, La Salette, and Hohenlohe devotions.

38. Examples include the shrine of the Señor de la Misericordia in Tepatitlán, Jalisco (Durand and Massey, *Miracles on the Border*, 52); and Nuestra Señora del Roble of Monterrey. In the case of Monterrey and Nuestra Señora del

Roble, the area suffered from droughts and flooding in the early 1850s, but the devotion is also thought to have been abetted by the papal declaration of the dogma of the Immaculate Conception in 1854 and no doubt was furthered also by completion of a new church for the image in 1853 (Israel Cavazos Garza, *La Virgen del Roble: Historia de una tradición regiomontaña* [Monterrey: Impresora del Norte, 1959], 13, and Ignacio Campero Alatorre, *Santuarios marianos en México* [Guadalajara: Populares, 1999], 98).

39. These conditions are described for the Tepalcingo shrine in María Cristina Toledano Vergara, *Tepalcingo, su historia y sus tradiciones* (Cuernavaca: PACMYC, 1996), 98ff, and Benson Collection, University of Texas at Austin, Mariano Riva Palacio Papers, docs. 3884 and 3927.

40. The availability and use of firearms during and after the independence period is a social change that deserves study. For an example of the circulation of firearms in provincial towns during the turbulent political times after independence, see Benson Collection, University of Texas at Austin, Muse Purchase, folder 9b, leaves 85 and 88, which documents Guadalupe Victoria's attempt in June 1839 to recover 541 *fusiles* and *carabinas* given to people in the district of Tlacotalpan, Veracruz, for defense against a possible French invasion of the interior during the Pastry War of 1838. Even in the distant central valleys of Oaxaca, firearms became available during the independence period and appear in the record of homicides there after the 1810s (William B. Taylor, "Homicidios en el distrito de Tlacolula, Oaxaca, 1700–1900: Un examen preliminar de las actas de defunción," in *Lecturas históricas del Estado de Oaxaca: Época colonial*, ed. María de los Ángeles Romero Frizzi, 477–505 [México: Instituto Nacional de Antropología e Historia, 1986]).

41. This is not an exhaustive list, but the secondary literature on other regional shrines does not give enough attention to the early nineteenth century to include them in this group. Yet other, more local shrines that began to develop in the second quarter of the nineteenth century are left out, as well; for example, the shrine to San Francisco at Magdalena de Kino, Sonora, where the present church was dedicated in 1832 (James S. Griffith, *Beliefs and Holy Places: A Spiritual Geography of the Pimería Alta* [Tucson: University of Arizona Press, 1992], 38); and the devotion to the Señor del Encino of Yahualica, Jalisco, remembered in a loving tribute by native son Agustín Yáñez. The image apparently was made in the 1820s and had its own cofradía and fervent following by 1832. Yáñez is quoted in Higinio Vásquez Santa Ana, *Cristos célebres de México* (México: n.p., 1950), 69–72.

42. Elio Masferrer Kan, coord., "Espacios, territorios y santuarios en las comunidades indígenas de Puebla," in *Diálogos con el territorio: Simbolizaciones sobre el espacio en las culturas indígenas de México*, vol. 2, ed. Alicia Barabas, 80–94 (México: Instituto Nacional de Antropología e Historia [hereafter INAH], 2003). The Señor del Huerto's fame began with its reported self-renovation in 1810. The chapel was completed in 1812 and stories of miraculous recoveries and escapes quickly spread and mounted after 1813 (Colín, *Retablos del Señor del Huerto*). Durand and Massey mention the Señor de la Misericordia's origin story, the shrine's beginnings in 1839, and its development from the 1850s (*Miracles on the Border*, 16, 51–52). For the Señor del Saucito's 1820 origin story and development as a pilgrimage site, see Rafael Montejano y

Aguiñaga, *El Señor del Saucito y su templo*, 4th ed. (San Luis Potosí: Talleres Linotipográficos "Evolucón," 1983), and Luis Mario Schneider, *Cristos, santos, y vírgenes: Santuarios y devociones de México* (México: Grupo Editorial Planeta, 1995), 118–22. For the Señor del Claustro of Tacuba, the triduo published in 1854 mentions that a new chapel was blessed by the archbishop in 1837 and that "desde entonces . . . el culto se aumenta sensiblemente . . . aun en partes muy remotas . . . [evidenced by] la multitud de presentallas de cera, plata, y algunas de oro" (*Religioso triduo consagrado a Jesús del Claustro, que se venera en Tacuba* [México: Impr. de M. Murguía, 1854], 4).

43. Javier Pescador, "Seeking the Holy Child of Tierra Adentro: The Historical Origins of the Santo Niño de Atocha, 1704–1848," in *Saints and Their Cults in the Atlantic World*, ed. Margaret Cormack, 68–89 (Columbia: University of South Carolina Press, 2007); Rosa María Sánchez Lara, "Niño peregrino, de los plateros y de las causas perdidas," in *Fe, arte, y cultura: Santo Niño de Atocha* (México: Consejo Nacional para la Cultura y los Artes [and other sponsors], 2000), 105–12; *Nueva novena dedicada al Milagrosísimo Niño de Ntra. Sra. de Atocha . . .*, for four editions between 1848 and 1867 (México: Tipografía de M. Murguía, 1867).

44. "las infinitas imágenes, copias de este milagroso retrato, que se han hecho en todo este dilatadísimo Reino, pues no se hallará en todo él, iglesia, capilla, casa ni choza de español ni indio, en que no se vean y adoren imágenes de Nuestra Señora de Guadalupe." He added, "I doubt, rather I don't doubt, that more copies of this image of Mexico's Guadalupe have spread throughout the world than of any other image of Mary" (Dudo, o por mejor decir, no dudo, se hayan sacado en el mundo más copias de otra imagen de María, que de ésta de Guadalupe de México) (Francisco de Florencia, *La estrella del norte de México* [1695] [Guadalajara: Imprenta de J. Cabrera, 1895], 133).

45. William B. Taylor, "Trouble with Miracles: An Episode in the Culture and Politics of Wonder in Colonial Mexico," in *Politics and Reformations: Communities, Polities, Nations, and Empires. Essays in Honor of Thomas A. Brady, Jr.*, eds. Christopher Ocker, Michael Printy, Peter Starenko, and Peter G. Wallace, vol. 1 (Leiden: Brill, 2007), 441–58. Civil and religious authorities had ample reason to withhold their support for long-distance pilgrimage until the coming of the railroads in the late nineteenth century. Popular exuberance of this kind was difficult to control. Even though pilgrimages might contribute to national loyalties, authorities did not want boisterous, unsupervised crowds on the roads, wasting their time and money, and commiserating about shared grievances. As Robert Orsi observed in an essay on Marian shrines, "nationalist sentiments are eclipsed [there] at least momentarily, in the shared experience and expression of common need before the Virgin. The shrines create alternative publics of men and women in need and distress. These sites, in other words, are characterized by their multiple instabilities," "Abundant History," 12.

46. For example, La Virgen de la Piedrita of Canalejas, Estado de México, found in 1868. See Jesús García Gutiérrez, *La Virgen de la Piedrita*, 2nd ed. (Canalejas, Estado de México: n.p., 1993).

47. "La Villa de Guadalupe," *Boletín de la Sociedad Mexicana de Geografía y Estadística*, primera época, tomo 7 (1859): 277–79, "para los mexicanos esta

imagen es el tesoro mayor que pueden tener, y por consiguiente es la Patrona de toda la Nación."

48. Solange Alberro speaks of a "Guadalupan fever" in the naming of infants in Mexico City's *sagrario* parish from the 1850s to 1890 in *El águila y la cruz: Orígenes religiosos de la conciencia criolla. México, siglos XVI–XVII* (México: El Colegio de México/Fondo de Cultura Económica, 1999), 169. The first surge in this naming "fever" dates from the 1750s to 1790s in parishes I examined for "The Virgin of Guadalupe in New Spain: An Inquiry into the Social History of Marian Devotion," *American Ethnologist* 14, no. 1 (February 1987): 9–33. A Spanish translation of this article is available in William B. Taylor, *Entre el proceso global y el conocimiento local* (México: UAM-Iztapalapa/CONACyT/Miguel Ángel Porrúa, 2003), 389–427.

49. Serge Gruzinski, *Images at War: Mexico from Columbus to Blade Runner (1492–2019)* (Durham, NC: Duke University Press, 2001), 215.

50. *Constituciones de la Imperial Orden de Guadalupe, instituida por la Junta Provisional del Imperio* ... (México: D. A. Valdés, 1822).

51. Beinecke Library, Yale University, The Mexico Collection, Part II, unit 2, folder 1385.

52. Their lapidary texts were printed by local presses, as well as by presses in Mexico City. For example, José María Barreda y Beltrán, *Sermón, que en celebridad de la maravillosa aparición de ... Guadalupe predicó en su santuario extramuros de la ciudad de la Puebla de los Ángeles* (Puebla: P. de la Rosa, impresor del gobierno, 1822): national independence "ser efecto de la protección de María en su milagrosa imagen de Guadalupe" and Guadalupe as "prenda de nuestra felicidad ... protejiendo nuestra libertad e independencia," and "no es ya la América una Nación inculta y salvaje"; José Antonio González Plata, *Sermón predicado en la santa iglesia catedral de Guadalajara* ... (Guadalajara: Impr. del Supremo Gobierno a cargo de d. Nicolás España, 1834); Luis Gutiérrez del Corral, *Sermón histórico-apologético de Nuestra Señora de Guadalupe predicado el dia 12 de diciembre de 1833* ... (Puebla: La Oficina del Hospital de San Pedro, 1846); Ignacio Sampallo, *Sermón político-religioso de María Santísima de Guadalupe que predicó en la santa iglesia parroquial de San Luis Potosí* ... (San Luis Potosí: Impr. de M. Escontria, 1847): "su fidelidad le asegura a México la Victoria," but in a premonition of defeat he laments that "México es devorada de las disenciones domésticas"; and José Juan Canseco, *Ocasión encomiástica de la aparición de María Santísima de Guadalupe* (Oaxaca: Manuel Rincón, 1850), unpaginated.

53. Diego [Aranda y Carpinteiro], Obispo de Guadalajara, ... *ha propuesto ultimamente a los illmos. Sres. Obispos y cabildos de la nación mejicana, el pensamiento de que se erijan en aquel santuario tantos altares cuantos son los obispados comprendidos en el territorio de la República* ... (Guadalajara: n.p., 1837), unpaginated. Available at the Indiana University Library.

54. Tomás Francisco López Rodríguez de Figueredo, *Oración panegírica, que en la festividad que el excelentísimo Ayuntamiento del Distrito Federal dedica anualmente a la Patrona de los Estados-Unidos Mexicanos* ... (México: Imprenta del Aguila, 1831); Luis Gutiérrez del Corral, *Sermón histórico-apologético de Nuestra Señora de Guadalupe predicado el dia 12 de diciembre de 1833,* ... (Puebla:

Hospital de San Pedro, 1836): "los buenos mexicanos, desde las más distantes costas de la California sobre el mar pacífico hasta las de Yucatán sobre el océano Atlántico y desde las orillas del Arkansas hasta los límites de Goatemala."

55. Rojas, *Los Huicholes*, 168, 173, 177: "si querían hacer un obsequio a la Virgen de Guadalupe, quemasen el Calihuey" (the thatched "templillo" they used for special rites). An 1852 report on the Franciscan missions described *calihueyes* as two types of "edificios o casas de jacales pajizos . . . en el que reunidos hacen sus fiestas llenas de supersticiosas ceremonias" (Rojas, *Los Huicholes*, 169).

56. Benson Collection, University of Texas at Austin, García Collection, Series IV: la Junta Guadalupana, 1831–1837, and Bancroft xF1232 B975, volume of actas and other printed tracts from the Junta Guadalupana, 1831, 1835, and 1836, collected by Carlos María Bustamante, who chaired these committees. In 1843 he published his *La aparición guadalupana de México* . . . (México: J. M. F. de Lara, 1843).

57. AGN Bienes Nacionales 465, exp. 62, fol. 87ff, 1837–1838. The early eighteenth-century projects, such as the new santuario and the bicentennial festivities, depended more on a few elite donors.

58. William B. Taylor, "La Virgen de Guadalupe, Nuestra Señora de los Remedios y la cultura política del período de Independencia," in *México en tres momentos: 1810-1910-2010. Hacia la conmemoración del bicentenario de la Independencia y el centenario de la Revolución Mexicana. Retos y perspectivas*, ed. Alicia Mayer and Juan Ramón de la Fuente, II:211–38 (México: Universidad Nacional Autónoma de México/Instituto de Investigaciones Históricas, 2008).

59. Brian Connaughton, *Clerical Ideology in a Revolutionary Age: The Guadalajara Church and the Idea of the Mexican Nation, 1788–1853* (Boulder: University Press of Colorado, 2003), 16–17, suggests that Our Lady of Guadalupe had not yet become the consensus or exclusive symbol of providential destiny of the nation, perhaps partly because of the association with both sides of the bloody civil struggle of 1810–1821.

60. The case file ends without a verdict (AGN Bienes Nacionales 638, exp. 84, and 1172, exp. 53, "aquella antigua inclinación que los indígenas tienen a levantar capillas en sus pueblos sin cuidar de que estén con el decoro debido").

61. For example, at Santa Rita, Texas, in 1851, Abbe Domenech, *Missionary Adventures in Texas and Mexico: A Personal Narrative of Six Years' Sojourn in Those Regions* (London: Longman, Brown, Green, Longman, and Roberts, 1858), 357–59, reprinted in Timothy Matovina and Gerald E. Poyo, eds., *¡Presente! U.S. Latino Catholics from Colonial Origins to the Present* (Maryknoll, NY: Orbis Books, 2000), 65–67. The Virgin of Guadalupe came to be a favorite devotion in northern New Mexico during the early nineteenth century judging by the number of household and church images recorded by William Wroth, *Christian Images in Hispanic New Mexico: The Taylor Museum Collection of Santos* (Colorado Springs: The Museum, 1982); Larry Frank, *New Kingdom of the Saints: Religious Art of New Mexico, 1780–1907* (Santa Fe: Red Crane Books, 1992); and E. Boyd, *Popular Arts of Spanish New Mexico*.

62. C. Dora Tabanico, "De Tuape a la Basilica de Guadalupe," in *Memorias: IV Simposio de la Sociedad Sonorense de Historia* (Hermosillo: Instituto

Sonorense de Cultura, 1991), 133–38. I thank José Refugio de la Torre Curiel for this reference.

63. Quoted in María Cristina Camacho de la Torre, *Fiesta de Nuestra Señora de Guadalupe: Celebración, historia y tradición mexicana* (México: CONACULTA, 2001), 15, "[es] una de las mayores fiestas del Catolicismo mexicano, la primera seguramente por su popularidad, por su universalidad"; "Es la ciudad de México entera que se traslada al pie del santuario, desde la mañana hasta la tarde."

64. Manuel Escandón, *Segunda exposición al público sobre el negocio del camino de fierro entre México y Veracruz* (México: Imp. de Ignacio Cumplido, 1861). I thank Rachel A. Chico for this reference.

65. The martial side of the Remedios devotion and its association with the Spanish Reconquista and American conquest were central themes during the colonial period. See p. 260, note 47, and pp. 146–57 in this volume. Other Marian images providentially associated with the sixteenth-century conquest in central Mexico include La Conquistadora and Our Lady of Defensa in Puebla, and Our Lady of Guanajuato.

66. On Remedios in the independence period, see William B. Taylor, "La Virgen de Guadalupe, Nuestra Señora de los Remedios y la cultura política del período de Independencia," in *México en tres momentos*, ed. Mayer and la Fuente, II:211–38. I hope to consider the colonial history of the Pueblito shrine in a future essay.

67. On elites promoting Remedios as the royalist Virgin in late 1810 and then veering away from the association, see David A. Brading, *Mexican Phoenix: Our Lady of Guadalupe: Image and Tradition Across Five Centuries* (Cambridge, UK, and New York: Cambridge University Press, 2001), 230.

68. For Nuestra Señora del Pueblito as the royalist generala protecting Querétaro, see Manuel Agustín Gutiérrez, *Discurso que en la solemne función que hacen anualmente a María Santísima en su Imagen del Pueblito . . .* (México: Oficina de A. Valdés, 1817).

69. There were other differences. The link between the Totoltepec Remedios and Mexico City was shaped by the city government's right of patronato over the shrine. This circumstance of an urban corporation, rather than the crown and its highest colonial officials, exercising patronato powers dated from a royal concession in 1574. In exchange for the privilege of appointing the chaplains, overseeing shrine affairs, and exercising some authority over uses of the image, the ayuntamiento agreed to underwrite the cost of construction and maintenance of a new and larger chapel on the site, and otherwise promote the culto. For the Pueblito image and shrine, the city of Querétaro's administrative role was much later and less direct. Franciscans managed the shrine during the colonial period.

70. The two *vecindarios* and rivalries between them have recently been described by Esteban López Frías in *El Pueblito: Sus calles y su gente* (Querétaro: Viterbo Editorial, 2000), especially 4–5.

71. Benson Collection, University of Texas at Austin, García Collection, G-13.

72. José María Ortiz de Alfaro, AGN Inquisición 1465, exp. 7, fols. 85–87, "despues de predicar con el mayor ardor y estrechar a los yndios a que aprendan

la doctrina, hasta cogerlos del brazo para llevarlos al curato y enseñarles yo mismo, no he podido desterrar inumerables supersticiones que tienen más intimamente arraigadas que la fe de Jesuchristo. Pero con especialidad te hago saber como a comisario del Santo Oficio que cada día toma más cuerpo un culto supersticioso que tributan a una Santa Cruz que llaman *la cruz de justicia* tienen sus juntas nocturnas algunos dias de la semana y concurren a ellas de varios pueblos los alumnos de esta supersticiosa congregación fundada en una capilla que tiene en su casa el yndio Patricio García."

73. Pedro José de Zubialdea, *Sermón que en el tercer dia del solemne novenario de Nuestra Señora del Pueblito conducida en secreto a la Iglesia del seráfico patriarca San Francisco* . . . (México: Casa de Arizpe, 1810). The secret transfer touched off a series of disputes between the Franciscans of Querétaro and the municipal council of the city over when the image would be brought to the city, by whose authority, and where it would be displayed while there (Vicente Acosta and Cesáreo Munguía, *La milagrosa imagen de Ntra Señora del Pueblito*, tomo I [Compendio histórico de su culto], 2nd ed. [México: Edit. Jus, 1962], 61–62, and AGN Clero Regular y Secular 87, exp. 7).

74. Diego Miguel Bringas y Encinas, *Sermón que en la solemne función hecha por el noble Cuerpo de artilleros . . . en obsequio de su portentosa Patrona y General María Santísima del Pueblito,* . . . (México: Impr. de María Fernández de Jáuregui, 1811); Francisco Núñez, *Sermón panegírico que en la solemne anual función con que se celebra en esta ciudad de Querétaro a su protectora y generala María Santísima del Pueblito* . . . (México: Impr. de J. M. de Benavente, 1816); Miguel Agustín Gutiérrez, *Discurso que en la solemne función que hacen anualmente . . .* (México: Oficina de A. Valdés, 1817).

75. José Rodolfo Anaya Larios, *La Virgen del Pueblito y su iconografía* (Querétaro: H. Ayuntamiento de Querétaro, 1995).

76. Gutiérrez, *Discurso*, 32.

77. Ignacio R. Frías y Camacho, *Semblanza y realidad a través de la Santísima Virgen del Pueblito* (Querétaro: n.p., 1997 [corrected and augmented edition of the 1923 edition of Valentín F. Frías's *Historia de la célebre y portentosa imagen . . .*]), 46.

78. Acosta and Munguía, *La milagrosa imagen*, 90–95. Wroth, *Christian Images*; Frank, *A Land So Remote*; and Boyd, *Popular Arts*, document early nineteenth-century images of Nuestra Señora del Pueblito in New Mexico.

79. The deterioration of the shrine and infrequent meetings of the archicofradía during the 1820s, 1830s, and 1840s are documented in AHDF 3904–8.

80. Administrative records for the burning of politically incorrect *estampas* and inspection of possibly offensive paintings and statues in 1829 are in AHDF 3904, exp. 129, and AHDF 3905, exp. 130, and the acta de cabildo deliberations on June 20. The *Salutación a la Virgen de los Remedios. ¡Salve Esther compasiva! Celestial atalaya de los mexicanos* . . . was published in Mexico City by R. Núñez in 1829. The venida of 1829 is documented in AHDF 3904, exp. 125.

81. AHDF 3907.

82. Jesús García Gutiérrez, *Datos históricos sobre la venerada imagen de Nuestra Señora de los Remedios de México*, 2nd ed. (México: Edición Ant-Val, 1940), 51–52.

83. Five hundred ex-voto paintings from San Juan de los Lagos are reproduced on the compact disk, *México en un espejo*.
84. AGN Alcabalas 105.
85. Luis Pérez Verdía, quoted in Remberto Hernández Padilla, *San Juan de los Lagos frente a su historia* (México: Edit. Egida, 2001), 266–68. According to Pérez Verdía, the thirty-five thousand visitors to San Juan during the fiesta to the Virgin in 1792 greatly exceeded the roughly ten thousand who went in 1736.
86. Pedro M. Márquez, *Historia de Nuestra Señora de San Juan de los Lagos y del culto de esta milagrosa imagen*, 5th ed. (San Juan de los Lagos: Imprenta "Alborada," 1966), 174ff. Another shrine, not mentioned elsewhere in this chapter, that suffered during the independence wars was Nuestra Señora de los Remedios of San Juan Zitácuaro, Michoacán (Moisés Guzmán Pérez, *Nuestra Señora de los Remedios de San Juan Zitácuaro: Historia y tradición de un culto mariano* [Morelia: Universidad Michoacana de San Nicolás de Hidalgo, 1999], 65–66).
87. Joaquín L. Aguayo, *Compendio de la historia de Nuestra Señora de San Juan de los Lagos* (San Juan de los Lagos: Imp. C. Gallardo, n.d. [1947?]), 45; "San Juan de los Lagos," *Boletín de la Sociedad Mexicana de Geografía y Estadística*, primera época, vol. 2 (1864): 84–92; Alberto Santoscoy, *Historia de Nuestra Señora de San Juan de los Lagos y del culto de esta milagrosa imagen*, edición conmemorativa del V centenario del la evangelización (publication data unknown), 283.
88. Santoscoy, *Historia*, 263–64.
89. Frank, *A Land So Remote*, reproduces nine different nineteenth-century copies of the Virgin of San Juan from chapels and private oratorios in New Mexico, I:94, 96, 109, 188, 273; II:301, 326, 399, 418.
90. Quoted in Salvador Ortiz Vidales, *La arriería en México: Estudio folclórico, costumbrista e histórico* (México: Impr. del Museo Nacional de Arqueología, Historia y Etnología, 1929), 49–54, "Siempre que barren el templo los sacristanes tienen mucho cuidado de las basuras que recogen del suelo. Cuando esta operación es concluida el sacristán reparte esta basura como una reliquia; pues la ignorancia de las gentes ha creido que la tierra, tiros de cigarro y porción de inmundicias son una medicina que, tomada en agua o a secas, sirve para curar toda clase de enfermedades."
91. Márquez, *Historia*, 186ff.
92. Ibid., 212ff; Hernández Padilla, *San Juan de los Lagos*, 213; Santoscoy, *Historia*, 302ff.
93. AGN Indiferente Virreinal 3885, exp. 5. Authorities considered the crowds that gathered at Chalma to be the human vectors that would spread the infection. I thank Paul Ramírez for this reference. Late colonial authorities were also concerned about regulating the sale and consumption of alcoholic beverages at the shrine. See AGN General de Parte 50, exp. 222 (1772), and AGN Clero Regular y Secular 185, exp. 6 (1796).
94. For details, see AGN Alcabalas 371, exp. 6, fols. 25, 32.
95. AGN Criminal 226, exp. 3, fol. 235v "dando de limosna la moneda de cobre que ellos usaban." Distinctive copper and silver coins stamped with the word

"Sud" and a date between 1811 and 1814 circulated among forces affiliated with José María Morelos.

96. Gilberto Giménez, *Cultura popular y religión en el Anáhuac* (México: Centro de Estudios Ecuménicos, 1978), 74–75.
97. AGN Civil 2059, exp. 4. This mission apparently did not include communities in the modern state of Morelos where the Lord of Chalma was (and is) especially popular.
98. Municipal archive of Capulhuac, caja 1, Presidencia, exp. 5.
99. Benson Collection, University of Texas at Austin, Mariano Riva Palacio Papers, doc. 4927.
100. Fortino Vera, *Itinerario parroquial del arzobispado de México y reseña histórica, geográfica y estadística de las parroquias del mismo* . . . (Amecameca: Tip. del Colegio Católico, 1880), 90.
101. "Una romería," *El Espectador de México*, tomo IV, núm. 14 (March 6, 1852): 330, quoted in Fortino Vera, ed., *Santuario del Sacromonte, o lo que se ha escrito sobre él desde el siglo XVI hasta el presente*, segunda edición (Amecameca: Tip. del Colegio Católico, 1881), 19–23: "El templo del Señor es una preciosísima capilla, rica, vistosa y majestuosamente adornada; haciendo resaltar más su grandeza, así el bello altar en que se halla colocada la venerable efigie, como la riqueza y primor de los adornos de ésta. . . . Sobre la frente de la imagen se ve una venda cuajada de hermosos diamantes, y entre las muchas colchas que ordinariamente la cubren, alguna hay que por su materia y grandes bordados de plata, se reputa su valor en más de tres mil pesos. En los tres días de Carnaval se reunen indígenas, que vienen en romería a visitar el santuario, hasta de ciento y más leguas de distancia: de la parte de la sierra que corresponde al Estado de Querétaro, de la de San Luis Potosí y de más adelante han concurrido algunas danzas y muchas familias en el presente año. Entre los millares de personas de todos sexos que suben al santuario en los tres días, hay muchos que suben toda la calzada de rodillas y llegan derramando sangre, otros se entregan a más duras penitencias, muchos vienen a confesar. . . . Aunque el culto del Señor del Sacro Monte, en fin, siempre había sido grande, puede asegurarse que no era la mitad de lo que es bajo el cura actual: el fomentarlo es su delirio, su único pensamiento."
102. E. Boyd, *Popular Arts*, 360–61, 364; and William Wroth, *The Chapel of Our Lady of Talpa* (Colorado Springs: Taylor Museum, 1979), says it was placed in a family chapel at Rio Chiquito near Taos by 1838.
103. Haydé Quiroz Malca, *Fiestas, peregrinaciones y santuarios en México: Los viajes para el pago de las mandas* (México, CONACULTA, 2000), 103.
104. Manuel Carrillo Dueñas, *Historia de Nuestra Señora del Rosario de Talpa*, 4th ed. (México: Impresos Alfe, 1982 [1st ed., 1961]); Mario Alberto Nájera Espinoza, *La Virgen de Talpa: Religiosidad local, identidad y símbolo* (Zamora: El Colegio de Michoacán, 2003). José Toribio Medina, *La imprenta en Guadalajara, 1793–1821* (Santiago de Chile: Imprenta Elzeviriana, 1904), 54, Fr. Francisco Solano de León, *Novena a la portentosa Imagen de Nuestra Señora de Talpa que se venera con la advocación del Rosario*, for 1803; for the 1739 and 1804 editions, see José Toribio Medina, *La imprenta en México: Edición facsimilar* (México: UNAM, 1989), IV:485, VII:330.

105. Carrillo Dueñas, *Historia de Nuestra Señora del Rosario de Talpa*, chap. 9, especially 157.
106. Nájera Espinoza, *La Virgen de Talpa*, 56.
107. Carrillo Dueñas, *Historia de Nuestra Señora del Rosario de Talpa*, 208. A project to add new lodgings for visitors was suspended in 1805.
108. Ibid., 218.
109. Ibid., 221.
110. Ibid., 223–44.
111. Ibid., 247–48.
112. Ibid., 249, 281.
113. The principal historical work on the Tepalcingo shrine is Constantino Reyes Valerio, *Tepalcingo* (México: INAH, 1960). Another work, *Tepalcingo, su historia y sus tradiciones* (Cuernavaca: PACMYC, 1996), by María Cristina Toledano Vergara, relies on Reyes Valerio for its historical discussion, but adds a relevant passage from a 1743 report for Cuernavaca that mentions the feria, and provides information on armed groups in the area during the 1850s and 1860s that led to damage to the pueblo and santuario and a decline in visitors to the santo.
114. Toledano Vergara, *Tepalcingo y su historia*, 208–11.
115. Reyes Valerio, *Tepalcingo*, 9–10. Reyes Valerio says that local Indians established the cofradía several years before 1681.
116. Toledano Vergara, *Tepalcingo y su historia*, 180, "En este partido y pueblo de Tepalcingo ay una imagen de Cristo Nuestro Señor que se venera por santuario de cuia efigie reciben los que le visitan y le claman infinitos beneficios. Celébranle su fiesta el día de la Santa Cruz y el tercero viernes de Quaresma una solemnísima procesión con tal concurrencia que suelen padecer algunas criaturas ogarse en la Iglesia.... Son copiosas las limosnas que se recogen para las mismas de dicha santa imagen."
117. The license is transcribed in Reyes Valerio, *Tepalcingo*, 94–105, from AGN Bienes Nacionales 627, exp. 10, "la multitud de gente que concurre expecialmente el terzer viernes de Quaresma a venerar la expresada sagrada Imagen, lo que no pueden executar a causa de lo pequeño de la iglesia."
118. AGN Bienes Nacionales 627, exp. 10, cuaderno 3.
119. Rosenbach Library (Philadelphia) manuscript 462/25, pt. 3, #4, relating to the 1810 petitions of Tepalcingo and Atlacahualoyan to be made separate parishes. In cuaderno 1 of this record Tepalcingo reportedly had four hundred "Indian" families and forty "de razón" families.
120. Reyes Valerio, *Tepalcingo*, 11, 1743 judgment of Rubio y Salinas confirmed Lanciego's in 1722.
121. AGN Bienes Nacionales 627, exp. 10, cuaderno 3.
122. Reyes Valerio, *Tepalcingo*, 95, "la mejora que a su pueblo resultara con el nuevo templo de cuya mayor veneración a la Santa Imagen redundava mayor concurso y de ay era el veneficio común al pueblo."
123. AGN Bienes Nacionales 627, exp. 10, cuaderno 6, "inmenso [es] el concurso de gentes que concurren a adorar la imagen de Jesús Nazareno que allí se venera."
124. Rosenbach Library, manuscript 462/25, pt. 3, #4, cuaderno 1, fol. 1.

125. José María Guzmán, the resident pastor in 1813 claimed that there was no need for additional priests because his jurisdiction extended beyond Tepalcingo to only one very small pueblo, Atotonilco, and a rancho with only a few residents. He claimed that the annual income was about two thousand pesos, of which he was paid a monthly stipend of eighty pesos. Twenty-five pesos a month went to the parish seat of Xonacatepec, and sixteen pesos a month went to support the Royalist forces stationed at Xonacatepec (Bancroft, June 2, 1813, MSS M-M 1700, Pt. I:218,"informe al Arzobispo Antonio Bergoza y Jordán").
126. AGN Bienes Nacionales 627, exp. 10, cuaderno 5, fol. 12r, "dándoles buen trato, pero que después que comenzaron a cuidar de los bienes de la cofradía de Jesús Nazareno ... se reunió con él [Mijar] a maltratarlos."
127. AGN Bienes Nacionales 627, exp. 10, cuaderno 5, fol. 21v, "que se les restituyan sus antigous derechos de fundadores y dueños."
128. AGN Bienes Nacionales 627, exp. 10, cuaderno 6.
129. AGN Bienes Nacionales 370, exp. 24. They added that the shrine had recently been robbed of a "large quantity" of silver ornaments and that the circumstances of the robbery were "mysterious" since the building was locked and only the parish priest had the keys.
130. A cycle of six ferias were held during Lent in this part of central Mexico: the first and sixth Fridays at Amecameca, with its Sacromonte shrine; the second in Cuauhtla; the third in Tepalcingo; the fourth in Atlatlahucan; and the fifth in Mazatepec (Toledo Vergara, *Tepalcingo y su historia*, 178–79).
131. AGN Bienes Nacionales 929, exp. 84; Bienes Nacionales 370, exp. 24; AHAM, caja for 1887, fondos del santuario de Tepalcingo. I was not able to consult the financial records for Tepalcingo for 1831–1833 in AGN Bienes Nacionales 645, exp. 9; 1001, exp. 7; and 1197, exp. 10.
132. One of the estampas, with a caption reading "Jesús de Tapzingo. Se venera en el pueblo at Atlatlahuca," was recently reported in a copy of Juan Romualdo Amaro, *Doctrina extractada de los catecismos mexicanos de los padres Paredes, Carochi y Castaño* (México: Impr. de Luis Abadiano y Valdés, 1840). (Advertised on the Philadelphia Rare Books & Manuscripts website, November 2008.)
133. Benson Collection, University of Texas at Austin, Mariano Riva Palacio Papers, docs. 3884 and 3927.
134. Taylor, *Magistrates*, chaps. 14, 15.
135. Michel de Certeau, *The Mystic Fable: The Sixteeth and Seventeenth Centuries* (Chicago: University of Chicago Press, 1992). Constance M. Furey's, "Troubling Presence," *Historically Speaking: The Bulletin of the Historical Society*, IX, no. 7 (September/October 2008): 22–25, was especially helpful to me on this point.
136. The governor of the Estado de México's 1828 circular to district prefects and alcaldes against "costly pilgrimages" and popular religious celebrations at Chalma exemplifies this rhetoric: these "abusos ... producidos por la superstición y muy estraños en el siglo presente" needed to be uprooted. He urged "que los mismos Alcaldes en cumplimiento de sus deberes, ecsorten a los ciudadanos para que se abstengan de semejantes esterioridades religiosas que en nada conducen para el culto." The governor apparently knew better than

to prohibit journeys to Chalma outright. In retrospect, his circular looks more like a hope than a policy that would redirect the history of this shrine (municipal archive of Capulhuac, caja 1, Presidencia, exp. 5).

137. An essay in 1799 by an unknown author on Indian life from central Mexico viewpoint considered Indians to be respectful of the church and obedient to their pastors, adding that in every house there was a "santocal" (UT Benson Collection, G-273, "*Apunte del genio, condición, y trabaxos de los Yndios*"). Oratorios and altars in homes often are mentioned incidentally in colonial criminal case records. Two seventeenth-century examples are AGN Criminal 29, exp. 2, 1652 Coyoacan, and AGN Criminal 187, fol. 276f, 1645, minas de Temascaltepec ("*oratorio en la casa del indio cantor Cristóbal ... con belas ensendidas en el altar y enrramado de rrosas y rramas*").

138. Orsi, "Abundant History," 13.

139. I wonder if votive offerings in times of grave danger were just commemorations or negotiations with God for health and prosperity. The prayer, voto, and ex-voto could also be seen as acts of contrition for personal and collective sins, and the hope for purification, forgiveness, and reconciliation—a way of making body and soul whole; restoring order in the world and a right relationship with God.

140. Solange Alberro offers a different view in the article cited in the first note in this chapter. While her title would seem to promise a discussion of ex-voto paintings for the study of popular religion, she leaves the paintings aside and speculates that evidence of religiosity then is lost to us because of the effects of political and social turmoil on collective memory. "Is it not possible," she asks, "that such bloodlettings and traumas also led to the loss, or at least to the impoverishment, of the collective memory, with its cultural equipment, representations, practices and traditions?" ("Retablos and Popular Religion," 65–66).

141. This is not to say that the message of visual depictions of divine favor was clear and unequivocal. See "Images and Immanence in Colonial Mexico," in this volume. Not surprisingly, the Mexican retablos usually had a written caption as well as the depiction of the miracle and/or the donor at prayer.

142. Max Weber, *The Sociology of Religion*, trans. Ephraim Fischoff (Boston: Beacon Press, 1963), chaps. 6 and 7, which build on his proposition that "the peasantry will become a carrier of religion only when it is threatened by enslavement or proletarianization, either by domestic forces ... or by some external political power" (80).

143. Santoscoy, *Historia*, 302; Pescador, "Seeking the Holy Child of Tierra Adentro"; and Bernardo del Hoyo Calzada, *Nuestra Señora de la Soledad de Jerez* (Zacatecas: Instituto Superior de Cultura Religiosa, 1988), 24.

144. Kathleen Norris, *Dakota: A Spiritual Geography* (New York: Ticknor & Fields, 1993), 229.

Index

Acatlán, Santa Cruz, 267n19
Acayucan (Veracruz), 39
Aguiar y Seixas, Archbishop Francisco, 16, 32, 67, 226nn16–17, 241n43
Albares, Ygnacio, pastor of Tepalcingo, 199
Alberro, Solange, 165, 239n25, 272n48, 280n140
alcalde mayor, in conflict, 78–79, 149, 160, 219n60
Alcozer, José Antonio, OFM, 56
Alfajayuca (Hidalgo), 72, 74, 84, 88, 91, 231n63
alms collecting, 36, 37, 39, 41, 73, 75–76, 78, 83, 88, 105, 119–20, 123, 138, 144–45, 183, 194–95, 198, 200, 220n69
Alphonsus Liguori, St., 167
Altamirano, Ignacio Manuel, 140, 185, 252n62
Amanalco (Hidalgo), 86
Amecameca, Sacromonte shrine, 160, 177, 179, 194–95, 202, 218, 279n130
ancestor veneration, 22, 24, 86–87, 134
Ángeles, Nuestra Señora de los, 47, 227n24
Antequera, 8, 38, 121, 252–53n67
apparitions, 15, 25–29, 31, 56, 58–59, 61, 82, 97, 172–73, 203, 212n12, 214nn29–30, 268n26, 268n29. *See also* Guadalupe
Aquila (Michoacán), 41
Arenal, El (Hidalgo), 81
Arias, Patricia, 176, 269n36
Ashanti golden stool, 213n19
Asunción, Isidro de la, 67, 58n36
Atenco, San Mateo (Estado de México), 29, 128
Augustine, St., 61
Augustinians, 27, 86, 149, 230n54, 233n73, 259n39
auto da fé, 129
ayuntamiento (Mexico City city council) and images, 102, 147–56, 190, 191, 245n13, 255–56n11, 259n37, 259n39, 259n44, 260n45, 261n53, 262n68
Azcapotzalco, 169–70

Bajío, 83, 88, 142, 173, 234n85, 245n16
Bala, Nuestra Señora de la, 59
baptism records, 98, 118, 127, 246n19, 249n46
Barbero, Jesús Martín, 92
Bargellini, Clara, 7, 252n66
baroque art, 20, 169, 252n66, 264n6
beauty and images, 7, 20, 22–23, 42–43, 61, 131–32, 212n13, 212n16
Becerra Tanco, Luis, 100, 111, 113, 115, 119, 215n33
Benedict XIV, 117, 243n2
Bergamo, Ilarione da, 128
Beristáin de Souza, José Mariano, 256n13, 257n17
Bienpica y Sotomayor, Salvador, Bishop of Puebla, 37
Bloch, Marc, 90
body, human, 24, 58, 69–70, 174–75, 214n25, 280n139; Christ's body, 69–70
Boturini, Lorenzo, 120, 246n24
Bourbon administrators, 169–70, 265n10
Bourdieu, Pierre, 91, 203, 264n4
Bouza, Fernando, 208n11, 211n9
Brading, David, 103, 142, 256n13, 264n6
brandea (holy keepsakes), 31, 192, 196, 216n33, 230n61. *See also* relics
bulls of the crusade, 40
Burkhart, Louise, 215n30
Bustamante, Anastasio, 182
Bustamante, Carlos María, 151, 260n49, 268n29, 273n56, 289n56

Cabañas, Juan Cruz Ruiz de, bishop of Guadalajara, 38
cabildo eclesiástico, Mexico, 102, 259n37
Cabrera, Miguel, 43–44, 55, 120, 127, 244n7
calendars of Galván Rivera, 114
Calpulalpan, 16, 17, 24
Calvino, Italo, 6, 19
Calvo, Thomas, 137
Camacho de la Torre, María Cristina, 258n28

281

Campeche, 50, 146, 173
Cancuc, Virgin of (Chiapas), 50, 52
candles, 7, 29, 41, 58, 62, 124, 129, 152, 166, 174–75, 196, 216n37. *See also* light
Cañada, La (Querétaro), 229n49
capellanías, 168, 265n9
Capuchin convent, 118, 122, 262n69
Carmelite friars and nuns, 66–67, 71, 72, 80, 122, 226n11, 227n18
Carranza, Francisco Javier, 1748 Guadalupan sermon, 142, 256n13
Carrasco, Davíd, 5, 214n25, 263n2
Carrillo Dueñas, Manuel, 195–96
Carrillo y Pérez, Ignacio, 227n24
casas de novenarios at Tepeyac, 102, 105–6, 108
Casey, Edward, 133
Castillo, Julián Cirilo de, 251n51
Cawley, Martinus, 215n33, 242n55
Certeau, Michel de, 65, 90, 92, 202
Cervantes, Miguel de, 136
Chakrabarty, Dipesh, 234n90, 236n107
Chalma, Nuestro Señor de, 39, 47, 85–86, 88, 104, 136, 160, 191, 193–94, 201, 266n16, 267n24, 276n93, 277n97, 279n136, 280n136
Chichimecs, 85, 228n24, 235n101
Chihuahua, 54, 179, 223n96, 252n67
Chimalpa el Grande (Tlaxcala), procession of the cross, 87–88
Chimalpahin, 111, 113, 241n49
Chimayó, 179, 266n13
Chowning, Margaret, 265n7
Christ, images of, 24–25, 31–32, 35, 47, 56, 58–60, 62, 64–65, 69, 70, 82–83, 88, 173, 177–78, 202, 205, 221n83, 225n7, 243n1, 267n22. *See also* cross; *and individual images of Christ*
Christian, William, 58, 60, 82, 232n72, 268n26
Cisneros, Luis de, 97, 115, 148, 154, 239n27
Clendinnen, Inga, xi, 214n27
cofradías (confraternities), 122–23, 148, 152, 155, 190, 195–200, 202, 241n44, 249n43, 265n7, 265n9, 267n19, 275n79, 278n115
Coire, 41
Colín, Mario, 174–75
Conde de Galve, 150, 259n40
Connaughton, Brian, 257n24, 264n6, 273n59
Conquistadora, La, 151, 190; image in Puebla, 25, 216n37
Constantine, Emperor, 86–87
continuities, 10, 30, 87, 134, 167, 172, 204, 205, 263n2
Copal, 39

Corpus Christi, 26, 38–41, 64, 150, 170, 229n49, 255n9
Cosamaloapan, Nuestra Señora de, 104
Council of Trent, and images, 18–19, 25, 32, 64
creoles, creole patriotism, 101, 103, 110, 112–13, 120, 125, 131, 140–41, 144, 160, 215n32, 239n25
Cristo Renovado de Ixmiquilpan (a.k.a. Cristo de El Cardonal, Cristo de las minas del plomo pobre, Cristo Renovado de Mapethé, Cristo Renovado de Santa Teresa), 8, 63–94, 143, 227–35 passim
cross, 26, 32–33, 36, 38, 50, 59, 86, 187, 217n42, 225n6; Cristo Renovado, 71; Huaquechula, 49–50; Huatulco, 8, 27, 59; natural, 31, 75, 217n42, 232n68, 233n82; Otomí understandings of, 85–88, 91, 93, 232n68, 234n86; in processions, 80, 85–86, 88, 91–92, 158, 232n68; Querétaro stone cross, 59, 86, 232n68; Tepic, 217n43; Tlaxcala, 59; Yucatán, 217n41
cross of El Maye, 230n59
crucifixes, 27, 35, 59, 64, 169–70, 178, 201, 213n20, 229n47, 230n59. *See also* Chalma, Nuestro Señor de; Cristo Renovado de Ixmiquilpan; *and individual images*
Cruz, José de la (playwright), 144–45
Cruz, Mateo de la, 100, 113
culto/cultus/cult, 100, 156; definition, 238n12

darsan, 20
decorous images, and devotion, 22, 49, 170–71, 213n18, 218n58, 229n48
Defensa, Nuestra Señora de la, 25
demandas. *See* alms collecting
Dewey, John, 1
Díaz Calvillo, Juan Bautista, 153–54, 262n66
divine presence, 7, 9–10, 18, 20, 23, 25, 27, 30–32, 39, 43, 46–47, 56, 58–60, 97, 118, 131, 132, 138, 145, 181, 200, 203–4, 209n4, 211n11, 212n13, 214n29, 224n114, 229n41, 264n3
Dolores, Nuestra Señora de los, 220n77
domination, resistance model, 89–90, 167, 264n5
Dominicans, 25, 53, 149, 259n39
dreams, 25, 27, 215n30
Duffy, Eamon, 136
Durand, Jorge, 176
Durango, 118, 179, 244n8
Durkheim, Émile, 10, 32, 87
Dutch interlopers, 50, 52

Ecatepec, San Cristóbal, 127, 144
Ecce Homo, 170

Echave Orio, Baltasar, 21, 111–13, 241nn50–51
Echeverría y Veytia, Mariano Fernández de, 120, 215–16n33, 243n7
Eguiara y Eguren, Juan José, 19, 119, 124
El Cardonal (Hidalgo), 66, 73, 76, 78–79, 82, 85, 88, 91, 194, 229n49, 229n51, 230n53, 231n65
Enríquez de Rivera, Archbishop-Viceroy Payo, 149, 259n37
epidemic of 1737, 68, 73, 114, 117, 119, 121
Escuelas de Cristo, 166
Esquípulas, Nuestro Señor de, 64, 266n13
estampas. See prints
Europe, comparisons and connections, 56, 59, 64, 67, 81, 102, 129–31, 136, 166–67, 172–74, 202–3, 205, 211n11, 215n29. *See also* Spain
ex-votos, 58, 102, 166, 174, 179, 191, 193, 202–3, 205, 268nn31–32, 269n36, 280n139, 280n141

family chapels (*oratorios*), 30, 86–87, 166, 169, 184, 233n76, 268n32, 276n89, 277n102. *See also* home altars
Febvre, Lucien, 90
Feijóo, Benito Jerónimo, 135–36
female figures, 24, 214n27. *See also* Virgin Mary; *and individual images of* Mary
ferias (trade fairs), 176–77, 179, 191–94, 196, 201, 278n113, 279n130
Fernando VII, portrait, 146, 157–58
fertility symbols, 24, 59, 86, 178
firearms, 177, 270n40
Flon, Manuel, 38, 219n60, 265n10
Florencia, Francisco de, 20, 22, 63, 99–100, 104, 106, 108–9, 145, 180, 213n17, 271n44
Folgar, Manuel, 68
Foster, George, 224n106
Fourth Mexican Synod, 47, 54, 222n88, 225n115
Franciscans, 15–17, 26, 29, 43, 53–54, 56, 82, 86, 119, 121, 149, 169, 173, 183–84, 188, 202, 215n29, 216n36, 223n96, 259n39, 262n68, 275n73
Freedberg, David, 212n13
Fresnillo, 39. *See also* Plateros
furta sacra, 67, 152, 227n24

Galinier, Jacques, 234n86
Gandhi, Mohandas, 91
García, Bartolomé, 111
Gemelli Carreri, Juan, 68
geography, devotional, 83–86, 88–89, 130, 133, 135, 137. *See also* place; space
Giménez, Gilberto, 39
Godínez Salas, Pedro Martín, 80

Gombrich, E. H., 23
Gonzales Escobar, Mariano, 200
González Dávila, Gil, 83
González del Campillo, Manuel, Bishop of Puebla, 49, 51
Gruzinski, Serge, 103–4, 182, 235n95, 240n35
Guadalajara, 5, 17, 31, 34, 38, 88, 131, 181, 182, 196, 219–20n69, 257n24, 258n29, 264n6, 265n7, 273n59
Guadalupe, Nuestra Señora de, 99–101, 104, 106, 108–14, 119–22, 127–28, 140, 145, 180, 243n2; *colegiata*, 122, 247n38, 248n40; eighteenth century, ch. 4 passim, 43–45, 241n44, 243n3, 244n9, 245n13, 247n34, 247n38, 247n39, 251n51; independence period, ch. 5 passim; as *la morena*, 126, 245n16, 250nn50–51, 251n54, 253n77; naming, 98, 118, 127, 244n8, 272n48; nineteenth century, 173, 179–86, 201, 273n61; oaths and anniversaries, 119, 122, 246n19, 247n34; and Querétaro, 43, 104, 123, 186, 244n8; rosary processions, 249n43, 249n44; and San Luis Potosí, 43, 45, 104, 123, 142, 182, 240n41, 240n45, 244n8, 247n39, 253n77; sermons, 98, 104, 109, 112, 114, 118–21, 125–26, 142, 151, 180, 183; sixteenth and seventeenth centuries, ch. 3 passim, 237n7, 239n21, 239n26, 240n38, 240n41, 241n53; villa, 122, 248n40. *See also under* Remedios, Nuestra Señora de (Totoltepec)
Guanajuato, Nuestra Señora de, 25, 154, 187
Guanajuato (state), 34, 83, 124, 192, 223n96
Guha, Ranajit, 53, 85, 88–89, 234n89, 267n22
Guijo, Gregorio, 102, 259n40

hagiography, 67, 97, 99, 102
Hell, 26, 53–56, 222n93, 224n103
hermandad. See cofradías (confraternities)
Hexter, J. H., 11
Hidalgo, Miguel, 71, 139, 146, 157, 159, 184, 188, 256n14, 261n63
Hidalgo (state), 75–76, 80, 83, 85–86, 91–92, 123, 142, 181, 194, 232n71, 234n85, 244n8, 253n67, 267n24
historical study, 1–3, 8, 90, 93, 115, 207n3, 211n11, 235n91, 263–64n2
Hoinacki, Lee, 134
Holy Week, 27, 41, 59, 64, 105, 107, 255n9
home altars, 24, 29–30, 47, 87, 132, 166, 181, 184, 203, 216n37, 216n38, 280n137. *See also* family chapels
Huaquechula, Cruz de, 49–51
Huatulco, cross of, 8, 27, 59
Huejutla, 137
Huetamo, 41

Huichol, 137, 169, 183–84, 202, 253–54n78
Huizquilucan, 87

Ibarra, José de, 43, 71, 227n23
Ibarra González, Ana Carolina, 255n5
Ignatius of Loyola, 6, 19, 211n9
images, 7, 18–61, 141–42; abuse of, 32–36, 38, 218n55, 219n59, 219n60; in Buddhist practice, 211n11; copies, 29, 41–52, 75, 126, 128, 131–32, 138, 180, 181–82, 184, 252nn65–67; in Eastern Orthodox practice, 43; originality, 19–20, 42–43, 46–47, 56, 131, 221n78, 221n85, 221n86; power of, 8, 43, 46–47, 53–56, 71–72, 87–94; promotion of, 32, 50, 117, 121, 123–24, 128–29, 147, 180–81; regulation of, 36, 38, 169–72, 217n46, 218n50, 218n58. *See also* divine presence; prints; processions; *and individual images*
Immaculate Conception, images, 136, 170, 180; dogma, 167, 170, 270n38
immanence. *See* divine presence
indulgences, 42, 109, 131, 181
Innocent XIII, 122, 247n33
inquietud, meaning, 2, 8, 207n4
Inquisition, 27, 33, 35, 37, 36, 45, 50, 52, 218n54, 265n10
insurgents, 16, 91–92, 139, 142–43, 146, 159, 193, 196, 204
Iturbide, Agustín de, 140, 142, 182, 188
Ixmiquilpan, 66, 73, 75–76, 78–79, 81, 83, 88, 91, 228n33, 231n65
Izamal, Nuestra Señora de, 104, 160
Iztapalapa, 235n101

Jacala, 83
Jackson, J. B., 133–35, 223n6
Jalahuy, 160
Jalapa, 39
Jansenism, 166, 169, 164–65n6
Jeronymites, 155
Jesuits, 47, 52–54, 56, 63, 68, 125, 142, 180, 215n29, 216n36, 223n96, 251n51, 264–65n6
Jesús Malverde, 179
John of the Cross, 122
John the Baptist, 49, 170
Juan Bernardino, 99, 101, 127
Juan Diego, 9, 28, 65, 99–101, 109, 111, 114, 119–21, 125–27, 129–30, 141, 144–45
Juan Soldado, 195
Juquila, Nuestra Señora de, 8, 160, 201

Kahn, Louis, 2
Kempe, Margery, 136
Kriegel, Annie, 10

Labastida y Dávalos, Archbishop Pelagio Antonio de, 228n30
Labouré, Catherine, 167
Lafaye, Jacques, 103–4, 108, 239n26, 240n37
Lagos, Nuestra Señora de San Juan de los, 17, 104, 160, 175, 179, 191–93, 195–96, 201, 204, 276n85, 276n89
Laguna de Términos, 50
laicization, 166, 168, 175, 202
Lal, Vinay, 234n90
Lanciego, Archbishop José (José Pérez de Lanciego Eguiluz y Mirafuentes), 197, 200
landscape, devotional, 26, 36, 63, 87, 92, 134–36, 147. *See also* geography, devotional
La Profesa (Jesuit church), 56
La Salette, Our Lady of, 172
Lasso de la Vega, Luis, 100–101, 103–4, 112–14, 242n55
Lazcano, Francisco Javier, 63–64
Lent, festivities, 73, 75, 77, 81, 83, 92, 197, 199, 279n130
León (Guanajuato), 53, 54
Leviathan, 54–56, 103, 222n93, 223n101
liberals and liberalism, 140, 146, 182, 184, 193, 203–4
light, as metaphor, 26, 29, 54, 60, 209n1, 223n98
Lizana y Beaumont, Archbishop Francisco Javier de, 243n2
Lockhart, James, 238n14, 241n49
López Gonzalo, Victoriano, Bishop of Puebla, 37
Lorenzana, Archbishop Francisco Antonio, 126, 246n28
lotteries and raffles, 71, 118, 123, 247n38
Lourdes, Our Lady of, 172
Luz, Nuestra Señora de la, 52–57, 222n94, 223nn95–96

Macana, Nuestra Señora de la, 59
Magdalena de Kino (Sonora), 270n41
maize, 24–25, 67, 214n27
Makata (Otomí divinity), 87
Malinalco, 88, 194, 220n69
Mapethé shrine, ch 2 passim, 226n12. *See also* Cristo Renovado de Ixmiquilpan
Maquilí, 41
Margil de Jesús, Antonio, 43, 121
Mary Magdalene, 49
Mass, 15, 17, 30, 33, 43, 68, 109, 129, 148, 152, 158, 183, 245n13, 255n11
Matamoros, Mariano, 144
material culture of devotion, 7, 20, 24, 124, 194, 202, 208n11, 215n29, 268n32. *See also brandea*; ex-votos; images;

medidas; milagritos; prints; relics; rosary; scapulary
matrix image, 43, 132, 138, 182, 220n69, 221n78
mayordomo, of a shrine, 75, 78, 198–99, 229n47
Maza, Francisco de la, 99, 104, 237n7
Mazapil, 39
McNair, Wesley, 11
medidas, 152, 196, 261n51
Meinig, Donald, 2
Melville, Elinor, 234n86
Melvin, Karen, 264n5
mendicants. *See* Carmelite friars and nuns; Dominicans; Franciscans; Mercedarians; *and individual friars*
Mendieta, Gerónimo de, 26–29
Mendoza, Archbishop García de, 112
Mercedarians, 149, 259n39
Mesoamerica and Mesoamericans, 4, 23–25, 58–59, 92–93, 120, 135, 236n105
mestizo, 16, 76, 119, 178, 235n101
Mexico (state), 88, 104, 127–28, 160, 174–75, 177, 179, 184, 234n85, 240n41, 251n54, 254n79, 279n136
Mexico City shrines and images, 33, 35, 45–46, 67, 104, 113–14, 122, 132, 144, 155, 157, 166, 183, 185, 243n1. *See also* Cristo Renovado de Ixmiquilpan; Guadalupe, Nuestra Señora de; Remedios, Nuestra Señora de (Totoltepec); *and individual shrines and images*
Mezquital Valley (Hidalgo), 83, 85–86, 231n65
Meztitlán, Sierra de, 32, 142–43, 145, 181
Michoacán, 39, 40–41, 147, 220n69, 234n85, 243n3. *See also* Aquila
Mier y Trespalacios, Cosmé, 154
Mijar, Joseph, 199–200
milagritos (wax, metal, or wooden votive offering figures), 58, 174–75, 269n32
Mink, Louis O., 207n3
miracles, 16, 22–23, 26, 30, 58–61, 102, 132, 172–79, 204, 209n1, 215n30, 224n110, 230n61, 242n60, 252n67, 267n24; healing, 25–27, 46, 67, 86, 118, 127, 129, 178, 195, 209n1, 221n83, 229n41, 239n27, 244n9. *See also individual shrines and images*
Mixtecs, 157, 177–78
Monaghan, John, 30
Monte de las Cruces, 154–55, 260n49
morada, 168
Mora y Peysal, Antonio de, 38
Morelos, José María, 139, 144, 146, 159, 184, 277n95
Morelos (state), 123, 139, 202, 223n101

Motolinía, 20, 26, 29, 211n12
movement, sacred, 10, 86, 92, 129, 135, 141, 145. *See also* pilgrimage; processions

Nandy, Ashis, 89–92, 235n91, 235n96
Nativitas Tepetlatcingo, 136, 220n76
Naucalpan, 25, 153–54, 157, 261n55
Navarro de San Antonio, Bartolomé, 151
Nebel, Richard, 233n72
New Mexico, 168–69, 195, 202, 273n61
Noche Triste, 151
Nochistlan, Oaxaca, 160
Noguez, Xavier, 242n56
Norberg-Shulz, Christian, 210n6
novenas, and their occasional booklets, 29, 68, 71–73, 97, 102, 121, 148, 150–53, 178–80, 188, 195
Nuevo León, bishopric, 38, 219n64

Oaxaca, 4, 8, 9, 38, 157, 159–60, 178, 263n79
Ocotlán, Jalisco, 173
Ocotlán, Nuestra Señora de, 104, 201
O'Gorman, Edmundo, 238n14
O'Hara, Matthew, 254n5
Omerick, José Hugo de, 126
Ópatas, 160, 185
oratorios. See family chapels; home altars
Orizaba (Hidalgo), 79, 230n53
Oroz Codex, 26
Orsi, Robert, 271n45
Ortner, Sherry, 93
Ostula, 41
Otomí (Ñähñu), ch. 2 passim, 187, 193, 201, 228n33, 231n64, 231n66, 234n85, 234n86. *See also under* cross
Oviedo, Juan Antonio de, 52, 63

Pachuca, 27, 49, 119, 121, 194, 215n29, 223n96, 262n68
Palafox y Mendoza, Juan Antonio de, Bishop of Puebla, 32, 218n47
Palma Gorda, 75, 77, 79, 230n54
Papantla, 39
parish priests and parishioners, 5, 17, 22, 49, 52, 61, 73, 77, 86, 94, 126, 157–59, 166, 170–71, 184, 185, 202, 229n48, 247n39, 253n77, 265–66n10, 267n21, 279n29
Parras, Coahuila, 47
Patiño, Pedro Pablo de, 18–19
Paz, Octavio, 8, 104, 114, 125
Penitentes, 168–69, 202
Pentecost, 194
peregrinación, Feijóo's definition, 135–36. *See also* pilgrimage; *romerías*
Pérez de la Serna, Archbishop Juan, 105, 112
Pérez de la Serna, Jacinto, 28
Pescador, Juan Javier, 179

INDEX 285

peyote, 36
Piedad, Nuestra Señora de la, 217n45
pilgrimage, 38–39, 65, 72, 78, 130–37, 142, 152, 181, 185, 193–94
place (sacred) and place-making, 3, 4, 8, 60, 132–38, 181, 207–8n6. *See also* space
Plateros, and Santo Niño de Atocha, 160, 177–78, 201, 204, 263n84
players-counterplayers-nonplayers, 90–94, 107, 235n96, 235n101, 236n105
Pois, Robert, 207n3
Pomposo Fernández de San Salvador, Agustín, 71, 143, 145, 257n17
Poole, Stafford, 103–4, 238n14, 257n17
popular and lay practices, 36–37, 61, 89, 92, 124, 165–69, 201, 203, 205, 263n2, 265n7
Porta Coeli, church of, 53, 223n95
Porter, James I., 212n13
Portuguese in Mexico, 36
prints (*estampas*), 29, 42, 45, 48–49, 51, 62, 69–70, 112, 118, 188, 192, 196, 201, 260n51; banned and destroyed, 47, 50, 52, 56, 156, 189, 275n80; defaced, 32–36, 143–44, 219n59; and divine presence, 41–47, 50, 221n83, 221n84, 221n86
private piety, 166–69, 202–3. *See also* family chapels; home altars
probabilismo, 265n6
processions, 24, 26, 36–42, 68, 72, 80, 83, 85, 87, 92, 102, 125, 136, 148, 152, 154, 169, 183, 197–98, 219n64, 219–20n69, 220n71, 227n20, 241n53; and sacred movement, 41–42, 71, 80, 86, 135, 227n20, 267n24. *See also* romerías
Puebla, 25, 32, 37, 38, 45, 49, 53, 83, 100, 120, 124, 145, 147, 177, 178, 180, 216n33, 216n37, 219nn60–61, 223n96, 229n50, 234n85, 244nn8–9, 265n9. *See also* Zacapoaxtla
Pueblito, Nuestra Señora de El, 154, 179, 187–88, 201, 258n29, 274n68, 274n69; compared to Remedios, 186–87, 274n69; in New Mexico, 275n78. *See also* Querétaro
Pueblo Nuevo (El Santuario, Hidalgo), 230n54. *See also* Cristo Renovado de Ixmiquilpan
pulque, 83, 249n44
purgatory, 27–28, 54, 215–16n33

Querétaro, 20, 43, 54, 59, 64, 68, 85, 86, 88, 104, 123, 188, 195, 229n49. *See also* Cañada, La (Querétaro); Pueblito, Nuestra Señora de El

railroads, and pilgrimage, 65, 130, 141, 185, 271n45
Ramos Medina, Manuel, 226n11, 227n18

Real del Chico, 194
Redonda, Nuestra Señora de la, 217n44, 223n96
regulation and surveillance. *See* Guadalupe; images; prints; processions
relics, 65, 67, 82, 97, 120, 128
Remedios, Nuestra Señora de (Cholula), 147
Remedios, Nuestra Señora de (Totoltepec): in the eighteenth century, 143, 147–51, 255n11, 260n45; finances and, 108, 152, 260n51; in the independence period, 144, 146–57, 274n65; Mexico City and *venidas* and, 147–49, 258n33, 260–61n51; patronato and, 39, 147–48, 259n37; and post-independence, 156–57, 170, 189–90, 201, 261n61, 261n63, 262n72; Remedios and El Pueblito, 186–91; Remedios and Guadalupe, 22, 71, 140, 144, 147, 174, 227, 256–57n11; in the seventeenth century, 28, 102, 104, 148, 239n19, 259n37, 259n39, 259n40, 259n44; in the sixteenth century, 25, 147–48; Spaniards and, 146–57, 259n40, 274n67
Remedios, Nuestra Señora de (Zitacuaro), 147, 276n86
Rendón, Silvia, 241n49
Richardson, Miles, 233n72
robbery of church possessions, 36, 176, 191, 266n10, 279n129
Roble, Nuestra Señora del, 269n38
Rodríguez, Jeannette, 98
romerías, 38, 135–36, 148, 152, 196. *See also peregrinación*; pilgrimage
Rosa Figueroa, Francisco de la, 213n17, 220n76
rosary, 41, 125, 128, 249n43, 249n44, 262n66
royalists, 16–17, 91–92, 139–40, 142–47, 153–58, 160, 187–88, 191, 256n13, 265n10, 279n125. *See also* Guadalupe, Nuestra Señora de; Remedios, Nuestra Señora de (Totoltepec)
Rubin, Patricia Lee, 210n6
Rubio y Salinas, Archbishop Manuel, 42, 76
Ruiz Guadalajara, Juan Carlos, 88

Sacred Heart of Jesus, 168
sacrilege, 32, 265n10. *See also* images; prints; robbery of church possessions
Sacromonte. *See* Amecameca
saints (other than the Virgin Mary), 19, 25, 30–31, 45, 82, 85–86, 112, 123, 127, 136, 215n29, 243n1. *See also* San Antonio de Padua; San Miguel del Milagro; San Pascual Bailón
Salamanca, Cristo de, 88
Salvatierra (Guanajuato), 53–54
San Antonio de Padua, 33

Sánchez, Miguel, 99–100, 103–4, 110–11, 114, 145, 184, 240n35
San Francisco Galileo (Querétaro). *See* Pueblito, Nuestra Señora de El
San Luis Potosí (state), 43, 83, 85, 104, 123, 182, 244n8. *See also* Guadalupe, Nuestra Señora de
San Miguel del Milagro (Tlaxcala), 58, 104, 201, 210n6, 215n32, 217n41, 218n47
San Pascual Bailón, 173
Santa Catarina parish (Mexico City), 171
Santa Teresa, Señor de. *See* Cristo Renovado de Iximiquilpan
Santa Teresa la Antigua (convent and church in Mexico City), 71–72, 226n18
Santo Entierro (Christ Entombed), 194
Santo Niño de Atocha. *See* Plateros
Santo Niño de San Juan de la Penitencia, 31
Satan/devil, 23, 26–28, 33, 36, 49, 52, 86–87, 188
scapulary, 50, 152, 214n23, 261n51
Schorske, Carl, 115
Señor de la Misericordia (Tepatitlán, Jalisco), 177, 270n42
Señor de la Paz (Mixteca Baja; a.k.a. Cristo Negro de San Pablo Anicano), 178
Señor de las Maravillas, 230n58
Señor del Calvario, Malinaltenango, 268–69n32
Señor del Claustro of Tacuba, 271n42
Señor del Encino of Yahualica (Jalisco), 270n41
Señor del Huerto of Atlacomulco (Estado de México), 268n32, 270n42
Señor del Saucito at Encinillas (San Luis Potosí), 177, 270n42
sermons, 19, 33, 68, 151, 188, 242n54, 243n6, 250n48, 160n49. *See also under* Guadalupe, Nuestra Señora de
Seven Years' War, 141, 151, 186, 245n13
shamans, 28, 29, 86–87, 169
shrines, in Mexico, 135; eighteenth-century growth of, 29, 60, 65, 118, 130, 136–37, 141–42, 186, 197; Guadalupe at Tepeyac's dominance in, 8–9, 63, 130, 136–37, 142, 160; and nineteenth-century growth, new shrines, and laicization, 172, 174, 176–79, 201–2, 205; origin stories of, 30, 58, 111, 178, 217n40, 217n41, 224n111; seventeenth-century formation of, 25, 29, 32, 58–60
Sierra Gorda, 54, 85
Silao (Guanajuato), 83
Simpson, Lesley B., 3
smells, 20, 27, 29, 58, 135
Socorro, Nuestra Señora del, 17, 219–20n69
Socorro, Nuestro Señor del, 171, 234n83

Soergel, Philip, 59
Soledad, Nuestra Señora de la, 172, 204; Oaxaca, 8, 201
Sombrerete, 38, 146
Souza, Lisa, 238n14
space, 8, 132–35, 207n7, 208n6. *See also* landscape, devotional; place
Spain, comparisons and connections, 25, 36, 56, 58–60, 71, 82, 118, 123, 126, 147, 150, 151, 180, 188, 208n11, 211n9, 212n16, 220n69, 225n7, 227–28n24, 232n72, 268n26
Spaniard/Indian, 52, 67, 78, 101, 109, 125, 144, 180, 229n41
Subaltern Studies, 89–90, 93, 234nn88–90, 236n105, 236n107
Sultepec, 127
synesthesia, 23, 211n11

Tacuba, 149, 153, 177, 195, 271n42
Talabarteros chapel, 170
Talpa, Nuestra Señora del Rosario de, 17, 160, 179, 191, 195–96, 201, 263n84
Tamasulapan (Oaxaca), 157–60
Tecaxic, Nuestra Señora de, 104
Tecolutla, 39
Tecomatlan, 158
Tecpan of Azcapotzalco, 169–71
Temamatla, 132, 181
Tepalcingo, 196–202, 278n113, 279n125, 279n129, 279n130
Tepejí del Rio, 83, 88
Tepetlaostoc, 194
Tepeyac. *See* Guadalupe, Nuestra Señora de
Tepic, green cross at, 31, 217n43
Teposcolula, 157
Terán, Marta, 254n2
Tescatepec, San Juan Bautista, 251n54
Texcoco, 15–17, 26, 137, 194, 253n77
Tezontepec (Hidalgo), 267n24
Theresa of Ávila, St., 122
Third Mexican Synod, 218n46
Tlacochahuaya, 263n79
Tlacolula, Señor de, 8
Tlatelolco, 99, 100, 125
Tlaxcala/Tlaxcalans, 16, 26, 37, 59, 83, 86–87, 146, 194, 232n69. *See also* Ocotlán, Nuestra Señora de; San Miguel del Milagro
Tlazintla, 75, 228n33, 230n53
Tolpetlac, 127
Toluca (valley and city), 28, 123, 125, 136, 177, 249n44
Torquemada, Juan de, 26–29, 36, 255n26
Totoloapa, Cristo de, 25, 59
touch, 20, 43–44, 71, 109, 132, 135, 153, 182, 196

INDEX   287

trade fairs. See *ferias*
Trexler, Richard, 235n101
triduo, 150
Tuan, Yi-fu, 133, 207–8n6, 211n11
Tulantongo, Nuestra Señora de, 15–16, 47, 49, 58, 61, 215n32, 216n36, 217n43
Turner, Victor and Edith, on pilgrimage and Guadalupe, 63, 130
Tutino, John, 265n7
Tututepec, 78, 85, 132, 137, 181, 235n101
Tuxtla, 39
Tzeltal Rebellion, 50, 52
Tzinguilucan, Señor de (Singuilucan, Hidalgo), 233n73

unimagined community/imagined community, 159–60
university theses, 53, 112, 118, 242n54, 244n8, 246n19
upstreaming/downstreaming, 263n2
urban centers, and devotion. *See* Antequera; Guadalajara; Guanajuato; Mexico City shrines and images; Puebla; Valladolid; Zacatecas; *and particular shrines*

Vargas Ugarte, Rubén, 63
Valdés, José Francisco, 221n85
Valladolid, 118, 121, 220n71
Valley of Mexico and Distrito Federal, 15–16, 26, 68, 87, 104, 125, 127, 137, 145, 147, 177, 181, 194, 235n101, 248n40. *See also* Cristo Renovado de Ixmiquilpan; Guadalupe, Nuestra Señora de; Mexico City shrines and images; Remedios, Nuestra Señora de (Totoltepec)
Van Young, Eric, 256n14
Varas y Gutiérrez, Fernando Bustillo, 31
Velasco, Alfonso Alberto de, 66–92 passim, 226n12, 226n18, 229n41
Venegas, Viceroy Francisco Xavier, 154, 157
Veracruz, 39, 49, 118, 173, 270n40. *See also* Acayucan
Vetancurt, Agustín de, 16, 29, 209n1, 216n36, 237n8, 260n47, 274n65
Villa Alta, 160
Villagrán, Julián, 91
Vincent de Paul, St., 167
Vincentian Sisters of Charity, 167

Virgin Mary, 10, 30–32, 46–48, 63–64, 82, 167, 203, 205, 215n30, 233n72. *See also individual Marian shrines and images*
Virgin Mary of the Miraculous Medal, 167, 172
Vizarrón y Eguiarreta, Juan Antonio de, 114, 119–21, 122, 128, 246n28, 246n29, 248n40
votive offerings. *See* ex-votos

War of Austrian Succession, 52, 141, 150, 151, 186
War of Spanish Succession, 141, 151, 157, 186
wars of independence, shrines and images during, 16–17, 36, 71, 91, 139–61 passim, 182–83, 186–88, 192–94, 196, 198, 201, 256nn14–15, 265n10, 267n21, 270n40, 276n86
White, E. B., 6, 11, 207–8n6
White, Richard, 114–15
white, symbolism of, 27, 29, 136
women's piety, 35, 41, 66, 126, 160, 166–67, 175–76, 183, 203, 215n29, 262n66, 265n7

Xalmolonga, Nuestra Señora de, 217n44
Ximeno y Planes, Rafael, 227n24
Xochimilco, 172, 242n60, 251n54
Xonacatepec, 179, 199, 266n10

Yndaparapeo, 40
Yraeta, Ana María de, 154–55, 262n66, 262nn68–69
Yxtatlaxco, 83

Zacapoaxtla (Puebla), 145
Zacatecas, 53, 137, 142, 169, 177, 179, 183, 202, 204, 219n64; Colegio de Nuestra Señora de Guadalupe, 43, 121, 173
Zacualtipan (Sierra de Meztitlan, Hidalgo), 142, 256n15
Zanquitlalpan (Estado de México), 184
Zapopan, Nuestra Señora de, 17, 34, 104, 195, 201, 220n69, 258n29
Zapotlán del Rey (Jalisco), 17–18
Zimapán, 77–79, 81, 83, 88, 231n66
Ziraquarétiro, 40
Zodíaco mariano, 63, 218n46, 219–20n69
Zumpango de la Laguna, 248n40
Zúñiga y Ontiveros, Felipe, 244n9, 245n13